PHILIP'S

STR...

C000293018

Suffolk

st published in 2003 by

ilip's, a division of
topus Publishing Group Ltd
4 Heron Quays, London E14 4JP

st edition 2003
cond impression with revisions 2004

3N-10   0-540-08335-6 (pocket)
3N-13   978-0-540-08335-0 (pocket)

Philip's 2004

OS Ordnance Survey

is product includes mapping data licensed
m Ordnance Survey® with the permission
the Controller of Her Majesty's Stationery
fice. © Crown copyright 2004. All rights
served. Licence number 100011710.

Contents

II	**Key to map pages**
IV	**Route planning**
VI	**Administrative and Postcode boundaries**
1	**Key to map symbols**
2	**Street maps** at 1¼ inches to 1 mile
109	**Street maps** at 2½ inches to 1 mile
154	**Street maps of centres of Bury St Edmunds and Ipswich** at 5 inches to 1 mile
156	**Index** of towns and villages
159	**Index** of streets, hospitals, industrial estates, railway stations, schools, shopping centres, universities and places of interest

Digital Data

The exceptionally high-quality mapping found in this atlas is available as digital data in TIFF format, which is easily convertible to other bitmapped (raster) image formats.

The index is also available in digital form as a standard database table. It contains all the details found in the printed index together with the National Grid reference for the map square in which each entry is named.

For further information and to discuss your requirements, please contact Philip's on 020 7644 6932 or james.mann@philips-maps.co.uk

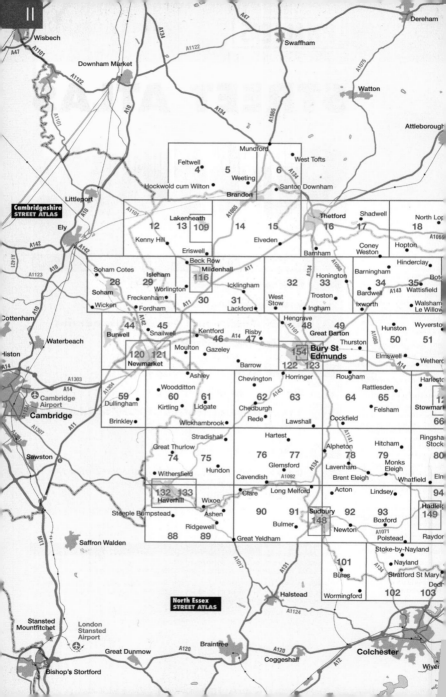

Wisbech
Downham Market
Swaffham
Dereham
Watton
Attleborough

A47
A1101
A47
A1122
A134
A1122
A1075
A10
A1101
A1065
A134

Littleport

Cambridgeshire STREET ATLAS

Ely
A142
A142
A10
A1421
A1123
A10

Mundford
West Tofts
Feltwell
4
5
6
Weeting
A134
Hockwold cum Wilton
Santon Downham
Brandon

A1101
A1065
Thetford
Shadwell
North Lop
12
Lakenheath
13 **109**
14
15
16
17
18
A1066
Kenny Hill
Elveden
Coney Weston
Hopton
Eriswell
Barnham
Hinderclay

Beck Row
Soham Cotes
Isleham
Mildenhall
116
Honington
Barningham
34
35
Bote
Soham
28
29
Worlington
Icklingham
32
33
Bardwell
Wattisfield
Freckenham
Troston
Ixworth
Walsham
Le Willow
Wicken
Fordham
30
31
West Stow
Ingham

Lackford

Hengrave
44
45
Kentford
Risby
48
49
Hunston
Wyversto
Burwell
Snailwell
A14
47
Great Barton
50
51
Moulton
Gazeley
Thurston
Elmswell
Wetherl
120 **121**
Barrow
154
BURY ST EDMUNDS
Newmarket
122 **123**

Ashley
Chevington
Horringer
Rougham
Harlesto
Wooddition
62
63
Rattlesden
64
65
Stowmar
59
60
61
Dullingham
Kirtling
Lidgate
Chedburgh
Felsham
66
Brinkley
Rede
Lawshall
Cockfield
Wickhambrook

Stradishall
Hartest
Alpheton
Hitcham
Ringsha
Stock
Great Thurlow
74
75
76
77
78
79
80
Withersfield
Hundon
Glemsford
Lavenham
Monks Eleigh
Cavendish
Brent Eleigh
Whatfield
Elm

132 **133**
Wixoe
Clare
Long Melford
Acton
Lindsey
94
Haverhill
90
91
92
93
Hadleig
149
Steeple Bumpstead
Ashen
Sudbury
Boxford
Ridgewell
Bulmer
148
Newton
Polstead
Raydor
88
89
Great Yeldham

Stoke-by-Nayland
101
Nayland
Bures
Stratford St Mary
Ded
102
103
Halstead
Wormingford

North Essex STREET ATLAS

A1124

Stansted Mountfitchet
London Stansted Airport
Braintree
Colchester
Bishop's Stortford
Great Dunmow
Coggeshall
Wiver

M11
A120
A120
A12
A1307
A131
A1017
A134

Saffron Walden
Sawston
Cambridge
Cambridge Airport
A1303
A14
Waterbeach
A142
Cottenham
Histon
A14
A11

A1304

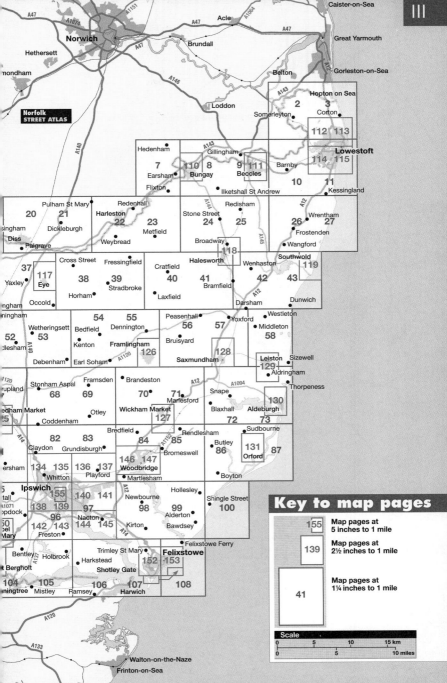

Caister-on-Sea
A47 Acle
Great Yarmouth
Norwich
Gorleston-on-Sea
Brundall
Hethersett
Belton
mondham
Loddon
Hopton on Sea
Somerleyton **2** **3** Corton
Norfolk
STREET ATLAS
112 **113**
Lowestoft
Hedenham **114** **115**
Gillingham
7 **110** **8** **9** **111** Barnby
Earsham **Bungay** **Beccles**
Flixton
10
Ilketshall St Andrew **11**
Kessingland
Pulham St Mary Redenhall
20 **21** Redisham
Dicklenburgh **Harleston** **22** **23** Stone Street **24** **25** **26** **27** Wrentham
singham Metfield Frostenden
Diss Weybread
Palgrave Broadway Wangford
37 Cross Street Fressingfield **118** **Southwold**
117 Cratfield **Halesworth** Wenhaston **42** **119**
Yaxley **Eye** **38** **39** **40** **41** **43**
Horham Stradbroke Bramfield A12
ngham Occold Laxfield Darsham Dunwich
ningham Peasenhall Westleton
54 **55** Yoxford Middleton
52 Wetheringsett Bedfield **56** **57** **58**
53 Dennington Bruisyard
Kenton **Framlingham**
Debenham Earl Soham **126** Saxmundham **128** Leiston Sizewell
dlesham **129** Aldringham
Framsden Brandeston Snape **130** Thorpeness
rupland **68** **69** **70** **71** Blaxhall Aldeburgh
edham Market Otley Marlesford **72** **73**
Coddenham Wickham Market **127** Sudbourne
Bredfield Rendlesham Butley **131**
Claydon **82** **83** **84** **85** Bromeswell **86** Orford **87**
ersham Grundisburgh **146** **147**
134 **135** **136** **137** Woodbridge
Whitton Playford Martlesham Boyton
Ipswich **155** **140** **141** Newbourne Hollesley
tall **138** **139** **97** **98** **99** Shingle Street
ppdock **96** Alderton **100**
Nacton Kirton
142 **143** **144** **145** Bawdsey
Mary Freston
Felixstowe Ferry
Bentley Holbrook Trimley St Mary **Felixstowe**
Berghot Harkstead **152** **153**
104 **105** Shotley Gate **108**
ningtree Mistley **106** **107**
Ramsey Harwich

Walton-on-the-Naze
Frinton-on-Sea

Key to map pages

155	Map pages at 5 inches to 1 mile
139	Map pages at 2½ inches to 1 mile
41	Map pages at 1¼ inches to 1 mile

Scale
0   5   10   15 km
0   5   10 miles

Route planning

Scale

| 0 | 5 | 10 | 15 km |

| 0 | 5 | 10 miles |

Administrative and Postcode boundaries

VI

Scale

0	5	10	15	20	25	30km
0	5	10	15	20 miles

County and unitary authority boundaries

District boundaries

Postcode boundaries

Area covered by this atlas

Motorway with junction number	
Primary route – dual/single carriageway	
A road – dual/single carriageway	
B road – dual/single carriageway	
Minor road – dual/single carriageway	
Other minor road – dual/single carriageway	
Road under construction	
Tunnel, covered road	
Rural track, private road or narrow road in urban area	
Gate or obstruction to traffic (restrictions may not apply at all times or to all vehicles)	
Path, bridleway, byway open to all traffic, road used as a public path	
Pedestrianised area	
DY7 **Postcode boundaries**	
County and unitary authority boundaries	
Railway, tunnel, railway under construction	
Tramway, tramway under construction	
Miniature railway	
Walsall **Railway station**	
Private railway station	
South Shields **Metro station**	
Tram stop, tram stop under construction	
Bus, coach station	

♦	**Ambulance station**
♦	**Coastguard station**
♦	**Fire station**
♦	**Police station**
✚	**Accident and Emergency entrance to hospital**
H	**Hospital**
✚	**Place of worship**
i	**Information Centre** (open all year)
P	**Parking**
P&R	**Park and Ride**
PO	**Post Office**
⋏	**Camping site**
⌒	**Caravan site**
►	**Golf course**
✕	**Picnic site**
Prim Sch	**Important buildings, schools, colleges, universities and hospitals**
River Ouse	**Tidal water, water name**
	Non-tidal water – lake, river, canal or stream
	Lock, weir, tunnel
	Woods
	Built up area
Church	**Non-Roman antiquity**
ROMAN FORT	**Roman antiquity**
87	**Adjoining page indicators and overlap bands**
228	The colour of the arrow and the band indicates the scale of the adjoining or overlapping page (see scales below)

Acad	**Academy**		Inst	**Institute**		Recn Gd	**Recreation**
ot Gdns	**Allotments**		Ct	**Law Court**			**Ground**
Cemy	**Cemetery**		L Ctr	**Leisure Centre**		Resr	**Reservoir**
C Ctr	**Civic Centre**		LC	**Level Crossing**		Ret Pk	**Retail Park**
CH	**Club House**		Liby	**Library**		Sch	**School**
Coll	**College**		Mkt	**Market**		Sh Ctr	**Shopping Centre**
Crem	**Crematorium**		Meml	**Memorial**		TH	**Town Hall/House**
Ent	**Enterprise**		Mon	**Monument**		Trad Est	**Trading Estate**
Ex H	**Exhibition Hall**		Mus	**Museum**		Univ	**University**
Ind Est	**Industrial Estate**		Obsy	**Observatory**		Wks	**Works**
IRB Sta	**Inshore Rescue**		Pal	**Royal Palace**		YH	**Youth Hostel**
	Boat Station		PH	**Public House**			

The small numbers around the edges of the maps identify the 1 kilometre National d lines

■ The dark grey border on the inside edge of some pages indicates that the mapping does not continue onto the adjacent page

he scale of the maps on the pages numbered in blue s 3.92 cm to 1 km • 2½ inches to 1 mile • 1: 25344

0	¼	½	¾	1 mile
0	250m	500m	750m 1 kilometre	

he scale of the maps on pages numbered in green s 1.96 cm to 1 km • 1¼ inches to 1 mile • 1: 50688

0	¼	½	¾	1 mile
0	250m 500m 750m 1kilometre			

he scale of the maps on pages numbered in red s 7.84 cm to 1 km • 5 inches to 1 mile • 1: 12672

0	220 yards	440 yards	660 yards	½ mile
0	125m	250m	375m ½ kilometre	

Norfolk STREET ATLAS

For full street detail of the highlighted area see pages 112 and 113.

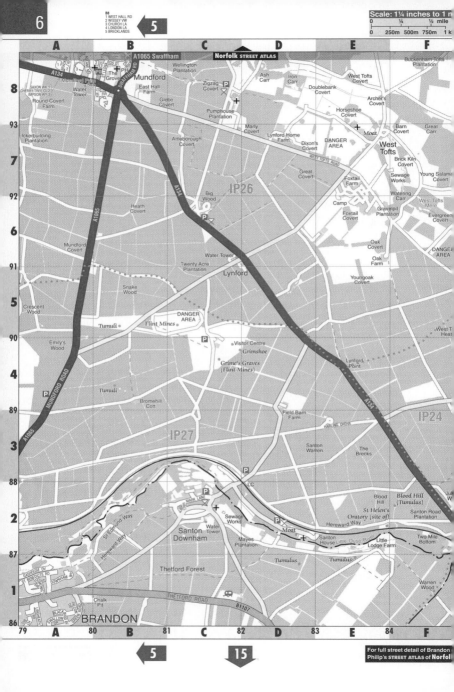

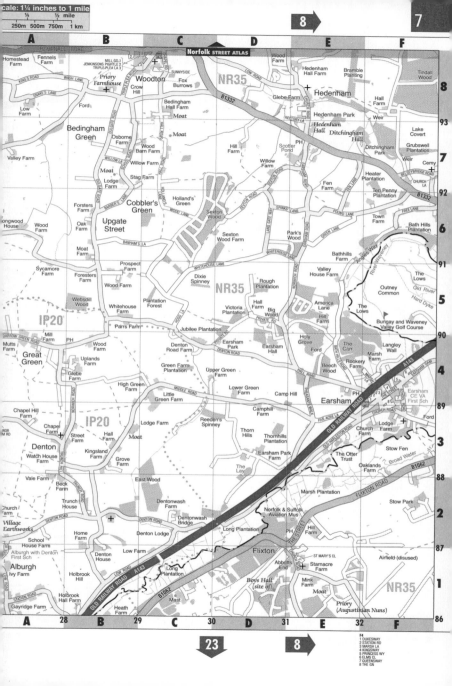

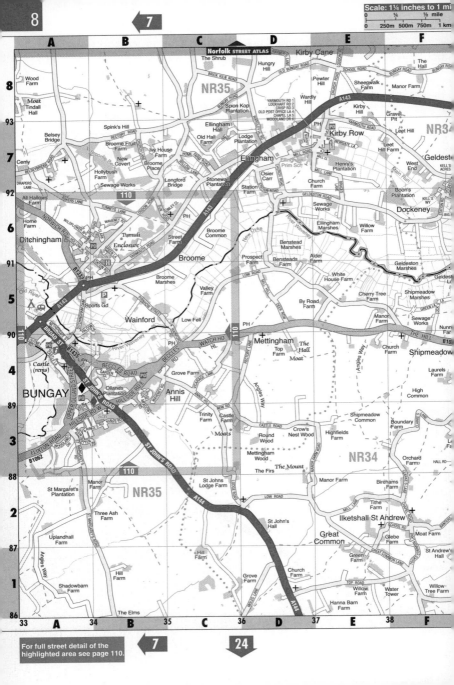

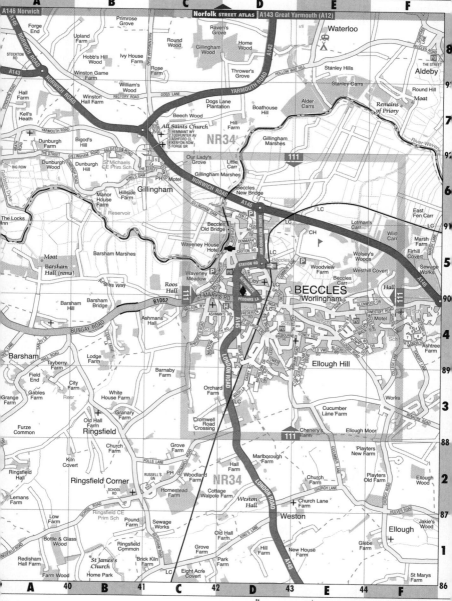

Scale: 1¼ inches to 1 mile

A146 Norwich

A143 Great Yarmouth (A12)

Waterloo

Aldeby

Forge End

Primrose Grove

Raven's Grove

Home Wood

Round Hill

STOCKTON RD

Upland Farm

Round Wood

Gillingham Wood

Thrower's Wood

Stanley Hills

Stanley Carrs

Moat

NORWICH ROAD

Hobb's Hill Wood

Ivy House Farm

Rose Farm

Remains of Priory

Winston Game Farm

William's Wood

Beech Wood

RECTORY ROAD

DOGS LANE

Dogs Lane Plantation

Hill Farm

Alder Carrs

River Waveney

Hall Farm

Kell's Heath

Winston Hall Farm

All Saints Church

1 HEMMANT WY
2 TODHUNTER AV
3 ASHFORD CL
4 KENYON ROW
5 FORGE DR

NR34

Gillingham Marshes

Dunburgh Farm

Bigod's Hill

THE STREET

St Michaels CE Prim Sch

Our Lady's Grove

Little Carr

BIG ROW

Dunburgh Wood

GILLINGHAM ROAD GELDESTON ROAD

Dunburgh Hill

THE STREET

KING'S DAM

PH

Motel

Gillingham Marshes

Beccles New Bridge

The Locks Inn

Manor House Farm

Hillside Farm

Gillingham

Reservoir

NORWICH ROAD

Beccles Old Bridge

FEN LA

GEORGE WESTWOOD WAY

LC

East Fen Carr

Moat

Barsham Marshes

GILLINGHAM DAM

Waveney House Hotel

DENMARK

CAXTON RD

Lotmant's Carr

Wild Carr

Marsh Farm

Firhill Covert

Barsham Hall (rems)

Angles Way

Roos Hall

B1062

Waveney Meadow

ST MARYS RD

PEDDARS LA

Sewage Works

Barsham Hill

Barsham Bridge

BUNGAY ROAD

Ashmans Hall

ASHMAN'S RD

WILSON RD

BECCLES

Worlingham

Woodview Farm

Beccles Carr

Westhill Covert

Wolsey's Woods

Hall

Motel

Barsham

Tayberry Farm

City Farm

Lodge Farm

Barnaby Farm

LONDON ROAD

RIGBOURNE HILL

Ellough Hill

GLENWOOD DR

LOWESTOFT RD

Ashtree Farm

Field End

Grange Farm

Gables Farm

White House Farm

Granary Farm

Orchard Farm

LC

Cucumber Lane Farm

Works

Furze Common

Old Hall Farm

Ringsfield

Church Farm

Grove Farm

Cromwell Road Crossing

Chenery's Farm

Ellough Moor

Players New Farm

Kiln Covert

FOLLS LANE

RUSSELL'S GN

PH

Woodland Farm

NR34

Marlborough Farm

Church Farm

CHURCH LANE

Players Old Farm

Ellough Wood

Ringsfield Hall

Ringsfield Corner

SCHOOL RD

Homestead Farm

Cottage Walpole Farm

Weston Hall

Ellough

Lemans Farm

Ringsfield CE Prim Sch

Pound Farm

Weston

Church Lane Farm

Low Farm

Ringsfield Common

Sewage Works

Old Hall Farm

KING'S LANE

Hill Farm

Glebe Farm

Jakie's Wood

Redisham Hall Farm

Farm Wood

Bottle & Glass Wood

Brick Kiln Farm

St James's Church

Home Park

Grove Farm

Park Farm

LC

Eight Acre Covert

New House Farm

A145

St Marys Farm

For full street detail of the highlighted area see page 111.

F4
1 PEPYS AVE
2 PAINS CL
3 ALL SAINTS GN
4 HOLM LA
5 WAINFORD CL
6 MIRBECK'S CL
7 BROOKWOOD CL
8 ASH TREE CL
9 MANOR CL

LOWESTOFT

Roman Hill
Town
Euroscope
Ness Point

A1144 NORMANSTON DR   ST PETER'S ST

NORMANSTON DRIVE

NR32

Oulton Broad North

LC
Liby
Mutford
Bridges
Lowestoft
Mus

NR33

Sports
Gd

Riverside
Business Park

COMMERCIAL RD

VICTORIA RD   A146   WAVENEY DR   HORN HILL

East Point
Pavilion

Suffolk Coast
& Heaths Path

BRIDGE RD

BECCLES ROAD

FOTIMER ROAD

A1117 ELM TREE RD

KIMBERLEY RD

NOTLEY RD

Meadow
Prim Sch

Claremont
Pier

South
Beach

Oulton Broad
South

Whitton
Green
Prim Sch

The Fairway

BELVEDERE RD

MARINE PDE

Kirkley

Cmty

BLOODMOOR RD

STRADBROKE ROAD

Pakefield

LONDON RD   PAKEFIELD   A12

KIRKLEY CLIFF ROAD

A118

St Marys
RC
Prim Sch

Government
Offices

Lowestoft
South Roads

LOWESTOFT

Carlton
Colville

B1384 LOWESTOFT RD

Recn
Gd

South Lowestoft
Industrial East

COOKE RD

HADENHAM RD

LINNET RD

JUBILEE WY

Pakefield Cliffs

Bell
Farm

Bloodmoor Hill

Gisleham
Middle Sch

Grange
Farm

114   115

Gisleham

CHURCH ROAD

Church
Farm

Glebe
Farm

Solar Mink
Farm

ROMANY LA

Heath
Farm

LONDON ROAD A12

Moat

Pakefield
Hall

Crazy Mary's
Hole

Lighthouse

White House
Farm

Moats

NR33

Hall Farm

CLIFF FARM LA

Suffolk Coast
& Heaths Path

Kessingland Cliffs

Briar
End

Laurel
Farm

Pond
Farm

B1437

HIGH

Kessingland

ck
reet

WHITE

CHURCH RD

PH

B1437

Water
Twr

Manor
Farm

War
Memorial

Suffolk Wildlife
Park

For full street detail of the
highlighted area see pages
112, 113, 114 and 115.

Scale: 1¼ inches to 1 mile

Norfolk STREET ATLAS

Cambridgeshire STREET ATLAS

A **B** **C** **D** **E** **F**

8
85
7
84
6
83
5
82
4
81
3
80
2
79
1
78

61 **A** 62 **B** 63 **C** 64 **D** 65 **E** 66 **F**

A1101 Littleport
MILDENHALL RD
A1101
B1382
MILE END ROAD

Letter F Farm
Flanders Farm
Cross Bank Farm
Redmere Fen
Decoy Farm
Decoy Fen

HEREWARD WAY
Peacock's Farm
Plantation Farm
Decoy Fen
LC

Burnt Fen
Bulldog Bridge
Shippea Hill
LC
Hereward Way
STATION HILL
Lodge Fen
SEDGEFEN ROAD
Sedge Fen

Shippea Hill Farm
LC
Willow Farm
FARTHING DROVE

Engine Drain
Sparrow Hall Farm
BURNT FEN TURNPIKE
Grosvenor House Farm
Elderberry Farm

DUCK DROVE
Engine Farm
A1101

CB7
Whistle Farm
Harris Farms

Spooner's Farm
River Lark
Friesland Farm
Mildenhall Drain
Townmoor Farm

Lark Grange

Great Fen
IP28

Kings Farm
Crossbank Farm
Poplar Farm
A1101
MILDENHALL DROVE

Great Fen
Row Fen
Baldwin's Lode
FIGGS DROVE
SNARE DROVE

B1104
Cock Inn Farm
County Farm
Summers Farm
NURSE DROVE
DUCK DROVE
Kenny Hill
P
BIRCHINHILL DROVE
Birchinhill Farm

Alder Farm

PRICKWILLOW ROAD
Isleham Fen
Forty Farm

Fen Bank Farm
FODDERFEN DROVE
Ranville Farm
Chestnut Farm
NEW DROVE
Stargate Farm

Sixteen Foot Drain
Cambria Farm
Fen Farm
Waverley Farm

Great Fen
Isleham Fen
Three Tree Farm
West Row Fen
Tree Farm
DELPH RD
Mildenhall Fen
High Post Farm
Mayfield Farm

NURSE DROVE

28 **29**

B1
1 KESTREL CL
2 ROOKERY DR
3 BLACKBIRD RD
4 PLOVER CL
5 HERON CL
6 VALIANT ST
7 WASHINGTON ST
8 SYCAMORE DR
9 MAGNOLIA CL
10 CEDAR CT
11 LINDEN WK

F2
1 YEW CL
2 OLIVE CL
3 NEWARK RD
4 COLCHESTER CL
5 NORWICH RD
6 NEWCASTLE CL
7 NEWPORT CL
8 WHITEWOOD WLK
9 PINE CL
10 ASH CL
11 BEECH CL RD
12 MAPLE CL
13 WALNUT CL
14 SPRUCE CL
15 THORNTON CL
16 THETFORD CL
17 DEREHAM CL
18 PORTLAND CL
19 PORTSMOUTH CL
20 SYCAMORE WLK
21 CHESTNUT WLK
22 ROSEWOOD CL
23 REDWOOD LA
24 BIRCH WLK
25 HAWTHORN LA
26 MYRTLE CL
27 LANCEWOOD WLK
28 APPLE CL
29 FIR WLK
30 ELM WLK
31 DOGWOOD WLK
32 CEDAR CL

For full street detail of the
highlighted area see page 109.

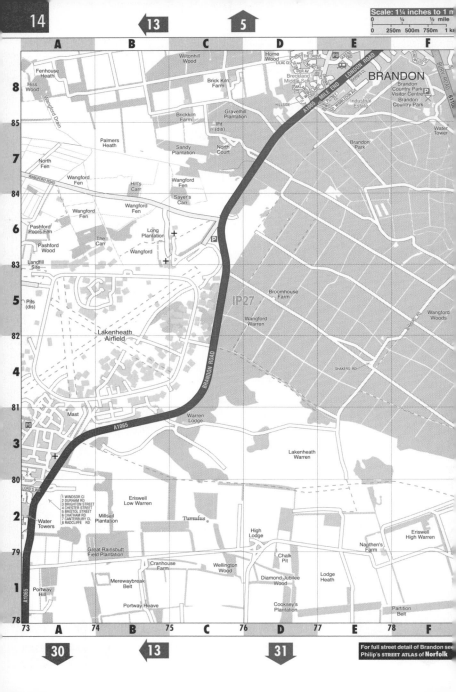

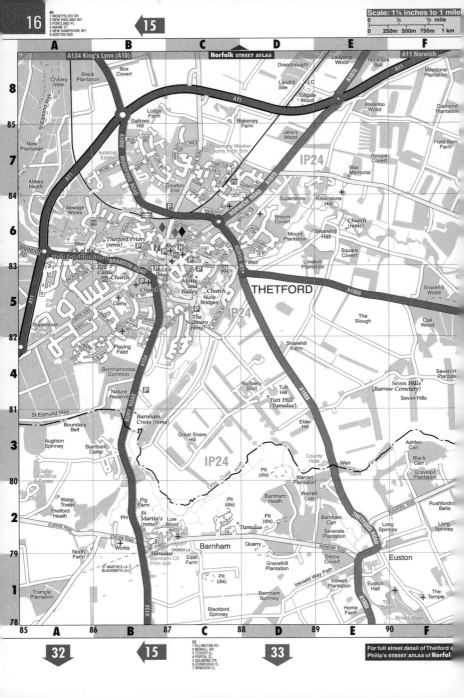

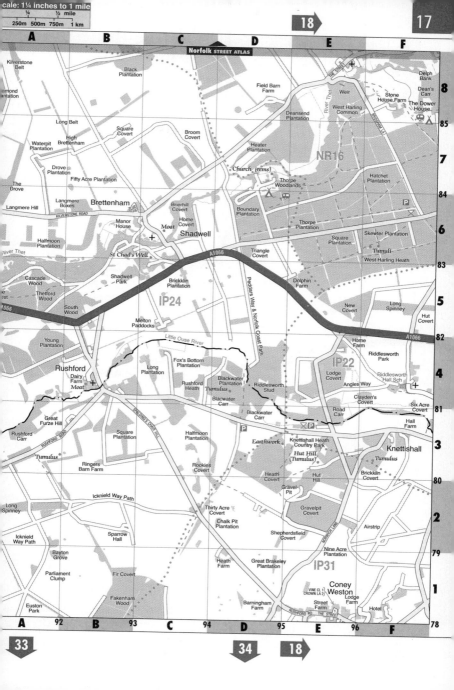

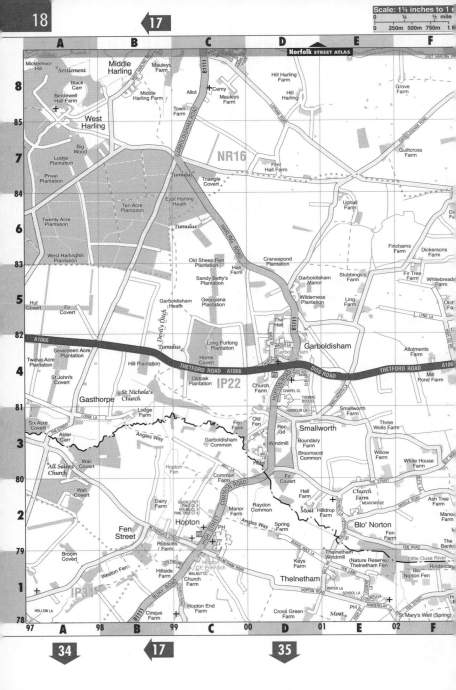

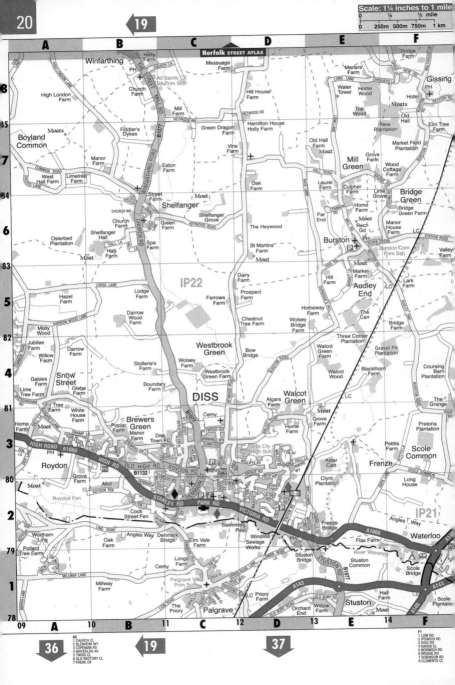

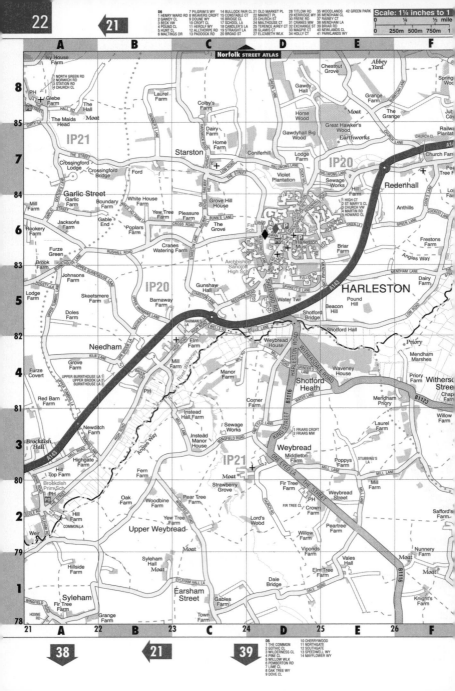

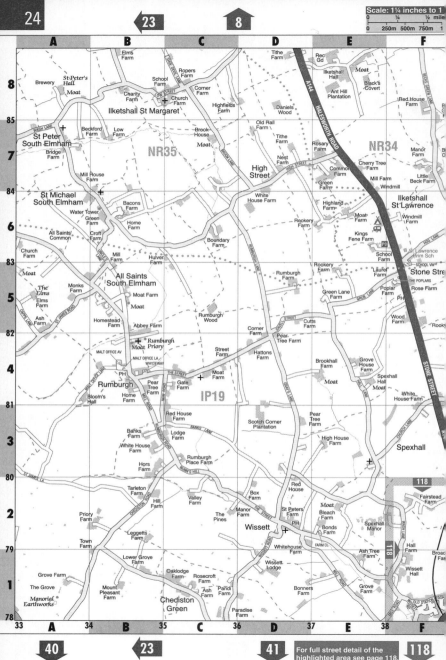

Scale: 1¼ inches to 1 mile

¼ mile   ½ mile
250m 500m 750m 1 km

A   B   C   D   E   F

Kessingland
Beach

Blackcap
Wood

Sewage
Works

HOLLY GRANGE
ROAD

PH
CHURCH
RD

MARSH

BEACH RD

Churchfarm
Marshes

NR33

Suffolk Coast & Heaths Path

8

85

Benacre

War
Memorial

Church Covert

Kessingland
Level

Beachfarm
Marshes

Northwalk
Plantation

Pumping
Station

The
Denes

Beach
Farm

7

84

Hall
Farm

Blackwater
Covert

Alder
Carr

Coney
Hill

Holly Hang

Craft
Plantation

Boathouse
Covert

Nature
Reserve

Benacre
Broad

6

83

NR34

od
m

Long
Covert

North
Common Wood

Chancel
Covert

lly
ve

St Andrew's
Church

Ausgates

Church
Farm

Covehithe

Covehithe Cliffs

82

5

4

Porter's
Farm

Green
Heath

Covehithe
Broad

Warren
House

The
Warren

Suffolk Coast
& Heaths Path

81

Easton
Wood

3

Easton Home
Covert

Easton
Broad

ttersbridge
Marshes

Easton
Marshes

80

2

P18

aston
vents

EASTON LN.

Easton Cliffs

79

1

78

A   52   B   53   C   54   D   55   E   56   F

Scale: 1¼ inches to 1 mi

0   ¼   ½ mile
0   250m   500m   750m   1 km

D5
1 NORTH DR
2 ST FELIX CL
3 CALIE REN CL
4 OLD SCHOOL LA
5 HOLMES LA
6 SNOWBERRY WY

7 FOX WOOD N
8 MARTIN CL
9 POPPY FIELDS
10 PRIMROSE LA
11 FOX WOOD ST

A   B   C   D   E   F

8   The Dunstalls
Mow Sides   Lay Clerks Farm   Nornea Farm   Hundred Acres   St John's Farm   Water Tower
SONIA LANE   Crooked Drain   Castles Farm   Great Fen
Harlock's Farm   Hithertree Farm   HASSE ROAD   Slack's Hill

77   Delph Bridge   Eye Hill Farm   Westfields Farm   Broadhill Farm   Great Hasse Farm
Turf Fen   Blockmoor Farm   Barcham Farm   Broad Hill   Longfield Farm

7   Blockmoor Fen   Orchard Farm   Crow Hall Farm   Saxon Farm   Hodson Farm
BARWAY ROAD   Orchard Farm Business Park   The Hasse

76   Barway Fen   North Field   North Horse Fen   Granary Farm
LC   BLOCKMOOR ROAD   Dolver Farm   LITTLE HASSE DROVE   Willow Farm

6   THE SHADE   Northfield Windmill   Mardon Farm   Soham Fen
Soham Cotes   Shade Common   Bancroft Field

75   Sedge Fen   Engine Farm   Sewage Works   THE BIRCHES 1   NORTHFIELD
Tiled House Farm   Pantile Farm   CLOVERFIELD DR 2   CAMPION CL 3   BLACKTHORN CT 4   THORN CL 5

5   Hotel
GREAT DV   Soham

74   Middlemere Farm   EAST FEN DROVE
SPENCER DV   Qua Fen Common

4   CB7   WEST OF CR   East Fen Farm
Soham Mere   Angle Common   Horse Bridge   East Fen Common
North Angle Farm   MILL DR   Soham Lode

73   Low Barn   South Angle Farm   The Ross Peers Sports Centre   Wet Horse Fen   Horse Fen
Wicken Dolves   Lilly   Allot

3   Cemy   Cherry Tree Farm   Small Path Hill
CHERRYTREE LANE   Windmill   Water Tower

72   Horse Croft   Ash Closes   Down Field
The Bracks   Down Field Windmill   Lark Hall Farm

2   Football Ground   North Corner   South Horse Fen   Horse Fen   WINDMILL CL   Lark Hall Bridge
HAWE'S LA   Hall Farm   Cemy   WICKEN ROAD   No Ditch Bridge   Block Farm

71   THE CRESCENT   Wicken   PH   CHURCH ROAD   No Ditch Field   Westside Farm
Visitor Centre   Windmill   Chancel Farm   A1123

1   National Trust   Moat   Little Fen   CB5

70   Cambridgeshire STREET ATLAS

56   A   57   B   58   C   59   D   60   E   61   F

D3
1 LODE CL
2 COLLEGE RD
3 REGENT
4 FRANK BRIDGES CL
5 REDHOUSE GD
6 THE CR
7 FORDHAM RD
8 MEADOW CL
9 MILL CFT

D4
1 ROSE BAY GD
2 BLUE BELL WK
3 HERBERT HUMAN CL
4 HONEYSUCKLE CL
5 NIGHTALL RD
6 CHESTNUT DR
7 GIMBERT RD
8 QUEENSWAY
9 WEATHERALLS CL

10 TEN BELL LA
11 BERRYCROFT
12 GUNTONS CL
13 BELL GD
14 FREDERICK TALBOT CL
15 CHURCHGATE ST
16 MKT ST
17 ADELAIDE CL
18 EASTERN AV
19 BREWHOUSE LA

20 WHITE HART LA
21 GARDENERS LA
22 BROOK DAM LA

44

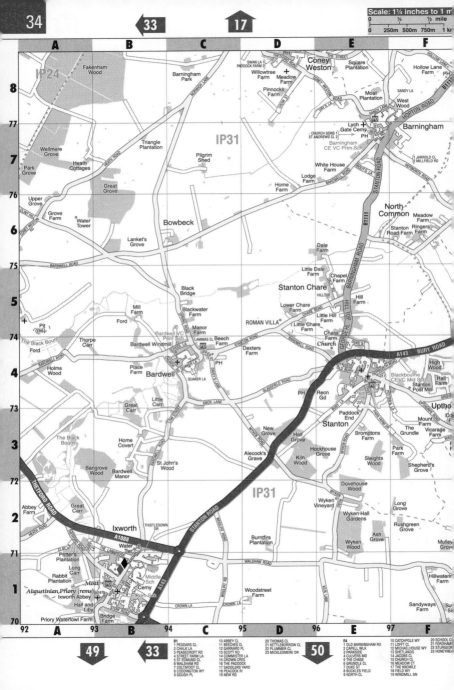

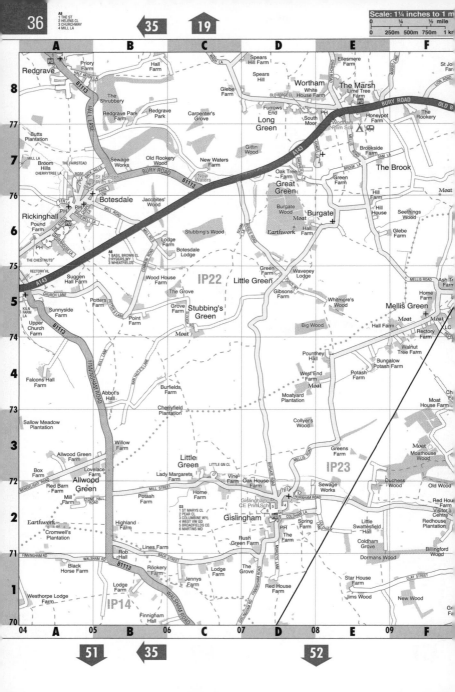

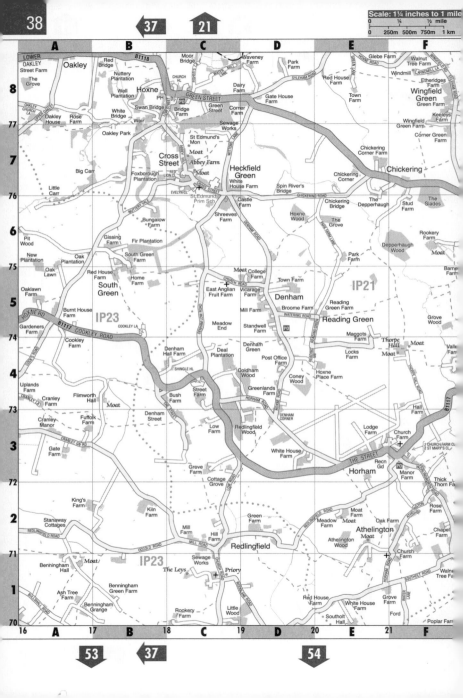

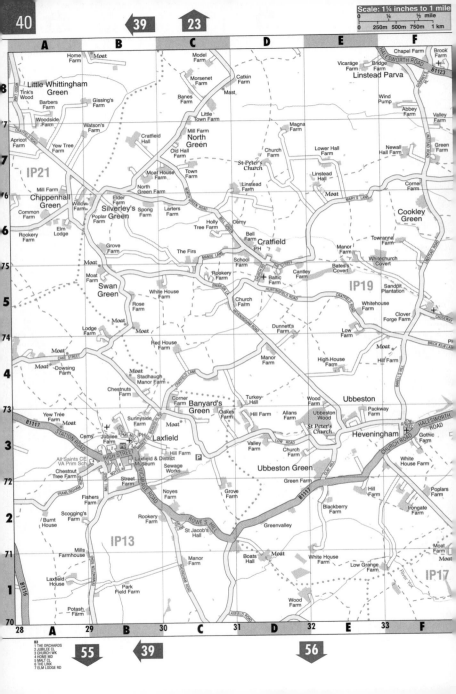

Scale: 1¼ inches to 1 mile

¼ mile ½ mile

250m 500m 750m 1 km

A | **B** | **C** | **D** | **E** | **F**

HILL ROAD
Alder Carr
Gravel Pit
Alder Carr Marshes
Wangford Common Covert

Mardle House

Lime Kiln Farm

NR34

Scotia End

Old Hall Farm

Reydon
Gorse Lodge Farm
Laurel Farm

119
Broadside Park Farm

B1127

Wolsey Bridge
Nature Reserve
Southwold Covert
A1095
Mile Walk Covert

HALESWORTH ROAD
B1126
Saint Georges Sch
Southend Warren
SEAVIEW RD

Reydon Marshes

Sch

Bridge Foot Farm
Sole End
NORTH RD
Pier

lcamp House

Tinker's Marshes

Wind Pump

IP18

Buss Creek

SOUTHWOLD

Tinker's House

Walberswick Common

CH
Wr Twr

Tinker's Barn

Squire's Hill

Town Marshes

Gunhill Cliff

Hill Covert

PH

The Denes

Deadman's Covert

Tinker's Covert
Eastwood Lodge Farm

Suffolk Coast & Heaths Path

Walberswick Nature Reserve

Tumulus

Tinker's Walks
Tumulus

IP19

Sallow Walk Covert

East Sheep Walk

Walberswick

THE STREET
B1387

Old Farm

PH

119

estwood Lodge

Old Covert

LODGE RD

East Hill

ADAM'S LA 1
CHURCH LA 2
SHORT LA 3

Hoist Covert

119

Dunwich River

Fen Hill

Westwood Marshes

Walberswick Nature Reserve

Dingle Great Hill

Dingle Farm

Foxburrow Wood

Sandymount Covert

Dunwich Corporation Marshes

Scheiller's Grove

IP17

Dingle Stone House

Reedland Marshes

Dingle Marshes

t Helena Farm

Little Dingle

Dunwich Forest

Hog's Grove

Suffolk Coast & Heaths Path

Dunwich River

Dunwich
Bridge Farm
Church Farm
BEACH RD

ST JAMES ST

Chapel
Dunwich
Mus
Franciscan Friary

Sandy Lane Farm

The Spinney
Broom Hill
Mound

A 47 | **B** 48 | **C** 49 | **D** 50 | **E** 51 | **F**

For full street detail of the highlighted area see page 119.

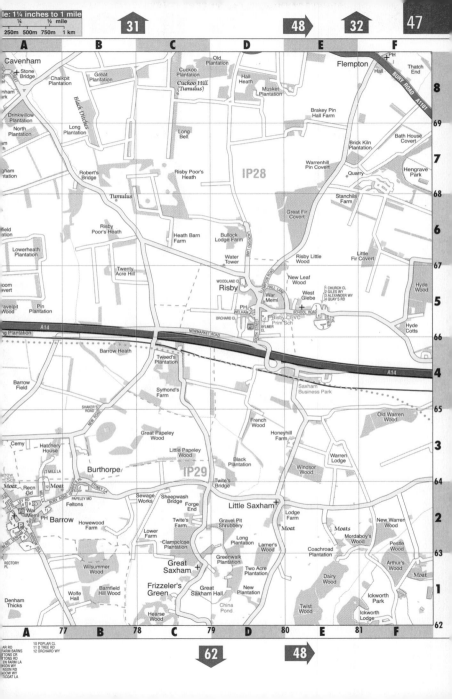

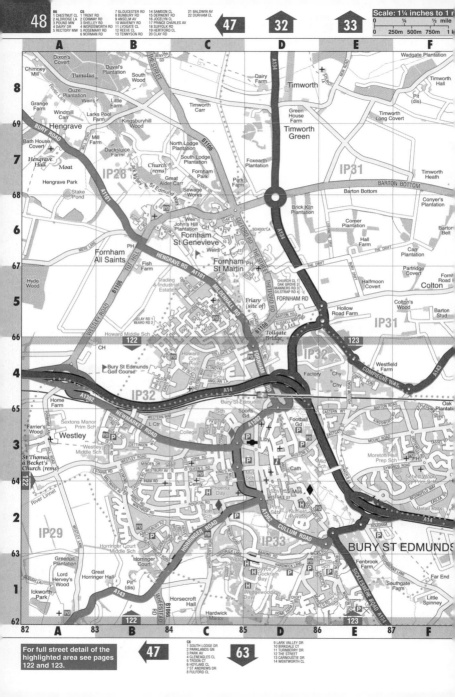

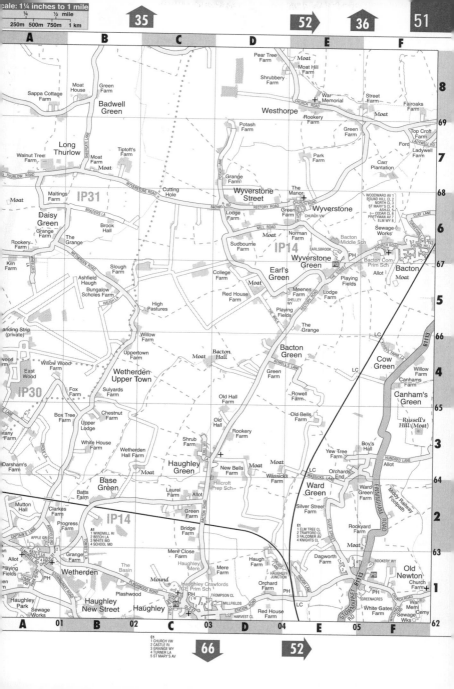

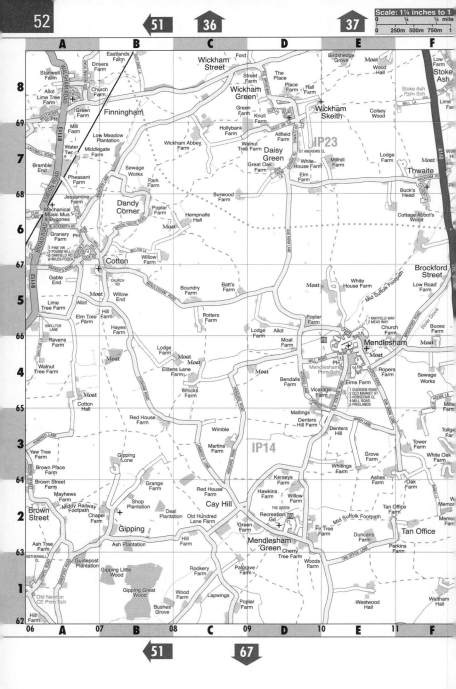

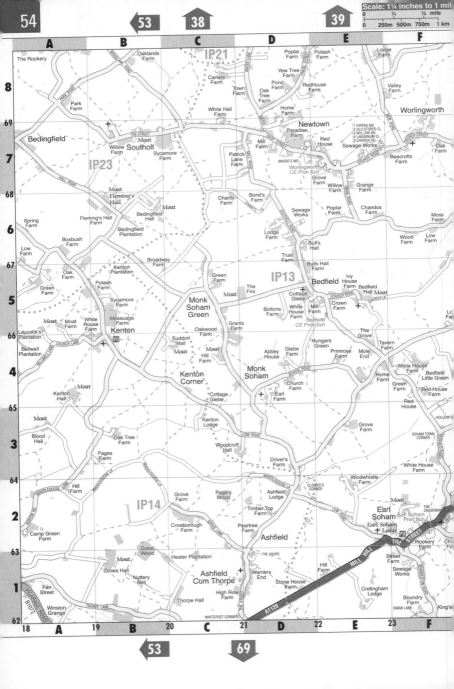

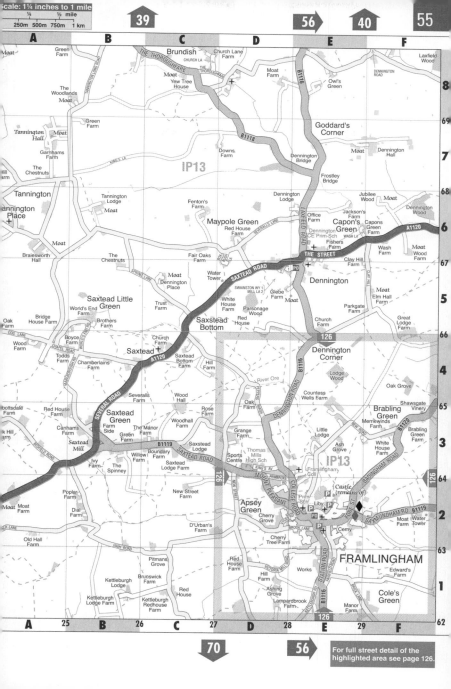

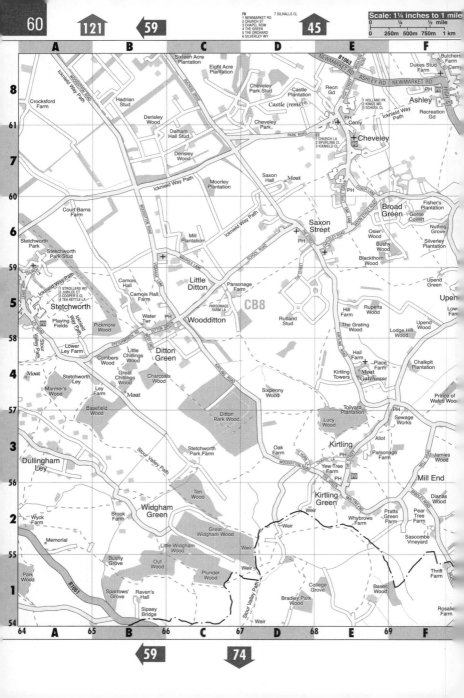

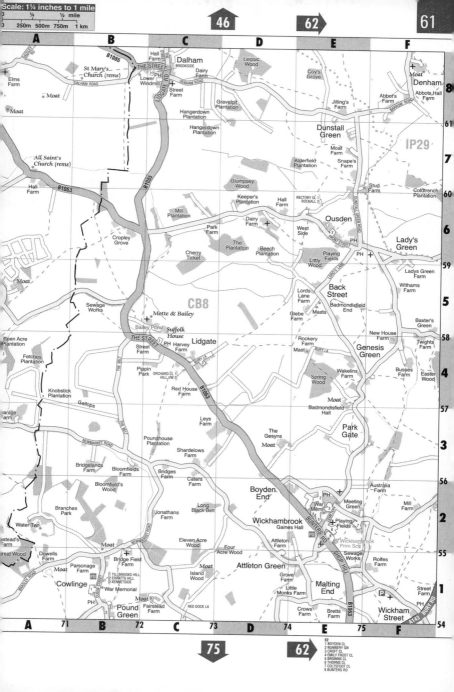

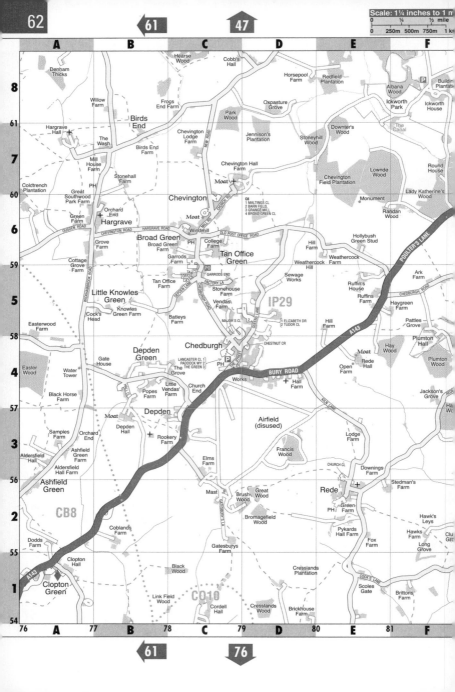

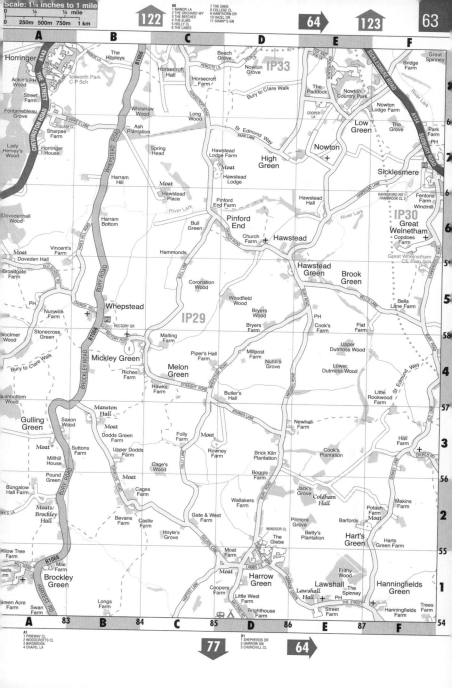

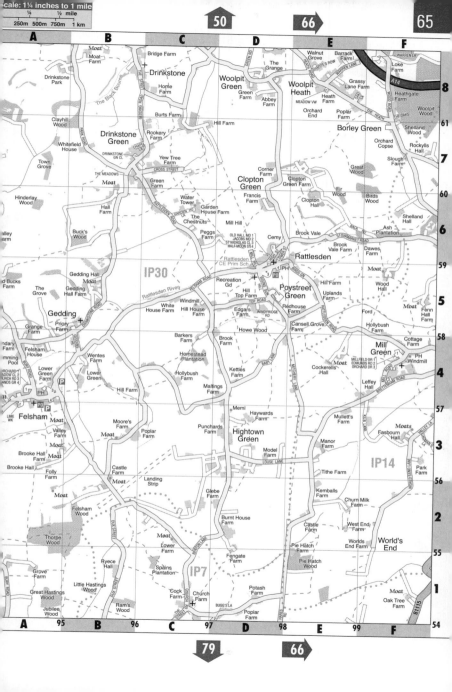

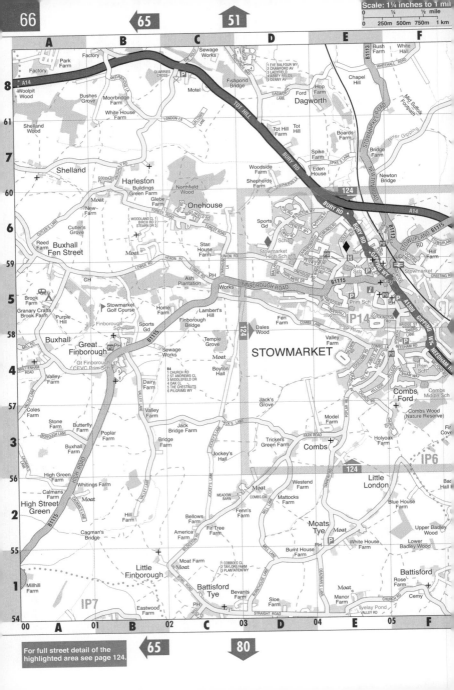

Cambridgeshire STREET ATLAS

A B C D E F

River Stour Ford
B1061 Weir

Carlton
Hall Farm Moat
BRINKLEY RD
CHURCH RD
CARLTON GREEN RD

Handy Bar Grove

Waterfield Barn Farm
Mill Farm

East Green
East Green Farm

BRADLEY RD

8

Church Farm
Carlton Wood

Matthews Farm
Evergreen La

THE STREET
WHITE ST

FOX GN
CB8

Moat

53

Great Bradley
Fox Farm

Doley Wood

Stour Valley Path

Ever Green
CLARENDALE EST

THURLOW ROAD

7

Hart Wood

Little Bradley

52

Lopham's Hall Farm

Mill Mound

Almshouses

Little Thurlow Green

BROAD ROAD

Carlton Green

Lopham's Wood

Moat

Church RD
Thurlow CE Prim Sch
School House

Waggell's Wood

6

Finchley Farm

Girton Farm

Sewage Works

Little Thurlow

Gover's Grove

Temple End Plantation

Temple End

Temple End Stream
TEMPLE END

PH

Drift Side

Great Thurlow

BURY ROAD

Grov

51

CB1

Manor Farm

PH

Foxburrow Wood

5

Temple End Farm

Wasteland Plantation

Goldings Farm

Great Thurlow Hall

Trundley Wood

The New Plantation

Dowsett Wood

Windmill
Moat
Glebe Plantation

Playing Fields

Ganwick Wood

50

Smoothies Plantation

WRATTING ROAD

WEST END LANE

Willow Hall Plantation

Cadge's Wood

Tuffill's Plantation

Hunts Park Farm

Gravel Pit Plantation

4

North Wood

The Spinney

High Noon Plantation

Hungry Hill Plantation

Nursery Plantation

Stour Valley Path

49

Exhibition Farm

Littley Wood

High Noon Farm

Abbacy Wood

Hill Wood

Pelican House Farm

Greenfields Farm

THE STREET
Maltings Farm

3

Lawn Farm

CB9

Moor Pasture Plantation

Jarvis Hill

Hall Farm
Ford
PH

Lawn Wood

SCHOOL RD

Moat
Charity Farm

Bittons Farm

Moor Pasture Farm

WITHERSFIELD ROAD

Rook Tree Farm

THURLOW RD
Was

Paradise Farm

PH
Great Wratting
Church End

Chimney
Factory

48

Sports Ground

Recreation Gd
Lilley Farm

PH
Withersfield

Church St

HOMESTALL CR

Church Farm
Hall Farm

Burton Ley Plantation

OLD HAVERHILL RD

P

2

Silver Street Farm

HOLLOW HL
PH
SILVER ST
HAVERHEATH RD

Sewage Works

Water Twr
Reservoir

Little Wratting

A143

Hilltop Farm

B1061

Sp

Howe Wood

Nomey Plantation

47

Spring Grove Farm

132

133

Keding

1

A1307 Cambridge

Hanchet End

Bridge End

A1307

WITHERSFIELD RD

Boyton Hall
Boyton Hall Farm

PH

HAVERHILL RD

Great Wilsey Farm

Hanchett Hall Farm

132

WRATTING RD

CHALK HILL

Samuel Ward Sch

Moat

Great Field Plantation

46

MELLIS CL 1
LANGHAM WY 2
MOTLEY DR 3
HOPTON RI 4

A1307

CHARITY Dr

64 A 65 B 66 C 67 D 68 E 69 F

88

132

For full street detail of the highlighted area see pages 132 and 133.

133

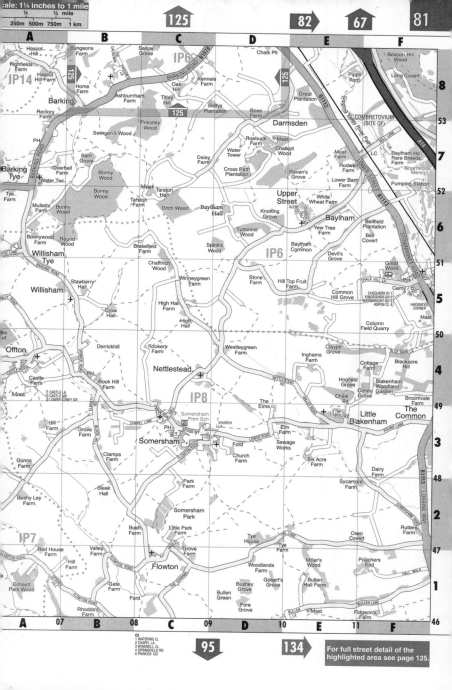

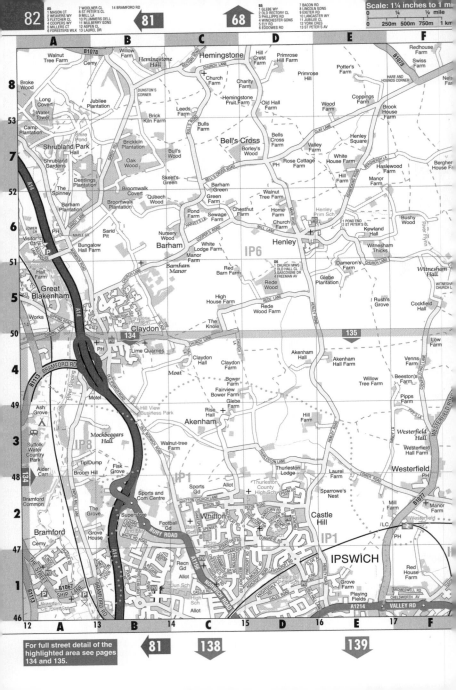

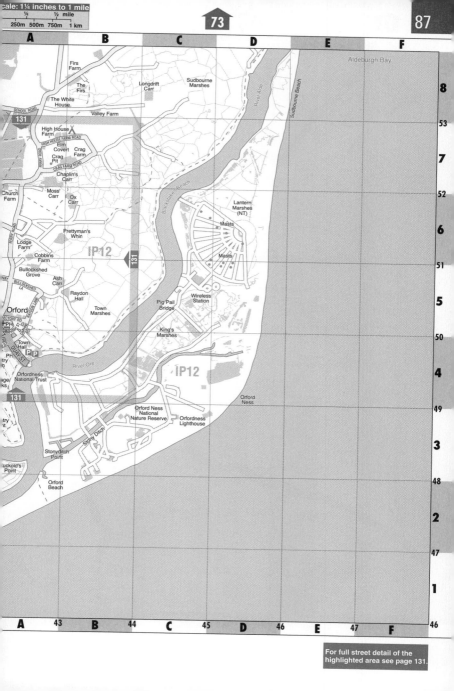

HAVERHILL

Mary Cole's Grove

Woodland Green

Hanchet End

Duncey Plantation

Hazel Stubb Farm

Hazel Stub

CB9

Nosterfield Farm

Goodwoods Farm

Poplar Wood

Ladygate Wood

Moat

Moon Hall Farm

Copse Hall Farm

Greatley Wood

Eastcott Farm

Eagles Farm

Hotel

Sports Gd.

Pope Mill Farm

Sturmer

Moat

PH

CB1

Horseham Hall

Hilltop Farm

Garland's Wood

Bex Grove

Abbott's Grove

Walton Farm

Copy Farm

132

133

Board Barn Farm

Draper's Farm

Wiggens Green

Whites Farm

Garlands Farm

Yew Tree Farm

Upper House Farm

Lancelots Farm

Catherines Wood

Haven Farm

Jacobs Farm

Wiggins Farm

Gable End

Lower House Farm

Pale Green

Meadow Side

Rolls Farm

Moss Farm

Helions Bumpstead

Wash Bridge

Sewage Works

Ford

Blois Road

Rylan

Sage's End

Helions Farm

Moat

Helions

PH

Rec Gd

Bumpstead Hall

New House Farm

NORTH CR 1
THE CHASE 2
LION MD 3

Freezes Farm

Steeple Bumpstead

Blois Farm

Devil's Grove

Recke Woo

Moyn's Park

Steeple Bumpstead Pottery

EDITH CAVELL WY

Cemy

Dock Plantation

Moyn's Park

Boblow

Balance Wood

Brook End

Rec Gd

Bower Hall

Smith's Green

CB9

Bower Hall Farm

Old Hall Farm

Moat

Arbour Grove

Syca Plan

CO9

Bulls Bridge Farm

Little Smith Green Farm

Mill Farm

Old Hall

Cootes Farm

Whiteho Farm

Round Wood

Hillside Farm

CB10

Little Bulls Farm

Moat

Latchley's Farm

Wildings Farm

Old Hall Wood

Ruses Farm

Hempstead Hall

Moat

Wakeland's Farm

Hophouse Farm

Hempstead Wood

Lakehouse Grove

CM7

Martin's Farm

Prouds Farm

Revels Fa

Lakehouse Farm

Moat

Mast

Herkstead Hall Farm

Moat

Messings Farm

For full street detail of the highlighted area see pages 132 and 133.

D3
1 CHURCHFIELDS DR
2 ST MARY'S WK
3 BARKER CL
4 JOHN TIBAULD CT
5 BORRADALE CT
6 WOOLNOUGH CL
7 GEORGE GENT CL

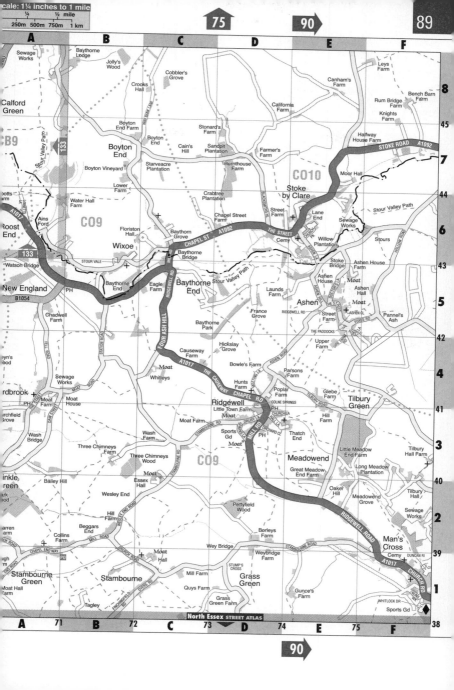

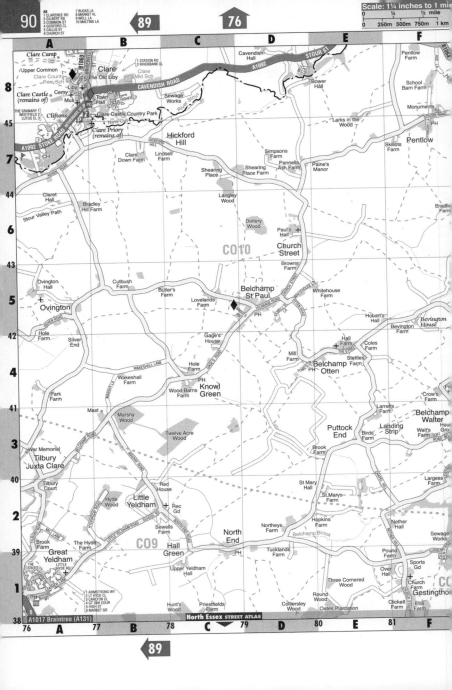

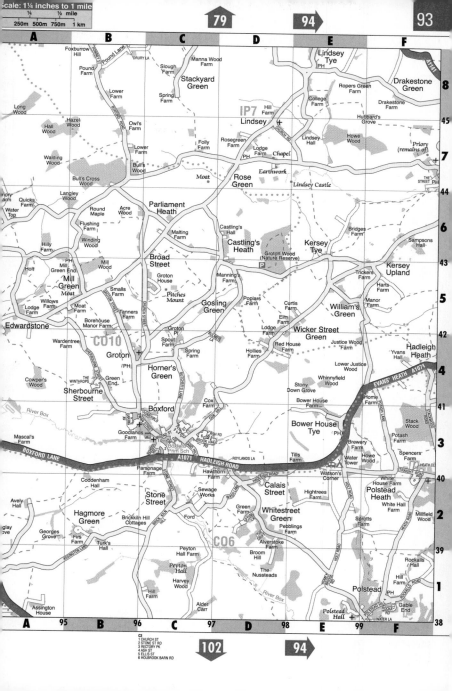

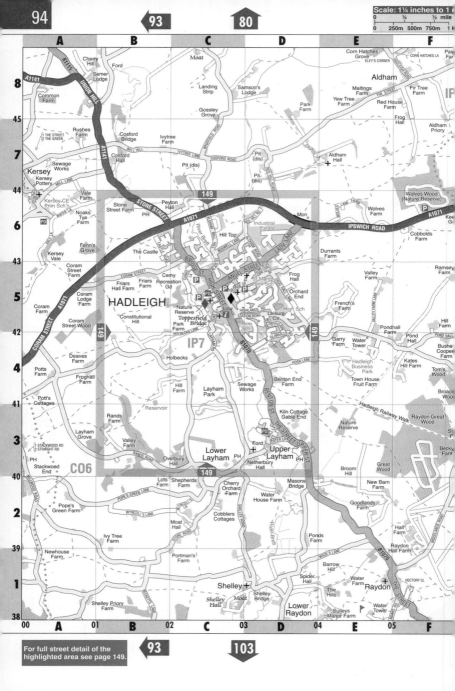

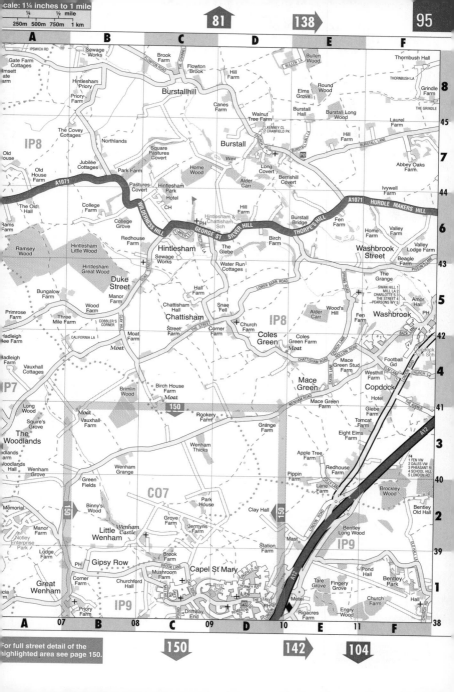

Scale: 1¼ inches to 1 mil

0   ¼   ½ mile
0 250m 500m 750m 1 km

| A | B | C | D | E | F |

8

Oak Hill

HM Prison

Sports Ground

Grove House

The Grove

IP12

River Ore

45

✠

7

Hollesley Bay Colony
(HM Young Offender Institution)

Hollesley Bay

Orford Haven

44

Sewage Works

Oxley Marshes

Oxley Dairy

North Weir Point

6

P

43

Shingle Street

5

Martello Tower

Suffolk Coast & Heaths Path

42

4

41

3

40

2

39

1

38

36 A 37 B 38 C 39 D 40 E 41 F

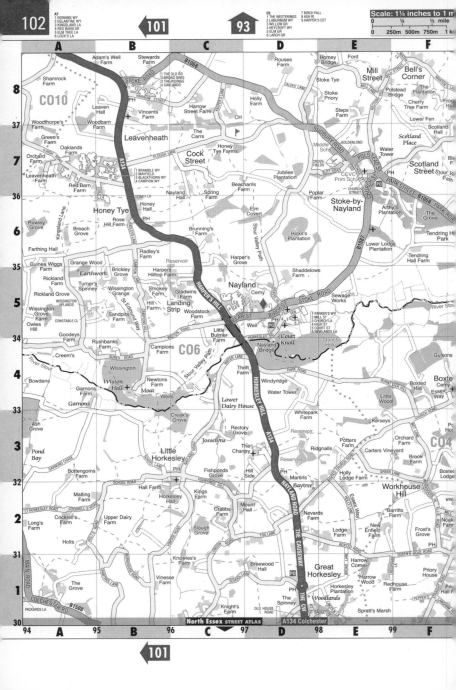

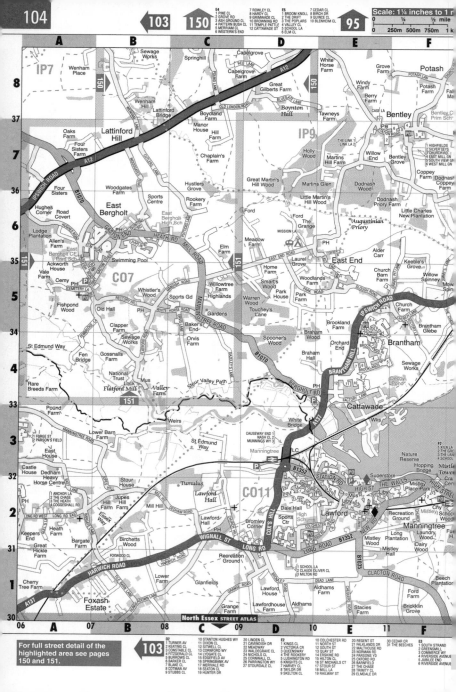

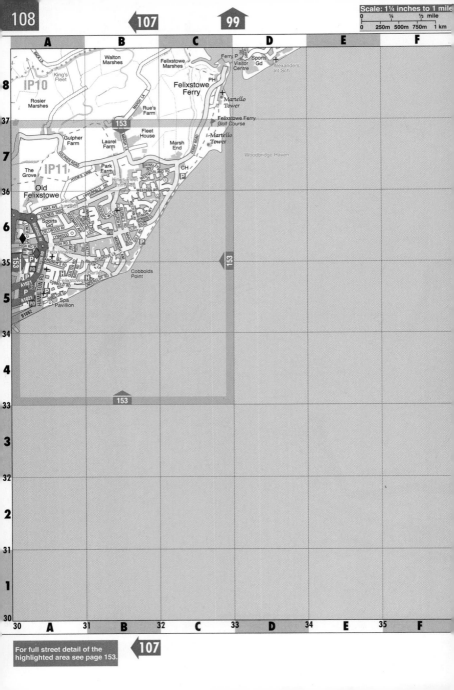

108

◄ 107

▲ 99

Scale: 1¼ inches to 1 mile
0   ¼   ½ mile
0   250m 500m 750m   1 km

A   B   C   D   E   F

8

IP10

King's
Fleet

Walton
Marshes

Felixstowe
Marshes

Ferry P
Visitor
Centre

Sports
Gd

Alexanders
Int Sch

Rosier
Marshes

PH

Felixstowe
Ferry

37

Marsh La

Rue's
Farm

Martello
Tower

153

Felixstowe Ferry
Golf Course

7

Gulpher
Farm

Laurel
Farm

Fleet
House

Marsh
End

Martello
Tower

Woodbridge Haven

The
Grove

IP11

Park
Farm

BRINLEY

CH

Old Felixstowe

36

King's Fleet Primary Sch

WESTMORLAND RD

Colneis Junior Sch

LINKS AVE

WESTERN

6

Sports
Gd

LYNWOOD

153

P

Felixstowe

Cobbolds
Point

35

P

ST ANDREW'S RD

153

5

A1021

A1021

H

Spa
Pavillion

34

B1092

4

33

153

3

32

2

31

1

30

30   A   31   B   32   C   33   D   34   E   35   F

◄ 107

For full street detail of the
highlighted area see page 153.

B6
1 BECCLESGATE
2 OLD MILL TR
3 POUND RD
4 CAXTON MS
5 SALTGATE
6 SMALLGATE
7 ROOK'S LA
8 MANORHOUSE LA
9

B5
1 MARKET ST
2 SMALLGATE
3 STEPPING HL
4 MIDMEADOW
5 HOMEFIELD AV
6 EXCHANGE SQ
7 CROWFOOT GD
8 TEMPERANCE PL
9

9

A · B · C · D · E · F

8

NORWICH ROAD
A146

Little Carr

Gillingham Marshes

Beccles Marshes

Worlingham Wall

7

Beccles New Bridge

91

PH

Superstore

LC

Lotman's Carr

Wild Carr

Beccles Old Bridge

PH

Boney's Island

CH

6

Hotel

Printing Museum

Football Ground

Sports Ground

Beccles Common

Beccles Golf Course

Wolsey's Woods

Westhill Covert

Town Hall

Chimney

Beccles

Sports Ground

NR34

Woodview Farm

Waveney Meadow

Beccles Liby

Works

MAPLE WY
MULBERRY CL
THE HARBOURAGE
KINGSTON DR

Beccles Carr

Horseshoe Covert

Worlingham Hall

5

Beccles & District Mus

St Benets RC Primary Sch

BECCLES

Recreation Ground

90

St Mary's Road

St Benet's RC Minst

PEDDARS LANE

Beccles and District War Meml

Albert Rye Prim Sch

Crowfoot Community Prim Sch

Motel

Worlingham Middle Sch

4

Sir John Leman High Sch

Beccles Sports Ctr

Cemy

Beccles Mid Sch

ORCHARD GREEN

CASTLE

Worlingham

Manor Farm

89

Works

Ellough Hill

1 FOXGLOVE CL
2 HILLTOP RI
3 HILLCREST CL
4 CHESTNUT CL

3

HILLCREST RD 1
CROMWELL CL2
WILLREDE CL3

Recn Gd

G2
1 ST MICHAEL'S CL
2 ST EDMUNDS CL
3 ST MATTHEW'S AV
4 ST PAUL'S CL
5 ST DAVID'S CL
6 RIGBOURNE HL LA

SIR JOHN LEMAN RD

2

1 JOHN LAWRENCE CL
2 DOWES HL CL
3 DOROTHY HODGKIN CT
4 RONDEN CL

Orchard Farm

Valley Farm

LC

LONDON ROAD
A145

CUCUMBER LANE

Cucumber Lane Farm

Ellough Moor

1

LC

CROMWELL RD

Chenery's Farm

88

42 · 43 · 44

C4
1 DUKES MD
2 BLYBURGATE
3 FREDERICK'S RD
4 GROVE MS
9

C3
1 McLAREN CT
2 HIGH LEAS CL
3 BOROUGH END
4 RUSSET CL
5 MARION CL
9

F4
1 CHERRY HL CL
2 FAIRMILE CL
3 THE RIDINGS
4 THE BRIDLES
5 SAMFORD CT
6 ALL SAINTS GN

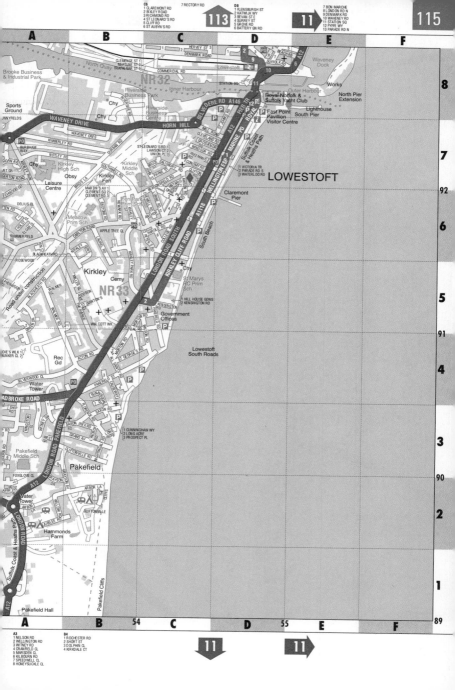

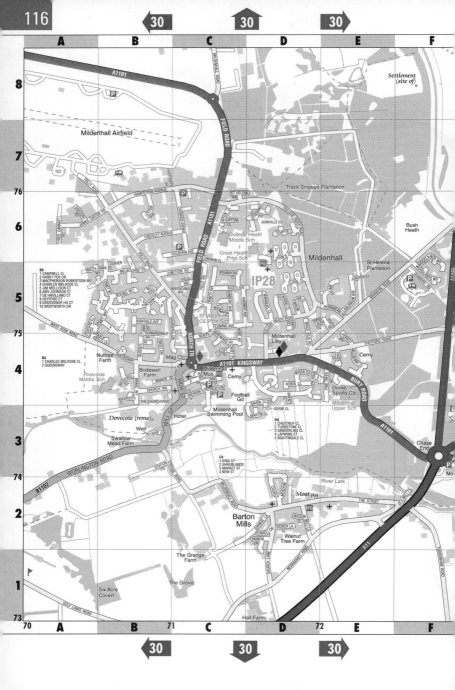

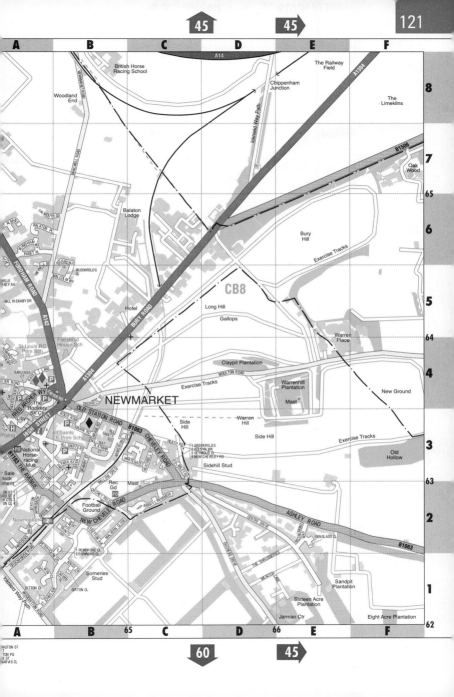

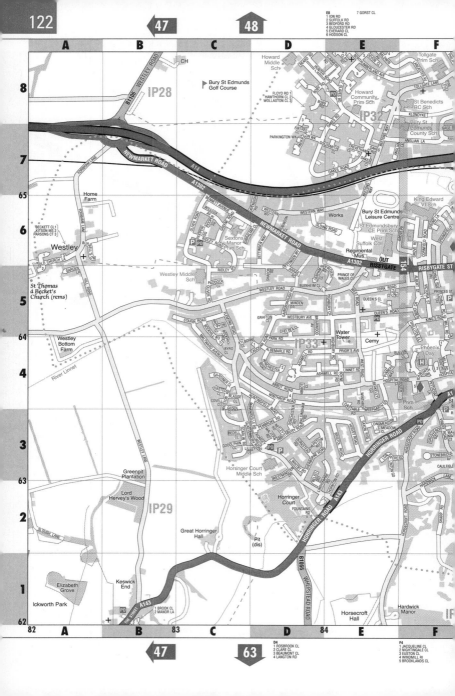

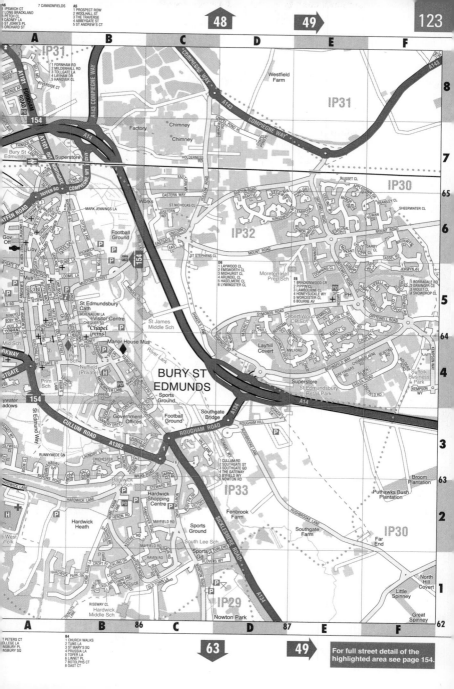

A5
1 PROSPECT ROW
2 WOOL HALL ST
3 THE TRAVERSE
4 ABBEYGATE ST
5 ST ANDREW'S CT

7 CANNONFIELDS

A6
1 IPSWICH CT
2 LONG BRACKLAND
3 PETO'S CL
4 CADNEY LA
5 ST JOHN'S PL
6 ORCHARD ST

IP31

A1101

Westfield Farm

IP31

A143

154

A14

Factory

Bury St Edmunds

Superstore

Chimney

Chimney

HOLDERNESS RD

COMPIEGNE WAY

A143

IP30

RUSSET CL

APPLEGROVE DR

SHEERWATER CL

TAYFEN RD

COMPIEGNE WY

154

MARK JENNINGS LA

Works

IP32

BARTON ROAD

MOUNT ROAD

IP30

MOUNT ROAD

Gov. Off

Liby

St Nicholas Cl

EASTERN WAY

UNICORN

ST STEPHENS CL

D6
1 LAYWOOD CL
2 EMSWORTH CL
3 MIDHURST CL
4 ARUNDEL CL
5 HASELMERE CL
6 LYMINGSTER CL

Moreton Hall Prep Sch

E6
1 BRACKENWOOD CR
2 PIPPIN CL
3 LAMBOURNE CL
4 HONEYSUCKLE WY
5 WORCESTER CL
6 BOURNE AV

F
1 BORRADALE RD
2 GRAINGER CL
3 VIOLET CL
4 SNOWDROP CL

JERMYN AV

Mus

St Edmundsbury Cath

Athenaeum La

Chequer Sq

Chapel Rems

Manor House Mus

Nuffield (Private)

Prim Sch

River Lark

St James Middle Sch

Robert Wood CE Sch

SYMONDS ROAD

Layhill Covert

MILFORD

Suffolk Business Park

KEMPSON WY

154

BURY ST EDMUNDS

Sports Ground

Football Ground

Government Offices

Southgate Bridge

CULLUM ROAD

A1302

Superstore

St Edmundsbury Retail Park

A14

ROUGHAM ROAD

Rougham Hill

A134

D3
1 CULLUM RD
2 SOUTHGATE ST
3 SOUTHGATE GD
4 THE GATEWAY
5 BYFIELD WY
6 NEWTON RD

RUNNYMEDE GN

CHICHESTER

Hardwick Prim Sch

Hardwick Shopping Centre

IP33

Broom Plantation

Puthawks Bush Plantation

IP30

HARDWICK LANE

Hardwick Heath

Fenbrook Farm

Southgate Farm

Far End

West Suffolk

H

Sports Ground

South Lee Sch

SICKLESMERE ROAD

North Hill Covert

Little Spinney

RISEWAY CL

Hardwick Middle Sch

IP29

Nowton Park

A134

Great Spinney

B4
1 CHURCH WALKS
2 TUNS LA
3 ST MARY'S SQ
4 PRUSSIA LA
5 TOPER LA
6 LINNET PL
7 BOTOLPHS CT
8 OAST CT

T PETERS CT
OLLEGE LA
NSBURY PL
NSBURY SQ

86   87

For full street detail of the highlighted area see page 154.

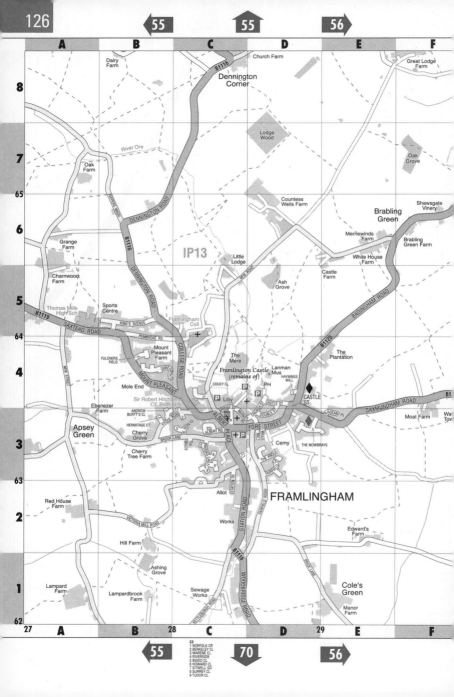

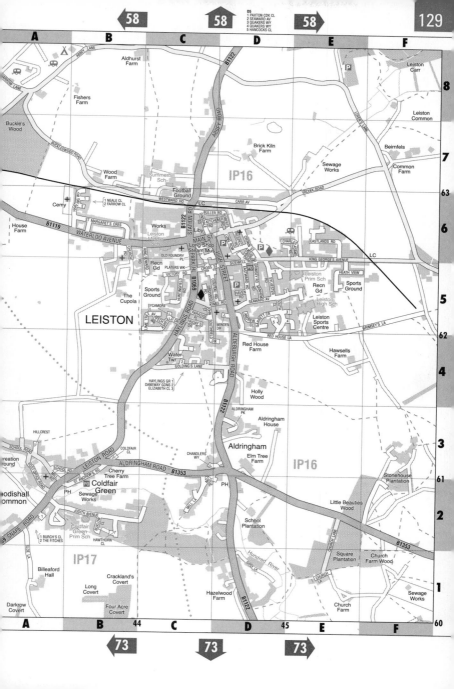

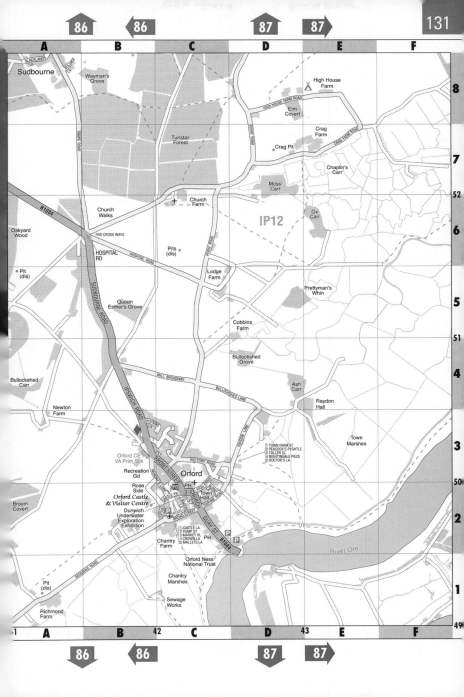

A B C D E F

A143
Hills Farm

Great Field Plantation

Great Wilsey Farm
Moat

Mill Road
RISBRIDGE DRIVE
SCHOOL DR
Kedington Prim Sch
WHITE HORSE LA
VILLAGE MEWS
B1061
DASH END LA
STATION RD
WESTWARD DEALS
Skips Wood
Ketton House
SIM'S LA

Kedington
PH
Liby

CB9

Mary Cole's Grove

Ruses Farm

Stour Farm

Sewage Works

Stour Valley Path

1 MILLFIELDS WY
2 SANDPIPER CL

PENTLOW HAWKE CL

REDSHANK CL 1
KESTREL RD 2
ROBIN CL 3

Coupals Prim Sch

ROMAN WY

Woodland Green

1 CLAUDIAN CL
2 HADRIAN CL
3 FLAVIAN CL
4 AUGUSTUS CL
5 TIBERIUS CL

Hotel
CH
P
JUSTINIAN CL
P

COUPALS ROAD

Eastcotts Farm

Calford Green

Eagles Farm

COUPALS CL

HUDSON CL 1
JUPITER CL 2
CHARRINGTON CL

A143

Sports Gd

Visitor Centre

Haverhill Golf Club

Pope Mill Farm

Kedington End

B1061

Willow Farm

FALCONER RD

Sturmer End Industrial Estate

STURMER ROAD

ROWLEY HILL

A1017

Tumulus

CB9

ROWLEY HILL

WATER LANE

1 ROWLEY CT
2 ABBOTTS CT
3 POPES CT
4 HICKS WY
5 ELM CT

CHURCH CE

PH

Sturmer

ROWLEY HILL

Abbotts Farm

Roost End

Stour Valley
Path
Water Hall Farm

Moat

CHURCH WALK

The Spinney

HILL LANE

Ains Ford

A1017

CO9

Greatley Wood

Bex Grove

Abbott's Grove

C8
1 ST PETER'S AV
2 QUOITS FIELD
3 MORGAN CT
4 POPLAR GR
5 LAUREL WY
6 WILLOW CL
7 LIMEKILN CL
8 OLD PAPER MILL LA

A   B   C   D   E   F

8

Claydon High Sch
Church Farm
Claydon
Lime Quarries
REDE LA
Claydon Farm

BLUE BARN LA
CHAPEL LANE
ADDISON WY
LODGE LA
BRAMFORD ROAD
B1113
STATION ROAD
CHESTNUT
NEWELL RD
THE BEECHES
CHURCH LANE
Claydon Hall

BRAMFORD ROAD
ORCHARD GR
IP6
Moat

7

Broomvale Farm
PAPER MILL LA
Motel
Bowe Farm

49

B1113
BRAMFORD ROAD
River Gipping
Hill View Business Park
Glebe Farm

6

Rise Hall
Akenham

Suffolk Water Park
Mockbeggars Hall

5

Paper Mill Farm
Walnut-tree Farm

48

Alder Carr
Tip/Dump
Fisk Grove
Broom Hill
IP1

4

Bramford Common
IP8
The Grove
WOODLANDS WY
A14
P&R
Retail Park
Sports Gd
Sports Centre
Recreation Gd
Allot
WHITTON CHURCH LANE
Whitton
Community Prim Sch
BYRON RD
HARDY CR
CHAUCER RD
THACKERAY RD
WORDSWORTH
SPENSER RD
BLAKE
BROWNING
ARNOLD CL
BURNS RD
BALLATER

Superstore
BURY ROAD
A1156 BURY ROAD
Football Gd

3

Grove House
Whitehouse Industrial Estate
Alpha Business Park
WHITE HOUSE ROAD
St.Pancras Catholic Prim Sch
CEDARCROFT RD
MEREDITH
CHARLTON
MANSFIELD AV
PO

47

Lawn Cemy
ACTON RD
CHAPEL FIELD
HILLCREST
Recreation Gd
Allot
OLYMPUS CL
TYRONE
CANAL RD
MASERATI
WEXFORD RD
RILEY AV
NELSON

2

Bramford
B1067
B1113
THE STREET
MILL FIELD
PACKARD
SHIP LANE
BRAMFORD ROAD
RILEY CL
LAGONDA DR
BASTON CL
The Gables Farm
White House
MAUDSLAY
DAIMLER RD
MARLOW RD
ANTRIM RD
CONNAUGHT RD
Chy
Whitehouse Junior Sch
Westbourne High Sch
Allot
HAYLEIGH
LISTER RD
KELVIN RD
DEBEN RD
NORWICH ROAD
A1156

1

LORAINE WY
Bramford CE Prim Sch
DUCKAMERE
FITZGERALD ROAD
VICARAGE LA
Woodlands Poultry Farm
1 CHURCH GN
2 ST MARY'S CL
A14
B1067
Recreation Gd
MOAT
CORAL DR
BROCKLEY CR
SHAFTO RD

46

LORAINE WY
Hazel Wood

12   A   13   B   C   14   D   E   F

A2
1 ACTON GDNS
2 LACON RD
3 BUSHMAN GDNS
4 WALNUT TREE CL
5 BULLEN LA
6 ORCHARD RD

D1
1 OPAL AV
2 AGATE CL
3 BRAMFORD LA

F1
1 HIGHFIELD APPROACH
2 MORNINGTON AV

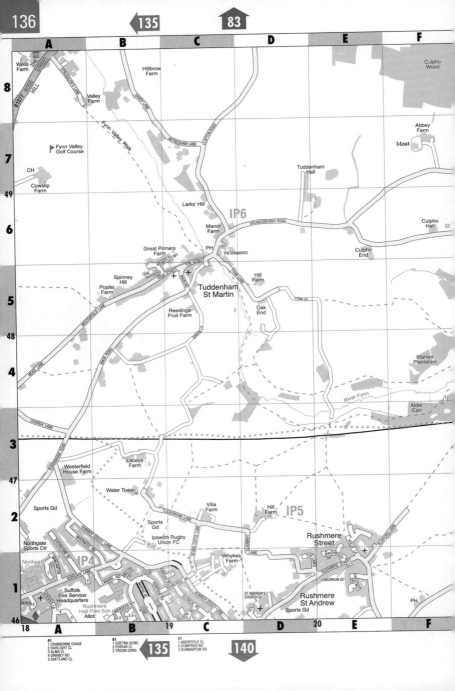

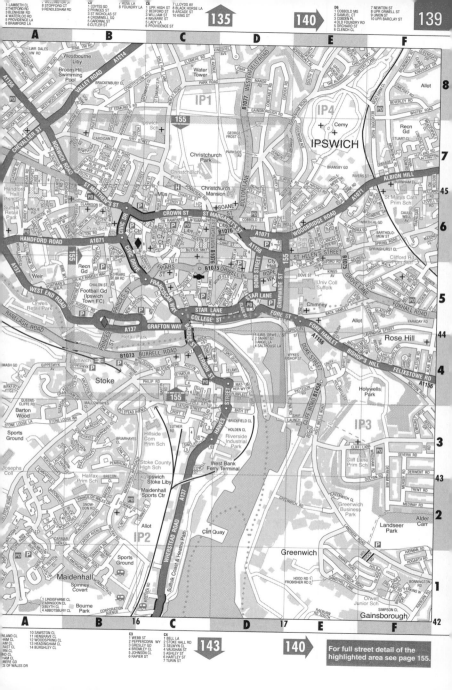

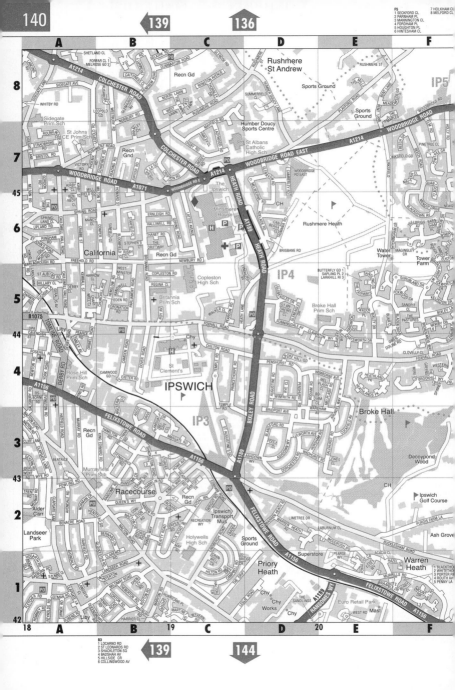

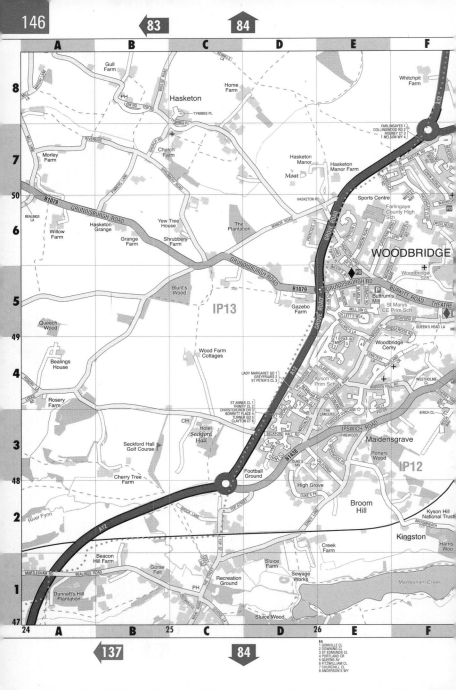

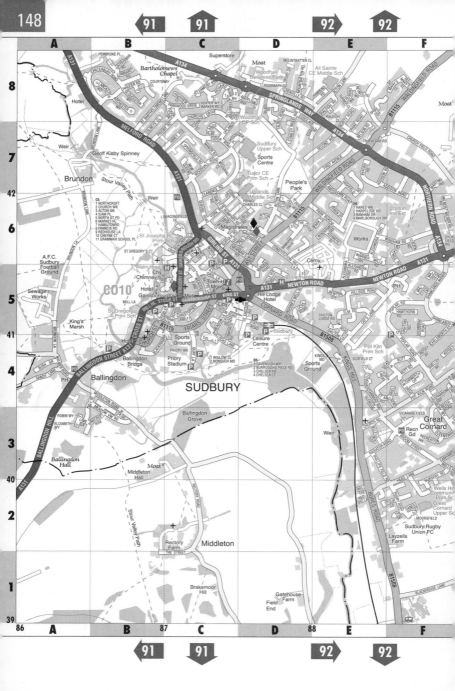

95
95
95

A B C D E F

8
7
40
6
5
39
4
3
38
2
1
37

Moat
Vauxhall Farm
Brimlin Wood
Rookery Farm
Cottage Farm
WENHAM ROAD
The Gra
IP8

Wenham Grange
Wenham Thicks

Green Fields
CO7

Park House

Binny's Wood
Grove Farm
Clay Hall

Little Wenham
Wenham Castle
Jermyns Farm

Lodge Farm

Binny's Wood
Brook Farm
IP9

PH
Gipsy Row
Churchford Farm
Mushroom Farm
Capel St Mary
THE PIGHTLE
PENN CL
LITTLE TUFTS
GREAT TUFTS

Corner Farm
Churchford Hall
WINDMILL RD
DAYS GN
DAYS GREEN
MILL CL
Capel St. Mary CE. Prim. Sch.
SNOWCROFT
Liby

Priory Farm
Driftway End
HOMEFIELD
PH

Great Wenham

AISTHORPE 1
LT GULLS 2
COOMBERS 3
RED SLEEVE 4
Capelgrove
Mast

Wenham Place
Sewage Works
Springhill
PEMBROW RD

Capelgrove Farm

CO7

Bush Farm
Great Gilberts Farm

Wenham Hill
RED LANE
Dovefield Farm
BLUEGATE LANE
Bluegate Farm

Boydland Farm
Manor House
OLD LONDON ROAD
Bradfield Farm
Boynton Hall

A12

E3
1 SCHOOL CL
2 CROTCHETS CL
3 PENNY MD
4 PETER'S GR
5 WINDING PIECE
6 TOLL GATE RD
7 CHALKNERS CL
8 STOCKMERS END
9 SMITHERS CL

1 GLEBE END
2 TWO ACRES
3 ROUNDRIDGE
4 FARTHINGS WH
5 THE QUEECH
6 JERMYNS CL

HAWBRIDGE 1
RYLANDS 2
THE SQUIRRELS 3

107
107

D5
1 KILN FIELD
2 CHILDERS FD
3 FEATHERS FD
4 REEDLAND WY
5 WINSTON CL
6 OTLEY CT

7 BREDFIELD CL
8 BRACKLEY CL
9 LARKHILL WY
10 EYNOLDS CT
11 WILLIAM BOOTH WY
12 GENERALS MS
13 ALDRINGHAM MS

14 SUDBOURNE RD
15 RENDLESHAM RD
16 MICKFIELD MS
17 WESTLETON WY
18 MELLIS CT
19 DARSHAM CL

E5
1 HALL FD
2 GARDEN FD
3 CROSSGATE FD
4 BEACON FD
5 BROOM FD
6 HAMILTON ST

7 JAMES BODEN CL

Great Street Farm

Candlet Farm

Hill House Farm

THURMANS LA

1 POUCH ML
2 THE WHEELWRIGHTS
3 CARRIAGE CL
4 HEATHGATE PIECE

Egypt Wood

Gulpher Business Park

Trimley St Mary

Trimley St Mary Prim. Sch.

LC

CANDLET ROAD

Cowpasture Farm

LC Trimley

Searson's Farm

Seasons Farm

1 LANGSTONS
2 THE KEMPSTERS
3 SPRITES END
4 EASTLAND CT

KINGSBURY RD 1
EATON CL 2

Chapman's Grove

LONGCROFT 1
CROSS ST 2

1 ST MARY'S CR
2 ROGERS CL
3 TAUNTON RD

Garden Wood

Searsons Farm

P

Clickett Hill

Causton Sch

Orwell High Sch

Walton

Recreation Gd

IP11

1 BARNFIELD
2 LONGFIELD

Christmasyards Wood

Superstore

Cerny Lawn

FELIXSTOWE

NURSERY WK
Deben High Sch

GARRISON LANE

Grange Prim Sch

HAVEN

MILL LANE

NEWRY AVE

MILL LA

PRINCES RD

WINDSOR RD 1
ANNE ST 2

ORWELL ROAD

UNDERCLIFF RD W

Leisu Cent

CORONATION LA

1 GLONCURRY GD
2 NEWBOURNE GD
3 LARKSWAY

ELIZABETH WAY

PHILIP AVE

DOVEDALE

MANNING RD

Langer Park

LC

Container Park

WALTON AVENUE

A154

Langer Cty Prim Sch

Suffolk Coast & Heaths Path

WALTON AVENUE

A154

HAULIERS RD

SUB STATION RD

The Port of Felixstowe

1 SHOTLEY CL
2 HOLBROOK CR
3 PARSONAGE CL

BEACH STATION RD 1
NACTON RD 2
PRETYMAN RD 3

Martello Tower

Jetty

STONEGROVE RD

LC

CARR RD

P

C3
1 NAYLAND RD
2 ICKWORTH CT

C4
1 LIDGATE CT
2 WICKHAMBROOK CT
3 SUDBURY RD
4 EUSTON CT
5 KENTFORD RD
6 THURSTON CT
7 BOXFORD CT

107
107

D3
1 SHOTLEY CL
2 HOLBROOK CR
3 PARSONAGE CL

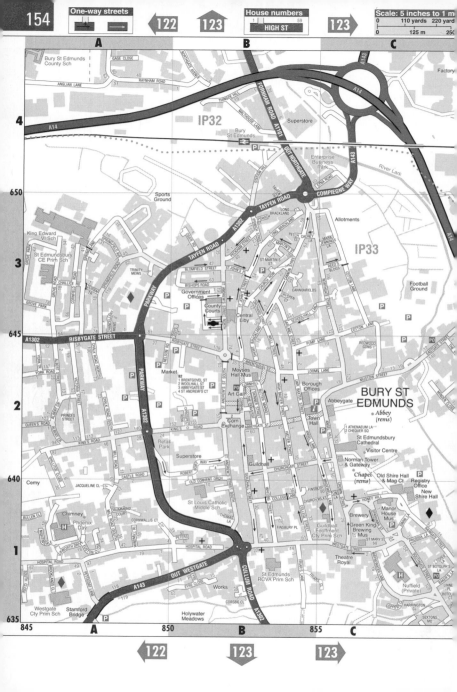

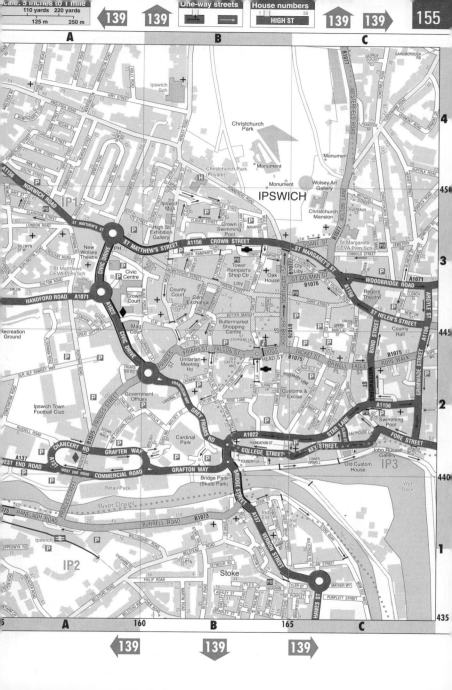

Index

Church Rd 🖸 Beckenham BR2..........**53** C6

Place name	Location number	Locality, town or village	Postcode district	Page and grid square
May be abbreviated on the map	Present when a number indicates the place's position in a crowded area of mapping	Shown when more than one place has the same name	District for the indexed place	Page number and grid reference for the standard mapping

Public and commercial buildings are highlighted in magenta. Places of interest are highlighted in blue with a star★

Abbreviations used in the index

Acad	**Academy**	Comm	**Common**	Gd	**Ground**	L	**Leisure**	Prom	**Promenade**
App	**Approach**	Cott	**Cottage**	Gdn	**Garden**	La	**Lane**	Rd	**Road**
Arc	**Arcade**	Cres	**Crescent**	Gn	**Green**	Liby	**Library**	Recn	**Recreation**
Ave	**Avenue**	Cswy	**Causeway**	Gr	**Grove**	Mdw	**Meadow**	Ret	**Retail**
Bglw	**Bungalow**	Ct	**Court**	H	**Hall**	Meml	**Memorial**	Sh	**Shopping**
Bldg	**Building**	Ctr	**Centre**	Ho	**House**	Mkt	**Market**	Sq	**Square**
Bsns, Bus	**Business**	Ctry	**Country**	Hospl	**Hospital**	Mus	**Museum**	St	**Street**
Bvd	**Boulevard**	Cty	**County**	HQ	**Headquarters**	Orch	**Orchard**	Sta	**Station**
Cath	**Cathedral**	Dr	**Drive**	Hts	**Heights**	Pal	**Palace**	Terr	**Terrace**
Cir	**Circus**	Dro	**Drove**	Ind	**Industrial**	Par	**Parade**	TH	**Town Hall**
Cl	**Close**	Ed	**Education**	Inst	**Institute**	Pas	**Passage**	Univ	**University**
Cnr	**Corner**	Emb	**Embankment**	Int	**International**	Pk	**Park**	Wk, Wlk	**Walk**
Coll	**College**	Est	**Estate**	Intc	**Interchange**	Pl	**Place**	Wr	**Water**
Com	**Community**	Ex	**Exhibition**	Junc	**Junction**	Prec	**Precinct**	Yd	**Yard**

Index of localities, towns and villages

A

Acton 92 B7
Acton Place 92 B8
Akenham 134 F6
Alburgh 7 A1
Aldeburgh 130 D4
Aldeby 9 F8
Alderton 99 E4
Aldham 94 E8
Aldringham 129 D3
All Saints South Elmham .24 B5
Allwood Green 36 A2
Alpheton 78 A5
Ampton 33 A2
Annis Hill 110 E3
Apsey Green 126 A3
Ardleigh Heath 103 F1
Ash Abbey 127 F3
Ashbocking 69 A1
Ash Corner 127 F7
Ashen 89 E5
Ashfield 54 D2
Ashfield Cum Thorpe ...54 C1
Ashfield Green Stradbroke .39 D4
Ashfield Green
  Wickhambrook 62 A2
Ashley 60 F8
Ash Street 80 A1
Aspall 53 E4
Assington 92 F1
Assington Green 76 B6
Athelington 38 E2
Attleton Green 61 D1
Audley End
  Burston and Shimpling ..20 E5
Audley End Lawshall ...77 D8

B

Babel Green 75 D3
Back Street 61 E5
Bacton 51 F5
Bacton Green 51 E4
Badingham 56 A6
Badwell Ash 50 E7
Badwell Green 51 B8
Ballingdon 148 B4
Banyard's Green 40 C4
Bardwell 34 C4
Barham 82 C6

Barking 125 A1
Barking Tye 81 A7
Barley Green 39 C5
Barnaby Green 26 C2
Barnardiston 75 B3
Barnby 10 B5
Barnham 16 C2
Barningham 34 F7
Barrow 47 A2
Barsham 9 A4
Barton Mills 116 D2
Base Green 51 B2
Bath Side 107 B3
Battisford 66 F1
Battisford Tye 66 C1
Battlesea Green 39 A6
Battlies Green 49 C3
Bawdsey 99 F3
Baylham 81 E6
Baythorne End 89 C5
Beacon Hill 137 F3
Beccles 111 D5
Beck Row 30 A8
Bedfield 54 E5
Bedingfield 53 F7
Bedingham Green 7 B7
Belchamp Otten 90 E4
Belchamp St Paul 90 D5
Belchamp Walter 90 F3
Bell's Corner 102 F8
Bell's Cross 82 D7
Belstead 142 C7
Benacre 27 A7
Benhall Green 72 C8
Benhall Street 71 F8
Bentley 104 F8
Beyton 49 F1
Beyton Green 49 F2
Bigsby's Corner 72 D8
Bildeston 79 F4
Billingford 21 B1
Birdbrook 89 A4
Birds End 62 B7
Bird Street 80 A7
Blackheath 42 C5
Blacksmith's Green 53 C5
Black Street 11 A2
Blackthorpe 49 C2
Blaxhall 72 B4
Bleach Green 39 A8
Blo' Norton 18 E2
Bloodman's Corner 3 A6
Bloodmoor Hill 114 E2

Blundeston 3 A4
Blyford 42 C7
Blythburgh 42 F6
Bobby Hill 35 C5
Boot Street 137 D6
Borley 91 C5
Borley Green Borley 91 B5
Borley Green Woolpit ...65 E7
Botesdale 36 B6
Bowbeck 34 C6
Bower House Tye 93 E3
Boxford 93 C3
Boxted 102 F4
Boxted 77 A6
Boxted Cross 103 A3
Boyden End 61 D2
Boyland Common 20 A7
Boyton 86 B2
Boyton End 89 B7
Brabling Green 126 E6
Bradfield 105 C1
Bradfield Combust 64 A4
Bradfield St Clare 64 C4
Bradfield St George 64 D7
Braiseworth 37 D2
Bramfield 41 F4
Bramford 134 A2
Brampton 25 E5
Brampton Street 25 E4
Brandeston 70 B7
Brandon 6 A1
Brantham 104 F4
Bredfield 84 C7
Brent Eleigh 79 A2
Bressingham 19 F4
Bressingham Common 19 F5
Brettenham 17 B6
Brettenham 79 C8
Brewers Green 20 B3
Bridge Green 20 F6
Bridge Street 77 F4
Brightwell 98 A6
Brinkley 59 E2
Broadgrass Green 50 C1
Broad Green Cheveley ...60 F6
Broad Green Chevington ..62 B6
Broad Green Creeting St Peter or
  West Creeting 67 C6
Broad Street 93 C5
Broadway 118 C6
Brockdish 21 F2
Brockford Green 53 A4
Brockford Street 52 F5

Brockley Corner 32 D2
Brockley Green Hartest ..63 A1
Brockley Green Hundon ..75 C2
Broke Hall 148 E3
Brome 117 B7
Brome Street 117 E8
Bromeswell 85 A5
Brook Green 63 E5
Brook Street 77 A3
Broome 110 D7
Broome Heath 110 D7
Broom Hill 146 E2
Broom's Barn 46 F4
Brown Street 52 A2
Browston Green 2 E8
Bruisyard 56 C5
Brundish 55 C8
Brundish Street 39 E1
Brundon 148 A7
Bucklesham 98 A5
Bulcamp 42 D7
Bulmer 91 C1
Bulmer Tye 91 D1
Bungay 110 B3
Bures 101 C5
Bures Green 101 D6
Burgate 36 E6
Burgh 83 F6
Burgh St Peter 10 B8
Burrough End 59 E2
Burrough Green 59 F2
Burstall 95 D7
Burstallhill 95 C8
Burston 20 E6
Burthorpe 47 B3
Burwell 44 A5
Bury St Edmunds 154 C2
Bush Green 64 D4
Butley 86 B5
Butley High Corner 86 C4
Butley Low Corner 86 B4
Button Haugh Green 50 F4
Button's Green 78 E8
Buxhall 64 A4
Buxhall Fen Street 66 A6

C

Calais Street 93 D2
Calford Green 133 D5
California 140 B6
Camps Heath 112 D3

Candle Street 35 F5
Canham's Green 51 F4
Capel Green 86 A4
Capel St Andrew 86 B3
Capel St Mary 150 E4
Capon's Green 55 E6
Carlton 74 A8
Carlton
  Kelsale cum Carlton ...128 C6
Carlton Colville 114 C3
Carlton Green 74 A6
Castle Hill 135 A3
Castling's Heath 93 D6
Cattawade 104 E4
Cavendish 76 C3
Cavenham 47 A8
Cay Hill 52 C2
Chantry 138 D2
Charles Tye 80 C7
Charsfield 70 B3
Chattisham 95 C5
Chedburgh 62 C4
Chediston 41 C8
Chediston Green 24 C1
Chelmondiston 106 C8
Chelsworth 79 E3
Chelsworth Common 79 E2
Cheveley 60 E7
Chevington 62 C6
Chickering 38 F7
Chillesford 86 C7
Chilton 92 B5
Chilton Street 75 F1
Chimney Street 75 C3
Chippenhall Green 40 A6
Chippenham 45 C8
Church End 106 F7
Church Street 90 D6
Clare 90 B8
Clay Common 26 B4
Claydon 134 C8
Claypits 109 B4
Clay Street 35 C2
Clopton Corner 69 E1
Clopton Green
  Wickhambrook 62 A1
Clopton Green Woolpit ...65 D7
Cobbler's Green 7 C5
Cock & End 75 C8
Cockfield 64 C1
Cocks Green 64 A5
Cock Street 102 C7
Coddenham 68 C1

Coddenham Green 67 F2
Colchester Green 64 E2
Coldfair Green 129 B2
Coles Green 95 D4
Cole's Green 126 E1
Colton 48 F5
Combs 124 C1
Combs Ford 124 D4
Coney Weston 17 E1
Conyers Green 49 B7
Cookley 41 A6
Cookley Green 40 F6
Cook's Green 79 D8
Copdock 95 C4
Cornard Tye 92 C4
Corton 3 C4
Cotton 52 B6
Cove Bottom 26 E3
Covehithe 27 B4
Cow Common 51 F4
Cowlinge 61 B1
Cox Common 25 A5
Crackthorn Corner 19 A1
Cranley 37 F3
Cranmer Green 35 E2
Cransford 56 B3
Cratfield 40 D6
Creeting Bottoms 67 F5
Creeting St Mary 125 F8
Creeting St Peter 67 C5
Cretingham 69 F7
Cross Green Cockfield 64 B2
Cross Green Hartest 77 A7
Cross Green Hitcham 79 E7
Cross Street 38 C7
Crowfield 68 C2
Crown Corner 39 D1
Crowland 35 D1
Cuckold's Green 26 C6
Cuckoo Green 3 A6
Cuckoo Tye 92 A7
Culford 32 D1
Culfordheath 32 F5
Culpho 137 A7
Curlew Green 128 C2

D

Dagworth 66 E8
Daisy Green Great Ashfield 51 A6
Daisy Green
Wickham Skeith 52 D7
Dalham 61 C8
Dallinghoo 70 D1
Dam Green 19 C8
Dandy Corner 52 B6
Darmsden 125 F1
Darsham 42 C1
Debach 70 A1
Debenham 53 E2
Dedham 103 F4
Dedham Heath 103 F2
Denham 61 F8
Denham Hoxne 38 D5
Denham End 46 F2
Dennington 55 D5
Dennington Corner 126 C8
Denston 76 A7
Denton 7 A3
Depden 62 B3
Depden Green 62 B4
Dickleburgh 21 B5
Dickleburgh Moor 21 D6
Diss 20 C4
Ditchingham 110 C7
Ditton Green 60 B4
Dockeney 8 F6
Dorking Tye 101 D7
Dorley's Corner 128 D8
Dovercourt 107 B2
Down Field 28 F2
Drinkstone 93 H8
Drinkstone 65 C8
Drinkstone Green 65 B7
Dublin 53 E8
Duke Street 95 B5
Dullingham 59 F5
Dullingham Ley 60 A4
Dunstall Green 61 E7
Dunwich 43 B1

E

Earl's Green 51 D5
Earl Soham 54 E2
Earl Stonham 67 E5
Earsham 7 E4
Earsham Street 22 C1
East Barton 49 C4
East Bergholt 151 C4
Eastbridge 58 D4
East End East Bergholt 104 E6
East End Stonham Aspal 68 D6
East Green Bradley 74 E8
East Green
Kelsale cum Carlton 57 E4
Easton 70 E5
Edge Green 19 88
Edwardstone 93 A5
Ellingham 8 D7
Ellough 9 F1

Ellough Hill 111 D3
Elmsett 80 F1
Elmswell 50 E2
Elveden 15 D3
Eriswell 13 F1
Erwarton 106 D5
Euston 16 F1
Exning 120 88
Eye 117 D3
Eyke 85 B6

F

Fakenham Magna 33 E7
Falkenham 98 E2
Falkenham Sink 98 F2
Farley Green 75 D8
Farnham 72 A7
Felixstowe 152 E4
Felixstowe Ferry 108 C8
Felsham 65 A3
Feltwell 4 D5
Fenstead End 76 E5
Fen Street Hopton 18 82
Fen Street Redgrave 19 C2
Fern Hill 77 B4
Fersfield 19 A2
Finkle Green 89 A2
Finningham 52 88
Flempton 47 F8
Flixton 7 D1
Flowton 81 C1
Foals Green 39 D2
Fordham 29 81
Fornham All Saints 48 86
Fornham St Genevieve 48 C6
Fornham St Martin 48 D6
Forward Green 67 E7
Foxash Estate 35 C1
Foxash 104 81
Foxearth 91 B7
Framlingham 126 D2
Framsden 69 86
Freckenham 29 F3
Frenze 20 F3
Fressingfield 39 D8
Freston 143 D3
Friday Street Benhall 72 B7
Friday Street Brandeston 70 A6
Friday Street Rendlesham 85 D7
Friston 72 F7
Fritton 2 B7
Frizzeler's Green 47 C1
Frostenden 26 C4
Frostenden Corner 26 C3

G

Gainsborough Ipswich 139 F1
Gainsborough Ipswich 144 88
Garboldisham 18 D4
Garlic Street 22 A6
Gasthorpe 18 B2
Gazeley 46 83
Gedding 65 A5
Geldeston 8 F7
Genesis Green 61 A1
Gestingthorpe 90 F1
Gillingham 9 C6
Gipping 52 82
Gipsy Row 150 A4
Gisleham 11 A3
Gislingham 36 D2
Gissing 20 F8
Glemsford 77 B2
Goddard's Corner 55 E7
Gosbeck 68 D2
Gosland Green 76 A5
Gosling Green 93 C5
Grass Green 89 D1
Great Ashfield 50 F6
Great Barton 49 B4
Great Bealings 137 E6
Great Blakenham 82 A5
Great Bradley 74 C7
Great Bricett 80 E5
Great Common 8 E2
Great Cornard 148 F3
Great Finborough 66 84
Great Glemham 71 D8
Great Green Burgate 36 D7
Great Green Cockfield 64 D2
Great Green Denton 7 A4
Great Green Thrandeston 37 C8
Great Horkesley 102 E1
Great Livermere 33 C2
Great Saxham 47 C1
Great Thurlow 74 E5
Great Waldingfield 92 C6
Great Welnetham 63 F6
Great Wenham 150 A3
Great Wratting 74 E3
Great Yeldham 90 A1
Greenstreet Green 80 D5
Greenwich 139 E1
Grimstone End 49 F8
Grinstead Hill 125 E3
Gromford 72 C5
Groton 93 84
Grundisburgh 83 D5
Gulling Green 63 A3

Gunton 113 C6

H

Hacheston 71 A6
Hadleigh 149 F6
Hadleigh Heath 93 F4
Hagmore Green 93 82
Halesworth 118 A4
Hall Green 90 C2
Hanchet End 132 A8
Hanningfields Green 63 F1
Hargrave 62 86
Harkstead 106 85
Harleston 22 E5
Harleston 66 87
Redenhall with Harleston 22 E5
Harrow Green 63 D1
Hartest 77 A7
Hartest Hill 77 C7
Hart's Green 63 E2
Harwich 107 A3
Haskelton 146 C8
Haughley 51 C1
Haughley Green 51 C3
Haughley New Street 51 C3
Haverhill 132 C6
Hawkedon 76 D7
Hawstead 63 D6
Hawstead Green 63 E5
Hazel Stub 132 A5
Hedenham 7 E8
Helions Bumpstead 88 84
Helmingham 69 84
Hemingstone 82 C8
Hemley 98 E5
Hemp Green 57 C8
Hengrave 48 A7
Henley 82 D6
Henny Street 91 F1
Henstead 26 E8
Hepworth 35 A6
Herringfleet 2 D4
Herringswell 46 C8
Hessett 64 F8
Heveningham 40 F3
Hickford Hill 90 C7
Higham 103 D6
Higham 46 E4
High Green 63 D7
High Rougham 49 E1
High Street Darsham 42 81
High Street Iken 73 82
High Street
'St Margaret, Ilketshall' 24 D7
High Street Green 66 A2
Hightown Green 65 D3
Hinderclay 35 E7
Hintlesham 95 C6
Hitcham 79 E6
Hobbies Green 75 A8
Hockwold cum Wilton 5 A3
Hoggard's Green 64 A3
Holbrook 105 E7
Hollesley 99 E2
Hollybush Corner 64 D6
Holly Hill 110 88
Holton 118 F4
Holton St Mary 103 F7
Holton St Mary 151 A8
Holywell Row 30 C8
Homersfield 23 88
Hone Tye 102 86
Honington 33 E5
Hoo 70 85
Hopton 18 C2
Hopton on Sea 3 C7
Horham 38 E3
Horner's Green 93 C4
Hornstreet 103 C3
Horringer 63 A8
Hoxne 38 88
Hulver Street 10 C1
Humble Green 92 F8
Hundon 75 E3
Hunston 50 D5
Hunston Green 50 D5
Huntingfield 41 A5

I

Icklingham 31 D4
Iken 72 F2
Ilketshall St Andrew 8 E2
Ilketshall St Lawrence 24 F6
Ilketshall St Margaret 24 88
Ingham 32 F1
Ipswich 155 83
Isleham 29 85
Ixworth 34 82
Ixworth Thorpe 33 F4

K

Kedington 133 E2
Kelsale 128 C2
Kennett 45 F7
Kenninghall 19 88
Kenny Hill 12 C1

Kentford 46 A5
Kenton 54 85
Kenton Corner 54 C4
Kersey 94 A7
Kersey Tye 93 E6
Kersey Upland 93 F5
Kesgrave 141 C8
Kessingland 11 C2
Kessingland Beach 27 C8
Kettlebaston 79 C5
Kettleburgh 70 C7
Kingshall Green 64 D8
Kingshall Street 64 D8
Kingston 146 F2
Kirby Cane 8 E8
Kirby Row 8 E7
Kirkley 115 85
Kirtling 60 E3
Kirtling Green 60 E2
Kirton 98 E2
Knaves Green 53 A5
Knettishall 17 F3
Knodishall 73 A8
Knodishall Common 129 A2
Knowl Green 90 C4

L

Lackford 31 F1
Lady's Green 61 F6
Lakenheath 109 E7
Lamarsh 101 A6
Lamb Corner 103 E2
Lambfair Green 75 A8
Lampardbrook 70 E8
Landwade 44 D6
Langham 103 C2
Langham 50 D8
Langton Green 117 D4
Lattinford Hill 151 D8
Lavenham 78 D4
Lawford 104 E2
Lawshall 63 E1
Lawshall Green 77 F8
Laxfield 40 C3
Leavenheath 102 87
Leiston 129 85
Letheringham 70 C4
Levington 145 E3
Lidgate 61 C4
Lindsey 93 D7
Lindsey Tye 93 E8
Linstead Parva 40 E8
Liston 91 D7
Little Bealings 137 E5
Little Blakenham 81 F3
Little Bradley 74 E6
Little Cornard 92 C2
Little Ditton 60 C5
Little Finborough 66 81
Little Glemham 71 D5
Little Green Burgate 36 D5
Little Green Gislingham 36 C3
Little Horkesley 102 83
Little Knowles Green 62 85
Little London 66 E2
Little Saxham 47 D2
Little Stonham 67 F6
Little Thurlow 74 E5
Little Thurlow Green 74 86
Little Waldingfield 92 D8
Little Welnetham 64 86
Little Wenham 150 85
Little Whittingham
Green 40 A8
Little Wratting 74 E2
Little Yeldham 90 82
Long Green 36 D8
Long Melford 77 F1
Long Meadow 91 E8
Long Thurlow 51 87
Lound 2 E5
Lower Common 25 83
Lower Falkenham 98 F1
Lower Green 46 E4
Lower Hacheston 127 F8
Lower Holbrook 106 A6
Lower Layham 149 D1
Lower Raydon 94 D1
Lower Street Stansfield 76 C6
Lower Street Stutton 105 D5
Lowestoft 113 F1
Low Green 63 E7
Lynford 6 C5

M

Mace Green 95 E4
Magpie Green 19 E1
Maidenhall 139 81
Maidensgrave 146 E3
Malting End 61 C1
Manningtree 104 F2
Man's Cross 89 F7
Market Weston 35 A8
Markeford 71 C5
Martlesham 84 A1
Martlesham Heath 98 87
Maypole Green
Bradfield St George 64 D6

Maypole Green
Dennington 55 D6
Meadowend 89 E3
Mellis 37 A5
Mellis Green 36 F5
Mells 118 E2
Melon Green 63 C4
Melton 147 C8
Mendham 23 A6
Mendlesham 52 E4
Mendlesham Green 52 D2
Metfield 23 C3
Mettingham 84 E1
Mettingham 8 D4
Mickfield 68 88
Mickley Green 63 84
Middle Green 46 E4
Middle Harling 18 88
Middleton 148 C2
Middleton 58 B6
Middleton Moor 58 A6
Middlewood Green 67 D8
Milden 79 81
Mildenhall 116 D6
Mile End 77 A7
Mill Common 25 C4
Mill End 60 F3
Mill Green
Burston and Shimpling 20 E7
Mill Green Buxhall 65 F4
Mill Green Edwardstone 93 85
Mill Green Stonham Aspal 68 B7
Mill Hill 77 E6
Mill Hills 147 A6
Mill Street 102 E8
Mistley 105 A3
Mistley Heath 105 A1
Moats Tye 66 E2
Monewden 69 E5
Monks Eleigh 79 82
Monk Soham 54 D4
Moulton 45 F3
Mount Bures 101 C3
Mount Pleasant 75 D2
Mundford 6 A2
Mutford 10 D2

N

Nacton 145 C5
Naughton 80 C3
Nayland 102 C5
Nedging 80 84
Nedging Tye 80 84
Needham 22 84
Needham Market 125 E5
Needham Street 46 84
Nether St 64 E8
Nettlestead 81 C4
Newbourne 98 C5
New England 89 A5
Newman's Green 92 A6
Newmarket 121 84
New Mistley 105 A2
Newton 92 D3
Newtown 54 D7
Normanston 113 83
North Common 34 F6
North Cove 10 C4
North End 90 C2
North Green Cratfield 40 C7
North Green
Kelsale cum Carlton 57 D5
North Green Parham 56 81
North Lopham 19 A5
Norton 50 84
Norton Little Green 50 D5
Nowton 63 E7

O

Oak Hill 100 A8
Oakley 38 A8
Occold 37 F1
Offton 81 A4
Old Felixstowe 153 C6
Oldhall Green 64 C3
Old Newton 51 F1
Onehouse 66 C6
Orford 131 C3
Otley 69 C2
Oulton 112 F5
Oulton Broad 114 C8
Ousden 61 E6
Ovington 90 A5

P

Page's Green 53 C4
Pakefield 115 83
Pakenham 49 F6
Pale Green 88 85
Palgrave 20 C1
Parham 71 A7
Parkeston 106 F3
Park Gate 61 E3
Park Green 53 83
Parliament Heath 93 C6
Parney Heath 103 D2
Peasenhall 56 E8

Peats Corner 69 B7
Pentlow 76 E1
Pentlow 90 F7
Pentlow Street 91 A8
Pettaugh 68 E6
Pettistree 127 B4
Pinford End 63 D6
Pitcher's Green 64 D5
Pitman's Corner 53 C5
Playford 137 B5
Polstead 93 F1
Polstead Heath 93 F2
Pooley Street 19 D4
Poslingford 76 A3
Potash 104 F8
Pound Green 61 B1
Poystreet Green 65 E5
Preston St Mary 79 A5
Priory Green 92 F6
Priory Heath 140 D1
Pulham St Mary 21 F8
Puttock End 90 E7

R

Racecourse 140 B2
Ramsey 106 C1
Ramsholt 99 A4
Rattlesden 65 E6
Raydon 94 E1
Reading Green 38 E5
Rede 62 E2
Redenhall 22 E7
Redgrave 36 A8
Redisham 25 B7
Redlingfield 38 D2
Red Lodge 30 B1
Rendham 56 E3
Rendlesham 85 D8
Reydon 119 C7
Reydon Smear 26 F1
Rickinghall 36 A6
Ridgewell 89 D4
Ringsfield 9 B3
Ringsfield Corner 9 B2
Ringshall 80 E7
Ringshall Stocks 80 F6
Risby 47 D5
Rishangles 53 D7
Rodbridge Corner 91 E6
Roman Hill 113 C7
Rooksey Green 78 E6
Roost End 133 E2
Rosedale Park 114 E4
Rose Green Assington .101 F8
Rose Green Lindsey ... 93 D7
Rose Hill 139 F4
Rotchfords 101 F1
Rougham 64 D8
Rougham Green 64 C8
Roydon 20 A3
Rumburgh 24 B4
Rushall 21 F5
Rushbrooke 64 B8
Rushford 17 B4
Rushmere 10 D1
Rushmere St Andrew .136 E1
Rushmere Street 136 E2
Russel's Green 39 C3

S

Sackers Green 92 D2
St Cross South Elmham .23 D7
St James South Elmham .23 F4
St Margaret
  South Elmham 23 E6

St Michael
  South Elmham 24 A6
St Nicholas
  South Elmham 23 E6
St Olaves 2 A6
St Peter South Elmham .24 A7
Santon Downham 6 C2
Sapiston 33 F6
Saxham Street 67 C8
Saxmundham 128 D3
Saxon Street 60 D6
Saxstead Bottom 55 C5
Saxtead 55 C4
Saxtead Green 55 B3
Saxtead Little Green .. 55 B5
Scole 21 A2
Scole Common 20 F3
Scotland Street 102 F7
Semer 79 F1
Shadingfield 25 E7
Shadwell 17 C6
Shelfanger 20 C6
Shelland 66 A7
Shelley 94 C1
Sherbourne Street ... 93 B4
Shimpling
  Burston and Shimpling ...21 A6
Shimpling 77 E6
Shimpling Street 77 E8
Shingle Street 100 A5
Shipmeadow 8 F4
Shop Corner 106 C5
Shotford Heath 22 D4
Shotley 106 F6
Shotley Gate 107 A4
Shottisham 99 C7
Sibton 57 A8
Sibton Green 41 D2
Sicklesmere 63 F7
Silverlace Green 71 C7
Silverley's Green 40 B6
Sizewell 58 F1
Slough Hill 77 E7
Smallwood Green 64 F5
Smallworth 18 D3
Smith's Green 88 C3
Smithwood Green 78 C7
Snailwell 45 A6
Snape 72 D4
Snow Street 20 A4
Soham 28 D4
Soham Cotes 28 B6
Somersham 81 C3
Somerton 76 F8
Sotherton 25 E2
Sotherton Corner 25 E1
Sotterley 26 A7
South Cove 26 F4
South Green Hoxne ... 38 B5
South Green
  Pulham St Mary 21 F6
South Lopham 19 B4
Southolt 54 B7
Southwold 119 C5
Sowley Green 75 A5
Spexhall 24 F3
Spratt's Street 85 D5
Sproughton 138 A7
Stackyard Green 93 C8
Stambourne 89 B1
Stambourne Green ... 89 A1
Stanningfield 64 A4
Stansfield 76 C7
Stanstead 77 C4
Stanton 34 E3
Stanton Chare 34 D5
Stanton Street 50 B5
Stanway Green 39 C1
Starston 22 C7

T

  White Horse 142 D1
Temple End Foxearth .91 A6
Temple End Little Thurlow ..74 C5
Theberton 58 B4
The Brook 36 E7
The Common 81 F3
The Heath 105 A7
Thelnetham 18 D1
Thelveton 21 A4
The Marsh 36 E8
The Port of Felixstowe ..152 C1
Thetford 16 D5
The Woodlands 95 A3
Thistley Green 29 E7
Thorington 42 C4
Thorington Street ... 103 A6
Thorndon 53 B8
Thorney Green 67 A7
Thornham Magna 37 A2
Thornham Parva 37 B3
Thorpe Abbotts 21 E2
Thorpe Common 107 C8
Thorpe Green 64 F1
Thorpe Morieux 79 A8
Thorpeness 73 E6
Thorpe Street 35 D8
Thrandeston 37 B7
Thurston 49 E3
Thurston End 76 D6
Thwaite 52 F7
Tilbury Green 89 E4
Tilbury Juxta Clare ... 90 A3
Timworth 48 A6
Timworth Green 48 D7
Toad Row 10 F1
Tostock 50 B2

Tannington 55 A6
Tannington Place 55 A6
Tan Office 52 F2
Tan Office Green 62 C6
Tattingstone 105 B8
Tattingstone

Steeple Bumpstead ..88 D4
Sternfield 72 D8
Stetchworth 60 A5
Stock Hill 50 E8
Stoke 155 B1
Stoke Ash 37 B1
Stoke by Clare 89 E6
Stoke-by-Nayland ... 102 E6
Stoke Park 138 F1
Stone Street Boxford .93 C2
Stone Street Spexhall ..24 F5
Stonham Aspal 68 A6
Stoven 25 F4
Stowlangtoft 50 C7
Stowmarket 124 E6
Stowupland 67 B6
Stradbroke 39 A5
Stradishall 75 F7
Stratford St Andrew ..71 F7
Stratford St Mary .. 103 D5
Stubbing's Green 36 C5
Sturmer 133 C2
Stuston 20 E1
Stutton 105 D6
Sudbourne 86 F8
Sudbury 148 C4
Sutton 85 A1
Sutton Street 99 A7
Swan Green 40 B5
Swefling 56 E2
Swilland 83 A7
Swingleton Green ... 79 C2
Syleham 22 A1

Tower Hill 107 C3
Trimley Lower Street .107 C7
Trimley St Martin ... 107 D8
Trimley St Mary 152 C8
Troston 33 D3
Tuddenham 30 F2
Tuddenham St Martin ..136 C5
Tunstall 71 F2

U

Ubbeston 40 E4
Ubbeston Green 40 D3
Ufford 127 B1
Ufford 84 F7
Uggeshall 25 F3
Undley 13 C4
Upend 60 F5
Upgate Street 7 B6
Upper Green 46 E3
Upper Holton 118 E7
Upper Layham 149 F2
Upper Street Baylham ..81 E6
Upper Street
  Dickleburgh and Rushall ..21 C2
Upper Street Stansfield ..76 C6
Upper Street Stutton ..105 B5
Upper Town 49 E7
Upper Weybread 22 B2
Upsher Green 92 D6
Upthorpe 34 F3

W

Wainford 110 D5
Walberswick 119 A2
Walcot Green 20 D4
Waldringfield 98 D7
Waldringfield Heath .. 98 C7
Wales End 76 D4
Walpole 41 C5
Walsham Le Willows .. 35 C2
Walton 152 F6
Wangford 26 B2
Ward Green 51 E2
Warren Heath 140 F1
Washbrook 95 F5
Washbrook Street ... 95 F6
Washmere Green 78 D2
Waterloo Aldeby 9 E8
Waterloo
  Dickleburgh and Rushall ..20 F2
Wattisfield 35 D5
Wattisham 80 B6
Wattisham Stone 80 A6
Weeting 5 E3
Wenhaston 42 C6
Westbourne 138 F7
Westbrook Green 20 C4
West End 26 B6
Westerfield 135 E4
Westhall 25 C4
West Harling 18 A8
Westhorpe 51 D8
Westleton 58 B7
Westley 122 A6
Westley Waterless ... 59 E3
Weston 9 D1
Weston Ditch 29 F7
West Row 29 F6
West Stow 32 B1
West Street
  Rickinghall Inferior ...35 E5
West Street
  Walsham-le-willows ..35 A1
West Tofts 6 E1
Wetherden 51 B1

Wetherden Upper Town ..51 B4
Wetheringsett 53 A5
Wetherup Street 53 C3
Weybread 22 D3
Whatfield 80 C1
Wheatacre 2 B1
Whelp Street 79 B4
Whepstead 63 B5
Wherstead 143 B6
Whitestreet Green ... 93 D2
Whitton 134 F3
Wicken 28 B1
Wicker Street Green .. 93 E5
Wickhambrook 61 E2
Wickham Green 52 C8
Wickham Market 127 B6
Wickham Skeith 52 E8
Wickham Street
  Wickhambrook 61 F1
Wickham Street
  Wickham Skeith 52 C8
Widgham Green 60 B2
Wiggens Green 88 C5
Wilby 39 C2
Wilde Street 13 D2
William's Green 93 E5
Willingham 25 B1
Willisham 81 A5
Willisham Tye 81 A6
Wilney Green 19 D4
Windsor Green 64 B2
Winfarthing 20 B8
Wingfield 39 B8
Wingfield Green 38 F8
Winston 68 F8
Wissett 24 D2
Withermarsh Green .. 103 A8
Withersdale Street ... 22 F4
Withersfield 74 B2
Witnesham 83 A6
Wixoe 89 B6
Woodbridge 146 F6
Woodbridge Walk ... 99 F8
Woodditton 60 C5
Woodland Green 133 C5
Woodton 7 C8
Woolpit 50 D1
Woolpit Green 65 D8
Woolpit Heath 65 E8
Woolverstone 144 B1
Wootten Green 39 B3
Wordwell 32 D3
Workhouse Green ... 101 C8
Workhouse Hill 102 F2
World's End 65 F2
Worlingham 111 F3
Worlington 30 A4
Worlingworth 54 F8
Wormingford 101 F2
Wortham 36 D8
Wortwell 23 B8
Wrabness 105 F2
Wrentham 26 E5
Wrentham West End ..26 C7
Wyverstone 51 E6
Wyverstone Green ... 51 E6
Wyverstone Street ... 51 D6

Y

Yaxley 37 B5
Yoxford 57 D7

390th Bomb Group Meml Air
  Mus* IP13 ....71 C7

A

Abbey Fields IP14 ....66 D8
Abbey La IP16 ....129 E8
Abbey Rd Flixton NR35 ....23 F8
  Leiston IP16 ....129 C7
  Sudbury CO10 ....148 C7
Abbeygate St **3** IP33 ....147 A4
Abbot Cl IP33 ....122 D4
Abbot Rd IP33 ....122 D4
Abbot's Hall Drift CO10 ..78 E2
Abbots Hall Prim Sch
  IP24 ....16 B6
Abbot's Hall Rd IP14 ....124 D5
Abbotsbury Cl IP2 ......139 A1
Abbotsbury Rd IP12 ......139 B3
Abbott Rd CO12 ....106 F1
Abbotts Ct CO10 ....133 C3
Abbotts Mdw **8** IP30 ....50 D1
Abbotts Rd IP13 ....132 E7
Abbotts Wlk IP33 ....122 B5
Abdy Ave **4** CO12 ....106 F1
Aberdeen Way IP4 ....136 B1
Aberfoyle Cl **1** IP4 ....136 C1
Abingdon Cl IP4 ....132 A3
Acacia Ave IP32 ....48 C5
Acacia Cl IP14 ....140 E1
Acer Gr IP14 ....138 C1
Acheson Way **2** IP15 ...130 E5
Acorn Cl **8** IP8 ....138 C1
Acorns The IP30 ....49 E3
Acre Cl IP6 ....83 A6
Acre Rd CO8 ....74 B8
Acton CE Prim Sch
  CO10 ....92 B7
Acton Cl Bramford IP8 ...134 A2
  Sudbury CO10 ....148 D6
Acton Gdns **1** IP8 .....134 A2
Acton La CO10 ....148 C5
Acton La Acton CO10 .....92 A6
  Sudbury CO10 ....148 D6
Acton Pl Ind Est CO10 ...92 A8
Acton Rd Bramford IP8 ...134 A2
  Newmarket NR33 ......115 A4
Adair Rd IP1 ....138 D8
Adam's La IP18 ....43 C5
Adams Pl IP5 ....141 C7
Adamson Rd IP18 ....119 B8
Adastral Cl
  Felixstowe IP11 ......153 H11
  Newmarket CB8 ......120 E4
Addington Rd IP11 .....152 C7
Addison Cl IP2 ....138 A8
Addison Rd CO10 ....148 E7
Addison Way IP8 ....134 A8
Adeane Mdw IP26 ....6 A8
Adelaide Cl **7** CB7 ....28 D4
Adelaide Rd IP4 ....140 D6
Admiral Rd IP8 ....142 E8
Admirals Jun Sch IP24 ..16 C7
Adrian Rd **8** NR32 ....113 D2
Aggage Cl **3** IP1 .....134 D1
Ailwin Rd IP32 ....123 C3
Ainslie Rd IP1 ....139 A6
Airedale NR33 ....114 E2
Airey Cl Lowestoft NR32 ..112 F5
  Newton CO10 ....92 A8
Airstation La IP21 .....21 E6
Aisthorpe IP9 ....150 D3
Akethorpe Way NR32 ....113 A3
Alabaster Cl **9** IP7 ...149 E6
Alan Rd IP3 ....140 E6
Alandale Dr **2** NR33 ...11 C1
Alban Sq **2** IP1 ....84 A1
Albany Rd **1** NR32 ....113 E2
Albany The IP4 ....139 E8
Albemarle Rd IP12 .....122 D4
Albemarle St **6** CO12 ..107 B3
Albert Cres IP13 ....154 A2
Albert Pye Prim Sch
  NR34 ....111 B4
Albert Rd IP13 ....126 C3
Albert Rolph Dr IP27 ...109 E4
Albert St IP33 ....154 A2
Alberta Cl IP5 ....141 A6
Albion Hill IP4 ....139 F7
Albion Rd NR35 ....110 D3
Albion St IP17 ....128 C3
Alburgh with Denton Fst Sch
  IP20 ....7 A1
Alde House Dr IP15 ....129 D4
Alde Rd IP15 ....130 E4
Alde Rd CB9 ....132 E7
Aldeburgh Cl CO10 ....132 C5
Aldeburgh Com Hospl
  IP15 ....130 E3
Aldeburgh Prim Sch
  IP15 ....130 E3
Aldeburgh Rd
  Friston IP17 ....72 F7
  Leiston IP16 ....129 D4
Aldecar La IP17 ....72 C7
Alder Dr **2** NR33 .....114 C4

Alder Way CO10 ....148 D6
Aldercroft Cl IP1 ......135 B3
Aldercroft Rd IP1 .....135 B3
Alderlee IP2 ....138 F8
Alderman Rd IP1 ......155 A2
Alderton Rd IP12 ......99 E6
Aldham Gdns IP14 .....124 E4
Aldham Mill Hill IP7 ...149 C7
Aldham Rd IP7 ....149 CE
Aldis Ave IP14 ....124 D4
Aldon Cl **14** CO12 ....106 E1
Aldous Cl CO7 ....151 C5
Aldous Ct **18** IP14 ...53 F2
Aldridge La **2** IP33 ..155 A5
Aldringham Mews **13**
  IP11 ....152 D5
Aldringham Pk IP16 ....129 C8
Aldringham Rd IP17 ....129 B3
Aldwyck Way NR33 .....114 F4
Alexander Cl NR34 .....111 C2
Alexander Dr
  8 Great Waldingfield CO10 .92 C6
  Needham Market IP6 ...125 C5
Alexander Way IP28 ....47 E5
Alexanders Int Sch
  IP12 ....108 D8
Alexandra Rd
  Beccles NR34 ....111 B5
  Felixstowe IP11 ......152 E6
  Ipswich IP4 ....139 E6
  Lowestoft NR32 ......113 E1
  Sudbury CO10 ....148 E5
Alexandra St **8** CO12 ..107 B2
Alfred Corry Mus*
  IP18 ....119 C2
Algar Dr IP8 ....134 D1
Alice Driver Rd **8** IP13 ..83 E5
Alicia Cl IP33 ....123 C3
All Hallows' Hospl
  NR35 ....110 C7
All Saints CE Mid Sch
  CO10 ....148 E8
All Saints CE Prim Sch
  CB8 ....121 A3
All Saints CE VA Prim Sch
  Laxfield IP13 ....40 A3
  Winfarthing IP22 .....20 B8
All Saints Dr IP14 ....114 D4
All Saints Dr NR34 ....111 C3
All Saints Gn
  3 Beccles NR34 .....9 F4
  Beccles NR34 ....111 F4
All Saints Rd IP4 .....125 F8
All Saints' Rd
  Ipswich IP1 ....139 A7
  Lowestoft NR33 .....115 B4
All Saints Rd CB8 ....121 B3
All Saints Wlk IP28 ...30 B8
Allen Rd IP17 ....112 D1
Allenby Rd IP7 ....138 F6
Alley Rd IP10 ....98 D2
Allfields **3** CO12 ....107 A3
Allington Cl IP4 ....139 F7
Allington Rd **7** IP19 ..139 F7
Allington Wlk CB9 ....132 C6
Allotment La IP6 ......69 A1
Allthorpe Rd **8** IP20 ...22 D6
Alma Cl **8** IP4 ....136 A1
Alma Pl IP17 ....128 D3
Alma Rd NR32 ....113 C1
Almond Gr IP24 ....16 A4
Almondhayes IP2 ......139 C3
Almshouse Rd IP30 ....49 C1
Alpe St IP1 ....155 A4
Alpha Bsns Pk IP1 ....134 D3
Alphamstone Rd CO8 ...101 A6
Alphamstone St CO10 ..106 E8
Alston Rd **2** IP14 ....124 D4
Alston Rd IP3 ....139 F4
Alton Hall La IP9 ......105 C6
Alton Wr Sports Ctr
  IP9 ....105 D6
Alton Wr Visitor Ctr*
  IP9 ....105 D6
Alvis Cl IP32 ....123 F5
Amber Mus The*
  IP18 ....119 C5
Amberfield Sch IP10 ...145 C6
Amberley Ct **3** IP14 ..112 F4
America Hill IP6 ....83 A6
Amy Johnson Ct **8**
  IP28 ....116 B5
Ancaster Rd IP2 ......155 A1
Anchor End **2** CO11 ..105 A2
Anchor La Burwell CB5 ..44 A6
  Dedham CO7 ....137 F5
  Lakenheath IP27 .....109 C6
Anchor St IP33 ....115 C6
Anchor Way NR33 .....114 B4
Ancient House Mus*
  CO10 ....90 A8
Anderson Cl IP26 .....125 C5
Anderson Rd IP22 ....122 D7
Anderson's Way **8** IP12 ..146 E4
Andrew Burtts Cl
  NR34 ....111 B4
Andrews Cl IP13 ......126 B3
Andrew Johnston Way
  IP19 ....118 B3
Andrew Rd CB8 ....120 E5
Andrews Cl NR34 .....114 D6
Andros Cl **8** IP33 ....53 F2
Anfield IP33 ....144 A7
Angel High
  Bury St Edmunds IP33 ..154 C2
Stonham Earl IP14 ....67 F5
Angel La Blythburgh IP19 ..42 F6

Angel La continued
  Bury St Edmunds IP33 ..154 A2
  Glemsford CO10 ......77 A2
  Ipswich IP4 ....155 C2
  2 Woodbridge IP12 ...147 A5
Angel Link IP19 ....118 B3
Angel Rd IP4 ....134 A2
Angel St IP7 ....149 D6
Angela Rd **4** CO12 ....107 C3
Angelgate Esp **4** CO12 ..107 C3
Angerstein IP27 ....5 E4
Anglesea Rd IP1 ......155 A4
Anglesey Pl **8** IP31 ..49 A5
Anglian La IP32 ....154 A4
Anglian Way IP1 ......3 B7
Angus Cl IP4 ....136 B1
Animal Health Trust Visitor
  Ctr* CB8 ....45 F5
Anita Cl **E** IP2 ....138 E5
Anita Cl W IP2 ....138 E5
Ann Beaumont Way
  IP7 ....149 C7
Ann Coles Cl CB9 .....88 B8
Ann St **1** IP1 ....155 A4
Ann Suckling Rd CB8 ..132 C3
Annandale Dr NR34 ....111 D4
Annbrook Rd IP2 ......138 A5
Anne Bartholomew Rd
  IP24 ....16 C7
Anne St IP1 ....155 A4
Annesons Cnr IP17 ....58 B6
Annis Hill La **4** NR35 ..110 E3
Annis Hill Rd NR35 ....110 D3
Annison Cl NR33 ......115 B5
Ansell Cl IP7 ....149 C6
Anselm Ave **8** IP32 ..48 C5
Anson Rd **8** IP5 .....98 A8
Anson Way NR32 ......10 A3
Antonia Cl CB9 ....133 C5
Antrim Rd IP1 ....134 D1
Anzani Ave IP11 ......152 C4
Apple Acre Rd IP33 ...13 F2
Apple Cl **6** IP27 ....51 A2
Apple Tree Cl NR33 ...115 B6
Appleby Cl IP3 ....138 C1
Appledore Dr NR33 ...114 D4
Appledown Dr IP30 ...114 C3
Appletree Gr **2** CB5 ..44 A6
Appletree La IP27 ....20 C3
Aragon Rd IP3 ....138 C1
Arbor La NR33 ....114 E2
Arcade St IP1 ....155 B3
Archangel Gdns IP2 ..155 B4
Archers' Ave **3** IP26 ..4 A5
Arderne Cl **12** CO10 ..106 F1
Ardleigh Rd CO7 .....137 D6
Argyle St IP4 ....155 C3
Ark Cl **7** NR33 ......11 B1
Arkwright Rd IP2 ....150 E6
Arlington Way IP24 ..16 C5
Arms La CB9 ....133 F7
Armstrong Cl
  Hundon CO10 ....75 D4
  Newmarket CB8 ....132 B5
Armstrong Way CO9 ..90 A1
Arnhem Ct NR32 .....113 C4
Arnhem Rd IP16 .....129 D5
Arnold Cl IP1 ....134 F3
Arnold St
  3 Lowestoft NR32 ..113 D2
  3 Lowestoft NR32 ..113 E1
Arras Rd **3** IP3 .....122 D5
Arrendene Rd CB9 ....132 D7
Arrowhead Dr IP27 ...109 C7
Artillery Dr **7** CO12 ..106 E1
Artillery Way **11** NR32 ..112 C1
Arundel Cl IP4 ......123 D6
Arundel Rd
  Ipswich IP3 ....140 E3
  2 Lowestoft NR33 ..114 D4
Arwela Rd IP11 ......152 F2
Ascot Dr
  Felixstowe IP11 .....152 E6
  Ipswich IP3 ....140 B3
Ash Ave **1** IP7 .....80 D6
Ash Cl Beccles IP14 ..51 F6
  2 Lakenheath IP27 ..109 D4
  7 Lowestoft NR33 ...114 D5
  Thetford IP24 ......16 A4
  Woodbridge IP12 ....146 F4
Ash Dr CB9 ....117 D3
Ash Gd Cl
  3 Brantham CO11 ...104 E4
  4 Felixstowe IP11 ...107 D8
Ash Gr
  Capel St. Mary IP9 ...150 E3
  Haverhill CB9 ....132 C7
  4 Sudbury CO10 ....92 B3
Ash Rd
  Campsey Ash IP12 ...71 C1
  Hacheston IP13 .....127 F7
  Onehouse IP14 ......66 C5
  Rendlesham IP12 ....85 C7
Ash Rise **8** CO6 ....102 C5
Ash Tree Cl
  8 Beccles NR34 .....9 F4
  18 Occold IP23 .....37 F1
Ash Wlk CB8 ....75 C6
Ashbocking Rd IP6 ...82 E6
Ashburnham Rd IP6 ..125 C4
Ashburnham Way
  NR33 ....114 D4

Ashby Rd NR32 ....113 C1
Ashcroft Rd IP1 ......135 A1
Ashdale Dr NR34 ....111 E4
Ashdale Rd IP5 .....141 D8
Ashdown Way IP1 ...140 D3
Ashe Rd IP12 ....71 F2
Ashen Cl CO10 ......89 E5
Ashen Gdns CO10 ...89 E5
Ashen Hill CO10 ....89 E6
Ashen La CO10 .....89 E6
Ashen Rd Ashen CO10 ..89 D7
  Ridgewell CO9 ......89 D4
Ashfield Cres IP33 ..114 F7
Ashfield Dr IP16 ....129 C5
Ashfield Hill IP16 ...50 F6
Ashfield Rd
  Elmswell IP30 ......50 F3
  Norton IP31 ....50 C4
  Wetherden IP14 .....51 A2
Ashford Cl NR34 .....9 B6
Ashlea Cl CB9 ....132 F4
Ashlea Rd CB9 ......132 F4
Ashley Downs NR32 ..113 C3
Ashley Rd Cheveley CB8 ..60 E8
  Harwich CO12 ......107 A2
Ashley St IP2 ....155 B1
Ashman's Rd NR34 ..111 B4
Ashmere Gr IP4 .....139 F6
Ashmere Rise CO10 ..148 E6
Ashness **2** NR32 ...113 A4
Ashwell Rd IP33 ....122 D4
Askins Rd CO12 ....151 C5
Aspal Cl **5** IP28 ...30 B8
Aspal Hall Rd IP28 ..30 C8
Aspal La IP28 ......30 C8
Aspal Pk IP28 ......30 B8
Aspall Rd IP14 .....53 F3
Aspen Ct Claydon IP6 ..83 D1
Aspen Cl
  Great Barton IP31 ..49 B6
  Haverhill CB9 ......132 C7
Aspinall Cl **4** NR33 ..114 F4
Assington La CO6 ...93 A1
Assington Rd CO10 ..92 D3
Astbury Rd **1** NR32 ..113 B5
Aster Rd IP2 ....138 E4
Aston Cl IP1 ....134 C1
Ataka Rd IP11 ......152 F6
Athelington Rd IP21 ..38 F2
Athenaeum La IP33 ..154 C2
Atherton Rd IP2 ....138 D5
Atterton Rd IP22 ...132 B7
Aubretia Cl **2** NR33 ..114 F7
Audley End IP27 ....20 B3
Augusta Cl **9** IP33 ..144 E7
Augustus Cl IP33 ...133 B5
Aureole Wlk CB8 ...120 E8
Austin Cl IP11 .....115 A4
Austin St IP2 ......155 B1
Aveley La IP29 .....77 D6
Avenue App IP32 ...123 A8
Avenue Rd IP27 ....109 E4
Avenue The
  Brome & Oakley IP23 ..117 E8
  8 Burwell CB5 .....44 B6
  Copdock & Washbrook
  IP8 ....95 F4
  Felixstowe IP11 ....152 B7
  Great Barton IP31 ..122 D3
  Halesworth IP19 ...118 B5
  Ipswich IP1 ....135 C1
  Ipswich IP3 ....140 B3
  4 Kessingland NR33 ..11 B1
  Lowestoft NR33 ....115 B5
  Newmarket CB8 ....132 C3
  Risby IP28 ....47 E5
  Ufford IP13 ....84 F7
  Woodbridge IP12 ...147 A4
Aves Cl IP4 ....29 C5
Avocet Cl NR33 ....115 C6
Avocet La **28** NR33 ..98 A8
Avondale Rd
  Ipswich IP4 ....140 A2
  Lowestoft NR32 ....113 A2
Aylmer Cl IP28 .....47 D5
Aylward Cl IP7 .....149 E4
Ayr Rd IP4 ....136 B1

B

Babb's La IP14 ....52 F2
Babergh Cl CO10 ....92 B7
Babington Dr IP2 ...118 B2
Baby La IP30 ....65 D4
Back Hamlet IP3 ...139 E5
Back Hill IP9 ......105 F6
Back Hills IP22 ....36 A7
Back La
  Badwell Ash IP31 ...50 F8
  Burrough Green CB8 ..59 F2
  Claydon IP6 ....134 C8
  Copdock & Washbrook
  IP8 ....95 F5
  Diss IP22 ....20 D7
  Falkenham IP10 ....98 F1
  Felixstowe IP11 ....152 F5
  Kettlebaston IP7 ...64 E3
  Lound NR32 ....2 F6
  Monks Eleigh IP7 ..79 C2
  St Mary, South Elmham
  Otherwise Homersfield
  IP20 ....23 C8
  Scole IP21 ....21 A5

Back La continued
  Tattingstone IP9 ...105 B7
  Wicken CB7 ....28 A1
Back Rd Brockdish IP21 ..11 E4
  Middleton IP17 .....58 B6
  Rattlesden IP30 ....65 E6
  Trimley St Martin IP10 ..98 D2
  Wenhaston With Mells Hamlet
  IP19 ....42 C6
Back St
  Garboldisham IP22 ..18 D5
  Gislingham IP23 ....36 B1
  Lavenham IP10 .....109 D6
Bacon Rd **7** IP6 ...82 B5
Bacon's Gn Rd IP19 ..25 D3
Bacton Com Prim Sch
  IP14 ....51 F6
Bacton Mid Sch IP14 ..51 E6
Bacton St
  Felixstowe IP11 ....152 F3
  Haughley IP14 .....51 C2
Bader Cl IP3 ....140 C2
Bader St IP8 ....98 A8
Badgers Bank IP19 ..138 E1
Badgers Gr CO6 ....102 D1
Badger's Holt **8** NR33 ..11 B1
Badingham Rd
  Badingham IP13 ....56 A4
  Framlingham IP13 ..126 E5
  Laxfield IP13 ......40 C1
  Peasenhall IP17 ...56 E7
Badley Hill IP6 ....125 B7
Badley Wlk IP6 ....125 A7
Badleys Cl **3** CO10 ..92 B3
Badlingham Rd CB7 ..29 E1
Badshah Ave IP4 ...140 B3
Badwell Ash VA Prim Sch
  IP31 ....50 E8
Badwell Rd
  Walsham-le-willows IP31 ..35 B1
  Wyverstone IP14 ...51 C6
Bagshaw La IP28 ...30 A6
Bahram Cl CB8 .....120 D4
Bailey Ave IP5 .....141 E7
Bailey Cl Haverhill CB9 ..133 B5
  Ipswich IP2 ....138 E6
Bailey La CO10 ....92 B3
Baileypool La IP31 ..49 F8
Baines Coney CB9 ..132 A7
Baird Cl IP2 ....138 F7
Bakehouse Hill CB8 ..59 F4
Baker Dr **2** CB5 ...44 B6
Baker Way IP9 .....107 A4
Baker's Cnr IP14 ...80 E6
Baker's Hill IP16 ...58 C4
Baker's La
  Bury St Edmunds IP33 ..154 C1
  Thornton IP23 .....53 C6
  Westleton IP17 ....58 C8
Bakers La
  Ditchingham NR35 ..110 B8
  Orford IP12 ....131 C2
  Winston IP14 ......68 E8
  Woodbridge IP12 ...147 A4
Baker's Score **8** NR32 ..3 C4
Bakers Way IP28 ...30 F2
Balaton Pl CB8 ....121 A6
Baldry Cl IP8 ......138 C1
Baldrys Wlk NR35 ..110 B7
Baldwin Ave
  18 Bury St Edmunds IP32 ..48 C5
  Bury St Edmunds IP32 ..48 C5
Baldwin Rd IP14 ...124 E4
Ballater Cl IP1 ....134 E4
Ballingdon Hall*
  CO10 ....148 A3
Ballingdon Hill CO10 ..148 A4
Ballingdon St CO10 ..148 A4
Ball's Chace CO6 ...102 C5
Balls Hill IP7 .....79 C5
Ballygate NR34 ....111 A5
Balmoral Cl IP2 ...138 F1
Balton Way **7** CO12 ..106 F1
Bancroft La CB7 ...28 D2
Bangor Rd IP27 ....13 F2
Banham Dr **3** CO10 ..148 D6
Banham Rd NR34 ..111 C2
Banham's La NR35 ..7 B6
Bank Alley **8** IP18 ..119 C5
Bank Rd IP4 ....139 E6
Banks' La IP19 ....24 C3
Bannocks La IP13 ..56 A4
Banters La NR34 ...8 F2
Bantocks Rd CO10 ..92 C5
Bantoff Terr IP23 ..140 C2
Banyard Cl **4** IP5 ..141 D7
Barbara Stradbroke Ave
  CB8 ....120 D1
Barber Cl **3** NR33 ..11 B1
Barber's La NR33 ..7 B6
Barcham Rd CB7 ...28 C2
Bardolph Rd NR33 ..110 B3
Bardwell Rd IP31 ..33 F5
Bardwell VC Prim Sch
  IP31 ....34 C5
Barell's Hill IP14 ..40 F4
Bargate La
  Beck Row, Holywell Row
  & Kenny Hill IP28 ...29 F5
  Dedham CO7 ....104 A2
Bargate Rd IP28 ...30 A6

Barham Picnic Site Visitor
Ctr* IP6 . . . . .82 A6
Barhams Way IP13 . . . . . .127 C7
Barker Cl Ipswich IP2 . . . .138 D5
🔟 Manningtree CO11 . . . .104 D2
🔒 Steeple Bumpstead CB9 .88 D3
Barker Rd CO10 . . . . .148 C8
Barking Rd
Barking IP6 . . . . .125 A1
Willisham IP8 . . . . .81 A5
Barkis Mdw NR32 . . . . .3 A4
Barkways 🔟 CB5 . . . . .44 B5
Barley Lands IP15 . . . . . . .130 E5
Barley Mdw 🔟 IP19 . . . . .118 A3
Barley Way NR33 . . . . .114 F2
Barlings Ct CB8 . . . . .121 A4
Barn Cl
🔟 Hopton on Sea NR31 . . .3 C7
Lowestoft NR33 . . . . .114 D5
Southwold IP18 . . . . .119 B8
Barn Field 🔟 IP29 . . . . . . .62 C6
Barn La NR33 . . . . .154 C3
Barn St 🔟 CO10 . . . . .78 D4
Barnardiston Hall Prep Sch
CB9 . . . . .75 B5
Barnards Way NR32 . . . . . .112 A1
Barnby & N Cove Prim Sch
NR34 .10 C4
Barnes Cl 🔟 Brandon IP27 .14 E8
🔒 Hadleigh IP7 . . . . .149 E6
Barnfield
Capel St. Mary IP9 . . . . . . .150 F3
Felixstowe IP11 . . . . .152 D6
🔟 Manningtree CO11 . . . .104 E2
Barnham CE Prim Sch
IP24 . . . . .16 B1
Barnham Pl IP5 . . . . .140 F6
Barnham Rd IP24 . . . . .16 E2
Barningham Rd IP31 . . . . .34 E5
Barons Cl
🔟 Felixstowe IP11 . . . . . . .153 D6
Halesworth IP19 . . . . .118 A2
Barons Rd IP33 . . . . .123 A2
Baronsdale Cl IP11 . . . . . . .135 B1
Barr Dr IP27 . . . . .109 D7
Barrack La
Harwich CO12 . . . . .107 C2
Ipswich IP1 . . . . .155 A3
Ufford IP13 . . . . .84 F7
Barrack Sq IP5 . . . . .98 A8
Barracks Rd CO10 . . . . . . .101 F8
Barrell's Rd IP11 . . . . .49 F3
Barrett's La IP6 . . . . .125 C4
Barrow Hill Acton CO10 . . .92 B8
Barrow IP29 . . . . .47 A2
Barrow Prim Sch 47 A3
Barrow Rd IP29 . . . . .46 F1
Barrow's Cnr IP24 . . . . . . .32 C8
Barry Lynham Dr CB8 . . . .121 C2
Barsey Cl CB9 . . . . .132 A7
Bartholomew St IP4 . . . . .139 F6
Bartholomew's La IP19 . . .42 B6
Bartlet Hospl IP11 . . . . . . .153 C4
Barton Bottom IP31 . . . . .48 E7
Barton Dr CB9 . . . . .133 F8
Barton Cir CB9 . . . . .133 F8
Barton Hamlet IP31 . . . . . .49 C6
Barton Hill IP31 . . . . .48 D5
Barton Rd
Bury St Edmunds IP32 . . . .123 D6
Felixstowe IP11 . . . . .152 D6
Thurston IP31 . . . . .49 D4
Woodbridge IP12 . . . . .146 F7
Bartons Pl CB8 . . . . .120 E5
Barvanes The IP8 . . . . .138 A1
Barway Rd CB7 . . . . .29 A1
Basil Brown Cl 🔟 IP22 . . .36 A6
Bates La IP22 . . . . .19 D6
Bath Hill IP11 . . . . .153 B4
Bath Hills Rd NR35 . . . . . . .7 F4
Bath Rd IP11 . . . . .153 B4
Bath St IP2 . . . . .139 D3
Battery Gn 🔟 NR32 . . . . . .113 E1
Battery Gn Rd
🔟 Lowestoft NR32 . . . . . . .113 E1
🔒 Lowestoft NR32 . . . . . .115 E8
Battery La 🔟 IP9 . . . . .107 A4
Battles La IP5 . . . . .141 D7
Battlesea Hill IP13 . . . . . . .39 A6
Baxter La CO10 . . . . .153 D7
Bay Rd 🔟 CO12 . . . . .107 B2
Bayfield Dr 🔟 CB5 . . . . . . .44 B5
Baylham House Rare Breeds
Farm* 🔟 IP6 . . . . .81 F7
Baynard's La IP16 . . . . .73 F6
Bays The 🔟 IP16 . . . . .73 F6
Beach Rd Dunwich IP17 . . .43 B1
🔟 Harwich CO12 . . . . . . .107 B1
Hopton on Sea NR31 . . . . . .3 C6
Kessingland NR33 . . . . .27 C8
Lowestoft NR32 . . . . .115 D8
Beach Rd E IP11 . . . . .153 C4
Beach Rd W IP11 . . . . .152 F2
Beach Sta Rd
Felixstowe IP11 . . . . .152 E1
Felixstowe IP11 . . . . .152 E1
Beacon Field 🔟 IP11 . . . . .152 E5
Beacon Hill Ave CO12 . . . .107 C2
Beacon Hill La IP16 . . . . . . .73 F3
Beacon La IP13 . . . . .137 F3
Beaconsfield Cl CO10 . . . .148 C6
Beaconsfield Rd
Aldeburgh IP15 . . . . .130 E3

Beaconsfield Rd continued
Ipswich IP1 . . . . .138 F7
🔟 Kessingland NR33 . . . .11 C1
Lowestoft NR33 . . . . .115 C6
Sudbury CO10 . . . . .148 C6
🔒 Woodbridge IP12 . . . . .147 A5
Bealings La IP13 . . . . .137 F8
Bealings Rd IP13 . . . . .137 D4
Bealings Sch IP13 . . . . .137 D4
Bear Mdw 🔟 IP30 . . . . . . .49 F2
Bear St CO6 . . . . .102 C5
Beard Rd IP32 . . . . .122 D8
Beardmore Pk 🔟 IP5 . . . .98 A8
Bear's La CO10 . . . . .78 D3
Beatrice Ave IP11 . . . . . . .153 A5
Beatrice Cl IP3 . . . . .140 A3
Beatty Rd Ipswich IP3 . . . .140 B2
Sudbury CO10 . . . . .148 E7
Beaufort Rd IP31 . . . . .32 F1
Beaufort St IP1 . . . . .139 A7
Beaumont Cl CB9 . . . . . . .132 A7
Beaumont Ct CB9 . . . . . . .132 F4
Beaumont Rd NR33 . . . . . .114 B2
Beaumont Vale CB9 . . . . .132 F4
Beaumont Way IP14 . . . . .124 B5
Beccles & District Mus*
NR34 .111 A5
Beccles & District War Meml
Hospl NR34 . . . . .111 A5
Beccles Bsns Pk NR34 . . . .10 A3
Beccles Mid Sch
NR34 . . . . .111 A5
Beccles Rd Aldeby NR34 . . .9 F8
Aldeby/Wheatacre/Burgh
St Peter NR34 . . . . .9 D8
Blyford IP19 . . . . .25 C1
Bungay NR35 . . . . .110 C4
Bungay NR35 . . . . .110 D4
Carlton Colville NR33 . . . . .114 A4
Fritton & St Olaves NR31 . . .2 C7
Holton IP19 . . . . .118 F4
Lowestoft NR33 . . . . .114 D7
Mutford NR34 . . . . .10 C3
Beccles Sports Ctr
NR34 . . . . .111 A3
Beccles Sta NR34 . . . . .111 C5
Becclesgate St IP13 . . . . . .111 B6
Beck Cl 🔟 IP12 . . . . .85 D8
Beck La CB7 . . . . .29 D4
Beck Row Prim Sch
IP28 .30 B8
Beck St IP22 . . . . .35 A7
Beck The IP26 . . . . .4 E5
Beckett Cl IP33 . . . . .122 A6
Becketts La IP7 . . . . .94 B1
Beckton Way IP11 . . . . . . .105 A2
Beckham Rd IP31 . . . . .32 D1
Becks Gn La NR34 . . . . . . .24 F8
Bedell Cl IP33 . . . . .122 C3
Bederic Cl IP32 . . . . .123 D4
Bedfield CE Prim Sch
IP13 .54 E5
Bedfield Rd IP13 . . . . .55 A3
Bedford Rd 🔟 IP32 . . . . . .122 E8
Bedford St IP1 . . . . .155 A3
Bedingfeld Way IP32 . . . . .123 E4
Bedingfield Cres IP18 . . . .118 A1
Bedingfield Rd IP32 . . . . . .53 E7
Beech Cir 🔟 IP7 . . . . .80 D6
Beech Cl
Halesworth IP19 . . . . .118 A3
🔟 Isleham CB7 . . . . .29 B5
🔒 Lakenheath IP27 . . . . . .13 F2
Sproughton IP8 . . . . .138 A6
Beech Croft CB8 . . . . .59 E3
Beech Gr Haverhill CB9 . . .132 C7
Ipswich IP3 . . . . .139 F3
Ipswich IP3 . . . . .140 F7
Beech La 🔟 IP14 . . . . .51 A1
Beech Paddocks 🔟 IP30 .64 F8
Beech Rd Ipswich IP5 . . . .140 F7
Lowestoft NR33 . . . . .114 D3
Sudbury CO10 . . . . .148 F4
Beech Rise IP33 . . . . .123 C3
Beech Row CB8 . . . . .46 F2
Beech Terr IP14 . . . . .124 D7
Beech Tree Ct NR34 . . . . .111 B4
Beech Way
Dickleburgh IP21 . . . . .21 C5
Woodbridge IP12 . . . . .146 F3
Beech Wlk IP16 . . . . .129 C5
Beechcroft IP29 . . . . .64 A3
Beechcroft Rd IP1 . . . . . . .134 F2
Beeches Cl 🔟 IP31 . . . . . . .34 B1
Beeches Rd IP28 . . . . .29 F7
Beeches The
Claydon IP6 . . . . .134 C8
Horringer IP29 . . . . .63 A8
Ipswich IP3 . . . . .139 F4
🔟 Lawford CO11 . . . . . . .104 E2
Little Blakenham IP8 . . . . . .81 E3
Beeching Dr NR32 . . . . . . .113 D4
Beechwood Cl CB8 . . . . . .120 C8
Beechwood Gdns
NR33 . . . . .115 A6
Beetons Way IP32 . . . . . . .122 E7
Belaugh Ave NR33 . . . . . .114 E5
Belchamp Hall* CO10 . . . .91 A3
Belchamp Rd CO9 . . . . . . .90 A3
Belgrave Cl IP4 . . . . .135 E1
Bell Cl IP7 . . . . .155 B1
Bell Gdns 🔟 CB7 . . . . .28 D4
Bell Gn IP19 . . . . .40 C6
Bell Hill CO8 . . . . .101 B6
Bell La
Barton Mills IP28 . . . . .116 D2
Ipswich IP2 . . . . .155 B1

Bell La continued
Marlesford IP13 . . . . .71 C4
Bell Mdw IP22 . . . . .123 A8
Bell St IP26 . . . . .4 E5
Bellands Way IP23 . . . . . . .117 C3
Belle Vue Rd
Ipswich IP4 . . . . .139 F6
Sudbury CO10 . . . . .148 D5
Bell's Cross IP14 . . . . .67 C6
Bell's Cross Rd IP6 . . . . . . .82 C7
Bells Hill CO8 . . . . .101 D2
Bell's La Hawstead IP29 . . .63 B8
Stowupland IP14 . . . . .67 C7
Bells La Glemsford CO10 . .77 A3
Hinderclay IP22 . . . . .35 C6
Bells Rd CO10 . . . . .90 F3
Bellwell La
Debenham IP14 . . . . .53 F4
Kenton IP14 . . . . .54 A4
Belmont Gdns NR32 . . . . .113 B3
Belmont Rd IP8 . . . . .138 C1
Belseybridge Rd NR35 . . . .7 F7
Belstead Ave IP2 . . . . .155 A1
Belstead Rd IP2 . . . . .155 A1
Belt The CB8 . . . . .61 B4
Belvedere Rd
Ipswich IP4 . . . . .139 F8
Lowestoft NR33 . . . . .115 C7
Benacre Rd
Ellough NR34 . . . . .9 F5
Henstead with Hulver Street
NR34 .26 E8
Ipswich IP3 . . . . .140 E4
Benefield Cl 🔟 CB8 . . . . . .45 F3
Benezet St IP1 . . . . .155 A3
Benjamin Britten High Sch
NR32 . . . . .113 A5
Bennett Ave
Bury St Edmunds IP33 . . . .122 C6
Elmswell IP30 . . . . .50 F2
Bennett Rd
Ipswich IP1 . . . . .134 E1
🔟 Red Lodge IP28 . . . . . .30 C1
Benouville IP13 . . . . .114 F3
Bensly's Drift IP19 . . . . . . .118 C4
Bent La IP4 . . . . .140 E8
Bentley CE VC Prim Sch
IP9 . . . . .104 F8
Bentley Dr NR32 . . . . .113 A6
Bentley La
Belstead IP8 . . . . .142 C5
Stutton IP9 . . . . .105 B6
Bentley Rd IP1 . . . . .134 C2
Benton Cl IP7 . . . . .65 C1
Benton St IP7 . . . . .149 D4
Benton Way IP10 . . . . .118 B4
Benyon Gdns IP14 . . . . . . .32 D1
Beresford Dr IP12 . . . . . . .146 F7
Beresford Rd NR32 . . . . . .113 D2
Bergamot Rd IP6 . . . . .132 A6
Berghersh La IP14 . . . . . . .66 F7
Berghorn Rd CO11 . . . . . . .104 D4
Berkeley Cl
🔒 Framlingham IP13 . . . .126 C3
Ipswich IP4 . . . . .135 E1
Berkeley Gdns
Bury St Edmunds IP33 . . . .122 C6
Lowestoft NR33 . . . . .114 A4
Bermuda Rd IP10 . . . . .144 D7
Bernard Cres IP3 . . . . .140 B2
Bernard Rooke Pottery Mill
Gall* IP6 . . . . .43 A8
Berners Rd IP1 . . . . .153 C4
Berners St IP1 . . . . .155 A3
Bernham Cl IP32 . . . . .123 D5
Berry Cl Ipswich IP3 . . . . . .140 F1
Lowestoft NR33 . . . . .112 A1
Berrycroft IP11 CB7 . . . . . .28 D4
Beryl Rd 🔟 CO12 . . . . . . .106 E1
Bethel Dr 🔟 NR33 . . . . . . .11 C1
Betts Ave IP5 . . . . .98 A8
Bevan St E 🔟 NR32 . . . . .115 D8
Bevan St W NR32 . . . . . . .113 C1
Beverley Cl NR33 . . . . .114 D6
Beverley Cr NR33 . . . . .114 C2
Beverley Rd IP4 . . . . .139 F8
Beversham Rd IP13 . . . . . .71 F5
Bexley Ave 🔟 CO12 . . . . .106 F1
Beyton Mid Sch IP30 . . . . .49 F7
Beyton Rd IP30 . . . . .49 F6
Bibb Way IP1 . . . . .139 A5
Bickers Hill Rd IP13 . . . . . .40 B3
Bickers Way CO6 . . . . .102 B7
Bier La IP22 . . . . .19 C1
Bigod Cl
🔟 Framlingham IP13 . . . .126 C3
Bigod Rd NR35 . . . . .110 C8
Bildeston Gdns 🔟 IP11 . .135 D1
Bildeston Prim Sch IP7 . . .79 F4
Bildeston Rd
Chelsworth IP7 . . . . .79 E3
Combs IP14 . . . . .65 F3
Offton IP7 . . . . .80 D4
Wattisham IP7 . . . . .80 A6
Bill Rickaby Dr CB8 . . . . . .121 A5
Billy's La CO7 . . . . .103 E5
Bilney Rd IP12 . . . . .146 E5
Birch Ave CO10 . . . . .107 A2
Birch Cl
Lowestoft NR32 . . . . .112 D2
🔟 Stowupland IP14 . . . . .67 A6
Wickham Market IP13 . . . . .127 C6
Woodbridge IP12 . . . . .146 F3
Birch Cres IP27 . . . . .109 D7
Birch Dr 🔟 CO11 . . . . . . .104 E5
Birch Fall 🔟 CO6 . . . . . . .102 C5

Birch Gr IP5 . . . . .98 A7
Birch Rd Onehouse IP14 . .66 C6
🔟 Thurstow IP31 . . . . . . .49 E4
Birch St CO6 . . . . .102 D5
Birch Wlk 🔟 IP27 . . . . . . .13 F2
Birches The CB7 . . . . .28 C5
Birchgrove IP23 . . . . .52 F7
Birchinhill Dro IP28 . . . . . .12 F2
Birchwood Cty Prim Sch
IP5 . . . . .98 A8
Birchwood Dr IP5 . . . . . . .136 E1
Birchwood Rd CO7 . . . . . .103 D8
Bird View Sq 🔟 IP28 . . . . .4 E5
Birdbrook 🔟 IP32 . . . . . . .63 A1
Birdbrook Rd CO9 . . . . . . .89 A2
Birdcage Wlk CB8 . . . . . . .120 F2
Birds Croft IP31 . . . . .33 C2
Birds End IP30 . . . . .63 A7
Birds Hill IP3 . . . . .65 E5
Birds La IP30 . . . . .64 D2
Bird's La Framsden IP14 . . .69 D5
Lowestoft NR33 . . . . .115 B6
Bird's Rd IP31 . . . . .48 C6
Birkdale Ave IP28 . . . . . . .116 B5
Birkdale Cl 🔟 IP28 . . . . . .48 C6
Birkfield Cl IP2 . . . . .139 A4
Birkfield Dr IP2 . . . . .138 E1
Biscay Cl CB9 . . . . .133 A5
Bishop Mews IP2 . . . . . . .138 B2
Bishops Cl 🔟 IP11 . . . . . .153 D6
Bishop's Hill IP3 . . . . .139 E4
Bishop's Palace E Elham
Hall* IP20 . . . . .23 D6
Bishops Rd IP33 . . . . .154 B3
Bishops Way IP21 . . . . . . .39 A4
Bishops Wlk
🔟 Hopton on Sea NR31 . . .3 B7
Lowestoft NR33 . . . . .113 D5
Bittern Cl IP2 . . . . .138 E3
Bittern Rd IP17 . . . . .128 B3
Bixley Dr IP4 . . . . .140 E5
Bixley La IP4 . . . . .140 F5
Bixley Rd Ipswich IP3 . . . .140 D3
🔒 Ipswich IP3 . . . . .155 C1
Black Barns IP11 . . . . .152 C7
Black Boy La CO11 . . . . . .106 A2
Black Boy Mdw NR34 . . . .111 B4
Black Dyke Rd IP26 . . . . . .4 E3
Black Gr La CB9 . . . . .75 E4
Black Hill (Tumulus)*
. . . . .33 C5
Black Horse La
Ditchingham NR35 . . . . . . .110 C7
Ipswich IP1 . . . . .155 A3
Black Mill Rd IP18 . . . . . . .119 C5
Black Slough IP17 . . . . . . .58 B7
Black St NR33 . . . . .10 F1
Blackberry Way
Lowestoft NR33 . . . . .112 A1
🔒 Red Lodge IP28 . . . . . .30 C1
Blackbird Ave IP27 . . . . . . .6 A1
🔒 Ipswich NR33 . . . . . . .112 A1
Blackbourne CE VC Mid Sch
IP31 .34 F4
Blackbourne Rd IP30 . . . . .50 F3
Blackdown Ave IP5 . . . . . .140 F6
Blackdyke Cl 🔟 IP26 . . . . .4 D5
Blackfriars CO10 . . . . .148 B4
Blackheath Rd
Lowestoft NR33 . . . . .115 A5
Wenhaston With Mells Hamlet
IP19 . . . . .42 C7
Blackhouse La CO10 . . . . .148 F1
Blacklands La IP31 . . . . . . .31 A2
Blackmore Cl CB9 . . . . . . .132 D7
Blacksmith La
Barnham IP24 . . . . .16 B2
Thorpe Morieux IP30 . . . . . .78 F7
Blacksmith Rd IP14 . . . . . .52 A6
Blacksmith's Cnr IP8 . . . .142 C6
Blacksmith's Corner CO10 .89 D6
Blacksmiths La
Bulmer CO10 . . . . .91 C1
Coddenham IP6 . . . . .68 B1
Stonham Earl IP14 . . . . . . .67 D6
Blacksmith's Loke NR32 . . .3 A4
Blackthorn Cl IP3 . . . . .140 F1
Blackthorn Ct CB7 . . . . . . .28 C5
Blackthorn Way CO6 . . . . .102 B7
Blacktiles La IP12 . . . . .84 A1
Bladen Dr IP4 . . . . .140 F6
Bladon Way CB9 . . . . .132 F7
Blagge Cl IP32 . . . . .122 C4
Blair Cl IP4 . . . . .140 E5
Blake Ave 🔟 IP9 . . . . .107 A5
Blake Cl IP1 . . . . .134 D2
Blake Rd Ipswich IP1 . . . . .134 F3
Stowmarket IP14 . . . . .124 B8
Blakenham Cl 🔟 NR32 . . .112 F4
Blakes Cl IP22 . . . . .147 C7
Blakesley La IP28 . . . . .29 F8
Blandford Rd IP4 . . . . .140 D3
Blaxhall Church Rd
IP12 .71 F2
Blaxhall Comm Nature
Reserve* IP12 . . . . .72 C3
Blenheim Cl
🔟 Brantham CO11 . . . . .104 E5
Bury St Edmunds IP33 . . . .122 F7
Haverhill CB9 . . . . .132 E7
Blenheim Dr IP7 . . . . .80 C6
Blenheim Rd 🔟 IP22 . . . . .20 A3
Blickling Cl 🔟 IP2 . . . . . . .139 B2

Blinco Rd NR32 112
Blind La IP29 77
Blo' Norton Rd
Blo' Norton IP22 18
South Lopham IP22 19
Block Rd CB7 28
Blocka Rd NR32 2
Blockmoor Rd CB7 28
Blofield Rd IP11 152
Blois Rd CB9 88
Blomfield St IP33 154
Blood Hill IP8 81
Bloodmoor La 🔟 NR33 . . .114
Bloodmoor Rd
🔟 Lowestoft NR33 114
Lowestoft NR33 114
Bloomfield St IP2 140
Bloomfield Way 🔟
NR33 114
Blooms Hall La CO10 77
Bloomsbury Cl NR32 112
Bloomsfield 🔟 CB5 44
Bluebell La NR33 10
Blue Barn Cl 🔟 IP11 107
Blue House La IP14 52
Bluebell Ave IP2 123
Bluebell Cl Ipswich IP2 . . .138
🔟 Lowestoft NR33 114
Bluebell Gr IP6 125
Bluebell Way NR31 111
Bluebell Wlk 🔒 CB7 28
Bluegate La IP9 150
Bluestem Rd IP3 144
Blundeston CE Prim Sch
NR32 .3
Blundeston Rd
Corton NR32 112
Somerleyton, Ashby &
Herringfleet NR32 112
Blyburgate
Beccles NR34 111
🔒 Beccles NR34 111
Blyford La Blyford IP19 . . .42
Holton IP19 118
Wenhaston With Mells Hamlet
IP19 42
Blyford Way IP11 152
Blyth Cl Ipswich IP2 139
Wenhaston IP19 42
Blyth Rd
Halesworth IP19 118
Southwold IP18 119
Blythburgh Rd IP17 58
Boathouse La
Carlton Colville NR32 114
Lowestoft NR33 114
Bobbits La
Pinewood IP9 142
Wherstead IP9 142
Boby Rd IP32 122
Bockhill Rd IP33 122
Bodiam Cl IP3 140
Bodiam Way 🔟 NR33 114
Bodmin Cl IP5 141
Boeing Way IP28 116
Boldero Rd IP32 122
Boleyn Cl CB9 132
Boleyn Wlk CB8 121
Bollard Way NR33 114
Bolton Cl 🔟 CB5 44
Bolton La IP1 155
Bolton St 🔟 CO10 78
Bon Marche 🔟 NR32 115
Bond Cl IP21 22
Bond St Stowmarket IP14 .155
Bonds Mdw NR32 112
Bond's Rd IP21 21
Bonnington Rd IP3 139
Bonsey Gdns NR34 26
Boon Cl IP33 123
Boon Dr NR33 114
Boot Drift IP9 106
Booth La IP6 141
Border Cot La IP13 127
Border La NR32 2
Borley Cres 🔟 IP30 50
Borley Rd CO10 91
Borough End 🔟 NR34 111
Borough La IP14 66
Borough La CO10 91
Borradale Rd 🔟 IP32 123
Borrett Pl IP22 146
Borretts Farm La IP13 70
Borrow Cl NR33 114
Borrow Rd NR32 112
Borrowdale Ave
🔟 Ipswich IP4 135
🔒 Ipswich IP4 140
Bosmere Prim Sch
IP6 125
Bosquet Cl 🔟 NR32 113
Boss Hall Rd IP1 138
Bostock Rd IP2 138
Boston End 🔟 IP14 51
Boston Rd Ipswich IP4 . . .139
Lowestoft NR33 113
Boswell La IP7 149
Botany La IP7 71
Botolphs Cl IP33 154
Bouchain Ct 🔟 IP19 118
Boulevard The NR32 114
Boulge Rd Burgh IP13 83
Haskeaton IP13 146
Boulters Cl IP14 124

Boulters Way IP14 . . . . . .124 B6
Boundary Cl IP26 . . . . .4 F3
Boundary Rd
  Haverhill CB9 . . . . .133 B3
  ■ Hockwold cum Wilton
  IP26 . . . . .5 A3
  Red Lodge IP28 . . . . .30 C1
Bourchier Cl IP7 . . . . . .149 E6
Bourne Ave IP32 . . . . . . .123 B3
Bourne Hill IP7 . . . . .143 B7
Bourne Rd
  Haverhill CB9 . . . . .132 F6
  Lowestoft NR32 . . . . .113 B3
Bowdens La CO6 . . . . . . .101 F3
Bower's La ■ CB7 . . . . . . .29 C5
Bowl Rd IP14 . . . . .66 C1
Bowman's La IP17 . . . . . . .42 D1
Bowthorpe Cl IP1 . . . . . .155 A4
Box Bush La IP13 . . . . .55 D5
Boxford Cl IP7 . . . . .124 E3
Boxford Ct ■ IP11 . . . . . .152 C6
Boxford La CO10 . . . . . . .93 A3
Boxford Prim Sch
  CO10 . . . . .93 C3
Boxford Rd IP7 . . . . .93 B8
Boxhouse La CO7 . . . . . . .103 D3
Boxted Church Rd
  CO6 . . . . .102 E2
Boxted Rd CO6 . . . . .102 E2
Boxted Straight Rd
  CO4 . . . . .103 A2
Boyden Cl ■ CB8 . . . . .60 F1
Boydlands IP9 . . . . .150 E3
Boyne Rd IP33 . . . . .122 E4
Boyscott La ■ NR35 . . . . .110 E3
Boyton Cl CB9 . . . . .132 E8
Boyton Rd
  Hollesley IP12 . . . . .86 A1
  Ipswich IP3 . . . . .140 B1
Boyton Vineyard★ CO9 . . .89 B7
Boyton's La CB10 . . . . .88 A1
Braces La NR35 . . . . .110 E3
Bracken Ave IP5 . . . . . . .137 E1
Bracken Rise IP26 . . . . .6 A8
Bracken Row ■ IP31 . . . . .49 D4
Brackenbury Sports Ctr
  IP11 . . . . .153 C5
Brackenhayes Cl IP2 . . . .139 B3
Brackenwood Cres ■
  IP32 . . . . .123 E6
Brackley Cl ■ IP11 . . . . . .152 D5
Bradfield Ave IP7 . . . . . .149 D7
Bradfield Cres IP7 . . . . . .149 D7
Bradley Rd Cowlinge CB8 . .60 F1
  Great Bradley CB8 . . . . . . .74 F8
  Kirtling CB8 . . . . .60 F2
Bradley St IP2 . . . . .139 A3
Braggon's Hill IP29 . . . . . .77 A5
Braithwaite Dr ■ CO10 . . .92 C6
Bramble Cl IP8 . . . . .140 E1
Bramble Dr IP3 . . . . .140 E1
Bramble Way CO6 . . . . . .102 B7
Brambles The IP5 . . . . . .130 C6
Bramblewood ■ IP8 . . . . .138 C2
Bramblewood Way
  IP19 . . . . .118 C4
Brames La IP20 . . . . .23 D3
Bramfield CE Prim Sch
  IP19 . . . . .42 A4
Bramfield House Sch
  IP19 . . . . .41 E4
Bramfield Rd
  Halesworth IP19 . . . . .118 B2
  Lowestoft NR32 . . . . .113 A4
  Walpole IP19 . . . . .41 C5
  Wenhaston With Mells Hamlet
  IP19 . . . . .42 B5
Bramford CE Prim Sch
  IP8 . . . . .134 A1
Bramford La
  ■ Ipswich IP1 . . . . .134 D1
  ■ Ipswich IP1 . . . . .139 A7
Bramford Rd
  Bramford IP8 . . . . .134 B1
  Claydon IP6 . . . . .81 A2
  ■ Great Blakenham IP6 . .82 A5
  Great Blakenham IP6 . . . .134 A8
  Ipswich IP1 . . . . .138 E8
Bramhall Cl IP2 . . . . .138 D1
Bramley Chase IP4 . . . . .140 B7
Bramley Cl IP32 . . . . .123 F6
Bramley Rd Diss IP22 . . . .20 A3
  Haverhill CB9 . . . . .132 A5
Bramley Rise IP4 . . . . . . .140 B7
Brampton CE Prim Sch
  NR34 . . . . .25 C5
Brampton Sta NR34 . . . . . .25 C6
Brand Rd IP31 . . . . .49 C7
Brandeston Cl ■ CO10 . . .92 C6
Brandeston Rd
  Cretingham IP13 . . . . .69 E7
  Earl Soham IP13 . . . . .54 F1
  IP27 . . . . .5 F8
Brandon Ctry Pk Visitor Ctr★
  IP27 . . . . .5 F7
Brandon Her Ctr★ IP27 . . .5 F1
Brandon Rd
  Felixstowe IP11 . . . . .152 C4
  Lakenheath IP27 . . . . .4 E4
  Methwold IP26 . . . . .5 B8
  Mildenhall IP28 . . . . .116 E5
  Thetford IP24 . . . . .16 F6
  Weeting IP27 . . . . .5 F1
  Wordwell IP28 . . . . .32 C3
Brandon St IP27 . . . . . . .109 F1
Brandon Sta IP27 . . . . .5 F2
Brands Cl ■ CO10 . . . . . . .92 B3

Brands La IP29 . . . . .63 D3
Bransby Gdns IP4 . . . . . .139 E7
Brantham Hill CO11 . . . . .104 E4
Brandy Rd ■ IP31 . . . . . . .33 D5
Brayfield Cl IP22 . . . . . . .123 D6
Braziers La IP7 . . . . .51 B6
Brazier's Wood Rd
  IP3 . . . . .144 B8
Breach Dro IP28 . . . . .13 C1
Breckland Way CO10 . . .109 D7
Breckland Mid Sch
  IP24 . . . . .14 D8
Breckland Way
  Lowestoft NR32 . . . . .113 A3
  Mildenhall IP28 . . . . .116 C5
Brecklands ■ IP26 . . . . . . .6 B8
Brecon Cl IP2 . . . . .139 B2
Bredfield Cl ■ IP11 . . . . .152 D5
Bredfield Rd IP12 . . . . . . .147 A7
Bredfield St IP12 . . . . . . .146 F5
Brendon Cl NR32 . . . . . . .112 E2
Brendon Dr IP5 . . . . .140 F6
Brent Cl IP28 . . . . .116 D4
Brent Eleigh Rd
  Lavenham CO10 . . . . .78 D3
  Monks Eleigh IP7 . . . . . . .79 B2
Brentgovel St
  ■ Bury St Edmunds IP33 . .154 B2
  Bury St Edmunds IP33 . . . .154 B2
Bressingham Prim Sch
  IP22 . . . . .19 E4
Bressingham Rd IP22 . . . .19 F4
Brett Ave IP27 . . . . .149 E7
Brett Gn IP7 . . . . .149 E2
Brettenham Cres ■
  IP1 . . . . .135 D1
Brettenham Rd
  Buxhall IP14 . . . . .65 F4
  Hitcham IP7 . . . . .79 E8
Bretts The IP5 . . . . .141 E8
Brewers Cl IP27 . . . . .109 C6
Brewers Gn La IP22 . . . . . .20 B3
Brewhouse La ■ CB7 . . . . .28 D4
Breydon Way NR33 . . . . . .114 F6
Briar Cl
  Halesworth IP19 . . . . .118 C4
  Lowestoft NR32 . . . . .113 B3
Briar Hill IP30 . . . . .50 D1
Briar La IP22 . . . . .35 F5
Briar Rd ■ IP20 . . . . .22 D6
Briardale Ave ■ CO12 . . .106 F2
Briarhayes Cl IP7 . . . . . . .149 B3
Briarwood Ave IP12 . . . . .139 B3
Briarwood Rd
  Lowestoft NR33 . . . . .114 F5
  Woodbridge IP12 . . . . . . .146 E3
Brices Way CB9 . . . . .77 A3
Bricett Bsns Pk IP7 . . . . . .80 E6
Bricett Gn IP7 . . . . .80 D5
Brick Kiln Ave NR34 . . . . .111 C4
Brick Kiln Cl ■ IP11 . . . . .107 D8
Brick Kiln Hill CO6 . . . . . .93 C2
Brick Kiln La
  Huntingfield IP19 . . . . .40 F4
  Melton IP12 . . . . .147 E7
Brick Kiln Rd
  Ellingham NR35 . . . . .8 C8
  Harkstead IP9 . . . . .106 B6
  Mildenhall IP28 . . . . .116 D5
Brick La
  Framlingham IP13 . . . . . . .126 D1
  Parham IP13 . . . . .71 A7
Brickfield Cl IP7 . . . . . . .155 C1
Brickfields Ave CB8 . . . . .120 D7
Brickfields The IP14 . . . . .124 C6
Brickkiln La IP12 . . . . .72 E7
Brickman's Hill CO11 . . . .105 B2
Bridewell La
  Botesdale IP22 . . . . .36 A6
  Bury St Edmunds IP33 . . . .154 C2
Bridewell St CO10 . . . . . . .90 B8
Bridge Cl ■ IP20 . . . . .22 D6
Bridge Cottage (National
  Trust)★ IP7 . . . . .151 D1
Bridge End Rd IP12 . . . . .146 F5
Bridge Foot Corner
  IP18 . . . . .119 C7
Bridge Pk (Skate Park)★
  IP1 . . . . .155 B1
Bridge St
  Bromeswell IP12 . . . . .85 A6
  Burston & Shimpling IP22 . .22 D7
  Felixstowe IP11 . . . . .153 A5
  Lavington IP12 . . . . .145 E4
  Lowestoft NR32 . . . . .112 E1
  Reydon IP18 . . . . .119 C7
  ■ Scole IP21 . . . . .22 D4
  Snape IP17 . . . . .72 D4
Bridge St Beccles NR34 . .111 A7
  Brandon IP27 . . . . .5 F1
  Bungay NR35 . . . . .110 B4
  ■ Bures Hamlet CO8 . . . .101 C5
  Carlton IP17 . . . . .128 D6
  Framlingham IP13 . . . . . . .126 C3
  Hadleigh IP7 . . . . .149 C7
  Halesworth IP19 . . . . .118 B4
  Huntingfield IP19 . . . . .40 A4
  Ipswich IP1 . . . . .155 B2
  Moulton CB8 . . . . .45 F3
  Needham Market IP6 . . . .125 D5
  Stowmarket IP14 . . . . . . .124 F5
  Thetford IP24 . . . . .16 B5
Bridge St Rd CO10 . . . . . .78 A4
Bridgewood Rd IP12 . . . .146 E5
Bridgham La NR16 . . . . . . .17 F8

Bridgwater Rd IP2 . . . . . .138 D2
Bridles The ■ NR34 . . . . .111 F4
Bridport Ave IP3 . . . . . . .140 D3
Bright Cl IP3 . . . . .123 C3
Brighton St ■ IP7 . . . . . . .47 A2
Bright's La CO10 . . . . .78 C4
Brights Wlk IP5 . . . . .141 E7
Brightlall Cl IP11 . . . . . . .152 C4
Brightwell Cl IP11 . . . . . .152 C4
Brimstone Rd IP8 . . . . . . .142 E8
Brindles The IP7 . . . . .149 A4
Brinkley Rd Brinkley CB8 . . .59 E1
  Carlton CB8 . . . . .74 A8
  Dullingham CB8 . . . . .59 F4
Brisbane Way IP11 . . . . . .153 D7
Brisbane Rd IP4 . . . . .140 D6
Bristol Hill IP1 . . . . .107 A4
Bristol Rd
  Bury St Edmunds IP33 . . . .122 C3
  Ipswich IP4 . . . . .140 A7
Bristol St ■ IP7 . . . . .14 A2
Britannia Prim Sch
  IP4 . . . . .140 B5
Britannia Rd IP4 . . . . .140 B6
Britten Ave IP14 . . . . . . .124 C7
Britten Cl IP15 . . . . .130 D5
Britten Rd NR33 . . . . .115 A6
Brittens Cres ■ IP29 . . . . .47 A2
Brittons Rd ■ IP29 . . . . . .47 A2
Broad Fleet Cl ■ NR32 . . .112 E4
Broad Gn Cl IP4 . . . . .62 C6
Broad La CO6 . . . . .102 E1
Broad Mdw
  ■ Ipswich IP8 . . . . .138 C2
  ■ Walsham-le-willows
  IP31 . . . . .35 C2
Broad Oaks CO6 . . . . . . .102 B8
Broad Piece CO7 . . . . .74 F6
Broad Rd Cotton CB9 . . . . .74 F6
  Little Thurlow CB9 . . . . . . .74 F6
  Lowestoft NR32 . . . . .112 D1
  Wickham Market IP13 . . . .127 B7
Broad St Stanford CO10 . . .93 C3
  Wickham Market IP13 . . . .127 B7
Broad View Rd NR32 . . . .114 C8
Broad Way IP21 . . . . .21 A4
Broadcroft Cres CO10 . . .132 C6
Broadfields Rd CB9 . . . . . .36 D2
Broadland Cl
  Beccles NR34 . . . . .111 E4
  Lowestoft NR33 . . . . .114 D7
Broadland Rd IP33 . . . . . .123 B1
Broadlands Way IP4 . . . . .140 F5
Broadmere Rd IP1 . . . . . .138 E8
Broadoak Cl ■ NR33 . . . .114 C4
Broads Rd CB5 . . . . .44 B8
Broads Rd Bsns Pk CB5 . .44 B7
Broadwater Gdns ■
  IP9 . . . . .107 A4
Broadwaters Rd NR33 . . .114 C5
Broadway
  ■ Fressingfield IP21 . . . . . .39 E8
  Pakenham IP31 . . . . .49 F8
  Wickham Market IP13 . . . .127 B7
Broadway The
  Dunwich Dr IP19 . . . . . . .118 C6
Broadway The
  Badwell Ash IP31 . . . . .50 F8
  Wickham Skeith IP23 . . . . .37 C7
Brock La IP13 . . . . .146 C2
Brockdish Prim Sch
  IP21 . . . . .22 A2
Brockford Rd IP14 . . . . . . .52 F4
Brockley Cres IP11 . . . . . .134 D1
Brockley La IP29 . . . . .46 F2
Brockley Rd IP14 . . . . .77 A8
  Whepstead IP29 . . . . .63 B4
Broke Ave IP8 . . . . .134 B2
Broke Hall Gdns IP4 . . . . .140 D4
Broke Hall Prim Sch
  IP4 . . . . .140 E5
Brome Ave IP23 . . . . .117 D5
Brome Hall La IP23 . . . . . .117 E7
Bromeswell Gn Nature
  Reserve★ IP12 . . . . .147 F7
Bromeswell Rd IP4 . . . . . .135 E1
Bromley Cl ■ IP7 . . . . . . .139 C3
Bromley Rd CO11 . . . . . . .104 D1
Bronyon Cl IP33 . . . . .122 C5
Brook Cl
  Horringer IP29 . . . . .122 B1
  Hundon CO10 . . . . .75 D3
  Ipswich IP3 . . . . .140 D3
  Lowestoft NR33 . . . . .114 D7
  Stowmarket IP14 . . . . . . .124 B7
Brook Dam La ■ CB7 . . . . .28 D4
Brook Dr ■ IP17 . . . . .56 F8
Brook Farm La ■ IP9 . . . .105 E7
Brook Farm Rd CO10 . . . .90 A8
Brook House Rd IP14 . . . . .52 B6
Brook Hall Prim Sch
  IP4 . . . . .140 E2
Brook La ■ IP14 . . . . .4 E6
  Capel St Mary IP9 . . . . . .150 C6
  Felixstowe IP11 . . . . .153 B5
  Framlingham IP13 . . . . . . .126 B3
  Mickfield IP14 . . . . .53 A2
  Needham IP20 . . . . .22 B7
  Playford IP6 . . . . .137 A4
  St Margaret, Ilketshall
  NR35 . . . . .24 C7
  Trimley St Martin IP10 . . . .98 E1
  Wortham IP22 . . . . .20 C7
Brook Service Rd ■
  CB9 . . . . .132 C6
Brook St Dedham CO7 . . .103 F4
Glemsford CO10 . . . . .77 A3

Brook St continued
  Soham CB7 . . . . .28 D3
  Woodbridge IP12 . . . . . . .147 A5
  Yoxford IP17 . . . . .57 D7
Brook Way IP8 . . . . .81 C3
Brooke Bsns & Ind Pk
  NR33 . . . . .115 A8
Brookfield Cl IP1 . . . . . . .138 F8
Brookfields Cl CB8 . . . . . .121 B5
Brookhill Way IP14 . . . . . .140 F4
Brookhouse Bsns Pk
  IP2 . . . . .138 F1
Brooklands Cl IP33 . . . . . .154 A1
Brooklands Rd CO11 . . . . .104 E4
Brooklands Rise CO11 . . .104 E4
Brooklyn Rd IP11 . . . . . . .107 B2
Brooks Castle IP13 . . . . . .126 C3
Brooks Hall Rd IP1 . . . . . .139 A7
Brooksfield ■ IP7 . . . . . . .79 F4
Brookside Dalham CB8 . . . .61 C8
  Moulton CB8 . . . . .45 F3
Brookview Ipswich IP7 . . .142 E8
  Pinewood IP7 . . . . .138 E1
Brookwood Cl ■ NR34 . . . .9 F4
Broom Cres IP3 . . . . .139 F1
Broom Field ■ IP11 . . . . .152 E5
Broom Hill La IP24 . . . . . . .2 A1
Broom Hill Rd IP1 . . . . . .139 A8
Broom Hill Swimming Pool
  IP1 . . . . .139 A8
Broom Knoll ■ CO11 . . . .104 E5
Broom Rd
  Lakenheath IP27 . . . . . . .109 E5
  ■ Lowestoft NR32 . . . . . .113 B2
Broom Rd CO10 . . . . .109 E5
Broom St CO10 . . . . .148 F3
Broom Way IP9 . . . . .150 E4
Broom Wlk ■ IP28 . . . . . . .30 B8
Broomfield
  Martlesham IP5 . . . . .141 F7
  ■ Martlesham Heath IP5 . .98 A8
Broomfield Comm
  IP8 . . . . .138 D4
Broomfield Mews ■ IP5 . .98 A8
Broomhayes IP2 . . . . .139 A2
Broomheath IP12 . . . . . . .146 C2
Broomhill Cl ■ IP28 . . . . . .30 C1
Broomhill La IP30 . . . . .50 C1
Broomspath Rd IP14 . . . . .67 A6
Brotherton Ave IP11 . . . . .152 B8
Broughton Rd IP1 . . . . . . .155 A4
Brown St IP14 . . . . .52 A3
Browning Rd
  ■ Brantham CO11 . . . . . .104 E4
  Ipswich IP1 . . . . .134 F3
Brownlow Rd IP11 . . . . . .153 A4
Browns Cl ■ Acton CO10 . .92 B7
  Hitcham IP7 . . . . .79 E6
  ■ Wickhambrook CB8 . . . .61 E2
Browns Gr IP5 . . . . .141 D7
Browns Cl IP22 . . . . .123 E4
Browston La IP32 . . . . . . .141 D7
Broxtead Cl IP12 . . . . .85 C2
Bruce St NR33 . . . . .114 B2
Brudenell St IP15 . . . . . . .130 E3
Bruges Cl ■ CO12 . . . . . .107 A1
Bruisyard Rd IP13 . . . . . . .56 C3
Bruisyard Vineyard★
  IP17 . . . . .56 C3
Brundon La CO10 . . . . . . .148 A5
Brunel Rd IP2 . . . . .138 E6
Brunel Way IP24 . . . . .16 B7
Brunswick House Cut ■
  CO11 . . . . .105 A2
Brunswick Rd IP4 . . . . . . .135 F1
Brunwyn Cl IP32 . . . . .123 F6
Brussels Cl ■ CO12 . . . . .107 A1
Brybank Rd CB9 . . . . .132 A7
Bryon Ave IP11 . . . . .152 B2
Bryony Cl Haverhill CB9 . .132 C7
  ■ Lowestoft NR33 . . . . . .114 F3
Buccaneer Rd IP31 . . . . . .33 D5
Buck La IP23 . . . . .117 E8
Buckanay La IP12 . . . . . . .99 E5
Buckenham Ct IP17 . . . . .119 D5
Buckenham Rd IP7 . . . . . .149 F4
Buckfast Cl ■ IP23 . . . . . .139 A2
Buckingham Cl IP12 . . . . .84 A1
Buckingham Rd CB9 . . . . .132 C4
Buckingham's Hill IP31 . . .39 E8
Buckles Field ■ IP31 . . . . .34 E4
Bucklesham Prim Sch
  IP10 . . . . .98 A4
Bucklesham Rd
  Ipswich IP3 . . . . .140 E2
  Kirton IP10 . . . . .98 D3
Buckleswood Rd IP16 . . . .58 A2
Bucknam Cl ■ NR33 . . . . .11 C1
Buck's Head La IP6 . . . . . .67 F2
Buck's Horns La IP8 . . . . .142 B6
Bucks La ■ CO10 . . . . .90 A8
Buckshorn La IP12 . . . . . .147 D8
Buddleia Cl ■ IP2 . . . . . .138 E4
Budds Cl IP5 . . . . .141 A6
Buggs Hole La IP22 . . . . . .18 D2
Bugg's La
  Brettenham IP7 . . . . .65 D1
  Hitcham IP7 . . . . .79 D8
Bugg's Rd IP22 . . . . .36 D6
Bugsby Way IP1 . . . . .141 E7
Bulcamp Drift IP19 . . . . . . .43 A7
Bull Hall La IP6 . . . . .83 A5
Bull La Acton CO10 . . . . . .78 A1
  Hawstead IP29 . . . . .63 C5
  Long Melford CO10 . . . . . .91 E8
  Rickinghall Superior IP22 . .36 F4
Bull Rd IP31 . . . . .49 F6
Bullace La IP12 . . . . .131 A8

Bullard's La IP12 . . . . . . .146 E5
Bullen Cl Bramford IP8 . . .134 A2
  Bury St Edmunds IP33 . . . .154 A1
Bullen La ■ IP8 . . . . .134 A2
Buller Rd IP8 . . . . .129 C6
Bullion's La NR34 . . . . . . .26 B2
Bullock Fair Cl ■ IP20 . . . .22 D6
Bullocks La CO10 . . . . . . .148 C5
Bullockshed La IP12 . . . . .131 C4
Bull's Ash Cnr IP7 . . . . . . .80 F5
Bull's Rd IP6 . . . . .82 C7
Bullshall Rd
  ■ Occold IP23 . . . . .37 F1
  Occold IP23 . . . . .53 E8
Bullswood La IP30 . . . . . . .64 D1
Bulmer La CO10 . . . . .93 C4
Bulmer Rd CO10 . . . . . . .148 A4
Bulmer St Andrews CE Prim
  Sch CO10 . . . . .91 C2
Bulstrode Rd IP2 . . . . . . .155 C1
Bulwer Rd IP1 . . . . .139 A6
Bumpstead Rd CB9 . . . . .132 F3
Bunbury Ave
  ■ Great Barton IP31 . . . . .49 A5
  Mildenhall IP28 . . . . .116 C5
Bunbury Rd ■ IP32 . . . . .123 F4
Bungay Castle (rems)★
  NR35 . . . . .110 A4
Bungay High Sch
  NR35 . . . . .110 C2
Bungay Mid Sch NR35 . . .110 D3
Bungay Mus★ NR35 . . . . .110 B4
Bungay Rd Barsham NR34 . .9 B4
  Beccles NR34 . . . . .111 A4
  Dickleburgh & Rushall
  IP21 . . . . .21 B1
  Ellingham NR35 . . . . .8 C8
  Halesworth IP19 . . . . .118 A4
  Scole IP21 . . . . .21 A1
  Stockton NR34 . . . . .8 F8
Bunker Cl NR33 . . . . .115 A5
Bunn's La IP20 . . . . .22 C6
Bunters Rd
  Bury St Edmunds IP32 . . . .123 F4
  Ipswich IP2 . . . . .138 D3
Bunting Rd
  Bury St Edmunds IP32 . . . .123 F4
  Ipswich IP2 . . . . .138 D3
Buntings Cres ■ CB5 . . . . .44 A6
Buntings Path CB5 . . . . . .44 A6
Buntry La CO10 . . . . .75 C2
Bunyan Cl IP1 . . . . .135 A3
Burch's Cl IP12 . . . . .129 A2
Burdock La IP26 . . . . .4 C3
Buregate Rd IP11 . . . . . . .152 F2
Bures La CO10 . . . . .124 E4
Bures Prim Sch CO8 . . . . .101 C4
Bures Rd
  Little Cornard CO10 . . . . .101 A8
  Nayland-with-wissington
  CO6 . . . . .101 A6
Bures Sta CO8 . . . . .101 C4
Burgate Rd
  Gislingham IP23 . . . . .36 D3
  Higham IP26 . . . . .46 E3
Burgess Cl ■ NR32 . . . . .112 F2
Burgess Pr ■ IP15 . . . . . .98 A8
Burgh Rd NR34 . . . . .2 C1
Burghley Cl ■ IP22 . . . . .139 A2
Burghley Rise ■ CB5 . . . . .44 B5
Burke Cl IP1 . . . . .135 A3
Burke Rd IP31 . . . . .135 A3
Burkitt Rd IP12 . . . . .146 E5
Burkitts La CO10 . . . . . . .148 C5
Burlington Rd IP1 . . . . . . .155 A3
Burnet Cl IP8 . . . . .142 D8
Burnham Cl
  Felixstowe IP11 . . . . .152 C7
  Ipswich IP4 . . . . .139 F7
Burnham Way NR33 . . . . .115 A5
Burns Cl IP23 . . . . .37 B5
Burns Rd IP1 . . . . .134 E3
Burnt Dick Hill CO4 . . . . .102 E4
Burnt Fen Turnpike
  IP29 . . . . .12 D6
Burnt Hill La IP14 . . . . . . .114 B7
Burnt Hill Way NR33 . . . . .114 D5
Burnt House La IP10 . . . . .98 D2
Burnt Oak La IP12 . . . . . .131 C2
Burnthouse La
  Battisford IP14 . . . . .66 D1
  Needham IP20 . . . . .22 B4
Burntoak La IP20 . . . . .22 C8
Burrell Cl ■ CO12 . . . . . . .106 E1
Burrell Cres IP32 . . . . . . .116 D2
Burrell Rd IP2 . . . . .155 B1
Burrell Way IP24 . . . . .16 A4
Burrell's Orch IP23 . . . . . .122 A6
Burroughs Piece Rd ■
  CO10 . . . . .148 D5
Burrows Cl IP11 . . . . .104 D2
Burrows Gn NR34 . . . . .2 A1
Burscough Rd IP12 . . . . . .84 E6
Burstall La IP8 . . . . .95 E7
Burston Com Prim Sch
  IP22 . . . . .20 F6
Burston Rd
  Dickleburgh & Rushall
  IP21 . . . . .20 F4
  Diss IP22 . . . . .20 D4
  Gissing IP22 . . . . .20 F7
Burton Cl CB9 . . . . .132 C5
Burton Dr IP6 . . . . .125 C5

Burton End CB9 .... **132** C5
Burton End Com Prim Sch
  CB9 .... **132** B5
Burton Hill CB9 .... 74 B3
Burton St NR32 .... **113** D2
Burwash 1 IP6 .... 83 A5
Burwell Mus* CB5 .... 44 B5
Burwell Rd CB8 .... **120** A8
Burwood P 7 NR32 .... **113** B6
Bury Bottom IP7 .... 15 A5
Bury Drift IP31 .... 48 E6
Bury Hill IP12 .... 147 A7
Bury Hill Cl IP12 .... 147 A7
Bury La Lidgate CB8 ..... 61 C8
  Moulton CB8 .... 45 F3
  Stanton IP31 .... 34 E3
  Wickhambrook CB8 .... 61 E4
Bury Pk Dr IP33 .... 123 C2
Bury Rd Alpheton CO10 . 78 A5
  Barrow IP29 .... 47 A2
  Beyton IP30 .... 49 B4
  Botesdale IP22 .... 36 B7
  Bradfield St Clare IP30 .. 64 C4
  Brandon IP27 .... 14 F8
  Brettenham IP7 .... 79 A2
  Brockley IP29 .... 63 A2
  Chedburgh IP29 .... 62 D4
  Felsham IP30 .... 65 A4
  Flempton IP28 .... 47 F8
  Great Barton IP31 .... 49 A5
  Great Thurlow CB9 .... 74 F5
  Great Whelnetham IP30 . 63 F4
  Haughley IP14 .... 66 D7
  Hengrave IP28 .... 48 A7
  Hepworth IP22 .... 35 A4
  Ipswich IP1 .... 134 D4
  Kentford CB8 .... 46 B5
  Lavenham CO10 .... 78 D5
  Lawshall IP29 .... 63 D2
  Market Weston IP22 ...... 18 B1
  Mildenhall IP28 .... 116 E4
  Newmarket CB8 .... 121 C5
  Rickinghall Inferior IP22 . 36 A5
  Stanton IP31 .... 34 F4
  Stowmarket IP14 .... 124 C8
  Stowmarket IP14 .... 124 C8
  Thetford IP24 .... 16 B3
  Thorpe Morieux IP30 ..... 64 E2
  Wickhambrook CB8 .... 61 F1
  Wortham IP22 .... 36 E8
Bury St 3 IP14 .... 124 D6
Bury St Edmunds Art Gall*
  IP33 .... 154 B2
Bury St Edmunds Cty Sch
  IP32 .... 154 B2
Bury St Edmunds Leisure Ctr
  IP33 .... 122 C6
Bury St Edmunds Sta
  IP32 .... 154 B4
Bush Cnr IP14 .... 53 E1
Bush Rd CO10 .... 148 A8
Bushel La CB7 .... 28 D4
Bushey Cl IP9 .... 150 E3
Bushman Gdns 3 IP8 .... 134 A2
Bushy La IP12 .... 99 E7
Bussock La IP12 .... 99 F7
Butchers La IP9 .... 150 F3
Butcher's La CO10 .... 93 C4
Butcher's Rd IP17 .... 128 E7
Butfield CO10 .... 92 E3
Butler Smith Gdns 6
  IP5 .... 141 C7
Butler's La CO11 .... 105 F1
Butlers Way CO9 .... 90 A1
Butley Cl IP7 .... 142 E8
Butley Dr 3 NR32 .... 113 A5
Butley Pottery* IP12 ...... 86 B6
Butt Rd
  Stoke-by-nayland CO6 ... 102 E7
  Sudbury CO10 .... 148 E4
Butter Mkt
  Bury St Edmunds IP33 .. 154 B2
  Ipswich IP8 .... 155 B3
Buttercup Cl
  Bury St Edmunds IP32 .. 123 F5
  Ipswich IP8 .... 138 C1
  3 Lowestoft NR33 .... 114 C4
Butterfly Gdns IP4 .... 140 D5
Button's Rd IP13 .... 71 D6
Buttrum's Mill* IP12 ...... 147 A4
Butt's Rd Holton IP19 ... 118 D8
  Spexhall IP19 .... 25 A4
Butts The
  Debenham IP14 .... 53 E2
  Soham CB7 .... 28 D3
Buxlow Cl IP17 .... 129 B2
Byfield Way IP13 .... 123 C3
Byford Rd CO10 .... 148 C7
Bylam La IP9 .... 106 A7
Byland Cl 3 IP22 .... 139 A2
Byng Hall Rd
  Pettistree IP13 .... 84 E8
  Ufford IP13 .... 127 A1
Byng La IP13 .... 127 A3
Byrd Cl IP33 .... 122 C4
Byron Rd IP1 .... 134 E4

Cabin Cl NR33 .... 114 B4
Caddie's Wlk IP33 .... 115 A5
Cadiz Way 1 NR31 .... 3 C6
Cadney La IP33 .... 154 B3

Cadogan Rd IP33 .... 122 D4
Cage La Boxted CO4 ..... 103 A3
  Felixstowe IP11 .... 152 E5
Cages Way 1 IP12 .... 84 E6
Cagman's La IP14 .... 65 F3
Caithness Cl IP4 .... 140 B8
Cake St IP13 .... 39 F4
Cakebridge La IP7 .... 79 D3
Calais St IP7 .... 149 D6
Caldecott Rd NR32 ...... 112 D1
Calder Rd 3 IP9 .... 84 E6
Caledonia Rd 8 IP9 ..... 107 A4
Calfe Fen Cl 3 CB7 ..... 28 D5
Calfe Fen Dro CB7 .... 28 D5
Calford Dr CB9 .... 132 A6
California IP12 .... 146 D3
California La IP9 .... 95 B4
California Rd 14 CO11 ... 105 A2
Calkewood La IP22 ...... 35 C5
Callis St 5 CO10 .... 90 A8
Calthorpe Cl IP32 .... 123 E6
Calves La CO6 .... 102 D8
Camberley Rd IP4 .... 140 D7
Camborne Rd IP5 .... 141 B7
Cambria Cl 3 CO11 ..... 105 A2
Cambrian Cres 2 NR32 . 112 D2
Cambridge Dr 2 IP14 ... 138 F2
Cambridge Rd
  Felixstowe IP11 .... 153 B4
  Ipswich IP5 .... 141 A7
  Lowestoft NR32 .... 113 D3
Cambridge Way
  Felixstowe IP11 .... 153 B4
  Ipswich IP5 .... 141 A7
  Lowestoft NR32 .... 113 D3
Camden Rd IP3 .... 140 B4
Camden St 5 NR32 ...... 113 E3
Camp Cl 2 IP29 .... 4 D5
Camp Rd NR32 .... 113 D1
Campbell Cl 1 IP28 ..... 116 B5
Campbell Rd IP13 .... 140 C1
Campion Cl IP7 .... 28 C5
Campion Cres IP14 ...... 124 C4
Campion La CO6 .... 102 B6
Campion Rd 2 IP28 ..... 138 F4
Campion Way CO6 .... 102 B7
Campions Hill CO6 ...... 102 B5
Camps Rd
  Haverhill CB9 .... 132 D5
  Helions Bumpstead CB9 . 88 A5
Camwood Gdns IP3 ..... 140 A4
Canaletto Cl 4 NR32 ... 113 B6
Canberra Cl
  Ipswich IP4 .... 140 D6
  2 Mildenhall IP28 .... 116 B3
Canberra Rd IP31 .... 33 D4
Candler's La 1 IP20 ..... 22 D6
Candlet Gr IP11 .... 152 F5
Candlet Rd IP11 .... 152 E7
Cangles La IP30 .... 49 F1
Canham St IP1 .... 155 A3
Canhams Rd CO10 ...... 148 F3
Cannon St IP3 .... 154 B3
Cannonfields IP33 .... 154 A1
Canon Cl CB9 .... 132 D7
Canon Pickering VC Jun Sch
  IP20 .... 22 D6
Canon Pugh Dr 6 CO10 . 92 B7
Canterbury Cl
  Ipswich IP2 .... 142 F8
  7 Lakenheath IP27 ...... 14 A2
Canterbury Gdns IP7 ... 149 E6
Canterbury Rd IP33 ..... 123 A3
Canterbury Inf Sch
  IP24 .... 16 A5
Canterbury Way IP24 ... 16 B6
Capel Cl
  6 Felixstowe IP11 .... 107 D8
  Troston IP31 .... 33 D3
Capel Dr IP11 .... 152 C4
Capel Hall La IP11 ...... 107 D6
Capel St Mary CE Prim Sch
  IP9 .... 150 D3
Capell Wlk 2 IP31 .... 34 E4
Capps La IP19 .... 23 F5
Captain's La IP14 .... 51 A2
Caraway Rd IP24 .... 16 D6
Carbonels CO10 .... 92 C6
Carders Cl IP7 .... 149 D4
Cardew Drift IP5 .... 141 D8
Cardiff Ave IP1 .... 139 B1
Cardigan St
  Ipswich IP1 .... 155 A4
  Newmarket CB8 .... 121 A3
Cardinal Cl IP32 .... 123 E6
Cardinal Pk IP1 .... 155 B2
Cardinal Way CB9 .... 132 D7
Cardinals Rd IP14 .... 124 D3
Carlford Cl 14 IP5 .... 98 A8
Carlton Cl
  Great Waldham CO9 ..... 90 A1
  Haverhill CB9 .... 132 D8
Carlton Colville Prim Sch
  NR33 .... 114 B2
Carlton Cross NR33 ..... 114 C3
Carlton Cr Hospl
  NR33 .... 114 C3
Carlton Gn Rd CB8 ...... 74 A7
Carlton Marshes Nature
  Reserve* NR33 .... 114 A7
Carlton Pk Ind Est
  IP17 .... 128 C5
Carlton Rd Brinkley CB8 . 59 F1
Carlton IP17 .... 128 C5
Ipswich IP5 .... 141 A7
Lowestoft NR33 .... 115 B6
Carlton Sq NR33 .... 114 C2

Caustons Cl 9 CO10 ..... 92 B3
Cautley Rd IP18 .... 119 D6
Cavan Rd IP1 .... 134 D2
Cavendish CE Prim Sch
  CO10 .... 76 E1
Cavendish Cl
  7 Lowestoft NR32 .... 113 A3
  12 Thurstow IP31 .... 49 D6
  Cavendish Dr 8 CO11 .. 104 D2
Cavendish La CO10 ...... 76 F2
Cavendish Rd
  Bury St Edmunds IP33 . 122 C6
  Clare CO10 .... 90 B8
  Felixstowe IP11 .... 152 F3
  Stowmarket IP14 .... 124 B6
Cavendish St IP3 .... 139 F4
Cavendish Way 1 CO10 . 148 D5
Cavenham Rd IP28 ...... 31 A1
Caville White CB9 .... 132 A6
Caxton Mews 4 NR34 .. 111 B6
Caxton Rd NR34 .... 111 B6
Cecil Lodge Cl CB8 ..... 120 E7
Cecil Rd IP1 .... 155 A4
Cecilia St IP1 .... 155 B2
Cedar Ave IP5 .... 141 A6
Cedar Cl Bacton IP14 ... 51 F6
  7 Brantham CO11 .... 104 E5
  8 Great Bricett IP7 ..... 80 D6
  55 Lakenheath IP27 .... 13 F2
  Occold IP23 .... 37 F2
Cedar Cres 50 CO10 .... 104 E2
Cedar Cl Alderton IP12 . 99 E5
  16 Beck Row, Holywell
  Row & Kenny Hill CB8 .. 13 B1
Cedar Dr
  Lowestoft NR33 .... 114 E5
  Worlingham NR34 .... 111 F3
Cedar Rd 1 Barrow IP29 . 47 A2
  7 Bentwaters Airfield IP12 . 85 E8
Cedarcroft Rd IP11 ...... 134 F2
Cedars La IP9 .... 150 D3
Cedarwood Prim Sch
  IP5 .... 141 C6
Celandine Cl NR33 ...... 114 C5
Cemetery La
  East Bergholt CO7 ...... 151 A4
  Ipswich IP4 .... 135 F1
  Woodbridge IP12 .... 146 E4
Cemetery Rd
  Ipswich IP4 .... 155 C3
  Lakenheath IP27 .... 109 D6
  Wickhambrook CB8 ..... 61 E2
Central Ave IP3 .... 144 D8
Central Rd IP16 .... 129 C5
Centre Cl NR34 .... 111 C3
Centre Dr CB7 .... 28 E2
Centre Dr CB7 .... 121 D2
Century Dr IP5 .... 141 C8
Century Rd IP23 .... 117 C4
Chadacre Rd IP29 .... 77 B7
Chaffinch Dr 14 CO12 .. 106 F1
Chaffinch Way IP8 ...... 138 C1
Chafford Dr IP6 .... 125 D3
Chalfont Dr 11 IP7 ...... 72 C8
Chalk Hill La IP6 .... 81 F5
Chalk Rd (N) IP33 ...... 154 A2
Chalk Rd (S) IP33 ...... 154 A2
Chalk Rd IP27 .... 5 D1
Chalkeith Rd IP6 .... 125 E3
Chalkners Cl IP7 .... 149 E3
Chalkstone Mid Sch
  CB9 .... 132 E6
Chalkstone Way 4 CB9 . 133 A6
Challice Rd IP33 .... 154 A3
Chalon St IP1 .... 155 A2
Chamberlain Way IP8 .. 138 C2
Chamberlayne Rd
  IP32 .... 123 E4
Chamberlin Cl 2 IP27 .. 79 F4
Champion Rd IP15 ...... 130 E3
Chancellery Mews
  IP33 .... 154 A3
Chancery La 5 IP14 ..... 53 F2
Chancery Rd IP1 .... 155 A2
Chandlers Ct 8 CB5 .... 44 A6
Chandlers Way IP16 .... 129 C3
Chandos Ct 8 IP3 .... 84 A1
Chandos Dr 5 IP3 .... 84 A1
Channel The IP8 .... 81 C2
Chantry Cl IP13 .... 71 D7
Chantry Gn IP7 .... 138 D3
Chantry High Sch IP2 .. 138 F3
Chantry Jun Sch IP2 ... 138 E2
Chantry Rd IP7 .... 128 C3
Chapel Cl
  Capel St. Mary IP9 ...... 150 E3
  4 Fressingfield IP21 .... 39 E8
  Garboldisham IP22 ...... 18 D4
  8 Great Waldingfield CO10 . 92 C6
Chapel Cut 18 CO10 .... 105 A2
Chapel End Way CO9 ... 89 A1
Chapel Farm La IP23 ... 37 A4
Chapel Field IP13 .... 134 A2
Chapel Hill
  Belchamp Walter CO10 . 90 B3
  Framsden IP14 .... 69 B7
  Thorpe Morieux IP30 ... 79 A8
  Botesdale IP22 .... 36 A6
  4 Brockley IP29 .... 63 A1
  Claydon IP6 .... 134 A8
  Copdock & Washbrook
  IP8 .... 138 A1
  Drinkstone IP30 .... 65 B7
  Great Glemham IP17 ... 56 D1
  18 Grundisburgh IP13 . 83 E8
  Horham IP21 .... 38 F2

Chapel La continued 8 E7
  Kirby Row NR35 .... 8 E7
  Kirtling CB8 .... 60 E3
  Little Cornard CO10 .... 92 B1
  2 Somersham IP8 .... 81 C3
  Stoke-by-nayland CO6 . 103 B7
  Wenhaston With Mells Hamlet
  IP19 .... 42 C6
  Wicken CB7 .... 28 A1
  Wickham Market IP13 .. 127 C5
  Wortham IP22 .... 36 D7
Chapel Pond Hill IP32 .. 123 C8
Chapel Rd
  Beck Row, Holywell Row
  & Kenny Hill CB8 .... 29 F6
  Bedingham NR35 .... 7 C8
  Boxted CO4 .... 103 A2
  Bradfield Combust with
  Stanningfield IP29 ...... 64 A3
  Bucklesham IP10 .... 98 B4
  Cockfield IP30 .... 64 D2
  Grundisburgh IP13 ..... 83 E5
  Langham CO4 .... 103 B2
  Lowestoft NR33 .... 114 B3
  Mendlesham IP14 ...... 52 E5
  Mutford NR34 .... 10 D3
  Old Newton with Dagworth
  IP14 .... 52 A1
  Otley IP6 .... 69 D3
  Rendham IP17 .... 56 E3
  Rougham CO10 .... 89 D4
  St Andrews, Ilketshall
  NR34 .... 8 F2
  Saxmundham IP17 ..... 128 C3
  Saxtead IP13 .... 55 A4
  Scole IP21 .... 18 E3
  Stoke Ash IP23 .... 37 B2
  Theberton IP16 .... 58 C5
  Wattisfield IP22 .... 35 A4
  Wrentham NR34 .... 26 D5
Chapel Row 33 CB8 ..... 60 F8
Chapel Stanton IP13 ... 79 F4
  Diss IP22 .... 20 B8
  Exning CB8 .... 120 B7
  Peasenhall IP17 .... 56 F8
  Steeple Bumpstead CB9 . 88 E4
  Stoke-by-clare CO9 .... 89 C6
  Woodbridge IP12 .... 147 A5
Chaplains Cl IP7 .... 132 D7
Chaplin Rd CO7 .... 151 C5
Chaplin Wlk 16 CO10 .. 92 B3
Chappel Rd CO6 .... 101 C2
Chapple Dr CB9 .... 132 F5
Chare Rd IP31 .... 34 D5
Charity La IP13 .... 54 D6
Charles Adams Cl
  IP14 .... 129 D6
Charles Ave 8 IP13 ..... 83 E5
Charles Burrell High Sch
  IP24 .... 16 B5
Charles Cl CB8 .... 120 E3
Charles Melrose Cl
  1 Mildenhall IP28 ...... 116 B4
  4 Mildenhall IP28 ...... 116 B5
Charles Rd IP11 .... 152 E3
Charlette's IP8 .... 95 F5
Charlton Ave IP1 .... 134 F2
Charrington Cl IP3 ...... 133 A4
Charsfield CE Prim Sch
  IP13 .... 70 B3
Charter Way 8 IP33 .... 114 C5
Chartres Piece NR34 ... 25 E3
Chartwell Cl IP4 .... 140 A5
Chase Cl CB9 .... 132 E7
Chase Ct CO10 .... 106 F1
Chase Rd IP28 .... 48 C5
Chase The
  Beccles NR34 .... 111 E5
  Brandon IP27 .... 104 F5
  Brantham CO11 .... 104 A2
  Dedham CO7 .... 104 A2
  Foxearth CO10 .... 91 B7
  20 Manningtree CO11 . 104 D2
  22 Martlesham Heath IP5 . 98 A8
  5 Steeple Bumpstead CB9 . 34 E4
  Steeple Bumpstead CB9 . 88 D4
Chase's La IP17 .... 72 F6
Chatham Rd 6 IP27 ..... 14 A2
Chatsworth Cl 5 NR32 . 113 A3
Chatsworth Cres
  Felixstowe IP11 .... 152 C7
  Ipswich IP2 .... 139 A2
Chatsworth Dr IP4 ...... 140 E4
Chattisham Rd IP8 ...... 95 E4
Chaucer Rd
  Felixstowe IP11 .... 152 F3
  Ipswich IP1 .... 134 F3
  Sudbury CO10 .... 148 B8
Chaucer St
  Bungay NR35 .... 110 A4
  Bungay NR35 .... 110 A4
Chaukers Cres NR33 ... 114 C5
Chauntry Rd CB9 .... 132 D5
Chedburgh Rd
  Chevington IP29 .... 62 C5
  Whepstead IP29 .... 62 F4
Chedgrave Rd NR33 .... 114 F5
Chediston Rd IP19 ...... 24 B2
Chediston St
  Chediston IP19 .... 41 D8
  Halesworth IP19 .... 118 A3
Chelmer Rd CB9 .... 132 F6
Chelmondiston CE Prim Sch
  IP9 .... 106 C8
Chelsea Cl
  Bury St Edmunds IP33 . 122 C5
  Ipswich IP1 .... 134 F1

Chelsea Ct 4 CO10 ....148 D5
Chelsea Rd 3 CO10 ......148 A5
Chelsworth Ave
  Ipswich IP4 ....135 E1
  Sudbury CO10 ....142 F4
Chelsworth Rd IP11 ......152 D3
Chelsworth Way IP14 .....124 E3
Cheltenham Ave IP1 ......135 B1
Chepstow Rd
  Bury St Edmunds IP33 ...122 D2
  Felixstowe IP11 ....152 F5
  Ipswich IP2 ....135 B4
Chequer Field 4 CO10 ....85 C2
Chequer Sq IP33 ....154 C2
Chequers La
  Bressingham IP22 ....19 E3
  Burston & Shimpling IP22 .20 E8
  Glemsford CO10 ....77 B3
Chequers Rd CO11 ....104 E1
Chequers Rise IP6 ....145 E5
Cherry Blossom Cl
  IP6 ....138 B2
Cherry Hill IP8 ....138 E2
Cherry Hill Rd 1 NR34 ...111 F4
Cherry La
  Belton with Browston NR31 ...2 D8
  Lakenheath IP27 ....13 F2
Cherry La Gdns IP4 ......140 F7
Cherry Tree La
  Mundford IP26 ....6 A8
  North Lopham IP22 .....19 A6
Cherry Tree La 1 IP3 ....53 F1
Cherry Tree Rd
  Stowmarket IP14 ....124 C8
Cherry Tree Row 3 IP31 ..35 C2
Cherrytree La
  Rickinghall Inferior IP22 ..36 A7
  Soham CB7 ....28 D3
Cherrytree Rd CO10 .....148 E5
Cherrywood 10 IP20 ......22 D5
Chesapeake Cl 3 IP9 ....106 C8
Chesapeake Rd 3 IP3 ....144 A8
Chesham Rd IP2 ....155 A1
Chessington Gdns IP1 ...138 F8
Chester Pl 5 IP3 ....144 A8
Chester Rd
  Felixstowe IP11 ....152 F5
  6 Southwold IP18 ......119 D5
Chester St 4 IP27 ....14 A3
Chesterfield Dr IP1 .....134 F2
Chesterton Cl 2 IP2 .....138 F1
Chestnut Ave
  Great Bricett IP7 ....80 D6
  Lowestoft NR32 ....112 E2
Chestnut Cl
  4 Beccles NR34 ....111 E3
  6 Bentwaters Airfield IP12 ..85 F8
  7 Fornham All Saints IP28 ..48 B6
  Great Barton IP31 ......49 B6
  3 Great Waldingfield CO10 ..92 C6
  Haverhill CB9 ....132 D6
  1 Mildenhall IP28 ......116 D4
  Rushmere St Andrew
  IP5 ....136 E1
  4 Stowupland IP14 ......67 A6
Chestnut Cres
  Chedburgh IP29 ....62 D4
  6 Lowestoft NR33 ....114 C3
Chestnut Dr
  Claydon IP6 ....134 C8
  2 Soham CB7 ....28 D4
Chestnut Gr 2 IP14 .....124 E5
Chestnut Rd
  Dickleburgh IP21 ....21 C5
  Glemsford CO10 ....77 A3
  Pulham St Mary IP21 .....21 F8
  Stradishall CB8 ....75 C6
Chestnut Way 2 IP11 ....137 D2
Chestnuts The
  5 Great Finborough IP14 ..66 B4
  1 Ipswich IP2 ....138 C2
  Rickinghall Superior IP22 ..36 A6
  Wrentham NR34 ....26 E5
Chevalier Rd IP11 ....153 B4
Chevallier St IP1 ....139 A7
Cheveley Rd
  Newmarket CB8 ....121 C3
  Woodditton CB8 ....60 E6
Chevington Rd
  Hargrave IP29 ....62 B6
  Horringer IP29 ....63 A7
Cheviot Rd 3 NR32 ......112 D2
Chevy Ct 3 CO12 ....107 A2
Cheyne Ct 6 CO10 ....148 C5
Chichester Cl IP33 ......123 B3
Chichester Dr NR33 .....114 C6
Chichester Rd IP19 .....118 A5
Chickering Rd IP21 ....38 D6
Childer Rd 1 IP14 ....124 D6
Childers Cl 7 IP7 ....107 A5
Childers Field 1 IP21 ...152 D5
Chiltern Cres NR32 .....112 D2
Chilton Ave IP12 ....124 C6
Chilton Ct CO10 ....148 E5
Chilton Hall * CO10 ......92 B5
Chilton Lodge Rd
  CO10 ....148 E5
Chilton Rd IP12 ....140 C4
Chilton Way IP12 ....124 C6
Chilton Way Sports Club
  IP14 ....124 A7
Chimer's La IP13 ....70 A4
Chimney Mills IP28 ......32 C1
Chimswell Way CB9 .....132 A6

Chippenham Rd
  Chippenham IP28 ....29 E2
  Fordham CB7 ....29 C1
  Moulton CB8 ....45 F3
  Snailwell CB8 ....45 F4
Chipperfield Rd 20 NR33 ..11 C1
Chippings The IP15 ......130 C6
Chislehurst Rd 8 NR33 ..114 C4
Chiswick Ave IP28 ......116 C6
Chivers Rd IP8 ....132 B5
Christ Church Sq
  NR32 ....113 E1
Christchurch Dr IP12 ...146 D3
Christchurch Mansion*
  IP1 ....155 C3
Christchurch Pk Hospl
  (private) IP1 ....155 B4
Christchurch St IP1 .....155 C3
Christmas La
  Lowestoft NR32 ....112 C1
  Metfield IP20 ....23 D3
Church Ave NR32 ....112 C0
Church Cl
  Aldeburgh IP15 ....130 E4
  Bucklesham IP10 ....98 A5
  Carlton IP17 ....128 D2
  4 Cavendish CO10 ......76 E1
  Creeting St Mary IP6 ...125 F8
  Dullingham CB8 ....59 F4
  Exning CB8 ....120 C8
  Fornham St Martin IP28 ..48 D5
  Hepworth IP22 ....35 A5
  Ipswich IP5 ....141 B8
  Pulham St Mary IP21 ....21 F8
  Rede IP29 ....62 E3
  Risby IP29 ....47 E5
  1 Roydon IP22 ....20 A3
  15 Stanton IP31 ....34 E4
  Wangford NR34 ....26 B2
  Wilby IP21 ....39 C3
  Wortwell IP20 ....22 F7
Church Cres IP28 ....138 A6
Church Dr IP13 ....71 E5
Church Farm Cl IP21 ....88 F3
Church Farm La IP8
  IP19 ....118 A3
Church Farm Rd
  Aldeburgh IP15 ....130 E5
  Bramfield IP19 ....41 F4
Church Field
  Monks Eleigh IP7 ....79 C2
  Walberswick IP18 ......119 A2
Church Field Rd CO10 ...148 F7
Church Gdns
  1 Barningham IP31 ......34 E7
  8 Beck Row, Holywell
  Row & Kenny Hill IP28 ..29 F6
Church Gn IP8 ....29 C2
Church Hill Beihall IP17 ..72 C8
  Burstall IP8 ....95 D7
  Cookley IP19 ....41 C5
  Helions Bumpstead CB9 ..88 B4
  Hoxne IP21 ....38 A2
  Kersey IP7 ....94 A6
  Lawford CO11 ....104 C2
  Monks Eleigh IP7 ....79 C2
  Pakenham IP31 ....49 E6
  Ramsey & Parkeston
  CO12 ....106 D1
  Saxmundham IP17 ......128 D2
  Starston IP20 ....22 C7
  Westhall IP19 ....25 D3
  Whepstead IP29 ....63 B5
  Wyverstone IP14 ....36 C5
Church La
  Aldeby/Wheatacre/Burgh
  St Peter NR34 ....2 B1
  Aldham IP7 ....94 D7
  Aldringham cum Thorpe
  IP16 ....129 E1
  Alpheton CO10 ....77 F5
  Arwarton IP9 ....106 C5
  Barnham IP24 ....16 C2
  Barton Mills IP28 ......116 D1
  Bayham IP6 ....81 E6
  Beck Row, Holywell Row
  & Kenny Hill IP28 ....29 F6
  Blo' Norton IP22 ....18 E2
  Brantham IP13 ....54 E5
  Brantham CO11 ....104 F5
  Bressingham IP22 ......19 E3
  Brockdish IP21 ....21 F2
  Bromeswell IP12 ....85 A5
  Broome NR35 ....8 F2
  Brundish IP13 ....55 C8
  Bucklesham IP10 ....98 A5
  Burrough Green CB8 .....59 F2
  4 Burwell CB5 ....44 A5
  Carlton IP17 ....128 D2
  1 Cheveley CB8 ....60 E7
  Claydon IP6 ....134 E8
  Clopton IP13 ....83 E8
  Codpeck IP30 ....64 C1
  Copdock & Washbrook
  IP8 ....142 A7
  Corton NR32 ....3 C4
  Creeting St Mary IP6 ...125 D7
  Dalham CB8 ....46 C1
  Ditchingham NR35 ......9 C7
  Dullingham CB8 ....59 F4
  Earl Soham IP13 ....55 A2
  Exning CB8 ....120 B8
  Felixstowe IP11 ....152 B8
  Finningham IP14 ....52 A8
  Fritton & St Olaves NR31 ..2 C7
  Frostenden NR34 ....26 C4

Church La continued
  Harkstead IP9 ....106 B6
  3 Harwich CO12 ....107 B3
  Hemingstone IP6 ....82 C8
  Hemley IP12 ....98 E5
  Henley IP6 ....98 B2
  Hepworth IP22 ....35 A5
  Hitcham IP7 ....79 E6
  Hockwold cum Wilton IP26 ..5 A2
  Hoo IP13 ....70 B6
  Ixen IP12 ....72 A2
  Kennett CB8 ....45 F6
  Kenton IP14 ....54 A4
  Kirton IP10 ....98 E2
  Levington IP10 ....98 C6
  Lowestoft NR32 ....112 C2
  Lowestoft NR32 ....114 B2
  5 Lowestoft NR33 ......114 C3
  Mundford IP26 ....6 B8
  Nayland CO6 ....102 D5
  Norton IP31 ....50 C4
  2 Occold IP23 ....37 F1
  Playford IP6 ....137 B4
  Preston St Mary CO10 ..79 A5
  Redenhall with Harleston
  IP20 ....22 E7
  Rendlesham IP12 ....85 C7
  Rickinghall Superior IP22 ..36 A5
  Ridgewell CO9 ....89 D3
  St James, South Elmham
  IP19 ....23 F4
  St Mary, South Elmham
  Otherwise Homersfield
  IP20 ....23 B8
  Semer IP7 ....79 F1
  Shottisham IP12 ....99 C7
  Somersham IP8 ....81 D3
  Spexhall IP19 ....24 F3
  Sproughton IP8 ....138 B6
  Stetchworth CB8 ....60 A5
  Stoke Ash IP23 ....37 B1
  Stonham Earl IP14 .....67 E6
  Stuston IP21 ....72 B8
  Swilland IP6 ....83 A7
  Thelnetham IP22 ....35 E2
  Thwaite IP23 ....52 F7
  Timworth IP31 ....48 E8
  Troston IP31 ....33 E3
  9 Ufford IP13 ....84 F7
  Walberswick IP18 ......119 A2
  Wenhaston With Mells Hamlet
  IP19 ....42 C6
  Westerfield IP6 ....135 F4
  Westley Waterless CB8 ..59 D3
  Weston NR34 ....9 E2
  Winfarthing IP22 ......20 B8
  Worlington IP28 ....30 B4
  Yaxley IP23 ....37 C4
Church La Cl IP28 ......116 D2
Church Mdw
  Barton Mills IP28 .....116 D2
  Rickinghall Inferior IP22 ..35 F6
Church Mdws 1 IP6 ......82 C6
  1 Boxford CO10 ....89 E6
Church Rd Alburgh IP20 ..7 A2
  Ashbocking IP6 ....68 E1
  Bacton IP14 ....51 A8
  Bardwell IP31 ....34 B4
  Barningham IP31 ....34 E7
  Barrow IP29 ....47 A3
  Battisford IP14 ....66 E1
  Bedfield IP13 ....54 E5
  Bentley IP9 ....142 A1
  Beyton IP30 ....49 F1
  6 Bildeston IP7 ....79 F4
  Blaxhall IP12 ....71 F4
  Blundeston NR32 ....3 A4
  Boxted CO4 ....103 A4
  Bradfield Combust with
  Stanningfield IP29 .....63 F3
  Bradfield St George IP30 ..64 D6
  Brandon IP27 ....15 C2
  Brettenham IP7 ....65 C1
  Brockdish IP21 ....21 F2
  Bruisyard IP17 ....56 C5
  Bulmer CO10 ....91 C2
  Butley IP12 ....86 B5
  Carlton CB8 ....74 A8
  Chevington IP29 ....62 D6
  Combs IP14 ....124 E2
  Cotton IP14 ....52 B5
  Cratfield IP19 ....40 D5
  Crowfield IP6 ....68 C4
  Dallinghoo IP13 ....70 C1
  Denham IP21 ....38 C5
  Dickleburgh & Rushall
  IP21 ....20 F3
  Earsham NR35 ....7 F3
  Ellingham NR35 ....8 D7
  Ellough NR34 ....111 F1
  Elmswell IP30 ....50 E2
  Felixstowe IP11 ....153 C6
  Felsham IP30 ....65 A4
  Flixton NR35 ....7 E7
  Friston IP17 ....72 F7
  Garboldisham IP22 .....18 D4
  Gillingham NR34 ....9 C7
  Gisleham NR33 ....11 A1
  Great Barton IP31 .....49 A5
  1 Great Finborough IP14 ..66 B4
  Great Yeldham CO9 .....89 F1
  Haskelon IP13 ....146 B7
  Hedenham NR35 ....7 E8
  Henstead with Hulver Street
  NR34 ....26 E8

Church Rd continued
  Heveningham IP19 ....40 E3
  Holbrook IP9 ....105 F6
  Honington IP31 ....33 F5
  Kessingland IP33 ....11 B1
  Kettleburgh IP13 ......70 C7
  Kirby Cane NR35 ....8 E8
  Knodishall IP17 ....58 A1
  Leiston IP16 ....129 B6
  Lindsey IP7 ....93 D7
  Little Glemham IP13 ....71 E5
  Little Thurlow CB9 .....74 D6
  Little Waldingfield CO10 ..92 E8
  Lowestoft NR32 ....113 C3
  Lowestoft NR32 ....113 D2
  Market Weston IP22 ....34 E8
  Marlesford IP13 ....71 C5
  Mendlesham IP14 ....52 E4
  Milden IP7 ....79 B1
  Mutford NR34 ....10 D3
  Nacton IP10 ....145 B4
  Newton CO10 ....92 D3
  North Lopham IP22 .....19 A5
  Old Newton with Dagworth
  IP14 ....51 F1
  Otley IP6 ....69 C1
  Pettaugh IP14 ....68 B6
  Playford IP6 ....137 B5
  Redlingfield IP23 ......38 C1
  Rushbrooke with Rougham
  IP30 ....49 C1
  Shelfanger IP22 ....20 B6
  Snape IP17 ....72 D5
  Stambourne CO9 ....89 B1
  Stowmarket IP14 ......124 D3
  Stowupland IP14 ....67 B6
  Stutton IP9 ....105 D5
  Sudbury CO10 ....148 E3
  Sutton IP12 ....85 A1
  Tattingstone IP9 ......105 B7
  Theberton IP16 ....58 B4
  Thistley Green IP28 ....29 F6
  6 Thrandeston IP21 .....73 F6
  Thurston IP31 ....49 E4
  Tostock IP30 ....50 B2
  Uggeshall NR34 ....26 A3
  Weybread IP21 ....22 D2
  Wheatacre NR34 ....2 A1
  Wicken CB7 ....28 B1
  Wilby IP21 ....39 A7
  Wingfield IP21 ....39 A7
  Worlingworth IP13 .....54 E7
  Wormingford CO6 ......101 F2
  Wortham IP22 ....19 A4
  Wrabness CO11 ....105 F2
  Wyverstone IP14 ....51 E6
Church Rd N IP21 ....21 F3
Church Row
  Bury St Edmunds IP33 ..154 B3
  Framsden IP14 ....69 C6
Church Sq 4 CO10 ......101 C4
Church St 2 Ashley CB8 ..60 F8
  Belcham Otten CO10 ....90 D5
  1 Boxford CO10 ....93 C3
  Boxted CO4 ....103 A4
  5 Chelmondiston IP9 ...106 C8
  6 Clare CO10 ....90 A8
  Diss IP22 ....20 C2
  Exning CB8 ....120 C8
  Fordham CB7 ....29 B1
  Framlingham IP13 .....126 D3
  2 Fressingfield IP21 ....39 E8
  Gestingthorpe CO9 .....90 F1
  Groton CO10 ....93 C5
  1 Hadleigh IP7 ....149 D5
  28 Harleston IP20 ....22 D6
  Hundon CO10 ....75 D3
  10 Isleham CB7 ....29 C5
  Kenninghall NR16 ......19 B8
  Lavenham CO10 ....78 D3
  Orford IP12 ....131 C2
  Peasenhall IP17 ....56 F8
  Saxmundham IP17 ......128 D3
  12 Southwold IP18 .....119 D5
  Steeple Bumpstead CB9 ..88 D4
  Stoke-by-nayland CO6 ..102 E6
  Stoke-by-nayland CO6 ..102 E7
  Stradbroke IP21 ....39 B4
  Sudbury CO10 ....148 B4
  Wangford NR34 ....26 B2
  Wetheren IP14 ....51 A1
  Wetheringsett-cum-brockford
  IP14 ....53 A6
  Withersfield CB9 ....74 A2
  Woodbridge IP12 ......147 A5
Church Terr IP13 ....127 C6
Church View
  Halesworth IP19 ......118 A4
  Harleston IP20 ....22 E6
  1 Haughley IP14 ....51 C1
  Stowlangtoft IP31 ......50 A8
  Weston NR34 ....51 E6
Church View Cl IP12 ...147 C7
Church Walks IP33 .....154 C1
Church Wlk
  Aldeburgh IP15 ....130 E4
  3 Lacfield IP13 ....40 B3
  Long Melford CO10 .....77 E1
  Mildenhall IP28 ....116 B4
  Shelfanger IP22 ....20 B6
  Stowmarket IP14 ......124 D6
  Sturmer CB9 ....133 D2
  2 Sudbury CO10 ....148 C5

Church Wood IP19 ....118 E4
Churchfields Dr 1 CB9 ...88 D3
Churchgate CO10 ....77 B3
Churchgate St
  Bury St Edmunds IP33 ..154 B2
  15 Soham CB7 ....28 D4
Churchill Ave
  Hadleigh IP7 ....149 D7
  Haverhill CB9 ....132 F7
  Ipswich IP4 ....140 B5
  Newmarket CB8 ....120 D5
Churchill Cl
  1 Lawshall IP29 ....63 D1
  Lowestoft NR32 ....113 C4
  Woodbridge IP12 ......146 E4
Churchill Cres IP12 ....127 C7
Churchill Dr
  Mildenhall IP28 ....116 B5
  Sudbury CO10 ....148 C8
Churchill Rd
  Halesworth IP19 ......118 B5
  8 Southwold IP18 .....119 C8
  Thetford IP24 ....16 C6
Churchman Cl IP12 .....147 B8
Churchway 3 IP22 ....36 A8
Churchyard The IP28 ...116 B4
Civic Dr IP1 ....155 A3
Clacton Rd CO11 ....105 E2
Clapgate La IP3 ....140 A1
Clapham Rd Central 3
  NR32 ....113 D1
Clapham Rd S NR32 ....113 D1
Clare Ave IP12 ....146 E4
Clare Castle (remains of)*
  ....90 A8
Clare Cl
  2 Bury St Edmunds IP33 .122 D4
  Mildenhall IP28 ....116 D5
  Stowmarket IP14 ......124 E3
Clare Cty Prim Sch
  CO10 ....90 A8
Clare Rd Hundon CO10 ...75 E2
  Ipswich IP4 ....139 F8
  2 Kessingland IP33 .....11 B1
  Poslingford CO10 ....76 A2
Claremont Rd 1 NR33 ...115 C6
Clarence Rd
  7 Clare CO10 ....76 A1
  1 Clare CO10 ....90 A8
  Ipswich IP3 ....140 B1
  8 Lowestoft NR32 .....113 D2
  Sudbury CO10 ....148 C6
Clarendale Est CB9 ......74 C7
Clarendon Rd CB9 ......132 D5
Clark Rd NR35 ....110 C7
Clarke Cl IP22 ....20 C1
Clarke's La NR34 ....8 F3
Clarkes La NR33 ....114 C6
Clarke's Rd 3 CO12 ....106 F2
Clark's Dro CB7 ....28 B4
Clarkson St 1 IP1 ......112 D1
Clarkson St IP1 ....155 A3
Claude Oliver Cl CO11 ..104 D1
Claude St IP1 ....155 B3
Claudian Cl CB9 ....133 B5
Claverton Way IP4 .....140 D5
Clay Hill Dennington IP13 ..55 F5
  Hintlesham IP8 ....95 B5
  Monks Eleigh IP7 ....79 D2
  Ubbeston IP19 ....40 E3
Clay La Bacton IP14 .....51 F6
  Henley IP6 ....82 E7
  Hepworth IP22 ....35 B5
  Ixworth IP31 ....34 A2
  Rushmere CO10 ....78 E4
  Stoke Ash IP23 ....37 B1
Clay Rd
  2 Bury St Edmunds IP32 .48 C5
  Bury St Edmunds IP32 .122 E8
  Fornham All Saints IP28 ..47 F7
Clay St Soham CB7 ......28 D4
  Thornham Magna IP23 ...36 F1
Claydon IP32 ....112 F3
Claydon High Sch IP6 ..134 C8
Claydon Prim Sch IP6 ...82 B5
Clayhall Rd CO10 ....92 C7
Clayhall Pl CO10 ....92 C7
Clayhall La Hitcham IP7 ..79 F6
  Wattisham IP7 ....80 A6
Clayhill Rd IP27 ....13 F7
Clayhills IP19 ....118 A3
Clayhive Dr 4 CB9 .....132 D5
Claypits Ave 1 CO8 ....101 D4
Claypits La CO10 ....91 B7
Clayton Ct IP12 ....146 D3
Clematis Cl 4 IP28 ......30 B1
Clemence St NR32 .....113 C3
Clement Rd NR33 ......115 B6
Clement Sq NR33 ......115 B6
Clements
  3 Haverhill CB9 ....132 C6
  Scole IP21 ....20 F1
Clements Dr 2 CB9 .....132 C6
Clements La CB9 ....132 C6
Clements Prim Sch
  CB9 ....132 D5
Clement's Rd 4 IP12 ....84 C6
Clement's Way 4 IP12 ..30 B8
Clench Cl IP9 ....155 C3
Clench Rd IP9 ....105 E8
Clerk's Piece NR34 .....111 D3

Clermont Ave CO10 ....148 C8
Cleveland Rd NR33 .....115 C7
Cleves Rd CB9 ....132 B4
Cricket Hill CO8 ....101 D4
Cliff Farm La NR33 ......11 B2
Cliff La
　Great Yarmouth NR31 .....3 B8
　Ipswich IP3 ....139 E3
Cliff La Prim Sch IP3 ..139 E3
Cliff Rd
　Felixstowe IP11 ....153 D6
　Harwich CO12 ....107 B2
　Ipswich IP3 ....139 E3
　Lowestoft NR33 ....115 C6
Clifford Dr NR3 ....114 E5
Clifford Rd IP4 ....139 F5
Clifford Rd Prim Sch
　IP4 ....139 F6
Cliffs The NR33 ....115 B2
Clifton Rd NR33 ....115 C7
Clifton Way IP2 ....138 D2
Clifton Wood 2 IP9 ....105 C7
Cliftonville NR33 ....115 B3
Cliftonville Rd NR33 ....115 B3
Clink The IP19 ....41 C5
Clint Hill 33 F6
Clint Rd IP23 ....97 D1
Clive Ave IP1 ....135 B2
Clockhall La CO10 ......75 D3
Clockhouse La IP14 .....67 F7
Cloncurry Gdns IP11 ...152 D3
Clopton Dr 2 CO12 .....91 E7
Clopton Gdns IP7 .....149 E4
Clopton Rd IP6 ....136 C7
Close The Corton NR32 ...3 D4
　5 Harwich CO12 ......107 A2
Kennett CB8 ....45 F7
　North Lopham IP22 ....19 A6
　Sudbury CO10 ....148 D6
　3 Tattingstone IP9 ...105 B8
Clough Dr 10 IP26 ......4 F3
Clovelly Cl IP4 ....140 F4
Clovelly Rise NR33 .....113 B3
Clover Field CB9 ......126 D3
Clover Field CB9 ......132 B6
Clover Way
　Lowestoft NR33 ....113 C5
　1 Red Lodge IP28 .....30 C5
Cloverfields 2 IP31 .....49 E4
Clowes's Cnr IP14 ......54 D2
Cluanie Orch CO10 .....76 F1
Clumps The IP12 ....86 A4
Coach La CB8 ....66 C7
Coachman's Paddock 3
　IP9 ....105 E7
Coakers La IP3 ....70 A1
Coalpit La IP29 ....46 F4
Coast Guards The 8
　IP16 ....73 F6
Coast Rd NR32 ....3 C5
Coastguard La 12 NR33 ..11 C1
Coates Dro 3 CB7 .....29 C5
Cobbler's Cnr IP18 ....95 B5
Cobbold Cl IP14 ....66 C1
Cobbold Mews IP4 ....155 C3
Cobbold Rd
　Felixstowe IP11 ....153 A4
　Woodbridge IP12 .....146 E7
Cobbold St Diss IP22 ...20 B2
　Ipswich IP4 ....155 C3
Cobden Pl IP14 ....54 C5
Cobham Rd IP3 ....140 C2
Coblers Way 3 CO10 ...92 B7
Cock & Bel La CO10 ....91 E8
Cock Rd IP14 ....52 A6
Cockfield Hall La IP16 .135 E7
Cockfield Rd IP30 ......65 A3
Cockpen Rd CB7 ....28 F1
Cockrell's Rd CO6 ....102 A2
Cocks Gn La IP30 ....64 A5
Cock's Rd IP23 ....117 F1
Coddenham Way 8 IP31 ...34 B1
Codling Rd IP32 ......123 E6
Cody Rd IP3 ....140 C1
Coggeshall Rd
　Dedham CO7 ....104 A2
　Foxash Estate CO7 ....103 F1
Colchester Cl IP27 .....13 F2
Colchester Rd
　Bures CO8 ....101 C4
　Dedham CO7 ....103 E2
　Ipswich IP4 ....135 F1
　10 Manningtree CO11 ..104 E2
　Wormingford CO6 ....102 A1
Cold Store Rd IP11 ....152 B2
Coldfair Cl IP17 ....129 B3
Coldfair Gn Prim Sch
　IP17 ....129 B2
Coldham La IP23 ....36 D2
Cole Ness Rd IP3 .....104 A8
Cole St IP21 ....39 B2
Coleman Cl IP20 ....21 C1
Coleridge Rd IP1 ......134 F3
Coles Hill IP19 ....42 C7
Coles La IP6 ....5 B2
Coles Oak La CO7 .....103 E3
Colethorpe La IP29 ....46 F3
College Cl 8 IP29 ......63 A8
College Gn IP11 ......153 C5

College Heath Mid Sch
　IP28 ....116 C6
College Heath Rd
　IP28 ....116 D6
College La
　Bury St Edmunds IP33 ..154 B1
　Worlingham NR34 .....111 F2
College Mdws 2 NR32 ..113 A3
College Rd
　Framlingham IP13 .....126 C4
　Hockwold cum Wilton IP26 ...4 F3
　Lowestoft NR33 ......115 C6
　2 Soham CB7 ....28 D3
College St
　Bury St Edmunds IP33 ..154 B1
　Ipswich IP4 ....155 B2
Colletts Chase CO6 ...101 F2
Colleymore Rd NR32 ....4 F4
Collett's Wlk IP12 ....146 E5
Collimer Cl 3 IP9 .....106 C8
Collings Pl CB8 ......120 E5
Collingwood Ave 8 IP5 .140 B3
Collingwood Fields
　CO7 ....151 B6
Collingwood Rd IP12 ..146 F7
Collin's Hill CB7 ....29 B1
Collinson's IP2 ....138 D5
Colman Rd 4 NR32 .....3 C4
Colne Rd CO8 ....101 C4
Colne Spring CO9 ......89 D4
Colne Valley Rd CB9 ..132 E5
Colneis Jun Sch IP11 ..153 B6
Colneis Rd IP11 ......153 B6
Colneys Cl CO10 .....148 B7
Colsterdale NR33 .....114 D3
Coltsfoot Cl IP32 ....123 F5
Coltsfoot Cl
　7 Ixworth IP31 ....34 B1
　8 Lowestoft NR33 ....114 F3
　7 Wickhambrook CB8 ..61 E2
Coltsfoot Rd IP2 .....138 C4
Columbia Cl IP5 ......141 A7
Columbine Cl 7 NR33 ..114 C5
Columbine Gdns IP2 ..138 E5
Columbine Way 3 IP23 ..36 D2
Columbines The CO10 ..76 F1
Columbyne Cl IP14 .....67 A7
Colville Rd NR33 ......114 C6
Colville Way NR33 ....114 C3
Colwyn Cl 21 IP2 .....21 A2
Combs Ford Prim Sch
　IP14 ....124 E4
Combs Gn IP14 ....66 D2
Combs La IP14 ....124 D4
Combs Mid Sch IP14 ..124 D3
Combs Wood Dr IP14 ..124 D3
Comet Way IP28 ....116 B5
Commerce Way 3
　CO11 ....104 E3
Commercial Rd
　Ipswich IP1 ....155 A1
　Lowestoft NR32 ......115 C8
Commister La 14 IP31 ...34 B1
Commodore Rd IP4 ....112 C1
Common Gate Dro CB7 ..29 A5
Common La
　Beccles NR34 ....115 C5
　Bromeswell IP12 .....147 F7
　Syleham IP21 ....22 A2
　Troston IP31 ....33 E3
Common La N NR34 ...111 B6
Common Rd
　Aldeby NR34 ....10 B7
　Botesdale IP22 ....36 B5
　Bressingham IP22 .....19 F4
　Hopton IP22 ....18 C2
　St James, South Elmham
　　IP19 ....23 D4
　Scole IP21 ....21 B4
　Shelfanger IP22 ......19 F7
Common St 3 CO10 .....90 A8
Common The 7 IP20 ....22 D5
Compass La IP12 ......147 A5
Compass St NR32 ......113 E2
Compiegne Way IP32 ..154 B3
Conach Rd IP12 ......146 E5
Coney Hill NR34 ......111 D3
Coney Weston Rd
　Coney Weston IP31 ....34 D8
　Fakenham Magna IP31 ..33 F6
　Sapiston IP31 ....34 A6
Congreve Rd IP1 ......135 A3
Coniston Cl IP11 .....153 E7
Coniston Rd IP3 ......140 B2
Connaught Rd
　Haverhill CB9 ....132 C5
　Ipswich IP1 ....134 D2
Conrad Cl NR33 ......114 D6
Conrad Rd NR33 ......114 D6
Consent La IP14 ....79 E4
Constable Cl
　Halesworth IP19 ......118 A2
　Lowestoft NR32 ......112 F1
　3 Manningtree CO11 ..104 D2
　Nayland-with-wissington
Constable Ct 8 IP20 ..22 D6
Constable Rd
　Bury St Edmunds IP33 ..122 E4
　Felixstowe IP11 ......153 A4
　Haverhill CB9 ....132 B7
　Ipswich IP4 ....155 C4
　Sudbury CO10 ....148 C6
Constable Way IP14 ..124 B7
Constantine Rd IP1 ...155 A2
Constitution Hill
　Ipswich IP1 ....155 A4
　2 Needham Market IP6 ..125 D5
　Southwold IP18 ......119 D4

Constitution Hill continued
　Sudbury CO10 ....148 D6
Convalescent Hill
　IP11 ....153 A3
Conway Cl
　Felixstowe IP11 ......153 C7
　Ipswich IP2 ....139 B2
Conway Rd 2 IP2 ......48 C5
Conyers Way IP11 ....153 A4
Cooke Cl NR33 ....114 F2
Cooke Rd NR33 ....114 C5
Cookley & Walpole CE Prim
　Sch IP19 ....41 C5
Cookley La IP23 ....38 B5
Cookley Rd Cookley IP19 ..41 B5
　Eye IP23 ....38 A5
Cooks Cl IP5 ....141 E8
Cook's Dro IP28 ....12 D2
Cooks Hill Boxted CO4 ..103 A4
　Letheringham IP13 ....70 D4
Cook's La
　Hawkedon IP29 ....62 E1
　Wortwell IP20 ....22 F6
Cooks Rd IP30 ....50 E2
Coombers IP9 ....150 D3
Cooper Cl 8 IP17 .....128 C4
Cooper La IP29 ....63 C8
Cooper Rd IP6 ....68 C1
Cooper's Cl CB8 ....60 A5
Coopers Cl IP6 ....83 A6
Coopers Dr 5 NR33 ...11 C1
Cooper's La CO7 .....103 F3
Coopers La NR33 ....11 B1
Cooper's Rd IP6 ......82 C6
Coopers St NR33 ......98 A8
Coopersfield 3 IP14 ...53 F2
Copdock Prim Sch IP8 .95 F4
Copellis Cl IP8 ....132 E8
Copeman Rd 8 IP22 ...20 A3
Copland Way NR34 ...100 A3
Copleston High Sch
　IP4 ....140 C5
Copleston Rd IP4 .....140 B5
Coplow Dale 5 NR33 ..114 C3
Copper Beech Dr 5
　NR33 ....114 D4
Copperfield Rd IP2 ..138 E5
Coppers Cl IP33 .....154 C1
Copperwheat Ave
　IP18 ....119 B8
Coppice Cl IP21 ......147 A6
Coppice The IP31 ......49 A6
Coprolite St IP3 .....155 C2
Cops Cl IP33 ....123 B1
Copswood Cl IP5 .....141 F7
Copy Hill CB9 ....132 C1
Coral Dr IP1 ....134 D1
Coram St IP7 ....149 A6
Cordell Pl CO10 ....91 E8
Cordell Rd CO10 ......91 E8
Corder Rd IP4 ....139 D8
Cordwinders CO7 .....151 F3
Cordy's La IP11 ......152 B6
Coriander Dr IP24 ....16 D6
Corks La IP7 ....149 C6
Corkway Dro IP26 ......5 D1
Corn Craft (Craft Centre)*
　IP7 ....79 D2
Corn Hatches La IP7 ...80 E1
Cornard Rd CO10 ....148 D5
Cornerth Cres CO10 ..148 F5
Cornfield Ave IP27 ...109 D7
Cornfield Cres 5 NR32 ..3 D4
Cornfield Rd IP3 .....154 A3
Cornfields IP7 ....148 D4
Cornflower Cl IP22 ..138 E4
Cornflower Way 1 CO10 .104 D2
Cornhill IP33 ....154 B2
Cornish Hall End Rd
　CO9 ....89 A1
Cornmills Rd IP30 .....50 D1
Cornwall Cl CB7 ......28 E2
Cornwall Cl 2 CO11 ..104 D2
Cornwall Rd IP11 ....152 F5
Cornwallis Cl IP28 ....32 C1
Cornwallis Ct IP33 ...154 A1
Cornwallis Dr 3 NR32 ..3 D4
Coronation Ave IP6 ...99 D6
Coronation Dr IP11 ..152 D3
Coronation Rd IP4 ...140 B5
Coronation Rise 1 CO10 ..92 C6
Corporation Ave IP2 ..139 B1
Corsican Pine Cl CB8 .120 F5
Corton CE VCP Sch
　NR32 ....3 D7
Corton Long La NR32 ..113 B8
Corton Rd Ipswich IP1 ..134 E1
　Lowestoft NR32 ......113 D6
Cosford Rd IP7 ....94 C7
Cotes The CB7 ....28 B6
Cotman Ave 8 CO11 ..104 D2
Cotman Cl 3 NR32 ...113 B6
Cotman Rd IP3 ......140 A1
Cotmer Rd NR33 .....114 D7
Cotswold Ave IP1 ....135 B1
Cotswold Dr 8 CO10 ..91 E7
Cotswold Way NR32 ..112 E2
Cottesford Cl IP7 ....149 E5
Cottingham Rd IP8 ..138 B2
Cotton End Rd CB8 ...120 C8
Cotton La
　Bury St Edmunds IP33 ..154 C3
　Cotton IP14 ....52 A6
Coucy Cl IP13 ....126 C4
Coupals Cl CB9 ......133 A3

Coupals Prim Sch
　CB9 ....133 B5
Coupals Rd CB9 ......133 C4
Courier Cl IP28 ......111 B5
Court Knoll (Earthworks)*
　CO6 ....102 D4
Court St CO6 ....102 D5
Courtenay Cl CO10 ..148 B8
Courts The
　Felixstowe IP11 ......153 B4
　Playford IP6 ....137 B5
Covell Cl IP33 ....122 C4
Coverdale 8 NR33 ...114 E3
Covert Cl CB9 ....132 E7
Covert Rd IP18 ......119 C8
Covey Dr IP27 ....109 E6
Covey Way IP27 .....109 E6
Cow and Sheep Dro
　IP28 ....29 E7
Cow Fair 7 IP30 ....50 D1
Cowell St IP2 ....139 C3
Cowle's Dro IP26 .....41 D1
Cowley Rd IP2 ....153 A4
Cowper St IP4 ....140 B6
Cowslip Cl IP2 ....138 E4
Cowslip Cres NR33 ...114 C5
Cowslip Way IP6 ....125 D3
Cox Hill CO10 ....93 C3
Cox La Great Barton IP31 ..155 C2
　Ipswich IP4 ....140 B6
Coxhall Rd IP9 ......142 E1
Cox's Cl NR34 ....111 C3
Coxs Cl CB9 ....132 A5
Cox's Hill CO11 .....104 D2
Cox's La IP18 ....119 C8
Coytes Gdns IP1 ....155 B2
Crabbe St
　Aldeburgh IP15 ......130 F4
　Ipswich IP4 ....140 A6
Crabbe's Cl 8 IP26 ....4 E5
Crabtree Cl IP19 .....118 B2
Crabtree La Aldeby NR34 ..9 F8
　Little Horkesley CO6 ..102 B1
Crabtree Mdw 8 IP30 ..50 F2
Crabtree Rise IP21 ....21 F2
Cracks La IP12 ....85 C6
Crag Farm Rd IP12 ..131 E7
Crag Path IP15 ......130 F3
Craig Cl 7 IP11 ......107 D8
Craig's La CO8 ....101 B3
Cramswell Cl IP30 ...132 B4
Cranberry Chase 1
　IP4 ....135 D1
Cranbrook La CO10 ...77 C1
Crane Cl IP12 ....146 D3
Crane Hill London Rd
　IP2 ....138 E4
Cranes Mdw 51 IP20 ..22 D6
Cranesbill Dr IP32 ...123 E5
Cranesbill Rd NR33 ..114 F3
Cranfield Cl 4 NR33 ..115 A3
Cranfield Pk IP8 ......95 D7
Cranleigh Rd NR33 ..114 F3
Cranley Gn Rd
　Eye IP23 ....117 D2
　Eye IP23 ....117 E1
Cranley La IP23 .....117 F1
Cranmeregreen La
　CO10 ....77 C1
Cranwell Cres IP3 ...140 C1
Cranwell Gr 1 IP3 ..141 C7
Cranworth Gdns 1
　NR32 ....112 F1
Cranworth Rd IP7 ...149 E4
Cratfield La IP19 ......40 C4
Cratfield Rd
　Bury St Edmunds IP32 ..123 E4
　Fressingfield IP21 ....39 F8
　Huntingfield IP19 ....40 F5
Craven Way CB8 ....120 D6
Crawford Ave IP14 ...66 D8
Crawford La 8 IP15 ..141 C7
Creeting La IP14 .....67 A7
Creeting Rd IP14 ....124 E6
Creeting St Mary Prim Sch
　IP6 ....125 F8
Crepping Hall Dr IP9 .105 C5
Crescent Rd
　Aldeburgh IP15 ......130 E4
　Felixstowe IP11 ......153 A4
　Felixstowe IP11 ......153 A4
　Ipswich IP1 ....155 A3
Crescent The
　Dullingham CB8 ......59 D5
　East Harling NR16 ....18 C8
　Great Hockham CB8 ..102 D1
　8 Soham CB7 ....28 D3
　Stowmarket IP14 ....124 D4
　7 Thurston IP31 ......49 D4
　Wicken CB7 ....28 A1
　Wickham Market IP13 .127 B6
Crescents The IP18 ..119 B8
Cresmedow Way IP30 ..50 F2
Crespigny Rd IP15 ...130 E3
Cresslands La IP29 ...76 D8
Crestland Bsns Pk
　CO10 ....92 A8
Crestview Dr NR32 ..113 B3
Cricket Field Rd CB8 .121 B2
Cricket Hill Rd CO11 ..95 C2
Crick's Rd
　Beck Row, Holywell Row
　& Kenny Hill IP28 ....30 A6
　Thistley Green IP28 ...29 F6
Crimbold's La IP30 ...64 D1
Crimp Cramp La NR34 ..10 B8
Crisp Cl 3 NR32 .....113 B4
Crisp Rd NR35 ....8 E7

Crispin Cl CB9 ....132 B5
Crockfords Rd CB8 ..121 A3
Crocus Cl IP2 ....138 F4
Croft Cl Beccles NR34 ..111 C6
　Diss IP22 ....20 C2
　10 Harleston IP20 .....22 D6
　3 Wickhambrook CB8 ..61 E2
Croft La Diss IP22 .....20 C2
　Haverhill CB9 ....132 F4
　Trimley St Martin IP10 ..98 C2
Croft Lea CO10 ....92 E8
Croft Pl IP28 ....116 C4
Croft Rd 8 Isleham CB7 ..29 E5
　Newmarket CB8 ......120 F7
　Sudbury CO10 ....148 C6
Croft Rise IP33 ......123 B3
Croft St IP2 ....139 C2
Croft The 8 Bures CO8 ..101 C4
　Great Yeldham CO9 ...90 A3
　1 Lowestoft NR32 ...113 C1
Crofton Rd IP4 ....140 B2
Cromarty Rd IP4 ....140 B8
Cromer Rd IP1 ....134 F3
Crompton Rd
　Ipswich IP2 ....138 F2
　Stowmarket IP14 ....114 E2
Cromwell Ave NR34 ..111 B3
Cromwell Cl NR34 ...111 B3
Cromwell Rd
　Ringsfield NR34 ....9 C1
　Weeting IP27 ....2 D1
　Weston NR34 ....111 B3
Cromwell Sq IP1 ....155 B2
Cropley Cl IP32 .....123 E4
Cross Cl CB9 ....132 E2
Cross Field Way CO4 .103 A2
Cross La CI IP27 .....109 De
Cross Rd IP20 ....22 C6
Cross St Bungay NR35 ..113 B4
　Drinkstone IP30 ......65 C7
　Elmswell IP30 ....50 E1
　Eye IP23 ....117 C2
　Felixstowe IP11 ......152 E2
　Hoxne IP21 ....108 C7
　Leiston IP16 ....129 C5
　Sudbury CO10 ....148 B4
Cross The IP23 ......117 C2
Cross Ways IP30 ......50 E1
Crossfields CO6 ......102 D5
Crossgate Field 3 IP11 ..152 E
Crossing Rd IP22 ....20 C
Crossley Gdns IP1 ...134 C3
Crotchets Cl 8 IP9 ..150 E2
Croutel Rd IP11 .....153 B
Crow St IP31 ....34 D
Crowbrook Pl IP30 ...78 C
Crowcroft Glebe IP7 ..80 B
Crowcroft Rd IP7 ....80 B
Crowe Hall La IP9 ...105 D8
Crowe St IP14 ....124 D6
Crowfield Rd IP14 ....68 C
Crowfoot Com Prim Sch
　NR34 ....111 D3
Crowfoot Gdns 7 NR34 ..111 D
Crowhurst Cl IP14 ...114 D
Crowland Cl 8 IP27 .139 A
Crowland Rd CB9 ...132 De
Crowley Rd IP6 .....125 D5
Crown Cl 10 IP12 .....84 A
Crown Corner IP6 ....68 B
Crown Cres 16 IP31 ..34 B
Crown Gn IP22 ....20 E
Crown La
　Coney Weston IP31 ....17 E
　Ixworth IP31 ....34 B
　Orford IP12 ....131 C
　Wickham Market IP13 .127 C
Crown Mdw Wlk
　NR32 ....113 C
Crown Mill 3 IP30 ...50 F2
Crown Pl IP12 ....147 A
Crown Rd IP26 ....6 B
Crown St Brandon IP27 ..14 E
　Bury St Edmunds IP33 ..154 B
　Dedham CO7 ....103 F
　Felixstowe IP11 ......152 E
　Ipswich IP1 ....155 B8
　Leiston IP16 ....129 Ct
　Needham Market IP6 ..125 De
　Stowmarket IP14 ....124 D
Crown St E 8 NR32 ..113 C
Crown St W NR32 ...113 C
Crown Swimming Pool
　IP1 ....155 B8
Crownfield Rd 8 CO10 ..77 A
Crownfields 2 IP13 ..84 F
Crownland Rd IP23 ...35 E
Crowswell Ct 6 IP11 .107 De
Croxton Cl IP10 ......98 C
Croxton Rd IP24 .....16 C
Crunch Croft CB9 ...133 C
Cryspen Ct IP33 .....154 B
Cuckfield Ave IP3 ....140 E
Cuckoo Hill (Tumulus)*
　IP27 ....40 C
Cuckoo Hill CO8 .....101 C
Cuckoo La IP20 ......22 C
Cucumber La NR34 ..111 D
Culford Rd
　Bury St Edmunds IP28 ..48 C
　Ingham IP31 ....33 A
Culford Sch CB8 ....32 D
Cullingham Rd IP1 ...155 A
Cullum Rd IP33 ......154 B
Culvers Mdw 4 IP31 ..34 E
Culzean Gdns 1 NR32 ..113 A

Cumberland Cl
4 Felixstowe IP11 ....153 D6
5 Southwold IP18 ....119 C5
Cumberland Mews IP12 ....147 A4
Cumberland Rd IP1 8 NR32 ....113 E2
Cumberland Rd IP18 ....119 C5
Cumberland St
Ipswich IP1 ....155 A4
Woodbridge IP12 ....147 A4
Cundle Gn La IP17 ....72 C5
Cundys Marsh 5 IP15 ....130 E5
Cunningham Way NR33 ....115 B3
Curlew Cl IP27 ....109 D5
Curlew Gn NR32 ....112 C5
Curlew Rd IP2 ....138 D4
Curlews The IP33 ....123 C1
Curriers' La IP1 ....155 A2
Curtis Cl IP8 ....138 C1
Curtis Dr 1 IP26 ....4 D5
Curwen Rd IP14 ....124 C6
Curzon Rd CO10 ....148 F6
Cutler Rd 8 NR32 ....112 D2
Cutler St 1 IP1 ....155 B2
Cutlers La CO7 ....151 D7
Cutler's La IP14 ....66 A6
Cutter's La IP31 ....49 E8
Cutting's Rd IP21 ....21 E4
Cypress Way 4 NR33 ....114 F7

D

Daffodil Cl IP2 ....138 E3
Dagworth La IP14 ....66 D8
Daimler Rd IP1 ....134 C2
Dains Pl IP11 ....152 C7
Daires La IP12 ....147 C3
Dairy Dr 4 IP28 ....48 B6
Dairy Hill IP19 ....38 F8
Dairy La Ixworth IP31 ....34 A2
Mutford NR34 ....10 C3
Dairy Rd IP7 ....80 A1
Daisy Cl IP27 ....109 D5
Daisy Hill IP21 ....39 F8
Daking Ave CO10 ....93 B3
Daking's Drift 6 IP19 ....118 A3
Dakota Rd 8 IP28 ....30 A8
Dale End NR33 ....114 E2
Dale Hall La IP1 ....135 B1
Dale Hall Prim Sch IP1 ....135 B2
Dale Hill IP14 ....53 A6
Dale Rd
Fressingfield IP21 ....22 D1
Stanton IP31 ....34 E5
Dale Tree Rd 11 IP29 ....47 A2
Dales Rd IP1 ....135 A1
Dales View IP1 ....95 F4
Dales View Rd IP1 ....135 A1
Dalham Ashley CB8 ....61 B8
Moulton CB8 ....59 E3
Dallinghoo Rd IP13 ....127 A6
Dalton Rd IP1 ....155 A3
Dam La Burgate IP22 ....36 E7
Kessingland NR33 ....11 A1
Damask Cl 3 NR33 ....114 E4
Damselfly Rd IP3 ....144 C8
Dandalan Cl IP1 ....138 E8
Dane Cl CB9 ....133 B8
Dane Hill Rd
Kennett CB8 ....45 E7
Kennett CB8 ....45 F7
Danes Cl IP1 ....124 C5
Danes Ct CO10 ....148 F2
Danescourt Ave IP14 ....124 C5
Daneway Gdns IP5 ....141 C6
Danforth Cl IP13 ....126 B4
Daniels Cl 8 CO10 ....92 B7
Daphne Rd IP12 ....131 C2
Darby Cl IP32 ....123 C4
Darby Rd NR34 ....111 B3
Darcy Cl IP32 ....123 E4
Dark La
Dicklesburgh & Rushall IP21 ....20 E2
Easton IP13 ....70 E7
Darkings La IP30 ....64 F2
Darrell Rd 1 IP11 ....153 H11
Darrow Gn Rd IP20 ....7 A4
Darrow Wood La IP22 ....7 B4
Darsham Cl 1 IP11 ....152 D5
Darsham Rd IP17 ....58 B8
Darsham Sta IP17 ....57 E8
Darter Cl IP3 ....144 A4
Darwin Cl IP28 ....116 C6
Darwin Pl CB8 ....121 B1
Darwin Rd IP4 ....139 F5
Dash End La CB9 ....133 F8
Dashwood Cl IP8 ....138 C3
Daundy Cl IP1 ....138 D5
Davall Cl 16 CO12 ....106 E1
Davey Cl Bungay NR35 ....110 E4
IP3 ....139 F1
Davey La IP13 ....34 C4
Davey's La IP13 ....34 C4
Davidson Cl CO10 ....92 B2
Daw St CO9 ....89 A3
Dawes Cl IP9 ....150 D4
Dawson Dr 1 IP15 ....152 C8
Dawson Drift 3 IP5 ....141 C7
Days Gn IP9 ....150 D3
Day's La IP31 ....34 E8
Days Rd IP9 ....150 D3
Dazeley's La CO7 ....151 F2
De Burgh Pl 8 CO10 ....76 A1
De Greys Ct 8 CO10 ....92 B3

De Havilland Ct 7 IP28 ....116 B5
De Vere Cl IP13 ....126 C3
Deacon Cl 8 IP11 ....153 D6
Deacon's Cl 2 CO10 ....78 D4
Dead La Ardleigh CO7 ....103 E1
Bures St Mary CO8 ....101 F5
Lawford CO11 ....104 E1
Deadman's La
Benhall IP17 ....128 A2
Combs IP14 ....66 E3
Rendham IP17 ....57 A3
Stoke Ash IP23 ....53 A8
Deane's Cl 1 CO12 ....107 A1
Deans Cl CB9 ....132 E7
Deben Ave Ipswich IP5 ....141 B8
Martlesham IP5 ....137 F1
Deben High Sch IP11 ....152 F4
Deben La
Waldringfield IP12 ....98 E7
6 Woodbridge Airfield IP12 ....85 B3
Deben Rd Haverhill CB9 ....132 F6
Ipswich IP1 ....134 F1
Saxmundham IP17 ....128 C4
Woodbridge IP12 ....147 B5
Deben Rise IP14 ....53 F1
Deben Valley Dr IP5 ....141 C7
Deben Way IP11 ....152 E5
Debenham CE High Sch IP14 ....53 E2
Debenham Rd
Crowfield IP6 ....68 C5
Winston IP14 ....53 F1
Debenside The IP12 ....147 C2
Decoy Rd IP27 ....12 F8
Dedham Ave 4 NR32 ....112 F3
Dedham Heavy Horse Ctr* CO7 ....104 A3
Dedham Meade CO7 ....103 E1
Dedham Rd
Ardleigh CO7 ....103 A3
Boxted CO4 ....103 A3
Lawford CO11 ....104 C2
Deepdale IP3 ....144 E2
Deepdale Rd 4 CO12 ....107 A1
Deer Row NR35 ....8 D5
Defoe Rd IP1 ....135 A1
Degas Gdns 1 NR32 ....113 B6
Delamere Gdns 6 IP5 ....98 A8
Dene Rd NR32 ....113 D4
Denes High's Sch NR32 ....113 D3
Denham Cl IP13 ....122 D5
Denham Cnr 38 D3
Denham La IP29 ....47 A2
Denham Low Rd Dalham CB8 ....61 B8
Hoxne IP21 ....38 D6
Denmark Gdns 1 IP5 ....105 E7
Denmark Hill IP22 ....20 C2
Denmark La IP22 ....20 B2
Denmark Rd
Beccles NR34 ....111 B6
Lowestoft NR33 ....115 C8
5 Lowestoft NR33 ....115 D8
Denmark St Diss IP22 ....20 C2
Diss IP22 ....20 C2
Denney's La IP17 ....128 D7
Dennington CE Prim Sch IP13 ....55 E6
Dennington Rd
Dennington IP13 ....55 F8
Framlingham IP13 ....126 B5
Laxfield IP13 ....40 B1
Denny Ave IP14 ....139 F3
Denny's Hill IP20 ....23 A6
Denton Cl IP22 ....138 D2
Denton Dr NR33 ....114 F5
Denton Rd IP22 ....7 C2
Depden La IP29 ....63 A2
Depot Rd CB8 ....120 E6
Derby Cl IP4 ....140 A5
Derby Pl 8 IP11 ....49 A5
Derby Rd Ipswich IP3 ....140 A4
Ipswich IP4 ....140 A4
Derby Way CB8 ....120 D5
Dereham Ave IP3 ....139 F3
Dereham Cl 2 IP7 ....149 E5
Derry Brook La IP14 ....53 F2
Derwent Gdns 8 NR32 ....113 A4
Derwent Rd
18 Bury St Edmunds IP32 ....48 C5
Ipswich IP3 ....139 F3
Desmond Cl IP3 ....144 D4
Dettingen Way IP33 ....122 D2
Devereaux Dr IP4 ....155 C3
Devils Dyke Nature Reserve* CO10 ....107 B1
Dowling Rd CO10 ....92 C1
Devil's La IP17 ....42 C1
Devlin Rd IP8 ....138 B1
Devon Cl IP32 ....122 E8
Devon Rd
Felixstowe IP11 ....152 A5
7 Stowupland IP14 ....67 A6
Devon Way 10 CO12 ....106 E1

Devonshire Rd IP3 ....139 F5
Dewar La IP1 ....141 C2
Dewarrene Dr IP27 ....5 E3
Dial La IP1 ....155 B3
Diamond Cl IP1 ....134 D1
Dickens Cl 8 NR32 ....112 F3
Dickens Rd IP2 ....138 E6
Dickinson Terr 8 IP15 ....141 D7
Dicky Hill IP20 ....22 D7
Didsbury Ct IP22 ....138 D2
Digby Cl IP5 ....98 A7
Digby Rd IP4 ....140 C7
Dighurn St W IP1 ....155 A3
Dinsdale Rd IP16 ....129 C6
Diomed Dr IP1 ....49 A5
Dirty La IP21 ....21 F7
Diss Church Jun Sch IP22 ....20 C2
Diss Cl IP2 ....138 D2
Diss Cty High Sch IP22 ....20 B3
Diss Mus* IP22 ....20 C2
Diss Rd
Burston & Shimpling IP22 ....20 C5
Garboldisham IP22 ....18 D4
Garboldisham IP22 ....18 D4
3 Scole IP21 ....20 F1
South Lopham IP22 ....19 C4
Wattisfield IP22 ....35 A5
Diss Sta IP22 ....20 C2
Diss Town FC IP22 ....20 B3
Ditchingham Dam NR35 ....110 B5
Ditchingham Gr IP4 ....140 F6
Ditton Cl CB8 ....121 A1
Ditton Gn CB8 ....60 B5
Dixon Cl 8 CO11 ....104 D2
Dixon Dr NR33 ....114 F2
Dobbs Drift IP5 ....141 F7
Dobbs La IP5 ....141 F7
Dock La IP12 ....147 C7
Dock St 1 IP4 ....155 B2
Dockfield Ave 8 CO12 ....106 F2
Dockings La 8 IP7 ....29 C5
Doctor Watson's La IP5 ....137 A1
Doctor's La Ashen CO10 ....89 E5
Orford IP12 ....131 C3
Pulham St Mary IP21 ....22 A6
Doctors La IP21 ....39 B4
Dodmans IP22 ....138 D2
Dodson Vale IP5 ....141 C7
Dodge Dr IP1 ....14 D8
Dog La Shelfanger IP22 ....19 E4
Tannington IP13 ....54 C6
Dogs Head St IP4 ....155 B2
Dogwood Wlk 5 IP12 ....146 A9
Doit La IP22 ....20 A3
Doit The IP22 ....19 F2
Dolphin Cl 8 NR33 ....115 B4
Dombey Rd IP2 ....138 E5
Domey Rd NR32 ....113 B4
Dome Sports Ctr IP28 ....116 E4
Donegal Rd IP1 ....138 D4
Donkey La
Bradfield Combust with Stanningfield IP29 ....63 F2
Wicken CB7 ....28 B1
Dooley Rd IP6 ....134 C8
Dorchester Rd
Bury St Edmunds IP33 ....122 D3
Ipswich IP3 ....140 D3
Doric Pl IP14 ....147 A4
Doris St CB8 ....120 F3
Dorking Rd NR32 ....3 A6
Dorley Dale NR33 ....114 E3
Dorothy Hodgkin Ct NR34 ....111 C4
Dorset Cl IP3 ....135 F1
Double St IP13 ....126 D3
Doug Smith Cl CB8 ....120 F6
Doughty Wylie Cres IP16 ....58 B4
Douglas Cl
Halesworth IP19 ....118 C5
Lowestoft NR33 ....114 D3
Douglas Rd 8 CO12 ....107 A2
Doune Way IP30 ....22 D6
Dove Cl 15 Debenham IP14 ....53 F2
Harleston IP20 ....22 D5
Saxmundham IP17 ....128 C4
Dove Cres 8 CO12 ....106 E1
Dove Gdns 2 IP14 ....67 A5
Dove House Rd CB8 ....132 E7
Dove La IP23 ....117 D2
Dover Rd IP8 ....119 B7
Dovest IP.. Ipswich IP3 ....139 E5
Lowestoft NR32 ....113 D2
Dovedale
Felixstowe IP11 ....152 D3
Ipswich IP4 ....140 F7
Dovehouse Hill IP29 ....77 D7
Dover Rd IP3 ....140 B4
Dovercourt Sta CO12 ....107 B2
Dovercourt Swimming Pool CO12 ....107 B1
Dowes Hill La NR34 ....111 B3
Downham Way IP27 ....6 A1
Downing Cl
Bury St Edmunds IP32 ....123 E5
Ipswich IP2 ....138 E2
Mildenhall IP28 ....116 D5
Newmarket CB8 ....121 B2
2 Woodbridge IP12 ....146 E4

Downing Dr 4 IP31 ....49 A6
Downing Prim Sch IP2 ....138 F2
Downing Rd IP7 ....80 F1
Downlands IP18 ....119 C6
Downs Cres CB9 ....132 D6
Downs Farm La IP20 ....23 B7
Downs The
Felixstowe IP11 ....152 D5
Rushbrooke with Rougham IP30 ....49 C2
Downside IP14 ....124 B6
Downside IP21 ....142 F8
Downton Dr CB9 ....132 D6
Dowson Dr 2 NR33 ....11 B1
Drab's La IP13 ....83 E7
Drage Rd IP14 ....124 A6
Drake Rd CO10 ....148 C8
Drake Sq S IP3 ....140 B2
Drake's Heath NR32 ....113 B2
Drapers Cl 7 IP17 ....149 E6
Drapers Hill IP21 ....39 B5
Drapers La
Ditchingham NR35 ....8 A7
Helions Bumpstead CB9 ....88 C4
Drapery Comm 3 CO10 ....77 A2
Drays The CO10 ....93 D2
Drift Rd IP27 ....109 C8
Drift The Botesdale IP22 ....36 A7
East Bergholt CO11 ....104 E5
Exning CB8 ....59 B5
Fornham St Martin IP31 ....48 D5
Holbrook IP7 ....105 E5
Ipswich IP4 ....140 A6
Ramsholt IP12 ....99 A3
Drinkstone Rd IP30 ....65 B7
Drinkstone Gn Cl IP30 ....65 B7
Drinkstone Rd
Beyton IP30 ....49 F2
Drinkstone IP30 ....65 B5
Drinkwater Cl CB8 ....120 E4
Drive The
Harwich CO12 ....107 A1
Heveningham IP19 ....41 B3
Hitcham IP7 ....80 A8
Lowestoft NR32 ....112 F2
Rushbrooke with Rougham IP30 ....64 B8
Southwold IP18 ....119 B7
Dro The IP27 ....14 D8
Drout's La IP31 ....34 E7
Drove La IP14 ....51 A3
Drovers Ave IP32 ....122 F8
Drover's Ct IP11 ....152 B8
Druids La IP22 ....20 A7
Druids' La IP22 ....20 A7
Drum Field 5 CO7 ....103 E5
Drummond Ct IP23 ....154 A1
Drury Cl 6 NR33 ....111 C1
Drury Rd CO10 ....148 D8
Drury La Milden IP7 ....79 B1
Ridgewell CO9 ....89 D3
Dryry Pk IP17 ....72 C4
Drury Pk IP6 ....134 C8
Drybridge Hill IP12 ....146 E4
Dryden Rd IP1 ....135 A3
Dublin Rd IP23 ....153 E8
Dublin Rd IP1 ....149 E6
Duchess Dr
Newmarket CB8 ....121 D2
Newmarket CB8 ....60 C8
Duck Dro CB7 ....22 A6
Duckamere IP8 ....134 A1
Ducks La CB8 ....120 C7
Ducksen Rd IP14 ....52 E4
Duddery Hill CB9 ....132 E5
Duddery Rd 6 CB9 ....132 E5
Dudley St IP27 ....109 F1
Duffs Hill CO10 ....77 A4
Duke Cl Beccles NR34 ....111 D3
4 Bildeston IP7 ....79 E4
Hadleigh IP7 ....149 D5
Haughley IP14 ....51 C1
Hintlesham IP8 ....95 C5
Ipswich IP3 ....139 E4
7 Stanton IP31 ....34 E4
Dukes Cl IP11 ....153 D6
Duke's Dr IP19 ....118 A2
Dukes Head St 8 NR32 ....113 E2
Dukes Mdw
1 Beccles NR34 ....111 C4
Cockfield IP30 ....64 B5
Duke's Mdw IP12 ....146 D3
Duke's Pk IP12 ....146 D2
Duke's Rd NR35 ....110 C2
Dukesway 8 NR35 ....7 F4
Dulgate Rd NR35 ....7 B7
Dullingham Rd
Newmarket CB8 ....120 C1
Woodditton CB8 ....59 F7
Dullingham Sta CB8 ....59 F7
Dumbarton Rd
3 Ipswich IP4 ....136 C1
Newmarket CB8 ....140 B8
Dumfries Rd 2 IP1 ....136 C1
Dumplingbridge La IP27 ....109 C6
Dun Cow Rd IP30 ....10 B8
Dunburgh Rd NR34 ....9 A6
Duncan Rise CO9 ....89 F1
Dunche's La IP6 ....67 E4

Dunhill La IP22 ....35 B5
Dunlin Rd IP2 ....138 E2
Dunlop Rd IP2 ....138 F6
Dunn Cl IP7 ....149 E5
Dunny Wood Cl CB9 ....132 C7
Dunstall Gn Rd CB8 ....61 A4
Dunster Dr CB9 ....132 C6
Dunston Rd IP32 ....132 E4
Dunston's Cnr IP6 ....82 B8
Dunton Gr IP7 ....149 C5
Dunwich Heath Nature Reserve* IP17 ....58 F7
Dunwich La IP17 ....41 A2
Dunwich Mus* IP17 ....43 B1
Dunwich Pl 8 IP11 ....49 A5
Dunwich Rd
Blythburgh IP19 ....42 F5
4 Felixstowe IP11 ....119 D5
Westleton IP17 ....58 D8
Dunwich Underwater Exploration Ex* IP17 ....
Durban Cl IP19 ....131 B2
Durban Rd IP33 ....115 B7
Durban Terr IP33 ....154 A3
Durbidge's Hill IP22 ....47 D3
Durham Rd 8 IP27 ....48 C5
Durham Rd IP27 ....14 A3
Durham Wlk CB8 ....120 E5
Durrant View IP5 ....141 E7
Durrant's Cl 8 NR33 ....11 C1
Dux St IP7 ....65 B5
Dyer Ct IP7 ....149 F5
Dyers La CO10 ....92 E2
Dyers Rd CO9 ....89 C1
Dyke St IP1 ....155 B3
Dyson's Dro CB5 ....44 A7

E

Eagle Ct NR34 ....26 E5
Eagle Dr IP15 ....130 C6
Eagle La CB8 ....59 E5
Eagle St 8 IP4 ....155 C2
Eagle Way IP5 ....98 A8
Eagles Cl 7 IP11 ....152 F4
Earl Soham Prim Sch IP13 ....54 F2
Earls Cl IP11 ....153 D6
Earl's Cl IP19 ....118 A2
Earlsbrook 1 IP4 ....51 E6
Earlsfield IP27 ....109 D4
Earlsford Rd Mellis IP23 ....36 F5
Wortham Pk IP23 ....37 A4
Earsham CE VA Fst Sch NR35 ....7 F4
Earsham Dam NR35 ....110 A4
Earsham Rd NR35 ....7 E6
Earsham St
Bungay NR35 ....110 A4
Bungay NR35 ....110 A4
Earth La NR32 ....2 F5
Easlea Rd IP32 ....123 E4
East Anglia Transport Mus* NR33 ....114 A3
East Barton Rd 3 IP31 ....49 B5
East Bergholt CE Prim Sch CO7 ....151 B5
East Bergholt High Sch CO7 ....151 D6
East Bergholt Pl Gdn* CO7 ....151 F3
East Dock Rd CO10 ....123 C6
East End Rd CO7 ....104 E6
East End La
East Bergholt CO7 ....151 F4
Stonham Aspal IP14 ....68 C6
East Fen Dro CB7 ....28 F4
East Fen Rd IP27 ....29 D5
East Hanningfield NR16 ....18 F8
East La Bawdsey IP12 ....99 A3
Dedham CO7 ....104 A2
Middleton IP17 ....58 B6
Ufford IP13 ....85 A7
East Lawn IP14 ....140 C8
East Mill Gn IP7 ....104 F7
East Point Pavilion Leisure Ctr* NR33 ....115 D8
East Rd CB7 ....29 C5
East Side CO4 ....103 B3
East St 6 Harwich CO12 ....107 B2
Southwold IP18 ....119 D5
Sudbury CO10 ....148 D5
East View IP8 ....29 E3
Eastcliff IP11 ....153 D7
Eastern Ave
Haverhill CB9 ....132 D6
Sharon IP4 ....28 D4
Eastern Ct IP4 ....140 F4
Eastern Way
Bury St Edmunds IP32 ....123 C6
Lowestoft NR32 ....50 F2
Lowestoft NR32 ....113 B1
Eastfen Dro IP28 ....22 D7
Eastfield Gdns 8 NR33 ....114 E4
Eastgate St IP33 ....154 C3
Eastland Cl 1 IP11 ....152 D7
Eastlands Rd IP21 ....39 B4
Eastlands St IP23 ....52 B8
Eastlands Rd IP16 ....129 C8
Eastlow Hill (Tumulus)* IP30 ....64 C8
Eastlowhill Rd IP30 ....64 B8

Easton La
Hacheston IP13 70 F5
Reydon IP18 27 A1
Easton Prim Sch IP13 70 E5
Easton Rd
Hacheston IP13 71 A4
Woodbridge Airfield IP12 85 B3
Eastward Ho IP16 129 D5
Eastward Pl IP14 124 C7
Eastwood Ave NR33 114 F6
Eaton Cl IP11 152 C7
Eaton Gdns IP11 152 E2
Eccles Rd IP2 138 D2
Economy Rd NR33 115 C7
Eddies The NR33 114 E4
Eddowes Rd 6 IP6 82 B5
Edelweiss Cl 1 NR33 114 C4
Eden Rd 5 Haverhill CB9 132 E5
Ipswich IP4 140 B5
Edendale NR32 112 D2
Edes Paddock 9 IP31 49 A6
Edgar Ave IP14 124 D3
Edgar Sewter Prim Sch IP19 118 B5
Edgeborough Cl CB8 46 A5
Edgecomb Rd IP14 124 D3
Edgefield Ave 15 CO11 104 D2
Edgerton Rd NR33 115 A7
Edgworth Rd CO10 148 C4
Edies La CO6 102 B7
Edinburgh Cl
6 Barnham IP24 16 C2
Stowmarket IP14 124 E6
Edinburgh Gdns IP6 82 B5
Edinburgh Rd
Lowestoft NR32 113 D3
Newmarket CB8 120 E4
Edith Cavell Way CB9 88 E3
Edmonton Cl IP5 141 A7
Edmonton Rd IP5 141 A7
Edmund Cl CB9 132 D6
Edmund De Moundeford VC Sch IP26 4 E6
Edmund Moundford Rd 11 IP26 4 E5
Edmund Rd IP27 14 D8
Edmunds Rd IP14 65 F4
Edward Cl IP1 138 F8
Edward St 6 CO12 106 F3
Edwards La IP19 41 F5
Edwin Ave IP12 146 F7
Edwin Panks Rd IP7 149 E6
Egglestone Cl IP2 138 F1
Eggshell La CO9 88 F1
Eglantine Way 2 CO6 102 A7
Egremont St CO10 77 A2
Ehringshausen Way CB9 132 F5
El Alamein Rd NR32 113 A4
Elder Crescen 2 IP7 80 D6
Elders The IP27 109 E5
Elderstub La IP30 49 B1
Eldith Ave CB7 29 C1
Eldo Gdns 8 IP28 29 F6
Eldo Rd IP28 29 F6
Eldon La IP28 30 D8
Eldred Cl IP32 123 E4
Eldred Dr CO10 92 B2
Eleanor Pl 6 IP31 49 A6
Eley's Cnr IP7 94 E8
Elgar Cl NR33 115 A6
Eliot Way 4 IP14 124 B8
Elizabeth Ave CB8 120 E5
Elizabeth Bonhote Cl 3 NR35 110 C2
Elizabeth Cl
Leiston IP16 129 C4
Lowestoft NR32 113 A3
Elizabeth Dr IP29 62 D5
Elizabeth Rd 15 CO12 107 A2
Elizabeth Way
Burrough Green CB8 59 F2
Eye IP23 117 C3
Felixstowe IP11 152 D3
Stowmarket IP14 124 E6
Sudbury CO10 148 A3
Elizabeth Wlk 27 IP20 22 D6
Ellenbrook Rd
Ipswich IP2 138 D1
Pinewood IP9 142 E8
Ellingham Prim Sch NR35 8 D7
Ellington Rd 1 IP24 16 C2
Elliott Ave IP18 119 C8
Elliott Cl CB8 121 A6
Elliott St IP1 139 A6
Ellis Rd CO4 102 F2
Ellis St CO10 93 C3
Elliston Cl 4 IP30 50 F2
Ellough Rd
Beccles NR34 111 D4
Worlingham NR34 111 F2
Ellwoods Cl 2 CB7 29 C5
Elm Cl
10 Bentwaters Airfield IP12 85 E8
6 Brantham CO11 104 E5
Dullingham CB8 59 E5
Haverhill CB9 132 D6
Lakenheath IP27 109 C7
Lowestoft NR33 114 C3
Elm Coppice 6 NR33 114 E4
Elm Ct CB9 133 C3
Elm Dr IP30 49 F1
Elm Gdns IP11 152 C7
Elm Gr
Garboldisham IP22 18 D4
5 Nayland CO6 102 C5
Elm La
Capel St. Mary IP9 150 E3
Copdock & Washbrook IP8 95 F4
Elm Lodge Rd 7 IP13 40 B3
Elm Rd
East Bergholt CO7 151 B5
Ipswich IP5 140 F7
Stowmarket IP14 124 C6
Sudbury CO10 148 E5
Thetford IP24 16 B4
Wickham Market IP13 127 B6
Elm St IP1 155 B3
Elm Tree Cl 1 IP14 51 E1
Elm Tree La 5 CO6 102 A7
Elm Tree Mid Sch NR33 114 E5
Elm Tree Prim Sch NR33 114 E5
Elm Tree Rd NR33 114 E5
Elm Tree Rd W NR33 114 E5
Elm Way IP14 51 F6
Elm Wlk 30 IP27 13 F2
Elmcroft La IP11 153 C7
Elmcroft Rd IP1 135 A2
Elmdale Dr
Lowestoft NR33 114 D4
29 Mistley CO11 104 E2
Elmers La IP5 141 D7
Elmham Dr IP10 145 B8
Elmhurst Ave NR32 112 E1
Elmhurst Cl CB9 132 F5
Elmhurst Dr IP3 139 F3
Elmhurst Rd 17 CO12 107 B2
Elms Cl 6 Earsham NR35 7 F4
Great Barton IP31 49 B6
Elms La NR34 26 E2
Elms Rd Cowlinge CB8 75 B7
Freckenham IP28 29 F2
Elms The 4 IP29 63 A8
Elmsett CE Prim Sch IP7 80 F1
Elmsett Cl IP14 124 F3
Elmsett Rd IP8 81 B3
Elmsley Way IP17 57 C8
Elmswell Rd
Great Ashfield IP31 50 F6
Wetherden IP14 51 A1
Elmswell Sta IP30 50 E3
Elmtree Bsns Pk IP30 50 E3
Elsmere Rd IP1 139 C8
Elton Pk IP2 138 D6
Elveden CE Prim Sch IP24 15 C2
Elveden Rd IP24 15 F2
Elvedon Way CB8 120 E5
Ely Cl IP33 123 B3
Ely Rd 5 Claydon IP6 82 B5
Ipswich IP4 135 F1
Soham CB7 28 B6
Embry Cres 10 IP7 80 D6
Emerald Cl IP5 141 C8
Emily Frost Cl 4 CB8 61 E2
Emlen St IP1 155 A3
Emmanuel Cl
Ipswich IP2 138 F2
Mildenhall IP28 116 D5
Emsworth Cl 2 IP32 123 D6
Endway The CB9 88 E4
Engine Rd CB7 28 B5
Ennerdale Cl 2 IP11 153 D6
Enstone Rd NR33 115 B6
Enterprise Bsns Pk IP33 154 C4
Entry The IP23 52 D8
Epsom Dr IP1 135 A4
Erbury Pl CO10 90 A8
Eriswell Dr IP27 109 D5
Eriswell Rd
Beck Row, Holywell Row & Kenny Hill IP28 13 E1
Haverhill CB9 132 F6
Lakenheath IP27 109 D4
Ernleigh Rd IP4 140 B6
Erratts Hill CB8 61 B1
Errington Way IP30 50 B2
Erskine Rd 14 CO11 104 E2
Erwarton Hall* IP9 106 E6
Erwarton Wlk IP9 106 E6
Eskdale Way NR32 113 A4
Essex Ave CO10 148 D7
Essex Rd NR32 113 B1
Essex Way IP3 140 E1
Estuary Cres 5 IP9 107 A4
Estuary Dr IP11 153 D7
Estuary Rd 7 IP9 107 A4
Ethel Mann Rd 5 NR35 110 C2
Ethel Rd NR32 113 D1
Etna Rd IP33 154 B4
Euro Ret Pk IP3 140 E1
Europa Rd NR32 113 C4
Europa Way
9 Harwich CO12 106 F2
Ipswich IP1 138 D8
Euroscope* NR32 113 E2
Eustace Rd IP1 138 E8
Euston Ave IP4 140 F6
Euston Cl IP33 154 A1
Euston Ct 4 IP11 152 C4
Euston Hall* IP24 16 E1
Evans Cl IP18 119 C7
Evans Dr NR32 113 B2
Evans' Heath CO10 93 F4
Eve Balfour Way IP14 66 D8
Evelyn Cl IP21 38 C7
Everard Cl 5 IP32 122 E8
Evergreen La CB8 74 C8
Evergreen Rd NR32 113 B2
Everitt Rd NR33 114 D8
Everton Cres IP1 134 F1
Eves Ct 12 CO12 106 E1
Evesham Cl 7 IP2 139 A2
Exchange Sq 6 NR34 111 B5
Exchange St 32 IP20 22 D6
Exeter Cres IP27 109 F1
Exeter Rd 9 Claydon IP6 82 B5
Felixstowe IP11 152 F5
Ipswich IP3 140 B4
Newmarket CB8 121 A4
Newmarket CB8 121 A4
Exmoor Rd IP11 152 F6
Exning Prim Sch CB8 120 B8
Exning Rd CB8 120 D6
Eye Airfield Ind Est IP23 117 A6
Eye Castle* IP23 117 D2
Eye Hill Dro CB7 28 B7
Eye Rd IP23 37 C5
Eyke CE Prim Sch IP12 85 B6
Eyke Rd IP12 85 A5
Eyre Cl IP33 154 B1

F

Factory La
Brantham CO11 104 E4
Chevington IP29 62 C5
Diss IP22 20 B3
Factory St NR32 113 D2
Fagbury Rd IP11 152 A4
Fair Cl Beccles NR34 111 B5
14 Feltwell IP26 4 E5
Fair View Rd IP19 118 C5
Fairbairn Ave 1 IP5 141 D7
Fairey Fox Dr 2 IP28 116 B5
Fairfax Ct NR34 111 B3
Fairfax Gdns IP6 125 E4
Fairfield Ave IP11 153 A5
Fairfield Cres IP13 126 D3
Fairfield Dr
Lowestoft NR33 114 D6
Saxmundham IP17 128 C3
Fairfield Hill IP14 124 D6
Fairfield Rd
Aldeburgh IP15 130 D5
Bungay NR35 110 C2
Framlingham IP13 126 D2
Ipswich IP3 140 A2
Lowestoft NR33 114 D6
Saxmundham IP17 128 C3
Saxmundham IP17 128 C3
Fairfield Way 12 IP26 4 E5
Fairfields IP24 16 C7
Fairhaven Way CB8 120 E5
Fairhead Loke NR33 114 B1
Fairlawns Rd CB8 120 F2
Fairlight Cl 2 IP4 136 A1
Fairmead IP30 50 F3
Fairmile Cl 2 NR34 111 F4
Fairstead House Sch CB8 121 B4
Fairstead The IP22 36 A7
Fairway The
Aldeburgh IP15 130 C6
6 Great Yarmouth NR31 3 B8
Lowestoft NR33 114 F5
Fairways The IP4 140 E5
Fakenham Hill IP31 33 F5
Falcon Ave IP22 20 D3
Falcon Cl CB9 133 A6
Falcon Dr IP27 6 A1
Falcon Inn Rd NR34 26 C7
Falcon La NR35 110 B5
Falcon Rd 15 IP26 4 E5
Falcon St
Felixstowe IP11 152 E6
Ipswich IP1 155 B2
Falcon Way IP28 13 B1
Falconer Ave 3 IP14 51 E1
Falconer Rd CB9 133 A3
Falkenham Rd IP10 98 E2
Falklands Dr 21 CO11 104 E2
Falklands Rd CB9 132 E7
Fallowfield 2 IP30 49 F2
Fallowfields NR32 112 F5
Falmouth Ave CB8 120 F3
Falmouth Cl IP5 141 B6
Falmouth Gdns CB8 121 A6
Falmouth St CB8 120 F3
Famona Rd NR33 114 C2
Faraday Rd IP3 139 F5
Farford Field 5 CO10 92 B3
Farina Cl IP1 138 F7
Farlingaye Cty High Sch IP12 146 E6
Farlingayes IP12 146 F7
Farm Cl Bungay NR35 110 D3
Bury St Edmunds IP33 123 B1
5 Lowestoft NR33 114 D5
Wissett IP19 24 E2
Farm Ct St IP20 23 A5
Farmerie Rd CO10 75 D3
Farmland Cl IP18 119 B8
Farnham Cl 5 NR32 112 F4
Farnham Rd
Blaxhall IP12 71 F5
Snape IP17 72 D6
Farriers Cl
15 Martlesham Heath IP5 98 A8
Stradbroke IP21 39 B4
Farrier's Rd IP14 124 C3
Farriers Went IP11 152 D7
Farrow Cl IP16 129 B6
Farthing Dro
Beck Row, Holywell Row & Kenny Hill IP27 12 E6
Lakenheath IP27 13 A6
Farthing Rd IP1 138 C7
Farthings The IP28 31 D3
Farthings Went IP9 150 F4
Fastnet Cl CB9 133 B6
Fastolf Cl 4 NR32 113 A3
Faulkeners Way IP11 152 C7
Fawcett Rd IP15 130 E4
Fawley Cl IP4 140 C7
Fayrefield Rd IP12 147 B7
Feast Cl 7 CB7 29 A1
Featherbroom Gdns IP13 127 C5
Feathers Field 3 IP11 152 D5
Feilden Way CB8 120 E5
Felaw St IP2 155 C1
Felix Cl IP5 141 B7
Felix Rd
Felixstowe IP11 153 B4
Ipswich IP3 140 C2
5 Stowupland IP14 67 A6
Felixstowe General Hospl IP11 153 B4
Felixstowe Mus* IP11 107 E2
Felixstowe Rd
Ipswich IP3 139 F4
8 Martlesham IP5 98 A8
Felixstowe Sta IP11 153 A5
Fell Rd CO9 89 A4
Fellbrigg Ave IP5 140 F6
Felsham Chase CB5 44 B5
Felsham Ct IP14 124 F3
Felsham Rd
Bradfield St Clare IP30 64 D4
Rattlesden IP30 65 C5
Felsham Rise IP17 128 C3
Feltons 6 CB7 29 A1
Feltwell Rd IP26 4 F3
Fen Bank CB7 29 C6
Fen Ct NR33 115 A6
Fen La Ardleigh CO7 103 E1
Beccles NR34 111 B7
Beck Row, Holywell Row & Kenny Hill IP28 13 D1
Braiseworth IP23 37 D3
Creeting St Peter or West Creeting IP6 125 D8
Ditchingham NR35 7 E7
Garboldisham IP22 18 D3
Hitcham IP7 79 E5
Rickinghall Inferior IP22 36 A6
Roydon IP22 19 F3
Stonham Earl IP6 67 D4
Thelnetham IP22 18 E1
Fen Mdw IP11 152 C8
Fen Pk Prim Sch NR33 115 B6
Fen Rd Blo' Norton IP22 18 F2
Pakenham IP31 49 F6
Fen St Boxford CO10 93 C3
Hinderclay IP22 18 F1
Nayland CO6 102 D5
Fen View
Copdock & Washbrook IP8 95 F4
Thorndon IP23 53 B8
Fenbridge La CO7 151 B3
Fengate Dro IP27 5 E2
Fenlands Cres NR33 114 F6
Fenn Cl
Halesworth IP19 118 A5
Stowmarket IP14 124 D3
Fenn La IP12 98 D6
Fenstreet Rd IP17 58 A7
Fenton Rd CB9 132 F6
Fentons Way IP5 141 C7
Ferguson Way IP5 141 B8
Fern Ave NR32 112 D2
Fern Gn Cl 1 NR32 112 E4
Fern Gr CB9 132 C6
Fern Hill CO10 77 A4
Ferndale Ave NR32 113 B3
Ferndale Cl CB8 121 B6
Ferndown Rd 3 IP11 153 C6
Fernhayes Cl IP2 139 A3
Fernhill Cl IP12 147 A7
Fernlea Rd 9 CO12 107 B3
Ferry La
Beck Row, Holywell Row & Kenny Hill IP28 29 F5
Felixstowe IP11 152 C3
Ferry Rd Bawdsey IP12 99 D1
Felixstowe IP11 153 D7
Southwold IP18 119 C3
Sudbourne IP12 131 C6
Walberswick IP18 119 B2
Fersfield Rd IP22 19 D5
Festival Cl 4 IP17 72 C8
Festival Rd 14 CB7 29 C5
Feveryears Yd 4 IP21 39 D8
Fiddlers La CO7 151 C5
Fiddler's La IP23 117 F2
Field Cl 3 IP30 49 F2
Field Fuller's IP6 135 E4
Field House Gdns IP22 20 D2
Field La NR33 11 B1
Field Rd
Mildenhall IP28 116 C5
Mildenhall IP28 116 C5
Field Stile Rd 2 IP18 119 D5
Field Terr Rd CB8 120 F5
Field View
Bucklesham IP10 98 A4
Field View *continued*
8 Thurstow IP31 49 E4
Field View Gdns NR34 111 D3
Field Way
Debenham IP14 53 F1
18 Stanton IP31 34 E4
Field Wlk IP28 116 C5
Fields View CO10 148 D6
Fieldview Cl IP18 119 B8
Fieldview Dr NR32 113 A1
Fife Rd IP4 136 B1
Finbars Wlk IP4 139 F5
Finborough Cl IP4 140 F6
Finborough Rd IP14 124 B6
Finborough Sch IP14 66 B5
Finch Cl 7 IP14 67 A5
Finch Hill CO10 91 D4
Fincham Rd IP28 116 B5
Finchingfield Rd
Stambourne CO9 89 B1
Steeple Bumpstead CB9 88 E3
Finchley Ave IP28 116 B6
Finchley Rd IP4 139 E6
Findley Cl IP9 105 C5
Fingal St IP13 39 A1
Finney's Drift IP10 145 C5
Finningham Rd
Gislingham IP23 36 D1
Old Newton with Dagworth IP14 51 F2
Rickinghall Superior IP22 36 A4
Walsham-le-willows IP31 35 D2
Finsbury Pl IP33 154 B1
Finsbury Sq IP33 154 C1
Fir Cl Barnby NR34 10 C4
Mundford IP26 6 B8
Wickham Market IP13 127 C6
Fir La NR32 113 A2
Fir Rd IP24 16 B4
Fir Tree Cl IP21 22 D2
Fir Tree Hill IP9 105 F7
Fir Tree La IP14 51 C3
Fir Tree Rise IP8 138 C2
Fir Wlk 29 IP27 13 F2
Fircroft Rd IP1 135 A2
Firebrass La IP12 85 C2
Firebronds Rd 7 IP9 105 E7
Firefly Way IP3 144 B8
Firfield Cl NR34 111 B3
Firs The Beccles NR34 111 F4
Lakenheath IP27 109 E6
Lowestoft NR33 114 C3
Southwold IP18 119 B8
First Ave
4 Glemsford CO10 77 B3
Sudbury CO10 148 E7
First Dro Burwell CB5 44 B8
Lakenheath IP27 109 A8
Firtree Cl IP32 122 D7
Fish Pond Hill IP9 106 B6
Fishbane Cl 9 IP3 144 A8
Fisher Cl Haverhill CB9 133 B5
2 Saxmundham IP17 128 C2
Fisher Rd IP22 20 D2
Fisher Row
Carlton Colville NR32 114 B8
Lowestoft NR32 112 B1
Fisherman's Way 13 NR33 11 C1
Fisher's Dro IP28 12 D3
Fisher's La
East Bergholt CO7 104 E6
Hoxne IP21 38 C8
Fishpond Rd IP12 98 D7
Fishponds Hill CO6 102 C3
Fishponds La IP9 105 F7
Fishponds Way IP14 66 C8
Fison Way IP24 16 B7
Fitches The IP17 129 A2
Fitzgerald Cl 4 CO11 104 D2
Fitzgerald Rd
Bramford IP8 134 A1
Woodbridge IP12 147 A6
Fitzmaurice Rd IP3 140 B3
Fitzroy St Ipswich IP1 155 B3
Newmarket CB8 120 F3
Fitzwilliam Cl
Ipswich IP2 138 F2
6 Woodbridge IP12 146 E4
Five Acre La NR35 7 E3
Five Acres 12 IP9 105 E7
Five Cross Ways
Butley IP12 86 B4
Sudbourne IP12 131 B6
Wetheringsett-cum-brockford IP23 53 A7
Flatford Cl IP14 124 E3
Flatford La CO7 151 D1
Flatford Mill (National Trust)* CO7 151 D1
Flatford Rd
East Bergholt CO7 151 D2
Haverhill CB9 132 A6
Flatts La IP30 50 B2
Flavian Cl CB9 133 B5
Flax La CO10 77 B2
Fleet Dyke Dr NR33 114 E5
Fleetwood Ave IP11 153 B5
Fleetwood Rd IP11 153 B5
Fleming Ave IP28 116 C5
Flempton Rd IP28 47 D5
Flemyng Rd IP33 122 C5
Fletcher Cl 3 IP6 82 A5
Fletcher Rd IP3 140 A4
Fletchers La IP5 141 E8
Fletcher's La IP17 58 B6
Flindell Dr IP8 134 A2
Flint Cl IP2 139 B2

Flixton Marsh La NR32 ....112 B6
Flixton Rd
Blundeston NR32 ....112 C8
Bungay NR35 ....110 A1
Flixton NR32 ....23 E2
St Mary, South Elmham
Otherwise Homersfield IP20 ....23 B8
Somerleyton, Ashby & Herringfleet NR32 ....2 F4
Flora Rd NR33 ....115 A3
Fiordon Rd IP4 ....125 E5
Florence Rd NR33 ....115 B3
Flowerday Cl 4 NR31 .....3 B7
Flowton Rd Elmsett IP7 ...81 A1
Flowton IP8 ....95 B8
Somersham IP8 ....81 C3
Floyd Rd IP32 ....122 D8
Flying Hospl C28 ....121 A3
Foal's Gn Rd IP21 ....39 D2
Fodderfen Dro
Beck Row, Holywell Row & Kenny Hill IP28 ....12 C1
Feltwell IP28 ....4 A3
Foden Ave IP1 ....134 C2
Folly Cl IP15 ....130 D5
Folly La
Bressingham IP22 ....19 F4
Copdock & Washbrook IP8 ....95 E2
Lawshall IP29 ....63 C3
Folly The Harleston NR16 ...66 C8
Haughley IP14 ....51 C1
Fonnereau Rd IP1 ....155 B3
Forbes Dr NR34 ....111 B3
Ford Cl
Beck Row, Holywell Row & Kenny Hill IP28 ....29 F7
Stowmarket IP14 ....124 E4
Ford Hill IP12 ....99 B7
Ford Rd IP12 ....71 C5
Ford View Rd IP14 ....99 B7
Fordham Cl NR34 ....29 A3
Fordham Pl IP4 ....140 F5
Fordham Road
Fordham C88 ....44 F7
Freckenham IP28 ....29 D2
Fordham Rd C06 ....101 C1
Fordham St 120 F7
Snailwell C88 ....45 A7
7 Soham C87 ....28 D3
Fordham Road C06 ....28 F2
Fordham Rd C06 ....126 F1
Fordhams Cl 2 IP31 ....34 E4
Fordley Rd IP17 ....57 F6
Fore Hamlet IP3 ....139 E5
Fore St
Framlingham IP13 ....126 D3
Ipswich IP4 ....155 C2
Forest End 46 A7
Forest Glade C89 ....132 D8
Forest La IP15 ....98 A7
Forest Mount NR31 ....4 F7
Forest Prim Sch IP27 ....5 F1
Forest Ret Pk IP24 ....16 A5
Forest La IP15 ....66 B6
Forester Cl IP8 ....142 E8
Foresters Wlk 6 IP6 ....82 A5
Forfar Cl 2 Ipswich IP4 ...136 B1
Ipswich IP4 ....140 B8
Forge Cl 28 Benhall IP17 ...72 C8
Bucklesham IP10 ....98 A4
Palgrave IP22 ....20 C1
Forge End IP28 ....48 B6
Forge Gr NR34 ....12 F6
Forge St C07 ....104 A3
Fornham La IP33 ....122 A7
Fornham Road
7 Bury St Edmunds IP32 ...123 A8
Bury St Edmunds IP32 ...154 B4
Fornham St Martin IP31 ...48 D5
Fornham Rd IP31 ....49 A5
Forties Cl IP9 ....133 B6
Fortress Rd NR33 ....114 E3
Foster Cl IP18 ....119 D6
Foster Rd IP12 ....106 F3
Foundation St IP4 ....155 B2
Foundry La IP1 ....155 B2
Fountain La C28 ....28 D4
Fountain Rd 6 IP32 ....122 A8
Fountain Way IP18 ....119 C8
Fountains La NR34 ....10 C4
Fountains Rd
Bury St Edmunds IP33 ...122 D2
Our Ash Hill C09 ....89 C4
Our Wheel Dr IP30 ....49 B2
Fourth Ave IP24 ....77 A3
Fowe's La C010 ....90 D4
Fowler's Cres 2 NR32 ...3 D4
Fox & Pin La IP29 ....63 E8
Fox Cl IP14 ....124 D6
Fox Gn C88 ....74 C8
Fox Hill Hollesley IP12 ...99 C7
St Cross, South Elmham IP20 ....23 C7
Fox La IP5 ....141 E8
Fox Lea IP5 ....142 B8
Fox Wood N 7 C87 ....28 D5
Fox Wood S 11 C87 ....28 D5

Foxborough Mid Sch NR32 ....113 A5
Foxborough Rd NR32 ...113 A5
Foxburrow Cl CB9 ....132 D7
Foxburrow Hill NR32 ...89 E5
Mendham IP20 ....23 B4
Foxes La Ashen C010 ...89 E5
Mendham IP20 ....23 B4
Foxes Cl C010 ....89 E5
Foxglade IP12 ....112 C2
Foxglove Ave IP6 ....125 D3
Foxglove Cl
Lowestoft NR33 ....115 B4
1 Worlingham NR34 ...111 E3
Foxglove Cres IP3 ....140 E1
Foxglove Rd IP24 ....16 C6
Foxgrove Gdns IP11 ...153 C5
Foxgrove La IP11 ....153 C5
Foxhall Cl C07 ....151 C6
Foxhall Fields C07 ....151 C5
Foxhall Rd Foxhall IP10 ...98 A6
Ipswich IP3 ....139 F5
Foxhall Stadium IP4 ...141 A5
Foxtail Rd IP3 ....144 D8
Foxwood Cl C011 ....144 A8
Foxwood Cres IP4 ....140 F5
Framfield Rd NR33 ....114 C4
Framlingham 4 IP12 ...85 B3
Framlingham Coll IP13 ....126 C5
**Framlingham Castle (remains of)* ** IP13 ....126 C5
Framlingham
Dennington IP13 ....39 F2
Easton IP13 ....70 E5
Laxfield IP13 ....40 A2
Framlingham Coll Jun Sch IP13 ....70 A7
Frampton Rd IP3 ....144 A8
Framsden Rd IP14 ....69 E7
Francis Cl
Haverhill CB9 ....132 D6
Ipswich IP5 ....141 E8
Francis Rd
16 Kessingland NR33 ...11 B1
3 Sudbury C010 ....148 C5
Franciscan Way IP1 ...155 B2
Frank Bridges Cl 4 CB7 ...28 C3
Franklin Cl IP15 ....130 D5
Franklin Rd
Aldeburgh IP15 ....109 A5
Ipswich IP3 ....140 B2
Fraser Rd
Bramford IP8 ....134 B2
Ipswich IP4 ....138 F7
Freckenham Rd IP28 ...29 D2
Fred Archer Way C88 ...121 A3
Fred Dannatt Rd IP28 ...29 F7
Frederick Talbot Cl 14 ....28 A4
Frederick's Rd 8 NR34 ...111 C4
Free La NR35 ....110 A8
Freehold Rd
Ipswich IP4 ....140 A6
Needham Market IP6 ...125 C6
Freelands IP14 ....138 E8
Freeman Ave 4 IP4 ...82 D6
Freeman Prim Sch IP14 ....67 B7
Freemantle Rd IP3 ....115 C7
Freewood St IP30 ....64 D6
Frenze Hall La IP22 ...20 D3
Frenze Rd IP22 ....20 D2
Frere Cnr IP22 ....20 A3
Frere Rd 12 IP22 ....22 C6
Freshfields
17 Harwich C012 ...106 F1
Newmarket C88 ....120 F4
Fressingfield CE Prim Sch IP21 ....39 D8
Fressingfield Rd IP20 ...23 C1
Freston Hill IP9 ....143 E4
Freston St IP9 ....143 F4
**Freston Twr* ** IP9 ....143 F4
Friar Cl IP33 ....132 D2
Friars Bridge Rd IP1 ...155 A2
Friars Cl
Bury St Edmunds IP33 ...154 B1
3 Felixstowe IP11 ....153 D6
Friars Croft 22 D3
Friar's La IP33 ....154 B1
Friars Mdw IP22 ....22 D3
Friars Rd IP7 ....149 C6
Friars St Ipswich IP1 ...155 B2
Sudbury C010 ....148 C5
Friday Mdw IP28 ....48 D5
Friday St
Beck Row, Holywell Row & Kenny Hill IP28 ....29 F6
Rendlesham IP12 ....85 D7
Friday's Orch IP14 ....126 B6
Friends Field 7 C08 ...101 C5
Friends Wlk IP5 ....141 D8
Friston Rd IP17 ....72 C2
Fristonmoor La
Knodishall IP17 ....57 E1
Sternfield IP17 ....72 E8
Fritillary Cl IP18 ....142 E8
Fritton Cl IP2 ....139 A1
**Fritton Lake City World* ** NR31 ....2 C6
Frobisher Rd
21 Harwich C012 ...106 F1
Stowmarket IP14 ....139 E1
Frog Hall La IP7 ....149 F6
Frogmore C88 ....120 B7
Frogs Alley IP9 ....106 F6

Frogs Hall Rd C010 ...78 D5
Frogs Hole NR32 ....2 C5
Fronk's Ave 8 C012 ...107 B1
Fronk's Rd C012 ....107 A1
Front Rd 144 D8
Front St
Mendlesham IP14 ....52 E4
Orford IP12 ....131 B3
Ousden C88 ....62 C6
Frostenden Cres 1 NR32 ....113 B4
Frowel Cl IP7 ....29 B1
Fryatt Ave 7 C012 ...107 A2
Fryth Cl CB9 ....132 D6
Fuchsia La IP14 ....140 A5
Fulchers Field IP13 ...126 B4
Fulford Cl 8 IP20 ....48 C6
Fuller Rd IP20 ....22 D5
Fullers Cl 2 IP7 ....149 E6
Fulmar Way IP14 ....140 A5
Fulmerston Rd IP24 ...16 B5
Furness Cl IP7 ....142 F8
Further St C010 ....92 E2
Furthen Dro IP27 ....4 D1
Furze Cl 4 IP11 ....153 D5
Furze Way IP22 ....36 D5
Fyfe Way 12 NR33 ....115 D8
Fynn La IP7 ....136 C5
Fynn Rd IP12 ....146 D3

G

Gaell Cres 6 IP7 ....149 D5
Gage Cl IP27 ....154 A4
Gage's Rd C010 ....90 C4
Gainsborough La IP3 ...143 F8
Gainsborough Rd
Bury St Edmunds IP33 ...122 D5
Felixstowe IP11 ....153 A4
Haverhill CB9 ....132 B7
Ipswich IP4 ....155 C4
Stowmarket IP14 ....124 B6
Sudbury C010 ....148 C5
Gainsborough St C010 ....148 C5
**Gainsborough's House Mus* ** C010 ....148 C5
Galley Rd C010 ....75 D3
Gallow La IP30 ....78 C7
Gallows Hill
Hadleigh IP7 ....149 B7
Hadleigh IP7 ....149 C7
Gallows La IP14 ....66 C7
Galway Ave IP4 ....134 E1
Gandish Rd C07 ....151 E4
Ganges Rd 8 IP9 ....106 B5
Gannet Cl IP3 ....133 A6
Gannet Rd IP2 ....138 E3
Ganwick Cl CB9 ....132 D8
Gaol La Beccles NR34 ...111 B5
Sudbury C010 ....148 C5
Gap The NR33 ....115 D5
Garboldisham Prim Sch 18 D4
Garboldisham Rd
Harling NR16 ....18 C7
Kenninghall NR16 ....18 F7
Garden Cl
Bungay NR35 ....110 A3
3 Great Barton IP31 ...49 A6
Garden Ct 2 C010 ....148 B6
Garden Field 2 IP11 ...152 E5
Garden Fields IP31 ...33 D3
Garden House La IP30 ...45 C6
Garden La
Beccles NR34 ....111 C4
Westley IP33 ....122 A5
Gardeners La 4 IP21 ...24 C8
Gardeners Rd IP14 ....53 F1
Gardeners Wlk IP30 ...50 E2
Gardenhouse La IP22 ...36 A2
Gardens The
8 Beyton IP30 ....49 F2
Lowestoft NR33 ....114 C2
Gardiner Cl IP13 ....122 C4
Gardner Rd IP18 ....119 D5
Garfield Cl IP11 ....152 F3
Garfield Rd IP11 ....152 F3
Garland Rd 8 C010 ...106 F3
Garland St IP33 ....154 B3
Garlic St IP21 ....22 A6
Garnons Chase 3 C06 ...101 F2
Garrard Pl 7 IP31 ....50 F1
Garrards Rd 3 IP7 ....80 F1
Garrett Cres IP16 ....129 D5
Garrick Way IP1 ....135 A3
Garrison La
Felixstowe IP11 ....152 F4
5 Great Waldingfield C010 ...92 C4
Garrod App IP12 ....84 E7
Garrod's Rd IP7 ....150 F3
Garrods End IP29 ....62 C7
Gas Works Rd IP18 ...119 D6
Gascoigne Dr 3 IP5 ...82 D6
Gashouse Dro IP27 ....5 F1
Gaston Cl C07 ....151 C5
Gaston St C07 ....151 B4
Gatacre Rd IP1 ....139 A7
Gate Farm Rd 2 IP9 ...107 A5
Gatesbury's La IP29 ...62 C2
Gateway The IP33 ....123 C3
Gavell St IP19 ....24 D5

Gawdy Cl 2 IP20 ....22 D6
Gaye Cres IP23 ....117 B3
Gaye St IP1 ....155 A3
Gayfer Ave IP5 ....141 F8
Gayford Sq IP7 ....80 C6
Gaymers La IP11 ....152 B8
Gazeley Prim Sch C88 ...46 B3
Gazeley Rd Ashley C88 ...46 A5
Kentford C88 ....46 A5
Gedding Hill IP30 ....65 B4
Gedding Rd IP30 ....65 B7
Gedge Cl IP33 ....122 C4
Gedgrave Rd IP12 ....131 A1
Geldeston Hill NR34 ...8 F6
Geldeston Rd
Geldeston NR34 ....8 D6
Gillingham NR34 ....9 B6
General Castle Way IP30 ....49 B2
Generals Mews 12 IP11 ...152 D5
Genesta Dr 2 IP31 ....49 D4
Geneva Gdns 4 NR31 ...3 D6
Geneva Rd IP1 ....155 A4
Gents La IP29 ....77 F7
George Baldry Way 2 NR33 ....110 C2
George Brown Way NR34 ....111 C3
George Cyprian 2 IP24 ...155 C4
George Gent Cl 7 C04 ...155 C3
George Gibson Cl 120 C8
George Hill IP31 ....34 E4
George La 3 C010 ....77 B2
George St Hadleigh IP7 ...149 E6
4 Harwich C012 ....107 B3
Hintlesham IP8 ....95 C6
George Westwood Way NR34 ....111 C6
Gerald's Ave IP1 ....140 A5
Gestingthorpe Rd C010 ...90 F2
Gibbon Cl IP12 ....123 E5
Gibraltar Cl IP33 ....122 C6
Gibraltar Rd IP6 ....82 C6
Gifford Cl 8 IP9 ....105 E7
**Gifford's Hall* ** C06 ...103 B8
Giffords Pl IP4 ....125 C5
Gilbert Cl IP4 ....125 C5
Gilbert Rd 2 C010 ....90 A8
Giles Way Risby IP28 ...47 A7
4 Withersham IP6 ....83 A5
Gillingham Rd NR34 ...9 A6
Gillingham Dam NR34 ...111 A2
Gilray Rd IP23 ....20 D2
Gilstrap Rd IP31 ....48 D5
Gimbert Rd 2 CB7 ....28 C5
Gin La IP13 ....40 C2
Gippeswyk Ave IP2 ...139 A4
Gippeswyk Rd IP2 ....155 A1
Gipping Pl IP14 ....132 C4
Gipping Rd IP14 ....124 A6
Gipping Rd Claydon IP6 ...82 A5
Stowupland IP14 ....67 A7
Gipping Way
Bramford IP8 ....134 A2
Sproughton IP8 ....138 B6
Stowmarket IP14 ....124 D7
Gipsy La
Aldringham cum Thorpe IP16 ....129 D1
Frostenden NR34 ....25 C6
Needham Market IP6 ...125 C6
Girling St C010 ....148 C6
Girton Cl
Mildenhall IP28 ....116 C6
Woodbridge IP12 ....146 A4
Woodditton C88 ....121 B1
Girton Rd C89 ....132 F5
Girton Way IP12 ....138 F1
Gisleham Mid Sch NR33 ....114 C1
Gisleham CE Prim Sch IP33 ....114 B1
Gislingham CE Prim Sch IP23 ....36 D2
Gislingham Rd IP14 ....36 C1
Gissing Rd IP22 ....20 F6
Glade Prim Sch IP24 ...5 F1
Glade The IP24 ....16 C7
Glades The IP12 ....112 D2
Gladstone Rd
1 Corton NR32 ....3 C4
6 Woodbridge IP12 ...147 A5
Glamis Cl IP30 ....22 D6
Glamorgan Rd IP2 ....139 B1
Glanville Pl IP5 ....141 B6
Glanville Rd IP7 ....149 E4
Glastonbury Cl IP14 ...134 D4
Glastonbury Cl IP2 ...138 F1
Glastonbury Rd IP2 ...122 C3
Glebe Cl Bayham IP6 ...81 E6
Horringer IP29 ....63 A7
Ingham IP31 ....32 F1
Lowestoft NR33 ....115 B4
Sproughton IP8 ....138 B6
7 Tattingstone IP9 ....105 B8
Glebe End IP9 ....150 F4
Glebe La IP29 ....62 C6
Glebe Mdws IP13 ....54 F2
Glebe Rd Bredfield IP13 ...84 C7
Gissing IP21 ....21 A8
Weeting IP27 ....5 E3
Glebe Rd E 18 NR33 ...11 C1

Glebe Rd W 18 NR33 ...11 B1
Glebe The
Haverhill CB9 ....132 E7
Lavenham C010 ....78 D3
Glebe Way 1 Claydon IP6 ...82 B5
Mendlesham IP17 ....72 D5
Glebes The IP17 ....140 F4
Glemham Dr 4 IP4 ...13 F3
**Glemham Hall* ** IP13 ...71 E6
Glemham Rd IP17 ....56 E2
Glemsford Cl IP11 ....153 C6
Glemsford Com Prim Sch C010 ....77 A3
Glemsford Rd
Lowestoft NR32 ....112 F4
Stowmarket IP14 ....124 E4
Glenavon Rd 2 IP14 ...140 D7
Glenbourne Wlk 2 NR33 ....114 C3
Glencoe Rd IP4 ....136 C1
Gleneagles Cl
4 Bury St Edmunds IP28 ...48 C6
6 Felixstowe IP11 ....153 D5
Gleneagles Dr IP4 ....140 D5
Glenfield Ave IP1 ....153 A6
Glenhurst Ave IP4 ....140 B8
Glenside C010 ....148 C6
Glenwood Dr NR34 ...111 E4
Gloster Rd IP5 ....98 A8
Gloucester Ave NR32 ...112 F3
Gloucester Pl 6 C010 ...76 A1
Gloucester Rd
7 Bury St Edmunds IP32 ...48 C5
2 Bury St Edmunds IP32 ...122 E8
Ipswich IP2 ....132 D5
Ipswich IP3 ....140 A2
Gloucester Way C010 ...148 B8
Gobbets La IP22 ....35 E7
Gobbett's Rd IP22 ....35 E8
Godbold Cl 8 IP5 ....141 D7
Goddard Pl IP14 ....66 B7
Goddard Rd IP1 ....134 C3
Goddard Rd E IP1 ....134 D3
Godetia Cl 2 NR33 ....113 B4
Godfrey's Hill IP19 ....40 D8
Godfrey's Wood IP12 ...147 A7
Godolphin Cl IP33 ....122 C3
Godyll Rd IP18 ....119 C5
Goldcrest Rd IP2 ....138 C2
Golden La IP29 ....63 C2
Golden Lion La 5 C012 ...107 B3
Golden Miller Cl C88 ...120 D7
Goldenlond C06 ....102 E7
Golding Way 8 C010 ...77 A2
Golding's CDR IP12 ...132 E8
Golding's La IP12 ....129 C4
Goldsmith Rd IP1 ....134 E3
Goldsmith Way IP21 ...21 B8
Golf Links Rd
Barton Mills IP28 ....30 C3
Worlington IP28 ....116 A1
Golf Rd IP11 ....153 D5
Gondree NR33 ....114 E3
Gonville Cl
Mildenhall IP28 ....116 D6
1 Woodbridge IP12 ...146 E4
Goodall Terr IP5 ....141 E8
Goodchilds Gdns 8 CB7 ...29 C5
Goodlake Cl C010 ....106 F1
Goodwood Cl IP1 ....135 B4
Goose Gn E NR34 ....111 C5
Goose Gn W NR34 ....111 C5
Gorams Mill La IP13 ...40 B3
Gordon Rd
5 Harwich C012 ....107 A1
Ipswich IP4 ....140 A7
Lowestoft NR32 ....112 E1
Gordon Richards Cl C88 ....120 C8
Goring Rd IP4 ....141 C8
Gorleston Rd
Blundeston NR32 ....112 C8
Corton NR32 ....3 B4
Gorse La
Lakenheath IP27 ....109 E4
8 Red Lodge IP28 ....30 C1
Gorse Hill Est IP12 ...36 C1
Gorse La IP18 ....119 B5
Gorse Rd Ipswich IP3 ...140 B2
Lowestoft NR33 ....114 C8
Gorse View IP17 ....58 C8
Gorsehayes IP2 ....139 B4
Gorselands Prim Sch IP5 ....141 F8
Gorselands IP22 ....99 F7
Gorst Cl IP32 ....122 E8
Gosford Cl IP14 ....90 A8
Gosford Way IP11 ....153 C6
Gosling Pl IP1 ....141 E8
Gothic Cl 8 IP20 ....22 D5
Gotsfield Cl 1 C010 ...92 B7
Gough Pl 8 IP31 ....34 E4
Gower St IP2 ....155 B1
Gowers Cl IP5 ....141 C7
Gowers End 8 C010 ...77 B3
Gowle Rd IP14 ....124 C8
Gowrie Cl IP4 ....152 F4
Gracchurch St IP14 ...53 E2
Grafton Way IP1 ....155 A2
Grafton Cl IP31 ....48 B8
Grafton Rd 2 C012 ...107 B2
Grafton Way IP1 ....155 B2

168 Gra - Har

Graham Ave IP1 139 B8
Graham Rd
Felixstowe IP11 152 F5
Ipswich IP1 155 A4
Grainge Way 3 IP14 51 C1
Grainger Cl IP32 123 F5
Grammar Sch Pl 11
CO10 148 C5
Grampian Way NR32 112 D2
Granaries The IP6 136 C6
Granary Crafts Brook Farm*
IP14 66 A5
Granary The CO10 90 A7
Granby St CB8 121 B3
Grand Ave NR33 115 B3
Grange Cl
Felixstowe IP11 152 E5
Ipswich IP5 141 F8
Grange Ct IP12 147 B6
Grange Farm Ave
IP11 152 D5
Grange La
Barton Mills IP28 116 D2
Ipswich IP5 141 E8
Grange Mill 3 IP29 62 C6
Grange Prim Sch
IP11 152 D4
Grange Rd
Beccles NR34 111 A4
Felixstowe IP11 152 D3
Flixton NR35 23 E8
16 Harwich CO12 107 A2
Ipswich IP4 139 E6
Lawford CO11 104 C1
Lowestoft NR32 112 D2
Wickham Skeith IP23 52 D7
Grange View IP17 58 B7
Grantchester Pl IP5 141 A8
Grantchester Rise CB5 44 A7
Grantham Cres IP2 155 A1
Granville Gdns IP28 116 A4
Granville Rd IP11 152 F3
Granville St IP1 155 A3
Granworth Cl IP13 83 E6
Grasmere Ave 5 IP11 153 D6
Gravel Dam NR32 112 B2
Gravel Dro IP28 29 E6
Gravel Hill CO6 102 D5
Gravel Hill Way CO12 106 F1
Gravel Pit La CO11 104 F5
Grayling Rd IP8 142 E8
Graylings The 10 NR33 114 E4
Gray's La IP19 24 D4
Gray's Orch IP10 98 E2
Grays Rd NR34 10 C7
Grayson Ave NR33 115 A3
Grayson Dr NR33 115 A2
Great Back La 4 IP14 53 F2
Great Barton Prim Sch
IP31 49 B6
Great Colman St IP4 155 C3
Great Comm La NR34 8 E1
Great Conard Ctry Pk*
CO10 92 B2
Great Cornard Mid Sch
CO10 92 B2
Great Cornard Upper Sch
CO10 148 F2
Great Dro CB7 28 A4
Great Eastern Rd
CO10 148 D5
Great Fen Rd CB7 28 D8
Great Field IP11 152 C8
Great Gipping St IP1 155 A2
Great Harlings IP9 107 A5
Great Heath Prim Sch
IP28 116 D6
Great Oak Cour CO9 90 A1
Great Tufts IP9 150 F3
Great Whelnetham CE Prim
Sch IP30 63 F6
Great Whip St IP2 155 B1
Grebe Cl Ipswich IP2 138 E2
Mildenhall IP28 116 D3
Stowmarket IP14 124 A6
Green Acre 2 CO10 92 C6
Green Cres IP10 98 A4
Green Dr NR33 115 A4
Green Farm La 5 IP29 47 A2
Green Fleet Dr NR32 112 E4
Green Hill IP6 68 B1
Green King Brewing Mus*
IP33 154 C1
Green La Boxted CO4 102 E3
Burgh St Peter NR34 10 C8
Cockfield IP30 64 D2
Creeting St Mary IP14 67 F5
Ditchingham NR35 110 C7
Earsham NR35 7 E6
6 Feltwell IP26 4 E5
Frostenden NR34 26 C4
Great Barton IP31 49 B5
Hundon CO10 75 D2
Kessingland NR33 11 C1
3 Martlesham IP12 84 A1
Pettistree IP13 127 D5
Redenhall with Harleston
IP20 22 E6
Reydon IP18 26 E1
Shipmeadow NR34 8 F5
Somerleyton, Ashby &
Herringfleet NR32 2 E4
Southwold IP18 119 B8
Starston IP20 22 D8
Stratford St Mary CO7 103 E6
Green La *continued*
Syleham IP21 38 E8
2 Tattingstone IP9 105 B8
Thelnetham IP22 35 C6
Thetford IP24 16 C6
Thrandeston IP21 37 B6
Troston IP31 33 C5
Tuddenham St Martin
IP6 136 C4
Wetheringsett-cum-brockford
IP14 53 A6
Green La Cl IP18 119 B8
Green Man Pl IP12 71 F2
Green Man Way IP12 147 B6
Green Oak Glade IP8 142 D8
Green Pk Brinkley CB8 59 E1
42 Harleston IP20 22 D6
Green Rd Brandon IP27 6 A1
Newmarket CB8 121 A2
Thorpe Morieux IP30 64 F1
Woolpit IP30 50 D1
Green St IP21 38 C8
Green The 4 Ashley CB8 60 F8
Beck Row, Holywell Row
& Kenny Hill IP28 29 E7
Chedburgh IP29 62 C4
8 Earsham NR35 7 F4
1 Grundisburgh IP13 83 E5
Hadleigh IP7 149 E6
Hessett IP30 64 F8
Kersey IP7 94 A7
Kirtling CB8 60 E3
Lound NR32 2 F6
Lowestoft NR33 114 F6
Mendlesham IP14 52 D2
2 Mistley CO11 104 F2
North Lopham IP22 19 A6
Snailwell CB8 45 A6
Green Willows CO10 78 C2
Greenacre Cres 1
NR32 113 B2
Greenacres IP14 51 F1
Greenbank IP19 118 C5
Greene Rd IP33 122 C6
Greenfield Rd NR33 114 F5
Greenfields CB8 121 C3
Greenfields Way CB9 132 C5
Greenfinch Ave IP2 138 D3
Greenhills CB7 28 E3
Greens The
Aldeburgh IP15 130 C6
Ipswich IP4 140 F4
Greensmill 2 CO11 104 E3
Greenspire Gr IP8 138 B2
Greenview IP29 77 B7
Greenway 4 IP31 49 A5
Greenway The NR34 111 B4
Greenways IP12 85 C2
Greenways Cl IP1 139 B8
Greenways Cres IP32 123 D6
Greenwich Bsns Pk
IP3 139 E2
Greenwich Cl IP3 139 E2
Greenwich Rd IP3 139 D2
Greenwood Cl CB9 132 C5
Greenwood Way 1
NR32 113 A6
Greenwoods The IP31 49 E6
Gregory Rd IP28 116 A6
Gregory St CO10 148 C5
Grenadier Rd CB9 132 A6
Grenville Rd CO10 148 D8
Gresham Ave NR32 112 F2
Gresham Cl NR32 112 F2
Gresham Rd NR34 111 C6
Gresley Gdns 3 IP2 139 C3
Gretna Gdns 1 IP4 136 B1
Greville Starkey Ave
CB8 121 A5
Grey Friars Rd IP1 155 B2
Greyfriars IP12 146 D4
Greyfriars Rd IP32 123 E4
Greyhound Hill CO4 103 C2
Greyhound La IP22 18 B1
Greyhound Rd 7 CO10 77 A2
Greys Cl 5 CO10 76 E1
Greys La CB9 75 A3
Grice Cl 3 NR33 11 C1
Griffith Cl 4 NR33 11 C1
Grime's Graves (Flint
Mines)* IP27 6 C4
Grimsey Rd IP16 129 D5
Grimsey's La IP16 129 E5
Grimston La IP11 107 C8
Grimwade Cl 9 CO11 104 E4
Grimwade St IP4 155 C2
Grinder's La IP21 22 D4
Grindle Gdns IP33 123 B3
Grindle The IP8 95 F8
Grinstead Gdns IP6 125 E3
Grinstead Hill IP6 125 E3
Gromford La IP17 72 C5
Groomes Cl 5 NR31 3 B7
Grosvenor Cl IP4 139 E8
Grosvenor Gdns IP33 122 F3
Grosvenor House Ct 9
IP28 116 B5
Grosvenor Rd
Lowestoft NR33 115 C7
Sudbury CO10 148 B8
Grosvenor Yd CB8 121 A3
Groton St CO10 93 B5
Grove Ave CO10 92 E8
Grove Cty Prim Sch
NR33 114 C4
Grove End IP21 39 B5
Grove Gdns
Fordham CB7 29 A2
Grove Gdns *continued*
Woodbridge IP12 146 E6
Grove Hill Belstead IP8 142 C7
Dedham CO7 103 E2
Langham CO4 103 C3
Grove La
Ashfield cum Thorpe IP14 54 C2
Elmswell IP30 51 A3
Harkstead IP9 106 C7
Ipswich IP4 139 E5
Mendham IP20 23 A2
Stanton IP31 34 F4
Thetford IP24 16 C6
Grove Mews 4 NR34 111 C4
Grove Pk
Bury St Edmunds IP33 154 A3
Fordham CB7 29 A2
5 Walsham Le Willows
IP31 35 C2
Grove Rd Beccles NR34 111 B5
2 Brantham CO11 104 E4
Brockdish IP21 21 F3
Bury St Edmunds IP33 154 A3
Felixstowe IP11 153 A6
Gissing IP21 21 A8
Knodishall IP17 72 F7
Lowestoft NR33 114 C4
Pettistree IP13 127 A4
Starston IP20 22 C6
Walsham-le-willows IP31 35 C2
Woodbridge IP13 146 E6
Grove Rd N NR33 114 D5
Grove The
Great Glemham IP17 56 F1
12 Martlesham Heath IP5 98 A8
Mildenhall IP28 29 F8
5 Woodbridge IP12 147 B6
Grove Wlk IP8 142 D8
Grove; Henley Rd The
IP1 135 C2
Grub La IP19 24 E5
Grundisburgh Cty Prim Sch
IP13 83 E5
Grundisburgh Hall*
IP13 137 C8
Grundisburgh Rd
Clopton IP13 83 D8
Great Bealings IP13 137 C6
Tuddenham St Martin
IP6 136 D6
Grundle Cl 6 IP31 34 E4
Gt Finborough CE VC Prim
Sch IP14 66 B4
Gt Waldingfield CE Prim Sch
CO10 92 C6
Guildhall Feoffment Cty Prim
Sch IP33 154 C1
Guildhall La NR34 26 D5
Guildhall of Corpus Christi
The* CO10 78 D4
Guildhall St IP33 154 B2
Guineas Cl CB8 120 E6
Gules Gn IP21 22 F1
Gull Hill IP19 25 C3
Gull La
Grundisburgh IP13 83 D6
Thornham Magna IP23 37 A2
Gull The IP13 70 C2
Gull's La CO7 104 A2
Gulpher Bsns Pk IP11 152 F8
Gulpher Rd IP11 152 E6
Gun Hill CO7 103 D4
Gun La NR32 113 E2
Gunton Ave NR32 113 A7
Gunton Church La
NR32 113 C5
Gunton Cliff NR32 113 D5
Gunton Dr NR32 113 D5
Gunton Prim Sch
NR32 113 C6
Gunton St Peter's Ave
NR32 113 C5
Guntons Cl 12 CB7 28 D4
Gurdon Rd 5 IP13 83 E5
Gurlings Cl CB9 132 E8
Guscot Cl NR32 113 A6
Gusford Prim Sch IP2 138 D1
Guston Gdns IP10 98 E2
Guthrum Rd IP7 149 D6
Guy Cook Cl CO10 92 B2
Guyatt Ct 6 CB5 44 A5
Gwendoline Rd IP4 140 E4
Gwynne Rd 4 CO12 107 B2
Gymnasium St IP1 155 A3

H

Hacheston Rd IP13 70 F5
Hackney Rd
Peasenhall IP17 56 E8
Woodbridge IP12 147 B6
Hackney's Cnr IP6 81 F5
Haddiscoe Sta NR31 2 A5
Hadenham Rd NR33 114 F1
Hadleigh Bsns Pk IP7 94 E4
Hadleigh Dr NR32 112 F3
Hadleigh High Sch
IP7 149 F5
Hadleigh Prim Sch
IP7 149 D5
Hadleigh Rd Aldham IP7 94 E8
Bildeston IP7 79 F3
Boxford CO6 93 D2
East Bergholt CO7 151 B4
Elmsett IP7 80 F1
Higham CO7 103 D7
Ipswich IP2 138 E6
Hadleigh Swimming Pool
IP7 149 D6
Hadrian Cl CB9 133 B5
Haggars Mead IP14 67 D7
Haglemere Dr IP4 139 E7
Halcyon Cres NR32 113 C1
Hale Cl IP2 138 D2
Halesowen Cl IP2 142 F8
Halesworth & District Mus*
IP19 118 B4
Halesworth Mid Sch
IP19 118 C5
Halesworth Rd
Brampton with Stoven
IP19 25 E3
Heveningham IP19 40 F3
Linstead Parva IP19 40 F8
Reydon IP18 119 B7
St Andrew, Ilketshall
NR34 25 A6
St Lawrence, Ilketshall
NR34 24 E8
Sibton IP17 41 B1
Uggeshall NR34 25 F3
Walpole IP19 41 C5
Wenhaston With Mells Hamlet
IP19 41 F6
Halesworth Sta IP19 118 B4
Half Moon La
6 Grundisburgh IP13 83 E5
Redgrave IP22 36 A8
Half Moon St IP30 65 D5
Halfar Rd 2 IP31 33 D5
Halfmoon La IP27 109 C7
Halford Ct 6 IP8 138 C2
Halford La IP22 19 D3
Halifax Prim Sch IP2 139 B2
Halifax Rd Ipswich IP2 139 B2
9 Mildenhall IP28 30 A8
Halifax St IP27 109 F1
Halifax Way CB8 120 E5
Hall Barn Rd CB7 29 B5
Hall Cl IP29 62 B4
Hall Cl The IP28 31 D4
Hall Dr 17 Feltwell IP26 4 E5
Lakenheath IP27 109 C7
Lowestoft NR32 112 C1
Santon Downham IP27 6 C2
Hall Farm Cl IP12 147 B8
Hall Farm La NR34 10 E1
Hall Farm Rd IP12 147 B8
Hall Field 1 IP11 152 E5
Hall La Blundeston NR32 3 A4
Bressingham IP22 19 D5
Brinkley CB8 59 F1
Burston & Shimpling IP21 21 A6
Burwell CB5 44 A5
Claydon IP6 134 E8
Harwich CO12 107 A1
Hawkedon CO10 76 C7
Otley IP6 69 C2
Oulton NR32 112 C4
Redgrave IP22 36 A8
Ridgewell CO9 89 D3
Risby IP28 47 D5
Roydon IP22 20 A3
Scole IP21 21 C4
Shelfanger IP22 20 B6
Somersham IP8 81 C3
Spexhall IP19 24 E4
Wetheringsett-cum-brockford
IP14 53 B4
3 Witnesham IP6 83 A5
Yaxley IP23 37 B4
Hall Pond Way IP11 152 D5
Hall Rd Barnardiston CB8 75 B5
Barsham NR34 8 F3
Bedingfield IP23 54 A7
Bedingham NR35 7 C7
Belchamp Walter CO10 91 A3
Blundeston NR32 112 C8
Borley CO10 91 D5
Brent Eleigh CO10 79 A3
Brockdish IP21 22 A3
Burston & Shimpling IP22 20 E7
Carlton Colville NR33 114 B2
Charsfield IP13 69 F3
Chelsworth IP7 79 E2
Cowlinge CB8 75 A7
Earsham NR35 7 E4
Ellingham NR35 8 C7
Foxhall IP10 141 E4
7 Hopton-on-sea NR31 3 B7
Hundon CO10 75 E4
9 Kessingland NR33 11 C1
Lavenham CO10 78 D4
Little Bealings IP5 137 E2
Lowestoft NR32 112 D1
Marlesford IP13 71 C5
Mount Bures CO8 101 C3
Parham IP13 71 B7
Pulham St Mary IP21 22 A8
Stowmarket IP14 124 B8
Thorndon IP23 53 C7
Wenhaston With Mells Hamlet
IP19 42 D5
Hall Rise CO10 148 A3
Hall St
Long Melford CO10 91 E8
Soham CB7 28 D4
Hall Wlk IP8 81 F1
Hallfields IP27 109 C7
Hallifax Pl IP29 77 F7
Halliwell Rd IP4 140 B6
Hall's La IP31 50 B5
Hallwong La IP20 22 D7
Hallwyck Gdns CB8 120 F2
Halton Cres IP3 140 C1
Hamblin Rd IP12 147 A
Hambling's Piece NR16 18 C
Hambrook Cl IP30 63 F
Hambros The 3 IP31 49 D
Hamilton Gdns IP11 153 A
Hamilton Rd
Felixstowe IP11 153 A
Felixstowe IP11 153 A
Ipswich IP3 140 B
Lowestoft NR32 113 E
Newmarket CB8 120 D
7 Sudbury CO10 148 C
Hamilton St
6 Felixstowe IP11 152 E
4 Harwich CO12 106 F
Hamilton Way
Ditchingham NR35 110 C
Stowmarket IP14 124 D
Hamiltons The CB8 120 F
Hamlet Ct 2 CO8 101 C
Hamlet Rd CB9 132 F
Hammond Cl CB8 120 E
Hammond's Cnr IP14 67 C
Hampstead Ave IP28 116 B
Hampton Rd IP1 138 F
Hanchet End CB9 74 A
Hancocks Cl 5 IP16 129 D
Handford Cut IP1 139 A
Handford Hall Prim Sch
IP1 139 A
Handford Rd IP1 155 A
Hankin Ave 18 CO12 106 E
Hanmer Ave IP28 116 C
Hanover Cl 5 IP32 123 A
Ha'penny Field 8 IP9 105 E
Ha'penny Pier Visitor Ctr*
CO12 107 E
Harbour Cres 7 CO12 107 C
Harbour La IP22 18 D
Harbour Rd NR32 112 E
Harbourage The NR34 111 C
Harcourt Ave 1 CO12 107 A
Harding's La IP31 50 E
Hardwick Cl IP4 140 E
Hardwick La IP33 122 F
Hardwick Mid Sch
IP33 123 E
Hardwick Pk Gdns
IP33 123 A
Hardwick Prim Sch
IP33 123 B
Hardwick Rd
Haverhill CB9 132 F
Starston IP20 22 C
Hardy Cl
8 Brantham CO11 104 E
Lowestoft NR33 115 A
Hardy Cres IP1 134 F
Hare & Hounds Cnr
IP6 82 F
Harebell Rd IP2 138 F
Harebell Way NR33 114 C
Harefield CO10 77 E
Hares La IP19 25 E
Hares Rd IP7 65 D
Hares Wlk 1 CO10 148 D
Hargrave Ave IP6 125 D
Hargrave Rd IP29 62 E
Harkstead La
Freston IP9 105 F
Woolverstone IP9 144 A
Harkstead Rd 3 IP9 106 A
Harleston Dove CE Fst Sch
IP20 22 D
Harleston Hill IP21 39 E
Harleston Mus* IP20 22 D
Harleston Rd
Metfield IP20 23 E
Pulham Market IP21 21 E
Scole IP21 21 D
Weybread IP21 22 D
Harling Dro IP27 6 E
Harling Rd
Garboldisham IP22 18 C
North Lopham IP22 19 A
Harling Way IP16 129 B
Harman's La IP20 22 C
Harold Rd NR33 115 C
Harpclose Rd 2 CO10 148 D
Harper's Est 9 CO6 102 C
Harper's Hill CO6 102 C
Harpers La IP17 128 D
Harp's Cl Rd NR32 113 F
Harpur's Rd 2 CO10 77 A
Harrier Cl IP3 140 B
Harriers Wlk IP13 70 F
Harrington Ave NR32 113 C
Harrington Cl IP33 154 C
Harris Ave NR32 113
Harris Ct 12 IP14 53
Harris Mid Sch NR32 113 D
Harrison Gn 3 IP18 119 C
Harrison Gr IP5 141
Harrison Rd NR32 112
Harrisons La IP19 118
Harrop Dale 10 NR33 114
Harrow Cl IP4 140
Harrow Gn 2 IP29 63
Harrow La Benhall IP17 72
Theberton IP16 129
Harrow Rd
Haverhill CB9 132
Troston IP31 33
Harrow St CO6 102
Harry Palmer Cl 1 CB7 29
Hart Cl CB9 132
Hartest Hill IP29 77
Hartest La IP29 63

Hartest Prim Sch IP29 . . . .77 B7
Hartest Rd IP29 . . . . .63 A1
Hartest Way
  Stowmarket IP14 . . . . .124 F3
  1 Sudbury CO10 . . . . .92 B3
  Sudbury CO10 . . . . .148 F4
Hartfield Rd CB8 . . . . .59 F2
Hartington Rd IP15 . . . . . . .130 E3
Hartismere High Sch
  IP23 . . . . .117 B3
Hartismere Hospl
  IP23 . . . . .117 C3
Hartley St IP2 . . . . .17 C5
Hart's La CO7 . . . . .103 E1
Harvard Rd **6** IP26 . . . . . . .4 D5
Harvest Cl IP14 . . . . .51 D1
Harvest Rd IP14 . . . . .114 F2
Harvesters Way
  Martlesham IP5 . . . . .141 F6
  2 Martlesham Heath IP5 . .98 A7
Harvey Cl **7** CO11 . . . . . . .104 E2
Harvey La IP31 . . . . .21 C5
Harvey's La IP14 . . . . .81 B1
Harwich Int Port CO12 . . . . .106 F3
Harwich Rd
  Foxash Estate CO11 . . . . . .104 A1
  Lawford CO11 . . . . .104 B1
  Mistley CO11 . . . . .105 A2
  Ramsey & Parkeston
    CO11 . . . . .106 A1
  Wrabness CO11 . . . . .105 F1
Harwich Town Sta
  CO12 . . . . .107 B3
Harwood Ave IP24 . . . . . . .16 C7
Hascot Hill Barking IP6 . . . .125 A1
  Battisford IP14 . . . . .81 A8
Haselmere Cl **5** IP32 . . . . .123 D6
Hasketon Rd Burgh IP13 . . . .83 F6
  Woodbridge IP13 . . . . . . .146 E6
Haskins Wlk IP5 . . . . .141 F7
Hasse Rd CB7 . . . . .28 E8
Hasted Cl IP14 . . . . .122 C4
Hatchley Cl IP12 . . . . .85 C3
Hatfield Rd IP3 . . . . .140 A3
Hatley Dr CB5 . . . . .44 A6
Hatter St IP33 . . . . .154 B2
Haugh La
  Great Ashfield IP31 . . . . . .50 F5
  Haughley IP14 . . . . .51 C6
  Woodbridge IP12 . . . . . . .146 F7
Haughgate Cl IP12 . . . . . . .146 E6
Haughley Crawfords CE Prim
  Sch IP14 . . . . .51 C1
Haughley Dr IP4 . . . . .140 F6
Haughley Junc IP14 . . . . . .51 D1
Haughley Rd IP14 . . . . .66 B7
Hauliers Rd IP11 . . . . .152 D2
Havell Ave NR32 . . . . .113 B3
Haven Cl IP11 . . . . .152 D4
Haven Rd IP16 . . . . .129 D5
Haven The IP16 . . . . .73 F6
Havens The IP10 . . . . .144 E7
Haverhill Rd
  Haverhill CB9 . . . . .132 F8
  Helions Bumpstead CB9 . . .88 B5
  Kedington CB9 . . . . .133 E8
  Steeple Bumpstead CB9 . . .88 D5
Haverhill Rovers FC
  CB9 . . . . .132 F4
Haward St **7** NR32 . . . . . .113 C1
Hawbridge IP9 . . . . .150 E4
Hawe's La Norton IP31 . . . . .50 B4
  Wicken CB7 . . . . .2 A3
Hawes St IP2 . . . . .155 C1
Hawk End La IP30 . . . . .50 E2
Hawke Rd IP3 . . . . .139 E1
Hawker Dr IP5 . . . . .98 A8
Hawkes La IP11 . . . . .63 A2
Hawkins Rd CO10 . . . . .148 E8
Hawks La IP29 . . . . .63 A2
Hawks Mill St IP6 . . . . .125 D5
Hawstead La IP29 . . . . .63 E6
Hawthorn Ave NR33 . . . . . .115 A7
Hawthorn Cl
  Beccles NR34 . . . . .111 E4
  Bury St Edmunds IP32 . . . .122 D8
  Knodishall IP17 . . . . .129 B2
  6 Stowupland IP14 . . . . .67 A6
Hawthorn Dr
  6 Horringer IP29 . . . . . .63 A8
  Ipswich IP2 . . . . .139 C1
Hawthorn La **2** IP27 . . . . .13 F2
Hawthorn Pl IP14 . . . . .146 E6
Hawthorn Rd
  Haverhill CB9 . . . . .132 B7
  Middleton IP17 . . . . .58 A5
  Sudbury CO10 . . . . .148 F5
  Theberton IP16 . . . . .57 F4
Hawthorn Way CB5 . . . . . . .44 B6
Hawthorn Wlk **10** IP28 . . . .30 B8
Hawthorns The **8** IP31 . . . .49 D4
Hay Barn Mdw **2** IP30 . . . .50 D1
Haycocks Rd CB9 . . . . .132 A7
Haygate IP23 . . . . .117 C3
Hayland Dro IP28 . . . . .29 D7
Haylings Gr IP16 . . . . .129 C4
Haylings Rd IP16 . . . . .129 C4
Hayman Rd IP3 . . . . .139 E1
Haymans Mill IP13 . . . . . . .129 E8
Haysborder Rd IP29 . . . . . .46 F3
Hayhill La IP26 . . . . .4 D6
Haywards Fields IP5 . . . . . .141 D8
Hazel Cl
  8 Bentwaters Airfield IP12 .85 E8
  Haverhill CB9 . . . . .132 C5
  Mildenhall IP28 . . . . .116 E4

Hazel Dr
  10 Horringer IP29 . . . . . .63 A8
  Ipswich IP3 . . . . .140 E1
Hazel Rise IP6 . . . . .134 C8
Hazelcroft Rd IP11 . . . . . . .135 B2
Hazels La IP17 . . . . .42 D5
Hazelville Cl **11** CO12 . . . . .106 F1
Hazelwood Rd 80 F1
Hazelwood Cl **3** IP31 . . . . .49 D4
Hazlitt Rd **8** IP11 . . . . . . .135 A8
Head La CO10 . . . . .148 F2
Headingham Cl **15** IP2 . . . .139 A2
Headland Ave CB8 . . . . . . .132 C5
Headland Dro IP26 . . . . . . .4 A1
Heasman Cl CB8 . . . . .120 F5
Heath Cl
  East Bergholt CO7 . . . . . .151 D5
  Hessett IP30 . . . . .64 F8
  Polstead CO6 . . . . .93 F3
Heath Ct **12** IP11 . . . . . . .107 D8
Heath Dr IP12 . . . . .99 C7
Heath Farm Rd IP28 . . . . . .30 B1
Heath La Blundeston NR32 . .3 A4
  Ipswich IP4 . . . . .140 C5
  Pakenham IP31 . . . . .49 D8
Heath Prim Sch IP5 . . . . . .141 B8
Heath Rd Burwell CB5 . . . . .44 C2
  East Bergholt CO7 . . . . . .151 D5
  Exning CB8 . . . . .120 A4
  Fritton & St Olaves NR31 . . .2 B5
  Geldeston NR34 . . . . .8 E8
  Hessett IP30 . . . . .64 F8
  Ipswich IP4 . . . . .140 C7
  Ixworth IP31 . . . . .33 E2
  Kenninghall NR16 . . . . . . .19 A7
  Lowestoft NR33 . . . . .114 F5
  Mildenhall IP28 . . . . .116 E5
  Mistley CO11 . . . . .105 A2
  Newmarket CB8 . . . . .121 C3
  Norton IP31 . . . . .50 B4
  Polstead CO6 . . . . .93 F3
  Sapiston IP31 . . . . .34 B7
  Swaffham Prior CB5 . . . . . .44 A1
  Thurston IP31 . . . . .49 D4
  Troston IP31 . . . . .33 D4
  Wenhaston With Mells Hamlet
    IP19 . . . . .42 B7
  Woolpit IP30 . . . . .50 D1
Heath The
  Dedham CO7 . . . . .104 A2
  Great Waldingfield CO10 . . .92 C6
  Woolpit IP30 . . . . .65 F8
Heath View
  Ipswich IP5 . . . . .141 A6
  Leiston IP16 . . . . .129 E5
Heath Way CO10 . . . . .92 C6
Heath Wlk IP12 . . . . .72 A4
Heathbell Rd CB8 . . . . .121 C3
Heather Ave IP3 . . . . .140 C2
Heather Cl
  1 Great Barton IP31 . . . .49 D4
  Martlesham Heath IP5 . . . .141 F6
Heather Rd NR34 . . . . .113 D4
Heather Way IP3 . . . . .135 A3
Heathercroft Rd IP14 . . . . . .124 C7
Heatherhayes IP2 . . . . .139 A3
Heatherset Way IP28 . . . . . .30 C1
Heathfield
  4 Martlesham Heath IP5 . .98 A7
  Martlesham Heath IP5 . . . .141 F6
Heathfield Mews IP5 . . . . . .141 F6
Heathfield Rd **9** IP9 . . . . . .105 E7
Heathfields IP11 . . . . .74 A3
Heathgate Piece IP11 . . . . .152 C8
Heathlands Pk IP4 . . . . . . .140 E4
Hedley La IP33 . . . . .114 A3
Heigham Dr NR33 . . . . .114 F5
Heights The NR34 . . . . .111 D3
Heldhaw Rd IP32 . . . . .123 E5
Helena Rd IP3 . . . . .139 E4
Helens Cl **2** IP22 . . . . . . .36 A8
Helions Bumpstead Rd
  CB9 . . . . .132 D3
Helions Pk Ave CB9 . . . . . .132 E6
Helions Rd CB9 . . . . .88 D4
Helions Service Rd **3**
  CB9 . . . . .132 E5
Helions Wlk CB9 . . . . .132 E5
Helmingham Hall & Gdns*
  IP14 . . . . .69 A4
Helmingham Prim Sch
  IP14 . . . . .69 B5
Helmingham Rd IP6 . . . . . . .69 C2
Helston Cl IP5 . . . . .141 B7
Hemmant Way NR34 . . . . . .9 B7
Hemplands The **2**
  NR32 . . . . .113 D2
Hempnall Rd IP6 . . . . .7 A8
Hempstead Rd CB9 . . . . . . .132 A7
Hencote La
  Horringer IP29 . . . . .63 C8
  Nowton IP29 . . . . .123 B1
Henderson Cl
  Bramford IP8 . . . . .134 A1
  Haverhill CB9 . . . . .132 A7
Hengrave Cl **1** IP32 . . . . . .123 D6
Hengrave Hall* IP28 . . . . . .48 A7
Hengrave Rd IP28 . . . . .48 B6
Henham Rd IP20 . . . . .113 A5
Henley Ave IP1 . . . . .135 B3
Henley Cl IP21 . . . . .21 C7
Henley Prim Sch IP6 . . . . . .82 E6
Henley Rd Henley IP6 . . . . . .82 D5
  Ipswich IP1 . . . . .135 B4
  Ipswich IP1 . . . . .155 A4
Henniker Rd
  3 Debenham IP14 . . . . . .53 F2
  Ipswich IP1 . . . . .138 C8

Henny Rd CO8 . . . . .101 A7
Henny Ward Rd **1**
  CO8 . . . . .101 A7
Henry Rd IP3 . . . . .140 B1
Henry St IP14 . . . . .53 E2
Henry Ward Rd **1** IP20 . . .22 D6
Henslow Rd IP4 . . . . .140 B5
Henstead Gdns IP4 . . . . . . .140 A2
Hepworth Ave IP33 . . . . . . .122 D5
Hepworth Rd
  Barningham IP31 . . . . .34 F7
  Hepworth IP22 . . . . .35 A7
  Stanton IP31 . . . . .34 E4
  Thelnetham IP22 . . . . .35 F3
Herbert Human Cl **3**
  IP3 . . . . .28 D4
Herbert Rd IP5 . . . . .141 E8
Hereward Ave IP28 . . . . . . .116 D5
Hereward Way
  6 Feltwell IP26 . . . . . . .4 D5
  Littleport CB7 . . . . .12 B7
  Weeting-with-broomhill
    IP27 . . . . .5 E3
Heritage Gn **8** NR33 . . . . .11 B1
Herivan Cl NR32 . . . . .112 E4
Herivan Gdns **8** NR32 . . . .112 E4
Hermitage Cr IP13 . . . . . . .126 B3
Hermitage Mdws CO10 . . . . .76 B1
Herolf Way **11** IP20 . . . . . .22 D6
Heron Cl
  8 Mildenhall IP28 . . . . . .13 B1
  Stowmarket IP14 . . . . . . .124 A6
Heron Hill IP14 . . . . .66 C6
Heron Rd
  Bury St Edmunds IP33 . . . .123 B2
  Ipswich IP2 . . . . .138 E3
  Saxmundham IP17 . . . . . .128 D4
Herons Cl IP32 . . . . .112 D2
Herring Fishery Score **2**
  NR32 . . . . .113 E1
Herringfleet Rd NR31 . . . . . .2 B5
Herringswell Rd
  Herringswell IP28 . . . . . . .30 D2
  Kentford CB8 . . . . .46 A6
Hertford Cl **2** NR33 . . . . . .114 C5
Hertford Pl IP15 . . . . .130 E3
Hertford Rd **5** CO10 . . . . . .76 A1
Hervey Cl IP20 . . . . .22 D6
Hervey La IP29 . . . . .107 A5
Hervey Rd IP23 . . . . .117 C3
Hervey St Ipswich IP4 . . . . .155 C4
  Lowestoft NR32 . . . . .115 C8
Hessett Cl IP14 . . . . .124 C7
Hethersett Cl CB8 . . . . .120 E8
Heveningham Long La
  IP17 . . . . .41 A1
Heveningham Rd IP19 . . . . .40 C5
Hewitt Rd **8** CO10 . . . . . . .106 E1
Hexham Cl **3** IP2 . . . . . . .139 A2
Heycroft Way **4** CO6 . . . . .102 C5
Heyford Cl **6** IP28 . . . . . . .30 A1
Heyford Rd IP22 . . . . .33 D5
Heywood Ave IP22 . . . . . . .20 C3
Heywood Cl IP22 . . . . .138 D1
Heywood Rd IP22 . . . . .20 C4
Hibbard Rd IP14 . . . . .134 C2
Hickford Hill CO10 . . . . .90 B7
Hickling Dr IP33 . . . . .123 B1
Hicks Way CB9 . . . . .133 C3
High Baxter St IP33 . . . . . .154 B2
High Beach IP11 . . . . .153 C4
High Comm Rd IP22 . . . . . .18 F5
High Ct IP20 . . . . .22 C6
High Hall Cl **2** IP11 . . . . . .107 D8
High House Farm Rd
  IP12 . . . . .131 D8
High House La IP7 . . . . .79 B5
High La IP14 . . . . .53 B6
High Leas NR34 . . . . .111 C3
High Lighthouse Wireless
  Mus* CO12 . . . . .107 C3
High Lodge Visitor Centre
  Thetford Forest Pk*
    IP27 . . . . .15 C7
High London La IP22 . . . . . .20 A8
High Rd Badingham IP13 . . . .56 C6
  Bressingham IP22 . . . . . . .19 F4
  Felixstowe IP11 . . . . .152 B8
  Great Finborough IP14 . . . .66 A2
  Kettleburgh IP13 . . . . . . .55 A4
  Leavenheath CO6 . . . . . . .102 A7
  Needham IP20 . . . . .22 B3
  Roydon IP22 . . . . .20 A3
  Swilland IP6 . . . . .83 A7
  Trimley St Martin IP11 . . . .98 C1
  Wortwell IP20 . . . . .23 A7
High Rd E IP11 . . . . .153 B5
High Rd W IP11 . . . . .152 F5
High Row Field IP31 . . . . . .153 C5
High St Acton CO10 . . . . . . .92 B7
  Aldeburgh IP15 . . . . .130 E3
  Ashley CB8 . . . . .60 F8
  Brandon IP27 . . . . .6 A1
  Brinkley CB8 . . . . .59 F1
  5 Bures CO8 . . . . .101 C5
  Burwell CB5 . . . . .44 A5
  Cavendish CO10 . . . . .76 E1
  Cheveley CB8 . . . . .60 E8
  Chippenham CB7 . . . . .45 C8
  Clare CO10 . . . . .90 A8
  Debenham IP14 . . . . .53 F2
  Dedham CO7 . . . . .103 F3
  Dunwich IP17 . . . . .43 B1
  Felixstowe IP11 . . . . .152 E6
  Feltwell IP26 . . . . .4 D5
  Flowton IP8 . . . . .81 C1
  Gislingham IP23 . . . . .36 D2
  Great Yeldham CO9 . . . . . .90 A1
  Hadleigh IP7 . . . . .149 D6

High St continued
  Harwich CO12 . . . . .107 B2
  Haverhill CB9 . . . . .132 E5
  Hemingstone IP6 . . . . .68 C1
  Hitcham IP7 . . . . .79 F4
  Honington IP31 . . . . .33 F4
  Hopton IP22 . . . . .18 C2
  Ipswich IP1 . . . . .155 B3
  Ixworth IP31 . . . . .34 B1
  Kessingland NR33 . . . . . . .11 B1
  Lakenheath IP27 . . . . . . .109 C6
  Lavenham CO10 . . . . .103 B2
  Lavenham CO10 . . . . .78 D4
  Laxfield IP13 . . . . .40 B3
  Leiston IP16 . . . . .129 C6
  Long Melford CO10 . . . . . .77 F2
  2 Lowestoft NR32 . . . . . .113 E2
  Lowestoft NR33 . . . . .113 E3
  Manningtree CO11 . . . . . .104 E2
  Mildenhall IP28 . . . . .116 C4
  Nayland CO6 . . . . .102 D5
  Needham Market IP6 . . . . .125 D5
  Newmarket CB8 . . . . .120 F2
  Orford IP12 . . . . .131 C2
  Pettistree IP13 . . . . .127 C5
  Rattlesden IP30 . . . . .65 D6
  St Margaret, Ilketshall
    NR35 . . . . .24 D7
  Saxmundham IP17 . . . . . .128 D3
  Soham CB7 . . . . .28 D8
  Southwold IP18 . . . . .119 D5
  Sproughton IP8 . . . . .138 A6
  Stansfield CO10 . . . . .76 C6
  Stetchworth CB8 . . . . .60 A6
  Thelnetham IP22 . . . . .18 E1
  Thorndon IP23 . . . . .53 C8
  Tuddenham IP28 . . . . .30 F2
  Tuddenham St Martin
    IP6 . . . . .136 B5
  Wangford with Henham
    NR34 . . . . .26 B2
  Wicken CB7 . . . . .28 A1
  Wickham Market IP13 . . . .127 C7
  Wrentham NR34 . . . . .26 E5
  Yoxford IP17 . . . . .57 D8
High St Sx Gall* IP1 . . . . . .155 B3
High View Rd IP31 . . . . . . .134 D1
Higham Hill IP7 . . . . .103 D8
Higham Race Course
  CO7 . . . . .103 D7
Higham Rd
  Higham CO7 . . . . .103 D6
  Tuddenham IP28 . . . . .31 A1
Highbridge Gravel Dro
  IP27 . . . . .109 E8
Highbury Cres IP33 . . . . . . .122 E5
Highbury Rd IP33 . . . . .122 E5
Highbury Way CO10 . . . . . .148 F4
Highclere Cl CB8 . . . . .120 D8
Higher Dr NR32 . . . . .112 F2
Highfield
  Blythburgh IP19 . . . . .42 F6
  Clare CO10 . . . . .90 B8
  Eye IP23 . . . . .117 C3
Highfield App **1** IP11 . . . . .134 F1
Highfield Ave CO12 . . . . . .107 A2
Highfield Cl NR34 . . . . .114 B1
Highfield Dr IP14 . . . . .53 E2
Highfield Rd
  Felixstowe IP11 . . . . .153 A4
  Halesworth IP19 . . . . .118 B2
  Ipswich IP1 . . . . .134 F2
  6 Stowupland IP14 . . . . .67 A6
  Sudbury CO10 . . . . .148 E2
Highfields Bentley IP9 . . . . .104 F7
  Great Yeldham CO9 . . . . . .90 A1
  Lakenheath IP27 . . . . . . .109 E6
Highfields Dr IP20 . . . . .109 D6
Highgate La IP13 . . . . .70 B2
Highgrove Cl NR32 . . . . . . .113 A3
Highland Dr NR34 . . . . .111 E4
Highland Way IP27 . . . . . . .14 B6
Highlands IP27 . . . . .109 C6
Highlands Cl NR33 . . . . . . .114 A4
Highlands Rd
  Hadleigh IP7 . . . . .149 E5
  Monks Eleigh IP7 . . . . . . .79 C7
Highlands The CB8 . . . . . . .120 D8
Highview Cl CO10 . . . . .148 C8
Highwood Cres CB8 . . . . . . .46 B2
Highwood La CO10 . . . . . . .92 E5
Highwood Rd CB8 . . . . .46 B2
Hill Cl
  6 Long Melford CO10 . . . .91 E8
  Newmarket CB8 . . . . .120 E8
Hill Cres CB9 . . . . .132 E7
Hill Farm La **8** IP9 . . . . . .106 C8
Hill Farm Rd
  Grundisburgh IP13 . . . . . .83 D6
  Halesworth IP19 . . . . .118 C3
  Playford IP6 . . . . .137 B4
  Rendham IP17 . . . . .56 E4
Hill House Gdns IP14 . . . . . .115 C5
Hill House La IP5 . . . . .136 C8
Hill House Rd IP4 . . . . .139 E5
Hill La CB9 . . . . .133 D1
Hill of Health (Tumulus)*
  IP28 . . . . .32 D2
Hill Rd Lowestoft NR32 . . . .113 C6
  Southwold IP18 . . . . .119 C6
  Wangford with Henham
    NR34 . . . . .26 B1
  Westley IP33 . . . . .122 A3
Hill Rise IP14 . . . . .124 D3
Hill St **20** IP20 . . . . .22 D6
Hill The North Cove NR34 . . .10 C4
  Shipmeadow NR34 . . . . . . .8 F4
  Westleton IP17 . . . . .58 C8
Hill Top IP31 . . . . .34 E5

Hill View CB8 . . . . .61 C4
Hill View Bsns Pk IP6 . . . . .134 C8
Hillary Cl IP14 . . . . .140 A5
Hillcrest IP17 . . . . .129 A3
Hillcrest App IP8 . . . . .134 B2
Hillcrest Cl **3** NR34 . . . . . .111 E3
Hillcrest Dr NR32 . . . . .113 B4
Hillcrest Gdns NR32 . . . . . .113 B3
Hillcrest Rd
  Beccles NR34 . . . . .111 B3
  Sudbury CO10 . . . . .148 C8
Hillcroft Prep Sch IP14 . . . .51 D2
Hilrise Cl NR34 . . . . .111 D3
Hillside Brandon IP27 . . . . .14 D8
  Stowmarket IP14 . . . . . . .124 D3
Hillside Ave NR34 . . . . .111 E4
Hillside Com Prim Sch
  IP3 . . . . .139 C5
Hillside Cres **3** IP13 . . . . .140 B3
Hillside Ct **1** NR35 . . . . . .110 C2
Hillside Mdw CB7 . . . . .29 B1
Hillside Rd
  Southwold IP18 . . . . .119 C7
  Sudbury CO10 . . . . .148 E5
Hillside Rd East NR35 . . . . .110 C3
Hillside Rd West
  NR35 . . . . .110 B2
Hilltop Way IP19 . . . . .118 B5
Hilltop Gn NR32 . . . . .113 A4
Hilltop Rise **2** NR34 . . . . .111 E3
Hilltop Way IP31 . . . . .34 E5
Hilly Cl IP21 . . . . .33 F5
Hilly Fields IP12 . . . . .146 E4
Hilton Cl **15** CO11 . . . . . . .104 E2
Hilton Rd Ipswich IP3 . . . . .140 C1
  Martlesham Heath IP5 . . . .98 A8
Hinderclay La IP22 . . . . . . .18 E1
Hinderclay Rd
  Redgrave IP22 . . . . .19 A1
  Rickinghall Inferior IP22 . . .35 F6
Hines Rd IP3 . . . . .140 C4
Hintesham Cl **6** IP14 . . . . .140 F5
Hintlesham & Chattisham
  Sch IP8 . . . . .95 C6
Hintlesham Cl **3** IP14 . . . . .124 E3
Hintlesham Dr IP11 . . . . . . .152 D4
Histon Cl IP5 . . . . .140 F7
Hitcham Causeway IP7 . . . .79 E6
Hitcham Rd
  2 Debenham IP14 . . . . . .53 F2
  Wattisham IP7 . . . . .80 B6
Hitcham St NR34 . . . . .26 E4
Hitchcock Pl CO10 . . . . . . .148 C7
HMS Ganges Mus*
  IP9 . . . . .107 B4
Hobart Cl NR32 . . . . .112 E3
Hobart Way NR32 . . . . .112 E3
Hobbies La IP14 . . . . .52 D4
Hobbs Dr CO4 . . . . .103 A3
Hobbs La CO10 . . . . .77 B2
Hobland Rd
  Belton with Browston NR31 . .2 F8
  Bradwell NR31 . . . . .3 A8
Hocket Cres IP12 . . . . .71 F2
Hockey Hill IP14 . . . . .53 A5
Hockney Gdns IP3 . . . . .144 A8
Hockwold Prim Sch
  IP26 . . . . .5 A2
Hodgkinson Rd IP11 . . . . . .152 C3
Hodson Cl IP32 . . . . .122 E8
Hoe La CO10 . . . . .90 B8
Hog La
  St Lawrence, Ilketshall
    NR34 . . . . .24 F6
  Wenhaston With Mells Hamlet
    IP19 . . . . .42 C5
  Westhall NR34 . . . . .25 A6
Hogarth Rd IP23 . . . . .139 F1
Hogarth Sq IP3 . . . . .140 A1
Hogarth Wlk NR32 . . . . . . .113 B6
Hogg La NR35 . . . . .7 C5
Hoggars Rd IP14 . . . . .52 C4
Hoggty La IP21 . . . . .22 A5
Holbecks La IP7 . . . . .149 C4
Holbein Way **2** NR32 . . . . .113 B6
Holborn Ave IP28 . . . . .116 B6
Holbrook Barn Rd **2**
  CO10 . . . . .93 C3
Holbrook Cres CO10 . . . . . .92 C6
Holbrook Cres IP11 . . . . . . .152 D4
Holbrook Cty High Sch
  IP9 . . . . .105 E8
Holbrook Prim Sch
  IP9 . . . . .105 E7
Holbrook Rd
  Haverhill CB9 . . . . .132 C4
  Holbrook IP9 . . . . .106 A5
  Ipswich IP3 . . . . .139 F1
  Lowestoft NR32 . . . . .113 D3
  Stutton IP9 . . . . .105 D5
Holcombe Cres IP2 . . . . . . .138 D2
Holdans La IP17 . . . . .56 D2
Holdans Mdw IP17 . . . . . . .56 D2
Holden Cl Ipswich IP2 . . . . .139 D3
  Lavenham CO10 . . . . .78 D4
Holden Rd IP28 . . . . .31 F1
Holderness Rd IP32 . . . . . .123 C7
Holeywall La IP31 . . . . .35 A1
Holfen Cl IP12 . . . . .84 B1
Holiday Village NR31 . . . . . .3 C7
Holkham Cl **2** IP24 . . . . . .140 F5
Holkham Mead **1** CB5 . . . .44 B5
Holland Dr NR32 . . . . .60 E8
Holland Pk CB8 . . . . .60 E8
Holland Rd
  Felixstowe IP11 . . . . .152 F3

Holland Rd *continued*
Ipswich IP4 .... 139 F6
Holland Rise IP19 .... 41 A4
Holland's La NR35 .... 7 C7
Hollands Rd CB9 .... 132 E4
Hollesley Ave CB9 ...... 132 A6
Hollesley Prim Sch
IP12 .... 99 F7
Hollesley Rd
Hollesley IP12 .... 99 D7
Rendlesham IP12 .... 85 D7
Hollingsworth Rd
Lowestoft NR32 .... 113 C3
3 Stowmarket IP14 .... 124 E5
Hollow Gr Way NR33 ... 114 C4
Hollow Hill CB9 .... 74 A2
Hollow Hill Rd NR35 .... 110 B7
Hollow La
Badingham IP13 .... 56 C6
Barningham IP31 .... 34 F8
Bures St Mary CO8 .... 101 C6
Carlton Colville NR33 ...... 114 C4
6 Chelmondiston IP9 ..... 106 C8
Coney Weston IP31 .... 18 A1
Earl Soham IP13 .... 54 F3
Mendham IP20 .... 23 A4
Thurston IP31 .... 49 F3
Tostock IP30 .... 50 A2
Hollow Rd Ashen CO10 .... 89 F6
Bury St Edmunds IP32 .... 123 C6
Copdock & Washbrook
IP8 .... 95 E4
Hollow Way Hill NR34 ..... 9 D8
Hollowell Cl 3 NR32 .... 112 E4
Hollows The IP6 .... 67 F2
Holly Blue Cl IP8 .... 142 E8
Holly Bush Corner
CO7 .... 103 E7
Holly Cl Beccles NR34 .... 111 E3
5 Horringer IP29 .... 63 A8
Little Bealings IP13 .... 137 D5
6 Red Lodge IP28 .... 30 B1
Holly Ct 34 IP20 .... 22 D6
Holly End IP5 .... 141 F6
Holly Gr NR34 .... 111 C4
Holly Hill NR32 .... 112 C3
Holly La Belstead IP8 .... 142 C7
Great Horkesley CO6 ...... 102 E2
Little Bealings IP13 .... 137 D5
Mutford NR34 .... 10 E3
Rushmere St Andrew
IP5 .... 136 E2
Stutton IP9 .... 105 C6
Holly Oaks 2 CO6 .... 101 F2
Holly Rd
4 Great Bricett IP7 .... 80 D6
Ipswich IP1 .... 155 A4
Lowestoft NR32 .... 112 E1
Willisham IP8 .... 81 A5
Holly Wlk 8 IP28 .... 30 B8
Hollybush D[illegible] IP1[illegible] .... 15[illegible] D7
Hollybush L[illegible] 64 D6
Hollycroft Cl 5 IP1 .... [illegible]35 A3
Hollydene Cl 4 NR32 .... 112 D2
Holm Cl 4 NR34 .... 9 F4
Holme Cl IP22 .... 18 C2
Holmere Dr 4 IP19 ...... 118 A3
Holme's Hill IP17 .... 41 A1
Holmes La 5 CB7 .... 28 D5
Holmsey Gn
Beck Row, Holywell Row
& Kenny Hill IP28 .... 13 C1
Mildenhall IP28 .... 30 B8
Holmsey Gn Gdns 7
IP28 .... 30 B8
Holst Cl NR33 .... 115 A6
Holst Mead IP14 .... 124 C8
Holt Rd CO6 .... 93 E2
Holton Ave NR32 .... 112 F4
Holton Rd IP19 .... 118 C3
Holton St Peter Prim Sch
IP19 .... 118 E4
Holt's La IP6 .... 125 F6
Holt's Rd CO6 .... 102 A2
Holy Wells Rd IP3 .... 139 E3
Holyhouse Drift 1 IP31 .... 49 A6
Holyrood 4 CO12 .... 106 F1
Holyrood Cl IP2 .... 138 F1
Holywell Cl IP33 .... 123 A3
Holywell Dro IP28 .... 13 C2
Holywells Cl IP3 .... 139 E4
Holywells High Sch
IP3 .... 140 C2
Home Cl CB9 .... 88 E4
Home Farm La IP33 ..... 123 B1
Home Farm Rd NR35 .... 8 C7
Home Mdw 4 IP13 .... 40 B3
Home Piece IP22 .... 35 A8
Homefield Boxford CO10 .. 93 C3
Capel St. Mary IP9 .... 150 F3
Homefield Ave
5 Beccles NR34 .... 111 B5
Lowestoft NR33 .... 114 F6
Homefield Paddock
NR34 .... 111 B5
Homefield Rd CB9 ..... 132 C4
Homefield Rd Ind Est
CB9 .... 132 D4
Homer Cl IP1 .... 134 F4
Homestall Cres CB9 ...... 74 A2
Homestead Dr 2 IP28 .... 30 B8
Homey Bridge Rd CO6 .... 93 E1
Honey Hill IP33 .... 154 C1
Honey La CO6 .... 102 B6
Honeymeade Cl 23 IP31 .. 34 E4
Honeypot La
Kelsale cum Carlton IP17 ... 57 E4
Mendham IP20 .... 23 C4
Monewden IP13 .... 69 F4
Wattisfield IP22 .... 35 D4
Honeypot Mdw 2 NR35 .. 110 B3
Honeysuckle Cl
Haverhill CB9 .... 132 C7
8 Lowestoft NR33 .... 115 A3
1 Red Lodge IP28 .... 46 A8
4 Soham CB7 .... 28 D4
Honeysuckle Gdns
IP2 .... 138 E4
Honeysuckle Way 4
IP32 .... 123 E6
Honington Rise IP31 ...... 33 E5
Honington VC Prim Sch
IP31 .... 33 F5
Hoo La IP12 .... 71 E4
Hood Dr IP6 .... 81 F5
Hood Rd IP3 .... 139 E1
Hood's La NR34 .... 25 F4
Hook La IP7 .... 149 F4
Hooper Sq IP33 .... 122 C6
Hop Mdw CO7 .... 151 B4
Hope Cres IP12 .... 147 A6
Hopelyn Cl 4 NR32 ..... 113 B4
Hopton CE Prim Sch
IP22 .... 18 C1
Hopton Fst Sch NR31 ...... 3 C6
Hopton Gdns NR31 .... 3 B7
Hopton Rd
Barningham IP31 .... 34 F8
Thelnetham IP22 .... 18 D1
Hopton Rise CB9 .... 132 A6
Horham Rd IP21 .... 38 E1
Horkesley Hill CO6 ..... 102 D4
Horkesley Rd CO6 ...... 102 D4
Horn Hill NR33 .... 115 C7
Horn La CB8 .... 60 D3
Hornbeam Cl NR34 ...... 111 E4
Hornbeam Dr IP29 .... 63 A8
Hornbeam Rd
Mildenhall IP28 .... 116 E5
2 Stowupland IP14 .... 67 A6
Horringer Ct Mid Sch
IP33 .... 122 D3
Horringer Rd IP29 ...... 122 D2
Horsecroft Rd
Bury St Edmunds IP33 .... 122 F2
Horringer IP29 .... 63 C8
Horsefair IP30 .... 50 D1
Horsefair Cl IP14 .... 52 E4
Horseheath Rd CB9 .... 74 A2
Horseshoe Dr IP28 .... 30 C1
Horseshoe La CB9 ...... 132 C5
Horsham Ave IP3 .... 140 D3
Horsham Cl CB9 .... 132 A7
Hospital Rd
Bury St Edmunds IP33 .... 154 A1
Orford IP12 .... 131 B6
Sudbourne IP12 .... 131 B6
Hossack Rd IP3 .... 144 A8
Hotson Rd IP18 .... 119 D6
Houghton Dr NR32 ...... 112 E4
Houghton Pl 5 IP4 ...... 140 F5
Houghtons La CB7 .... 29 D5
Houldsworth Valley Prim Sch
CB8 .... 120 F4
How Hill (Tumulus)*
IP27 .... 31 B7
Howard Cl
6 Framlingham IP13 ..... 126 C3
Harleston IP20 .... 22 E6
Howard Com Prim Sch
IP32 .... 122 E8
Howard De Walden Way
CB8 .... 121 A4
Howard Mid Sch IP28 ... 122 D8
Howard Rd 1 NR35 ...... 110 D3
Howard St IP4 .... 140 B7
Howards Way IP5 .... 141 D8
Howe Ave IP3 .... 140 C3
Howe La Cockfield IP30 ... 64 C1
Thornham Parva IP23 .... 37 A3
Howe Rd CB9 .... 132 D7
Howes Ave IP31 .... 49 D4
Howlett Cl IP5 .... 141 E7
Howlett Way IP24 .... 16 B7
Howley Gdns NR32 ..... 113 A6
Hoxne Cl 5 IP14 .... 124 E3
Hoxne Rd Eye IP23 ...... 117 E2
Hoxne IP21 .... 38 D3
Syleham IP21 .... 21 F1
Hoxter Way CO10 .... 148 C8
Hoylake Cl 6 IP28 .... 48 C6
Hubbard's Ave 2 NR32 .. 113 C6
Hubbard's Hill IP17 .... 41 B1
Hubbard's La IP30 .... 64 F8
Hubbard's Loke NR32 ... 113 C6
Hudson Cl
10 Harwich CO12 .... 107 A1
Haverhill CB9 .... 133 A4
Hudson Way 6 IP29 .... 47 A2
Hudsons La CO6 .... 103 A7
Huggins La IP23 .... 37 B1
Hughes Cnr CO7 .... 151 A6
Hughes Rd CO7 .... 151 B6
Hull St IP27 .... 109 F1
Hulver La IP17 .... 72 C6
Hulver Rd NR34 .... 9 F2
Humber Doucy La IP4 .. 136 A2
Humber Doucy Sports Ctr
IP4 .... 140 D7
Humphry Rd CO10 ...... 148 C6
Hundon Cl CB8 .... 75 B6
Hundon Prim Sch
CO10 .... 75 D3
Hundon Rd
Hundon CO10 .... 75 B1
Kedington CB9 .... 133 F8
Hundred La
Boxted CO4 .... 103 B2
Old Newton with Dagworth
IP14 .... 51 F3
Hungate NR34 .... 111 B5
Hungate La NR34 .... 111 B5
Hungerdown La CO11 .. 104 B1
Hunston Rd IP31 .... 50 E7
Hunt Cl
5 Redenhall with Harleston
IP20 .... 22 D6
Stowmarket IP14 .... 124 D3
Hunter Dr
19 Manningtree CO11 .... 104 D2
18 Thurstow IP31 .... 49 D4
Hunter Rd
Bury St Edmunds IP32 .... 122 D8
Honington IP31 .... 33 D5
Ipswich IP3 .... 144 C8
Hunter's Chase CO7 .... 103 F1
Hunters End IP11 .... 152 C7
Hunter's La IP20 .... 23 A3
Hunters La IP20 .... 23 B2
Hunters Ride 21 IP5 .... 98 A8
Huntingdon Cl 9 NR33 .115 A3
Huntingfield Rd
Bury St Edmunds IP33 .... 122 C4
Cratfield IP19 .... 40 D5
Leiston IP16 .... 129 C5
Huntley Cres IP19 ...... 118 C5
Hunts Hill CO10 .... 77 A2
Hurdle Dro IP28 .... 29 F8
Hurdle Makers Hill IP8 .. 95 F6
Hurn Crag Rd IP18 ...... 119 C7
Hurricane Pl IP3 .... 140 B1
Hurstlea Rd IP6 .... 125 F5
Hurth Way IP24 .... 16 C6
Hurts Croft 3 CB7 .... 29 A1
Hut Hill (Tumulus)*
IP31 .... 17 E3
Hutland Rd IP4 .... 139 F7
Hyams La IP9 .... 105 E7
Hyam's La IP9 .... 105 C5
Hyde Rd CO10 .... 148 C5
Hydewood Rd CO9 .... 90 A2
Hyem's La IP11 .... 153 B7
Hyntle Cl IP2 .... 138 E5
Hyperion Way CB8 ...... 120 D8
Hythe Cl 9 CB5 .... 44 A6
Hythe La CB5 .... 44 A6
Hythe Rd IP26 .... 4 E7

I

Iceni Way CB8 .... 120 B8
Icepits Cl IP31 .... 49 C6
Icewell Hill CB8 .... 121 A4
Icklingham Rd IP28 .... 32 B2
Icknield Cl 3 CB8 .... 60 E7
Icknield Way IP24 .... 16 B5
Ickworth Cres IP4 ...... 140 F5
Ickworth Ct 2 IP11 ...... 152 C3
Ickworth Dr IP33 .... 154 A1
Ickworth House Pk & Gdn*
IP29 .... 62 F8
Ickworth Pk CP Sch
IP29 .... 63 A8
Ilex Cl IP33 .... 123 A3
Iliffe Way IP14 .... 124 D6
Imperial Mews NR31 .... 3 B6
Impson Way IP26 .... 6 A8
Ingate NR34 .... 111 C4
Ingestre St 1 CO12 ..... 107 B2
Ingham Rd
Haverhill CB9 .... 132 E6
West Stow IP28 .... 32 C1
Ingram's Rd IP21 .... 21 F3
Ingram's Well Rd
CO10 .... 148 D5
Inkerman Cl 4 IP7 ...... 149 D6
Inkerman Terr 3 IP7 .... 149 D6
Innes End 4 IP8 .... 138 C2
Inverness Rd IP4 .... 136 A2
Inworth La CO6 .... 101 B1
Ion Rd 1 IP32 .... 122 E8
Ipswich Ave 3 IP12 .... 85 B3
Ipswich Cl 1 IP12 .... 85 B3
Ipswich Ct IP33 .... 154 B3
Ipswich High Sch IP9 .. 144 C2
Ipswich Hospl The
IP4 .... 140 C7
Ipswich Mus* IP1 .... 155 B3
Ipswich Rd
Brantham CO11 .... 104 E5
Charsfield IP13 .... 70 B2
Dedham CO4 .... 103 D3
East Bergholt CO7 .... 151 A6
Elmsett IP7 .... 95 A8
Grundisburgh IP13 .... 83 E5
Hadleigh IP7 .... 149 F7
Hadleigh IP7 .... 149 F8
Harkstead IP9 .... 106 A6
Holbrook IP9 .... 105 E8
Lowestoft NR32 .... 113 D3
Nacton IP10 .... 145 A5
Nedging-with-naughton
IP7 .... 80 C4
Needham Market IP6 ..... 125 E4
Newbourne IP12 .... 98 C6
Orford IP12 .... 131 B4
Otley IP6 .... 69 B2
2 Scole IP21 .... 20 F1
Scole NR15 .... 21 C7
Stowmarket IP14 .... 124 E4
Ipswich Rd *continued*
Stratford St Mary CO7 .... 103 E4
Waldringfield IP12 .... 98 D7
Willisham IP8 .... 81 B4
Winston IP14 .... 53 F1
Woodbridge IP12 .... 146 E3
Yaxley IP23 .... 37 B4
Ipswich Rugby Union FC
IP5 .... 136 C2
Ipswich Sch IP1 .... 155 B4
Ipswich St
Bury St Edmunds IP33 .... 154 B3
Lakenheath IP27 .... 109 F1
Stowmarket IP14 .... 124 D6
Ipswich Sta IP2 .... 155 A1
Ipswich Transport Mus*
IP3 .... 140 C2
Ipswich Way IP14 .... 68 E6
Ireland Rd IP3 .... 139 F1
Irex Rd NR33 .... 115 B3
Iris Cl IP2 .... 138 F5
Irlam Rd IP2 .... 138 D2
Isaacson Rd CB5 .... 44 B4
ISCA Maritime Collection*
NR32 .... 112 D1
Isinglass Cl CB8 .... 121 E2
Isleham Rd CB7 .... 29 B2
Ivry St IP1 .... 155 A4
Ivy Cl IP13 .... 54 E7
Ivy La NR33 .... 114 C7
Ivy Lodge Rd IP12 .... 71 D1
Ivytree La IP7 .... 94 C7
Ixer La IP30 .... 64 B5
Ixworth Abbey IP31 .... 34 A1
Ixworth CE Prim Sch
IP31 .... 34 B1
Ixworth Mid Sch IP31 .... 34 B1
Ixworth Rd
Haverhill CB9 .... 132 C4
Honington IP31 .... 33 F5
Stowlangtoft IP31 .... 50 B6
Walsham-le-willows IP31 ... 35 A1

J

Jack Jarvis Cl 5 CB8 ..... 121 A3
Jack's Gn Rd IP6 .... 125 E6
Jack's La IP14 .... 124 A2
Jackson Rd IP12 .... 98 C5
Jackson Way IP6 .... 125 D4
Jacob Way 11 IP12 .... 147 A5
Jacobs Cl 14 IP31 .... 34 E4
Jacobs Mdw IP30 .... 65 D5
Jacobs St 7 NR32 .... 113 D2
Jacqueline Cl
Bury St Edmunds IP33 .... 154 A1
7 Grundisburgh IP13 .... 83 E5
James Boden Cl 7
IP11 .... 152 E5
James Carter Rd IP28 .. 116 A6
Janus Cl CB9 .... 133 B4
Jaques Cl 3 CO10 .... 77 B3
Jarman Cl IP33 .... 123 C3
Jarman's La IP28 .... 29 F7
Jarrold Cl 1 IP31 .... 34 F7
Jarvis Way CB8 .... 120 E5
Jasmine Cl
9 Felixstowe IP11 .... 107 D8
Ipswich IP2 .... 138 F3
Java Lodge Rd IP13 .... 127 B3
Jay Cl CB9 .... 133 A5
Jay La NR32 .... 3 A6
Jays Croft Rd 2 IP12 ...... 85 E8
Jay's Gn IP20 .... 22 E6
Jay's Hill Rd
Ellough NR34 .... 10 B2
Sotterley NR34 .... 10 B1
Willingham St Mary NR34 ... 26 A8
Jaywick Rd 2 CB9 ...... 132 E6
Jeavons La IP5 .... 141 E7
Jefferies Rd IP4 .... 139 E6
Jellicoe Ave NR33 .... 114 D6
Jenkins Gn NR32 .... 113 A5
Jenkinsons Pightle
NR35 .... 7 B8
Jenner Cl NR35 .... 110 C2
Jenners Cl 1 IP12 .... 147 B6
Jennings Way IP22 .... 20 C3
Jermyn Ave IP32 .... 123 F5
Jermyn Way IP19 .... 118 A2
Jermyns Cl IP9 .... 150 F4
Jermyns Rd IP18 .... 119 B8
Jervis Cl 10 IP9 .... 105 E7
Jewell View IP5 .... 141 D8
Jim Mollison Ct 5 IP28 .. 116 B5
Jimmy's La CO11 .... 104 F5
Jocelyn Cl 16 IP32 .... 48 C5
Jockey's La Combs IP14 .. 66 C2
Framsden IP14 .... 69 B7
Joes Rd CO10 .... 92 C3
John Childs Way
NR35 .... 110 C2
John Lawrence Cl
NR34 .... 111 B2
John Russell Gall*
IP3 .... 155 C2
John Shepherd Rd 1
IP21 .... 39 D8
John St Leiston IP16 ..... 129 C5
Lowestoft NR33 .... 115 C7
John Swain Cl IP6 ...... 125 C5
John Tibauld Ct 4 CB9 ... 88 D3
Johnson Cl 5 IP2 .... 139 C3
Johnson Rd 7 IP29 .... 47 A2
Johnson Way NR32 ...... 113 A5
Jolly's Way IP31 .... 35 C1
Jones Rd CO10 .... 76 C3
Jordan Cl IP6 .... 125 E7
Jordayn Cl 5 IP7 .... 149 E6
Jordayn Rise IP7 .... 149 E6
Joshua Ct 5 NR31 .... 3 B8
Josselyns The IP11 .... 152 B8
Joyce Rd NR35 .... 110 D3
Jubilee Ave IP14 .... 124 D4
Jubilee Cl 11 Claydon IP6 .. 82 B5
11 Felixstowe IP11 .... 107 D8
10 Harwich CO12 .... 106 F1
13 Isleham CB7 .... 29 C5
2 Laxfield IP13 .... 40 B3
Weeting IP27 .... 5 E3
Jubilee Cres IP14 .... 67 A7
Jubilee Ct CB8 .... 60 A5
Jubilee End 5 CO11 .... 104 E3
Jubilee Rd
Bungay NR35 .... 110 B2
Lowestoft NR33 .... 115 A2
Sudbury CO10 .... 148 D6
Jubilee Terr 10 IP30 .... 50 F2
Jubilee Way NR32 ...... 113 E2
Judas La IP23 .... 37 B5
Judith Ave IP17 .... 129 B2
Julian Cl CB9 .... 133 B5
Julian Way 12 NR31 .... 3 B7
Julius Martin La CB7 ...... 28 C4
Junction Rd IP28 .... 116 B5
June Ave Ipswich IP1 ... 135 B2
Lowestoft NR32 .... 113 B3
Juniper Cl IP28 .... 116 E5
Jupes Hill CO7 .... 104 B3
Jupe's Hill CO6 .... 101 B1
Jupiter Cl CB9 .... 133 B4
Jupiter Rd IP4 .... 140 B7
Justinian Cl CB9 .... 133 B4

K

Karen Cl Ipswich IP1 .... 135 B1
4 Scole IP21 .... 20 F1
Kate's La IP14 .... 51 A1
Katwijk Way 2 NR32 .... 115 D8
Keating Cl 2 CO11 ...... 104 D2
Keats Cres IP1 .... 134 F3
Kebbles 9 CO10 .... 77 A3
Kedington Hill CO10 .... 92 A1
Kedington Prim Sch
CB9 .... 133 E8
Keel Cl NR33 .... 114 B4
Keens La IP18 .... 119 B7
Keeper's La
Marlesford IP13 .... 71 D5
Stoke-by-nayland CO6 .... 102 C8
Trimley St Mary IP11 ..... 152 A7
Keightley Way IP6 ...... 136 B5
Kell's Acres NR34 .... 8 F7
Kell's Way NR34 .... 8 F6
Kelly Rd IP2 .... 138 E5
Kelly-pain Ct NR32 ..... 113 D3
Kelsale CE VCP Prim Sch
IP17 .... 128 D5
Kelso Rd IP33 .... 122 D2
Kelvedon Dr IP4 .... 140 F5
Kelvin Rd IP1 .... 134 F1
Kemball St IP4 .... 140 A5
Kembold Cl IP32 .... 123 E5
Kemps La NR34 .... 111 B3
Kempson Dr 7 CO10 ...... 92 B3
Kempson Way IP30 ..... 123 F4
Kempsters The IP11 .... 152 D7
Kempton Cl 4 IP1 .... 135 A3
Kempton Cross NR34 ... 111 E4
Kempton Rd IP1 .... 135 A3
Kemsley Rd IP11 .... 152 F5
Kendal Rd NR33 .... 115 B5
Kennedy Ave IP19 ...... 118 A1
Kennedy Cl
Halesworth IP19 .... 118 B1
Ipswich IP4 .... 140 A6
Kennedy Rd 9 CB7 .... 29 C5
Kennel Loke NR31 .... 3 B8
Kennels La IP13 .... 146 C8
Kennels Rd
Brightwell IP10 .... 98 A6
Foxhall IP10 .... 141 F2
Kennetside CB8 .... 61 B1
Kennett Rd Or Moulton
CB8 .... 45 F3
Kennett Sta CB8 .... 45 F6
Kenney Cl IP8 .... 95 D7
Kenninghall Prim Sch
NR16 .... 19 A8
Kenninghall Rd NR16 .... 19 A7
Kennyhill Dro IP28 .... 13 A3
Kensington Rd
Ipswich IP1 .... 139 A8
Lowestoft NR33 .... 115 C5
Lowestoft NR33 .... 115 C5
Stowmarket IP14 .... 124 D5
Kent Rd Lackford IP28 ..... 31 F1
Lowestoft NR32 .... 113 B1
Stowmarket IP14 .... 124 C7
Kentford Rd 5 IP11 .... 152 C4
Kenton Rd IP14 .... 53 F2
Kents La Bungay NR35 .. 110 D3
Soham CB7 .... 28 D4
Kentwell Cl IP4 .... 140 F4
Kentwell Hall* CO10 .... 77 E2
Kentwell Pl 3 CB5 .... 44 B5
Kenyon Cl 7 CO7 .... 103 E5
Kenyon Dr 9 CO10 .... 92 C6
Kenyon Row NR34 .... 9 B6
Kenyon St IP2 .... 155 B1
Kerridge Way 20 IP20 ..... 22 D6
Kerridges NR16 .... 18 C8
Kerridge's Cut 15 CO11 .. 105 A2

Kerrison Con Ctr IP23 ....37 D1
Kerrison Rd NR35 ......110 D2
Kerry Ave IP11 ....134 D1
Kerrys Farm La IP14 ......51 F4
Kersey Ave CO10 ......148 F4
Kersey CE Prim Sch
IP7 ....94 A6
Kersey Rd IP14 ....124 E3
Kersey Pottery* IP7 ....94 A7
Kersey Hall IP21 ....152 D4
Kersley Hall La IP21 ....39 A3
Kesgrave Cty High Sch
IP5 ....141 C8
Kesgrave Dr NR32 ......113 B2
Kesteven Rd IP2 ....155 A1
Kestrel Cl ■ IP28 ....13 B1
Kestrel Dr IP14 ....67 A5
Kestrel Rd
Bury St Edmunds IP33 ...123 B2
Haverhill CB9 ....133 A5
Ipswich IP2 ....138 D3
Keswick Cl IP11 ....153 C6
Kettle La IP6 ....67 E1
Kettleborough CI ■ IP31 ..34 E1
Kettleburgh Rd IP13 ....126 C1
Kettlefields CB8 ....59 F5
Kevington Dr NR32 ......112 C2
Key St IP3 ....155 C2
Keynes Way ■ CO12 ....106 F1
Keyrtoun Rd IP4 ....139 F7
Kilbourn Rd ■ NR33 ....115 A3
Kilback NR34 ....111 C5
Kilbrack Gdns NR34 ....111 C5
Kildare Ave IP7 ....134 D2
Kilmaine Rd ■ CO12 ....106 F1
Kiln Dr CO10 ....148 E4
Kiln Farm La IP22 ......35 F5
Kiln Field ■ IP11 ......152 D5
Kiln La Benhall IP17 ....128 C1

Kings Rd continued
Leiston IP16 ....129 C5
King's Way IP3 ....140 B2
Kingsbury Rd IP11 ......152 C7
Kingsfield Ave
■ Ipswich IP1 ....135 D1
Ipswich IP1 ....139 D8
Kingsgate Dr IP4 ....139 F8
Kingshall St IP30 ....64 D8
Kingsland IP9 ....106 F5
Kingsland La ■ CO6 ....102 A7
Kingsley CI ■ IP35 ......115 A3
Kingsmead CI ■ IP14 ....124 C7
Kingston Bridge NR32 ...112 C8
Kingston CI NR33 ....115 A3
Kingston Dr NR34 ......111 C5
Kingston Farm Rd
IP12 ....147 A4
Kingston Pas ■ CB8 ....121 A3
Kingston Rd
Ipswich IP1 ....138 F8
Woodbridge IP12 ......147 A4
Kingsway ■ Earsham NR35 ..7 F4
■ Harwich CO12 ....107 B2
Mildenhall IP28 ....116 C4
Newmarket CB8 ....120 F4
Woodbridge IP12 ......147 B5
Kingsworth Rd ■ NR33 ..114 D4
Kingsworth Rd IP23 ....123 D6
Kinross Rd IP4 ....136 B1
Kipling Cl ■ NR33 ......115 C1
Kipling Rd IP1 ....134 E3
Kipling Way IP14 ....124 E6
Kirby Cane Wlk NR32 ..113 A3
Kirby CI ■ IP14 ....140 A7
Kirby St IP4 ....140 A8
Kirkdale CI ■ NR33 ....115 B4
Kirkham CI ■ IP2 ......139 A2
Kirkley Cliff Rd NR33 ...115 C5
Kirkley Gdns NR33 .....115 B4
Kirkley High Sch
NR33 ....115 A7
Kirkley Mid Sch NR33 ..115 B7
Kirkley Pk Rd NR33 ....115 B7
Kirkley Run NR33 ......115 B6
Kirkley St NR33 ....115 C5
Kirkstead Rd IP28 ......116 C6
Kirkstone Way ■ NR32 ..113 A4
Kirkton CI IP3 ....107 A5
Kirkwood Dr ■ NR33 ...114 C3
Kirtling Rd CB8 ....60 E5
Kirton Rd IP11 ....153 A6
Kitchen Hill CO10 ......91 D4
Kitchener Rd
Ipswich IP1 ....138 F8
Leiston IP16 ....129 C5
Kitchener Way ■ IP9 ...107 A5
Kitson Mdws IP13 ......122 A5
Kittiwake CI
Ipswich IP2 ....138 E3
Lowestoft NR33 ....114 D5
Klondyke IP32 ....122 F8
Knaves Acre Dro CB7 ...29 B6
Knights CI
■ Debenham IP14 ......53 F2
■ Felixstowe IP11 ......153 D6
■ Manningtree IP11 ....104 E2
■ Old Newton with Dagworth
IP14 ....19 C5
Knights La ■ IP5 ......141 D7
Knightsdale Rd IP1 ....134 E5
Knightswood ■ NR32 ...113 B5
Knoll The IP13 ....126 D3
Knowle The ■ IP31 ....34 C4
Knox La IP31 ....34 C4
Knutsford Cl IP4 ......140 F5
Kreswell Gr ■ CO12 ...107 A1
Kylborne CI IP3 ....140 B2
Kyson Hill National Trust*
IP12 ....146 F2
Kyson Prim Sch IP12 ..146 D4

Lakeland ■ IP26 ....5 A3
Lakeland ■ NR32 ......112 F1
Lakenheath Airfield
IP27 ....14 B5
Lakenheath American High
Sch IP27 ....109 F1
Lakenheath Prim Sch
IP27 ....109 D6
Lakenheath Sta IP27 ....4 F1
Lakeside Ave IP6 ......118 D3
Lakeside CI IP28 ......119 B7
Lakeside Pk Dr IP18 ...119 B6
Lakeside Rd IP2 ....138 E2
Lakeside NR32 ....112 C8
Laksford IP30 ....64 D8
Lamarsh Hill CO8 ......101 C5
Lamarsh Rd CO8 ......101 A6
Lambert CI ■ IP2 ......139 A2
Lambert Dr CO10 ......92 B7
Lamberts CI ■ IP26 ....4 E5
Lambert's La
Mendlesham IP14 ......52 C3
Sudbourne IP12 ....73 B1
Lamberts La IP5 ......136 D2
Lambeth Way IP1 ......139 E3
Lambeth CI ■ IP14 ....139 A7
Lambeth Rd IP2 ....30 B8
Lambourne CI ■ IP32 ..123 E6
Lambourne Rd IP1 ....135 A1
Lambs La IP29 ....63 D1
Lambuse Mdw IP17 ....128 D4
Lambseth St IP23 ......117 C3
Lamdin Rd IP32 ....48 C5
Lammas CI IP31 ....34 C4
Lanark Rd IP4 ....136 B1
Lancaster Ave IP32 ....122 F8
Lancaster CI IP1 ......62 C4
Lancaster Dr ■ IP5 ....98 A7
Lancaster Rd
■ Feltwell IP26 ....4 E5
Ipswich IP4 ....139 E6
■ Mildenhall IP28 ......13 C2
Sudbury CO10 ....148 B8
Lancaster Way
■ Lowestoft NR32 ....112 F3
■ Stradishall IP14 ....124 E3
Lancers The IP12 ......146 E3
Lancewood Wlk ■ IP27 ..13 E7
Lancing Ave IP4 ....140 B8
Landguard Fort*
IP11 ....107 E2
Landguard Nature Reserve*
IP11 ....107 C2
Landmark Dr CO10 ....148 D7
Landsdown Rd IP11 ...153 B6
Landseer CI IP3 ....140 A1
Landseer Rd IP3 ....140 A1
Landspring La NR33 ...114 E6
Landwade Rd CB8 ......44 C6
Lane The
Creeting St Peter or West
Creeting IP6 ....67 B5
■ Mistley CO11 ....104 F2
Wrentham NR34 ....26 E5
Yoxford IP17 ....57 C8
Lanercost Way IP3 ....139 A1
Lang Gate Way NR35 ...7 D6
Langdale CI ■ IP1 ....153 D6
Langdale Pk NR32 ....113 B5
Langer Cty Prim Sch
IP11 ....153 E2
Langer Rd IP11 ....153 D5
Langford CI IP4 ....124 D3
Langham La CO4 ......103 B1
Langham Rd
Blaxhall IP12 ....72 B4
Boxted CO4 ....102 C1
Langham Way CB9 ....74 A1
Langley Ave IP11 ......152 E4
Langley Gdns NR33 ....114 F5
Langley Hill CO8 ......101 B6
Langmere Rd IP21 ....21 C4
Langridge Rd IP21 ....34 B2
Langstons IP11 ....152 D7
Langton Rd ■ IP33 ....126 D4
Lanman Mus* IP13 ....126 D4
Lansbury Rd IP19 ....118 B3
Lansdowne Rd
Felixstowe IP11 ....153 B6
Ipswich IP4 ....140 A5
Lowestoft NR33 ......114 E3
Lanwades Bsns Pk CB8 ..46 A5
Lapwing CI ■ IP31 ....49 D4
Lapwing Ct IP8 ....142 D4
Lapwing Way ■ IP2 ...138 D3
Larch CI IP27 ....109 D7
Larch Gr CO6 ....102 C5
Larch Rd IP28 ....13 B3
Larch Way IP6 ....125 B3
Larchcroft CI IP1 ......135 A2
Larchcroft Rd IP1 ....135 A2
Larches The NR34 ......26 E5
Larchwood CI IP8 ......138 C5
Largent Gr ■ IP5 ......141 E8
Lark CI
■ Stowmarket IP14 ....67 A5
Worlington IP28 ....30 B4
Lark Hill CB8 ....45 F3
Lark Rise
■ Martlesham Heath IP5 ..98 A8
Sudbury CO10 ....148 B3
Lark Valley Dr ■ IP28 ...48 C6
Larkhall CB8 ....28 F1
Larkhill Rise IP4 ......140 B8
Larkhill Way ■ IP3 ....152 D5
Larks CI CB9 ....133 A5
Larks Rise IP19 ....118 C3

Larksfield Cres ■ CO12 ..107 A2
Larksfield Rd IP9 ......105 D5
Larkspur CI
Corton NR32 ....113 B8
■ Red Lodge IP28 ......30 B1
Larkspur Rd IP2 ......138 F3
Larksway IP11 ....152 D3
Larters La IP14 ....67 D8
Larch Ct ■ NR32 ......112 F3
Lattice Ave IP4 ....140 C6
Laud's CI IP11 ....152 B8
Laundry La
Bury St Edmunds IP33 ..123 B3
Huntingfield IP19 ......41 A4
Laureate Gdns CB8 ....120 E6
Laureate Paddocks
CB8 ....120 E6
Laureate Prim Sch
CB8 ....120 E6
Laureate Sch Rd CB8 ..120 E6
Laurel Ave
■ Harwich CO12 ......106 F1
Ipswich IP5 ....141 A7
Laurel CI ■ IP30 ......50 F2
Laurel Dr ■ Claydon IP6 ..82 A5
■ Long Melford CO10 ..91 E8
Laurel Rd NR33 ......115 B6
Laurel Way ■ IP6 ....134 C8
Laurelhayes IP2 ......139 A3
Laurels The
■ Hopton on Sea NR31 ..3 B7
Worlingham NR34 ......111 F3
Lavender CI ■ IP28 ....30 B1
Lavender Hill IP32 ....138 F4
Lavenham Prim Sch
CO10 ....78 D4
Lavenham Rd
Great Waldingfield CO10 ..78 D1
Ipswich IP2 ....138 E5
Lavenham Way
■ Lowestoft NR32 ....112 F3
■ Stowmarket IP14 ....124 E3
Lawn Way IP11 ....152 E5
Lawns The IP4 ....140 C8
Lawrence Dr NR32 ....113 B6
Law's Drift NR33 ......98 C2
Lawshall Rd
Hartest IP29 ....77 B8
Hawstead IP29 ....63 D4
Lawshall Row IP29 ....63 D2
Lawson Cl IP32 ....123 E5
Lawson Cour NR33 ...114 D4
Lawson Pl IP32 ....123 E5
Lawson Rd NR33 ......115 C7
Laxfield & District Mus*
IP13 ....40 B3
Laxfield Rd
Badingham IP13 ....56 B8
Dennington IP13 ......55 E6
Fressingfield IP21 ....39 F7
Laxfield IP13 ....40 A6
Stradbroke IP21 ......39 E4
Laxfield Way NR33 ....114 F4
Layer Rd IP9 ....132 C5
Layham CI ■ IP32 ....123 A8
Layham Dr IP14 ......124 F3
Layham Rd IP7 ....149 D4
Layhill CI IP32 ....123 A8
Laywood CI ■ IP32 ....123 D6
Layzell Croft CO10 ....92 B2
Lazar Cotts IP3 ....140 A4
Lea Way CO10 ....92 D3
Leader's Way CB8 ....120 E4
Leader's Drift ■ NR33 ..114 C5
Leas The NR32 ....112 F5
Leather La
Great Yeldham CO9 ....90 A1
Haverhill CB9 ....132 C5
Leathes CI NR32 ......112 F1
Lee Rd Aldeburgh IP15 ..130 E3
Harwich CO12 ....107 D2
■ Lowestoft NR32 ....112 F1
Leeks Hill IP12 ....147 A7
Leggatt Dr IP8 ....134 A2
Leicester CI IP2 ....138 F1
Leighton Rd IP3 ......140 D5
Leighton Sq IP3 ......140 D5
Leighton Sq IP3 ......144 A8
Leiston Abbey* IP16 ...58 C3
Leiston High Sch IP16 ..129 E5
Leiston Mid Sch IP16 ..129 C6
Leiston Prim Sch
IP16 ....129 C5
Leiston Rd
Aldeburgh IP15 ......130 D7
Cakfair Green IP17 ....129 B3
Haverhill CB9 ....132 C5
■ Lowestoft NR32 ....113 D1
Theberton IP16 ....58 B5
Theberton IP17 ....58 B5
Leiston Sports Ctr
IP16 ....129 E5
Leisure Way NR33 ....113 B7
Lely Rd IP3 ....143 F8
Lemons Hill IP9 ......106 B6
Lentins The IP14 ......68 E6
Leona Cres NR34 ......114 C2
Leonard Dr ■ NR32 ...113 A6
Leonard's La IP26 ......30 B1
Leopold Gdns IP4 ....140 B8
Leopold Rd
Felixstowe IP11 ......153 A3
Ipswich IP4 ....140 B7
Leslie Rd IP3 ....140 C1
Lester Piggott Way
CB8 ....120 F6
Letton CI IP1 ....150 E3
Leverett's La IP18 ....119 B2

Levington La IP10 ......98 A3
Levington Rd
Felixstowe IP11 ......152 E1
Ipswich IP3 ....140 A4
Nacton IP10 ....145 C4
Lewes CI IP3 ....140 E3
Lewis CI
Ditchingham NR35 ....110 C8
Hopton IP22 ....18 C2
Lewis La IP9 ....105 B5
Ley Rd Barrow IP29 ....47 B2
Stetchworth CB8 ......60 A5
Leys La IP23 ....37 B5
Leyton Ave IP30 ......50 B2
Leyton Ave IP28 ......116 B6
Lidgate Ct ■ IP11 ....152 C4
Lidgate Rd CB8 ....61 C8
Lifeboat Mus* IP18 ...119 D4
Lighthouse Score ■
NR32 ....113 E3
Lilac CI IP27 ....14 D8
Lilac Dr
Lakenheath IP27 ......109 D6
Lowestoft NR32 ......113 B3
Lilac Wlk IP6 ....125 D3
Lilley CI IP13 ....122 C3
Lily La NR34 ....10 A7
Lily Way NR32 ....114 C5
Lime Ave
Harwich CO12 ....107 A2
Lowestoft NR32 ......112 D2
Lime CI ■ Harleston IP20 ..22 D5
Lakenheath IP27 ......109 D5
Mildenhall IP28 ......116 E5
■ Ufford IP13 ....84 F7
Wickham Market IP13 ..127 B6
Lime Gr CO10 ....148 A3
Lime Kiln Quay Rd
IP12 ....147 B5
Lime Tree CI IP6 ......129 C5
Lime Tree ■ IP30 ......64 F8
Lime Tree PI IP9 ......124 E5
Lime Wlk IP30 ....65 A3
Limecroft CI ■ IP1 ....135 A3
Limekiln CI ■ IP6 ....134 C8
Limerick CI IP1 ......134 E2
Limes Ave IP8 ....134 C2
Limes The
Halesworth IP19 ......118 A3
■ Horringer IP29 ......63 A8
Long Melford CO10 ....91 E8
Rushmere St Andrew
IP5 ....136 D1
Limetree CI IP6 ......125 E4
Limetree Dr IP3 ......140 D2
Limmer Ave IP21 ......21 C5
Lincoln Ave IP17 ....128 B2
Lincoln CI IP2 ....135 B3
Lincoln CI NR33 ......11 B1
Lincoln Gdns ■ IP6 ...82 B5
Lincoln Gn IP23 ......123 B2
Lincoln La CO6 ......102 E1
Lincoln Terr IP11 ....152 F3
Linda CI ■ NR32 ......3 D4
Lindbergh Rd IP3 ....140 C1
Linden CI
Aldeburgh IP15 ......130 D6
■ Manningtree CO11 ..104 D2
Linden Rd IP15 ....130 C5
Linden Wlk IP28 ......13 B1
Lindisfarne Cr IP2 ....139 A1
Lindisfarne Rd IP33 ..122 D2
Lindsey CI IP33 ......148 F4
Lindsey Rd IP4 ....140 C7
Lindsey Way IP14 ....124 E3
Ling Rd Palgrave IP22 ..20 B2
IP19 ....19 F2
Lingfield Rd IP1 ......135 B4
Lingheath Rd IP27 ....6 A1
Lings Field IP3 ....70 C7
Ling's La IP9 ....106 B7
Lingside ■ IP9 ....98 A7
Link La IP9 ....104 E2
Links Ave IP11 ....153 B6
Links CI
Bury St Edmunds IP33 ..123 B1
Lowestoft NR33 ......114 F5
Worlington IP28 ......30 B4
Links Rd
Great Yarmouth NR31 ..3 B8
Lowestoft NR33 ......114 F5
Links The Flempton IP28 ..32 B1
Woodditton CB8 ......59 E8
Links View CO10 ......92 D3
Linksfield CO10 ......140 E7
Linksfield Gdns IP5 ..146 F2
Linkwood Rd IP30 ....64 B7
Linnet CI CB9 ....133 A5
Linnet Rd
Bury St Edmunds IP33 ..122 C4
Ipswich IP2 ....138 D4
Linnett La CB8 ....133 E2
Linstead Rd IP19 ......40 F5
Linton CI CB8 ....120 F5
Linton Gdns IP33 ....122 E3
Link The ■ IP13 ......140 A8
Lion La IP6 ....125 E3
Lion Mdw CB8 ....88 C4
Lion Rd Glemsford CO10 ..77 A3

Lion Rd continued
Palgrave IP22 ....20 B1
Wortham IP22 ....34 D6
Lion St IP1 ....155 B3
Lionel Hurst Cl 13 CO10 ....92 B3
Lisburn Rd Hadleigh IP7 ....149 F5
Ipswich IP1 ....134 F1
Liston La CO10 ....91 D7
Lithgo Paddock 3 IP31 ....49 A6
Little Back La 3 IP14 ....53 F2
Little Fen Dro C85 ....44 A7
Little Gipping St IP1 ....155 A3
Little Gn C88 ....60 E6
Little Gn Cl IP23 ....36 C3
Little Gr IP9 ....150 D3
Little Gulls IP9 ....150 D3
Little Hasse Dro C87 ....28 E6
Little Horkesley Rd
  CO6 ....102 A2
Little Hyde Cl CO9 ....90 A1
Little Hyde Rd CO9 ....90 A1
Little London Hill IP14 ....53 E3
Little London La CB7 ....29 B5
Little Mdws Dr IP6 ....69 A2
Little Mill La IP29 ....23 A7
Little Oulsham Dro IP26 ....4 B6
Little St IP17 ....57 C8
Little St John's St 8
  IP23 ....147 A5
Little St Mary's CO10 ....91 E7
Little Tufts IP9 ....150 F3
Little Whip St IP2 ....155 B1
Little Yeldham Rd CO9 ....90 B2
Littlemoor Rd IP17 ....57 E6
Little's Cres IP2 ....155 B1
Livermere Drift IP31 ....48 E6
Livermere Rd
Bardon Eston IP31 ....49 A6
Troston IP31 ....33 D2
Lloyd Rd 3 IP9 ....107 A4
Lloyds Ave Ipswich IP1 ....155 B3
15 Kessingland NR33 ....11 C1
Lloyds The IP5 ....141 C7
Loam Pit La IP19 ....118 C4
Locarno Rd 1 IP3 ....140 B3
Lock Cl 1 IP14 ....53 F2
Lockhart Rd NR35 ....6 B7
Lockington Cl IP14 ....124 D5
Lockington Cres IP14 ....124 D5
Lockington Rd IP14 ....124 D5
Lock's La
6 Leavenheath CO6 ....102 A7
Shipmeadow NR34 ....8 F5
Wrentham NR34 ....26 C5
Lock's Rd NR34 ....25 C6
Lockwood 1 IP12 ....147 A3
Loddon Rd
Ditchingham NR35 ....110 C7
Gillingham NR34 ....9 B6
Kirby Cane NR35 ....
Lode Cl CB7 ....28 D3
Lode La CB7 ....28 A1
Lodge Farm Dr IP13 ....153 C5
Lodge Farm La
Barsham NR34 ....9 B4
1 Melton IP12 ....84 E6
Lodge Farm Rd CO10 ....77 B1
Lodge La Claydon IP6 ....134 A8
Riddlesworth IP22 ....18 A3
Shelfanger IP22 ....20 B8
Lodge Rd Fellwell IP26 ....4 F6
Great Bealings IP13 ....137 E5
Hollesley IP12 ....99 D7
Holton IP19 ....118 E5
St John, Ilketshall
  NR35 ....110 C7
1 Ufford IP13 ....84 F7
Walberswick IP18 ....119 A2
Lodge Way IP24 ....16 B7
Loff Cl 1 IP31 ....34 E4
Loftus Rd IP19 ....119 C7
Loggers La IP22 ....35 C8
Loke The
Blundeston NR32 ....3 A4
Ditchingham NR35 ....110 C7
Lombardy Rd CO10 ....148 B8
Lonbarn Hill CO11 ....105 D1
London City Rd IP21 ....39 C3
London La
Harleston IP20 ....66 C7
4 Mundford IP26 ....6 B8
London Rd
Beccles NR34 ....111 B2
Blythburgh IP19 ....42 E5
Brampton with Stoven
  NR34 ....25 E6
Brandon IP27 ....14 E8
Capel St. Mary IP9 ....150 F2
Copdock & Washbrook
  IP8 ....138 A1
Elveden IP24 ....15 C2
Great Horkesley CO6 ....102 C1
Halesworth IP19 ....118 A3
Halesworth IP19 ....118 B3
Harleston IP20 ....22 D5
Icklingham IP27 ....31 E8
Ipswich IP1 ....155 A3
Kessingland NR33 ....11 B2
Lowestoft NR33 ....115 A2
Pinewood IP8 ....138 B2
Thetford IP24 ....16 A5
Westley Waterless CB8 ....59 A4
Weston NR34 ....9 D2
Wrentham NR34 ....26 E4

London Rd N NR32 ....113 D1
London Rd Pakefield
  NR33 ....115 A2
London Rd S NR33 ....115 C5
Lone Barn Cl IP1 ....138 D8
Lonely Rd IP21 ....21 C6
Long Acre
Lowestoft NR33 ....115 B3
Southwold IP18 ....119 B7
Long Bessels IP7 ....149 D6
Long Brackland IP33 ....154 B3
Long Dolver Dro CB7 ....28 D6
Long Field IP11 ....152 D6
Long La Bawdsey IP12 ....99 E3
Burston & Shimpling IP22 ....20 E8
Helmingham IP14 ....69 B6
Long Mdw Wlk NR33 ....114 D5
Long Mdws 2 CO12 ....106 F1
Long Melford CE Prim Sch
  CO10 ....91 E8
Long Pastures 2 CO10 ....77 B2
Long Perry IP9 ....150 F3
Long Rd
Lowestoft NR33 ....114 E3
Lowestoft NR33 ....114 E3
Manningtree CO11 ....104 D1
Manningtree CO11 ....104 D2
Long Rd E CO7 ....104 A2
Long Rd W CO7 ....103 F2
Long Row IP16 ....129 D6
Long Shop Steam Mus*
  IP16 ....129 C6
Long St IP3 ....139 E5
Long Thurlow Rd IP31 ....51 A7
Longacre Gdns IP33 ....122 E3
Longbeach Dr NR33 ....114 D3
Longcroft IP11 ....152 E6
Longden Ave NR32 ....112 E2
Longfield Rd IP9 ....150 E4
Longfield Way 6 NR32 ....112 D2
Longfulans La NR31 ....3 B6
Longmeadow IP13 ....122 E3
Longmere La CB7 ....28 C5
Longrigg Rd NR35 ....110 C7
Lonsdale Cl IP4 ....139 F7
Looe Rd IP11 ....153 C5
Looms La IP33 ....154 B2
Lopham Rd NR16 ....18 D8
Lophams Cl IP30 ....132 D8
Loraine Way
Bramford IP8 ....134 A1
Bramford IP8 ....134 A2
Lord Rd IP22 ....20 D2
Lord's Croft La CB9 ....132 E5
Lord's Highway The
  IP11 ....67 E5
Lord's La CB8 ....61 E5
Lord's Wlk IP17 ....13 F2
Lorne Pk Rd NR33 ....115 C6
Lorne Rd
Lowestoft NR33 ....115 C6
Southwold IP18 ....119 D5
Lothing St NR32 ....112 F1
Lothingland Mid Sch
  NR32 ....3 A5
Lotus Cl IP1 ....134 C1
Loudham Hall Rd
  IP13 ....127 D3
Loudham La IP13 ....85 A7
Louie's La IP22 ....20 C3
Lound Dam NR14 ....2 A3
Lound Rd
Belton with Browston NR31 ....2 E8
Blundeston NR32 ....2 A4
Louse La Dedham CO7 ....103 F2
Rattlesden IP30 ....65 D3
Louvain Rd 16 CO12 ....107 A1
Lovat Cl IP20 ....22 E6
Love La Lowestoft NR33 ....114 F4
Thorndon IP23 ....53 B8
Westleton IP17 ....58 C7
Love Rd NR32 ....113 C1
Lovers La IP19 ....106 B6
Lover's La IP16 ....129 E8
Lovetofts Dr IP1 ....134 D1
Lovewell Rd NR33 ....115 C6
Low Comm IP22 ....19 B3
Low Comm La NR34 ....22 C4
Low Comm Rd IP22 ....19 B3
Low Farm Dr NR33 ....114 C3
Low La Brandeston IP13 ....70 A7
Creeting St Mary IP6 ....125 E8
Low Lighthouse Maritime
Mus* CO12 ....107 C3
Low Rd Alburgh IP20 ....7 A1
Bramfield IP19 ....42 A5
Brampton with Stoven
  NR34 ....25 D5
Burwell CB5 ....44 A5
Carlton IP17 ....128 C6
Cransford IP17 ....57 F8
Darsham IP17 ....57 F8
Debenham IP14 ....53 E1
Denham IP21 ....38 C2
Denton IP20 ....7 B1
1 Dickleburgh & Rushall
  IP21 ....20 F2
Earl Soham IP13 ....54 E2
Eyke IP12 ....85 B7
1 Fressingfield IP21 ....39 E8
Friston IP17 ....57 F6
Great Glemham IP17 ....56 C1
Harwich CO12 ....106 F1
Hasketon IP13 ....146 B8
Hedenham NR35 ....7 D8
Marlesford IP13 ....71 C5
Mettingham NR35 ....110 F5
Monk Soham IP13 ....54 D3

Low Rd continued
Redenhall with Harleston
  IP20 ....22 F5
St John, Ilketshall NR34 ....8 D2
Starston IP20 ....22 C7
Stratford St Andrew IP17 ....71 F7
Swefling IP17 ....56 E3
Ubbeston IP19 ....42 D3
Wenhaston With Mells Hamlet
  IP19 ....42 C7
Worlingham IP20 ....23 A7
Low St Badingham IP13 ....56 A7
Bardwell IP31 ....34 C3
Glemsford CO10 ....77 B3
Hoxne IP21 ....38 B8
Kettleburgh IP13 ....70 B7
St Margaret, Ilketshall
  NR35 ....24 B8
Low Wr La IP22 ....20 A1
Lower Barn Rd IP8 ....95 D5
Lower Baxter St IP33 ....154 B2
Lower Brook St IP4 ....155 B2
Lower Broom Rd IP30 ....50 C1
Lower Byfield IP7 ....79 C2
Lower Coney Gr IP8 ....81 A4
Lower Cres IP4 ....82 A6
Lower Dales View Rd
  IP1 ....139 A8
Lower Drag Way IP27 ....19 A4
Lower Farm Rd
Boxted CO4 ....103 A4
Ringshall IP7 ....80 E6
Lower Harlings 4 IP9 ....107 A4
Lower House La IP12 ....98 C5
Lower Houses NR9 ....106 B5
Lower Marine Par
  CO12 ....107 B1
Lower N St CO10 ....75 D3
Lower Oakley IP21 ....37 F8
Lower Olland St NR35 ....110 B4
Lower Orwell St IP4 ....155 C2
Lower Pk Wlk IP19 ....118 E4
Lower Rd Borley CO10 ....91 D6
Falkenham IP10 ....98 F1
Glemsford CO10 ....77 B1
Grundisburgh IP13 ....83 E5
Hemingstone IP6 ....68 D4
Hundon CO10 ....75 D3
Lavenham CO10 ....78 D4
Little Blakenham IP8 ....81 D3
Melton IP13 ....84 F6
Mount Bures CO8 ....101 D3
Onehouse IP14 ....66 B5
Westerfield IP6 ....135 D4
Wicken CB7 ....28 A2
Lower Rose La IP21 ....20 D1
Lower St Bayham IP6 ....81 E7
Cavendish CO10 ....76 E1
Great Bealings IP13 ....137 E6
Rattlesden IP30 ....65 D6
Sproughton IP8 ....138 A4
Stansfield CO10 ....76 C6
Stanstead CO10 ....77 C3
Stratford St Mary CO7 ....103 E5
Stutton IP9 ....105 D5
Ufford IP13 ....85 A6
Wickham Market IP13 ....127 C7
Lower Ufford La IP13 ....127 D3
Lower Ufford Rd IP13 ....127 C1
Lowes Hill IP12 ....128 E7
Lowestoft & Suffolk
Maritime Mus*
  NR32 ....113 E3
Lowestoft & N Suffolk Hospl
  NR32 ....113 D1
Lowestoft Coll NR32 ....113 C2
Lowestoft Mus*
  NR33 ....114 D8
Lowestoft Rd
Beccles NR34 ....111 E4
Blundeston NR32 ....112 E8
Hopton-on-sea NR31 ....3 C6
Lowestoft NR33 ....114 D3
Reydon IP18 ....119 C8
Worlingham NR34 ....10 A4
Lowestoft Sta NR32 ....113 E3
Lowestoft Town FC
  NR32 ....113 C2
Lowgate St IP23 ....117 D2
Lowlands Cl 7 NR33 ....11 C1
Lowry Cl CB9 ....132 E7
Lowry Gdns 6 IP3 ....144 A8
Low's La IP22 ....20 C1
Loxley Rd NR33 ....114 E6
Lucas Rd CO10 ....148 D5
Lucena Ct IP14 ....124 C6
Lucerne Cl
Lowestoft NR33 ....114 C5
5 Rudgate Cswy IP23 ....117 C2
Ludlow Cl IP11 ....135 B4
Luff Mdw IP6 ....125 D5
Lugano Ave IP14 ....98 B8
Lulworth Ave IP3 ....140 D3
Lulworth Dr CB9 ....132 C6
Lulworth Pk 8 NR32 ....113 A4
Lummis Vale IP5 ....141 C7
Lundy Cl CB9 ....133 B5
Lunnish Hill CO12 ....106 C2
Lupin IP18 ....119 B6

Lupin Rd IP2 ....138 E4
Lupin Way IP6 ....125 D3
Lushington Rd 6 CO11 ....104 E2
Luther Rd IP2 ....155 B1
Lutus Cl CO10 ....90 A7
Lydgate Cl
1 Bury St Edmunds IP32 ....48 C5
6 Lawford CO11 ....104 D2
Lydgate Rd IP14 ....124 C7
Lymingster Cl 6 IP32 ....123 D6
Lymn Rd NR32 ....112 E1
Lyncroft Rd NR33 ....115 B3
Lyndhurst Ave IP4 ....140 C5
Lyndhurst Rd NR32 ....113 D4
Lyng La IP22 ....18 F5
Lynn's Cl IP19 ....118 C4
Lynn's Hall Cl CO10 ....92 C6
Lynton Gdns NR32 ....113 C3
Lynwood Ave IP1 ....153 B5
Lynx Bsns Pk CB8 ....44 F7
Lyon Cl IP23 ....37 C4
Lysander Dr IP3 ....144 C8

M

Macaulay Rd IP1 ....134 F3
Mackenzie Dr IP5 ....141 B8
Mackenzie Rd IP3 ....78 C8
Mackenzie Rd IP24 ....16 A5
Macpherson Robertson Way
  3 IP28 ....116 B5
Magdalen Cl 3 NR32 ....113 A3
Magdalen Dr IP12 ....146 D3
Magdalen Rd IP12 ....146 D3
Magdalen St IP23 ....117 C2
Magdalene Cl IP2 ....138 F2
Maginley Cres IP4 ....140 F6
Magnolia Cl
8 Beck Row, Holywell
Row & Kenny Hill IP28 ....13 B1
2 Red Lodge IP28 ....30 B1
Magnolia Ct 6 NR32 ....113 B2
Magpie Cl 3 IP6 ....138 C2
Magpie Ct 8 IP20 ....22 D6
Magpie Hill IP29 ....19 E1
Maid Marion Ct IP33 ....122 F3
Maidenhall App IP2 ....139 B2
Maidenhall Sports Ctr
  IP2 ....139 B1
Maids Cross Hill IP27 ....109 E6
Maids Cross Way
  IP27 ....109 D6
Maidstone Rd
Felixstowe IP11 ....152 E5
Lowestoft NR32 ....113 C2
Main Rd Benhall IP17 ....72 C8
Bucklesham IP10 ....141 F1
Chelmondiston IP9 ....106 B8
Darsham IP17 ....42 A1
Hacheston IP13 ....71 C4
Harwich CO12 ....106 F1
Henley IP6 ....82 D6
Ipswich IP5 ....141 A8
Kelsale cum Carlton
  IP17 ....128 C8
Marlesford IP13 ....71 D4
Martlesham IP12 ....146 C1
Parham IP13 ....70 F8
2 Ramsey & Parkeston
  CO12 ....106 D1
Somersham IP8 ....81 C3
Tuddenham St Martin
  IP6 ....136 B4
Woolverstone IP9 ....143 F2
Wormingford CO6 ....101 F2
Main St
Hockwold cum Wilton IP26 ....4 F3
Leiston IP16 ....129 C6
Maine St 3 IP24 ....16 A5
Maisie's Mdw IP23 ....54 D7
Maitland Rd IP6 ....125 E3
Major La IP23 ....37 A2
Major's Cl IP20 ....22 E5
Makins Rd 2 CO12 ....106 F3
Malcolm Way C88 ....121 A5
Maldon Ct CO10 ....148 F5
Malin Cl CB9 ....133 B5
Mallard Rd IP18 ....119 B7
Mallard Way
Hollesley IP12 ....99 F7
Ipswich IP2 ....138 F3
Stowmarket IP14 ....124 A6
Sudbury CO10 ....92 B3
Mallards The IP27 ....109 D5
Mallets La IP22 ....131 C2
Mallow Rd IP24 ....16 C6
Mallow Way NR33 ....114 C4
Mallowhayes Cl IP2 ....139 B3
Malmesbury Cl IP2 ....139 B3
Malt Cl 5 IP13 ....40 B3
Malt Office Ave IP19 ....24 B4
Malt Office La IP19 ....24 A4
Malthouse Cl 4 IP20 ....22 D6
Malthouse La
Bury St Edmunds IP32 ....154 B4
Gissing IP22 ....20 B8
Martlesham Rd 2 CO11 ....104 E2
Malting End CB8 ....60 E2
Malting Farm La CO7 ....103 E1
Malting La 8 Clare CO10 ....90 A8
Isleham CB7 ....29 C5
Malting Row IP31 ....33 F5
Maltings IP11 ....152 D3
Maltings Cl
2 Bures Hamlet CO8 ....101 C5
1 Chevington IP29 ....62 C6
Halesworth IP19 ....118 B4

Maltings Cl continued
Moulton CB8 ....45 F3
Maltings Dr 6 IP20 ....22 D6
Maltings Garth 8 IP31 ....49 D4
Maltings The NR35 ....110 C4
Malt's La IP29 ....4 F3
Maltsters' Way
8 Lowestoft NR32 ....112 D1
Lowestoft NR32 ....114 D8
Maltward Ave Ipswich IP3 ....122 D5
Malvern Cl Ipswich IP3 ....140 B3
Newmarket C88 ....121 A4
Malvern Rd IP3 ....122 D3
Malvern Rise NR32 ....113 A3
Manchester Rd IP2 ....138 D2
Mandale Rd IP2 ....138 C6
Mandeville Rd IP23 ....122 C4
Mandeville 4 C85 ....44 A5
Mandy Cl IP4 ....140 A6
Mannall Wlk IP5 ....141 E8
Manning Rd IP11 ....48 D5
Manning Rd IP11 ....152 E2
Manning's La IP22 ....35 D5
Mannings La IP22 ....144 D4
Mannington Cl 3 IP4 ....140 F5
Manningtree High Sch
  CO11 ....104 D2
Manningtree Mus*
  CO11 ....104 A3
East Bergholt CO7 ....151 F3
Stutton IP9 ....105 C5
Manningtree Sports Ctr
  CO11 ....104 D2
Manningtree Sta
  CO11 ....104 D3
Manor Ash Dr IP32 ....123 E6
Manor Cl 8 Beccles NR34 ....9 F4
8 Cavendish CO10 ....76 E1
Walberswick IP18 ....119 A2
Worlingham NR34 ....9 F4
Manor Farm Cl 1 IP18 ....119 D5
Manor Farm Rd
St John, Ilketshall NR34 ....8 D3
1 Thistley Green IP28 ....29 F6
Manor Garth IP31 ....49 E6
Manor Gdns
2 Hopton on Sea NR31 ....3 C6
Saxmundham IP17 ....128 E3
Manor House Mus*
  IP33 ....154 C1
Manor La Gosbeck IP6 ....68 D2
1 Harwich CO12 ....107 A2
Horringer IP29 ....63 A8
Horringer IP29 ....122 B1
Stutton IP9 ....105 C5
Manor Pk Rd
Corton NR32 ....3 C4
5 Southwold IP18 ....119 D5
Manor Rd 8 Bildeston IP7 ....79 F4
Brandon IP27 ....5 E1
Bungay NR35 ....110 B2
Clopton IP13 ....69 E1
Elmsett IP7 ....80 F2
Felixstowe IP11 ....152 B8
Harwich CO12 ....107 A2
Hasketon IP13 ....146 D6
Haverhill CB9 ....132 F5
Hessett IP30 ....64 F7
Hopton-on-sea NR31 ....3 B6
Ipswich IP4 ....139 D8
1 Martlesham Heath IP5 ....98 A8
Mildenhall IP28 ....116 B4
Roydon IP22 ....20 B8
Sudbury CO10 ....148 C7
Trimley St Martin IP11 ....153 D11
Manor Terr IP11 ....107 F3
Manor View IP20 ....116 D2
Manor Wlk 8 NR31 ....11 B1
Manorhouse La 8
  NR34 ....111 B6
Manse La IP19 ....40 C6
Mansfield Ave IP1 ....134 F2
Manthorp Cl IP22 ....147 B8
Manwick Rd IP11 ....152 E2
Maple Cl
6 Great Bricett IP7 ....80 D6
Ipswich IP2 ....139 A3
3 Lakenheath IP27 ....13 F2
Yaxley IP23 ....37 B5
Maple Gn 8 IP31 ....49 A6
Maple Gr IP6 ....82 A6
Maple Hill CO10 ....75 E1
Maple Rd
5 Lowestoft IP11 ....114 F7
Stowupland IP14 ....67 A6
Sudbury CO10 ....148 F3
Maple Way
Beccles NR34 ....111 C5
Eye IP23 ....117 D3
Leavenheath CO6 ....102 B7
Maples The IP5 ....140 E8
Marbled White Dr IP2 ....138 E8
March Pl 8 IP24 ....76 A1
Marcus Cl CB9 ....133 B5
Marcus Rd IP11 ....153 D5
Mardle Rd Reydon NR34 ....43 A8
Wangford with Henham
  NR34 ....26 C1
Mardle The NR33 ....114 C2
Mare Hill CO10 ....75 D3
Margaret Rd 3 IP14 ....124 C7
Margaret St IP11 ....152 E5
Margate Rd IP3 ....140 B3
Marham Rd IP11 ....48 D5
Maria St 7 CO12 ....107 A3
Marigold Ave IP2 ....138 E3

Marigold Dr 3 IP28 .....46 A8
Marina 6 NR32 .....113 E1
Marina Gdns IP11 .....152 E2
Marine Ct 8 NR31 .....3 B8
Marine Par
    12 Harwich CO12 .....107 B2
    Harwich CO12 .....107 B2
    Lowestoft NR33 .....115 D7
Mariners CI 8 NR31 .....3 B8
Mariner's Compass NR31 .....3 B8
Mariners Pk CI 1 NR31 .....3 B7
Mariners St NR32 .....113 C1
Mariners Way IP15 .....130 D5
Marion CI 6 NR34 .....111 C3
Mark Jennings La
    IP33 .....154 C3
Mark La IP7 .....6 C2
Markant CI IP32 .....123 E6
Market Cross PI IP15 .....130 F4
Market Gr CO9 .....90 A1
Market Hill 4 Clare CO10 .....90 A8
    Diss IP22 .....83 D8
    Framlingham IP13 .....126 C3
    Haverhill CO9 .....132 E6
    Orford IP12 .....131 C2
    4 Sudbury CO10 .....148 C5
Market La
    Blundeston NR32 .....3 A4
    Burston & Shimpling IP22 .....20 E5
Market Rd
    Somerleyton, Ashby &
    Herringfleet NR32 .....2 C4
Market PI Hadleigh IP7 .....149 D5
    2 Halesworth IP19 .....118 A3
    Harleston IP20 .....22 D6
    3 Lavenham CO10 .....78 D4
    Saxmundham IP17 .....128 D3
Market Row NR34 .....111 B5
Market St
    8 Beccles NR34 .....111 B5
    Fordham CB7 .....29 A1
    3 Harwich CO12 .....107 C3
    Laxfield IP13 .....40 B3
    3 Mildenhall IP28 .....116 B6
    2 Newmarket CB8 .....121 A3
    10 Soham CB7 .....28 D4
Market Weston Rd
    IP22 .....35 A7
Markhams CI IP26 .....4 D5
Marlborough Ct NR32 .....112 F1
Marlborough Dr 4
    CO10 .....148 B6
Marlborough Rd
    Ipswich IP4 .....140 A5
    Lowestoft NR32 .....112 F1
    Saxtead IP13 .....55 A4
    Southwold IP18 .....119 D6
Marlesford Rd IP13 .....71 B5
Marlow Rd IP1 .....134 D1
Marriott's Wlk 5 IP14 .....124 D5
Marsden CI 3 NR33 .....115 A3
Marsh La Aldeby NR34 .....114 A4
    Carlton Colville NR33 .....114 A4
    8 Earsham NR35 .....7 F4
    Felixstowe IP11 .....153 C8
    25 Kessingland NR33 .....11 C1
    Kessingland IP13 .....27 C8
    North Cove NR34 .....10 B5
    Reydon IP18 .....26 D2
    Somerleyton, Ashby &
    Herringfleet NR32 .....2 C4
    Worlingham NR34 .....9 F1
    Wortham IP22 .....20 A1
Marsh Rd Boxford CO10 .....93 C3
    Fritton & St Olaves NR31 .....2 C3
    Stoke-by-nayland CO6 .....103 C7
Marsh View NR34 .....11 D5
Marshall CI IP5 .....141 C8
Marshalls Mdw 3 IP14 .....67 A6
Marshams Piece 4
    IP33 .....114 C5
Marshy La CO10 .....90 B4
Martello La IP11 .....153 D5
Martello Rd NR32 .....113 B4
Marten's La CO6 .....102 F8
Martin CI
    Lowestoft NR33 .....114 D3
    Mildenhall IP28 .....116 D3
    8 Soham CB7 .....28 D5
Martin Rd 2 Burwell CB5 .....44 A6
    Harleston IP20 .....22 E6
    Ipswich IP2 .....155 B1
Martinet Gn IP3 .....140 C1
Martin's Ave IP3 .....115 B6
Martins La IP13 .....55 A4
Martins Mdw 3 IP23 .....36 D2
Martins Rd CO10 .....148 F7
Martinsyde 9 IP5 .....141 D7
Martlesham Beacon Hill Prim
    Sch IP12 .....42 A5
Martlesham Heath Control
    Twr Mus* IP5 .....98 A8
Martlesham Rd IP13 .....137 F3
Martyns Rise 8 CO10 .....91 E7
Mary La CO10 .....92 A8
Maryon Rd IP3 .....140 B1
Mary's La IP19 .....40 E6
Masefield Rd Diss IP22 .....20 D2
    Stowmarket IP14 .....124 B8
Mashay Rd CO9 .....90 B3
Maskell's La IP7 .....80 E4
Mason Ct 1 IP6 .....82 A5
Mason Gdns 8 IP28 .....29 F6
Mason Rd IP5 .....44 A7
Masons Ct IP14 .....139 F6
Mason's La 5 IP30 .....50 D1
Mast CI NR33 .....114 B4

Masterson Gr IP5 .....141 C6
Mat Dawson CI CB8 .....120 F6
Mather La IP20 .....22 B5
Mather Way IP2 .....155 C1
Matlock CI 2 IP8 .....138 C2
Matlock Dale 11 NR33 .....114 F5
Matson Rd IP1 .....138 F8
Matthews La CB8 .....74 C7
Maudslay Rd IP1 .....134 C2
Mauthy Way NR33 .....114 F5
May Rd Ipswich IP3 .....140 C2
    Lowestoft NR32 .....113 C1
Maybury Rd IP3 .....140 B1
Maybush La IP11 .....153 C5
Maycroft CI IP1 .....135 A3
Mayes La CO12 .....106 D1
Mayfair Rd NR35 .....110 C3
Mayfield CI IP7 .....149 C8
Mayfield Ave IP18 .....11 C1
Mayfield La 7 IP5 .....98 A7
Mayfield Rd
    Bury St Edmunds IP33 .....123 B3
    Ipswich IP4 .....140 C7
    Lowestoft NR33 .....114 C4
Mayfield Way IP14 .....52 E5
Mayfields
    Lakenheath IP27 .....109 C7
    8 Martlesham Heath IP5 .....98 A7
Mayflower Ave
    8 Harwich CO12 .....107 C3
    Saxmundham IP17 .....128 B2
Mayflower Way
    14 Harleston IP20 .....22 D5
    Sudbury CO10 .....148 D8
Maynewater La IP33 .....154 C1
Maypole La CB8 .....60 C6
May's La CO10 .....103 F2
Mccalmont Way CB8 .....121 C2
Mclaren Ct 1 NR33 .....111 C3
Mclean Dr 2 NR33 .....11 B1
Mead The CO10 .....148 F2
Mead Way IP14 .....52 E5
Meadow Barn IP14 .....66 A2
Meadow Ct
    Bury St Edmunds IP33 .....122 E3
    8 Felixstowe IP11 .....107 D8
    4 Great Yarmouth NR31 .....3 B8
    16 Stanton IP31 .....34 E4
Meadow Dr
    Horringer IP29 .....63 A8
    Lakenheath IP27 .....109 D7
Meadow Gdns NR34 .....111 A3
Meadow La
    Newmarket CB8 .....121 D1
    Sudbury CO10 .....148 C5
    Thurston IP31 .....49 E4
Meadow Prim Sch
    NR33 .....115 B6
Meadow Rd
    Bungay NR35 .....110 D2
    Lowestoft NR33 .....112 F4
Meadow Valley IP7 .....80 D5
Meadow View
    Needham Market IP6 .....125 C5
    Woolpit IP30 .....65 E8
Meadow View Rd
    CO10 .....148 B4
Meadow Way
    Assington CO10 .....92 F1
    8 Barrow IP29 .....47 A2
    Lowestoft NR33 .....114 E3
    Wickham Market 3 IP17 .....72 C8
Meadowlands
    11 Blundeston NR32 .....3 A4
    Burwell CB5 .....44 A5
    Kirton IP10 .....98 D2
    4 Woolpit IP30 .....50 D1
Meadowlands Gdns
    IP4 .....140 E8
Meadowsweet
    Haverhill CB9 .....132 C7
    3 Lowestoft NR33 .....114 D5
Meadowvale CI
    Beccles NR34 .....111 B2
    Ipswich IP4 .....139 F8
Meads The NR32 .....113 D5
Meadway 22 CO10 .....104 D2
Mear CI IP12 .....45 F3
Mechanical Music Mus &
    Bygones* IP14 .....52 A6
Medway Rd IP3 .....139 F2
Meekings Rd CO10 .....148 F6
Meeting Field 10 CO10 .....91 E7
Meeting La
    Grundisburgh IP13 .....83 E5
    Ridgewell CO9 .....89 D4
Melbourne Ct 2 IP20 .....22 D5
Melbourne Rd
    Ipswich IP4 .....140 D7
    Lowestoft NR32 .....113 D3
Melford CI 8 Burwell CB5 .....44 B5
    8 Ipswich IP4 .....140 F5
Melford Hall* CO10 .....92 A8
Melford Rd Acton CO10 .....92 A8
    Cavendish CO10 .....76 F1

Melford Rd continued
    Lavenham CO10 .....78 C3
    Lawshall IP29 .....63 D1
    Stowmarket IP14 .....124 F4
    Sudbury CO10 .....148 F5
Melford Way IP11 .....152 C3
Mellis CI CB9 .....74 A1
Mellis Ct 10 IP21 .....152 D5
Mellis Rd
    Gislingham IP23 .....36 D3
    Thrandeston IP21 .....37 B6
    Wortham IP22 .....36 E7
    Yaxley IP23 .....37 B5
Melplash CI IP3 .....140 E4
Melplash Rd IP3 .....140 E4
Melrose CI NR32 .....112 F5
Melrose Gdns
    Ipswich IP4 .....140 B8
    Lowestoft NR32 .....120 E4
    Stowmarket IP14 .....124 B8
Melton Grange Rd
    IP12 .....147 A6
Melton Hill IP12 .....147 B6
Melton Mdw Rd 4 IP12 .....147 B6
Melton Prim Sch IP12 .....147 B7
Melville Rd IP4 .....139 F5
Mendham 3 NR20 .....22 D6
Mendham La
    8 Harleston IP20 .....22 D6
    St Cross, South Elmham
    IP20 .....23 C6
Mendham Prim Sch
    IP20 .....23 A6
Mendham Rd IP20 .....23 A6
Mendip Dr IP5 .....140 E6
Mendip Rd NR32 .....112 E2
Mendlesham Prim Sch
    IP14 .....52 E4
Mendlesham Rd IP14 .....52 B5
Mercers Rd IP32 .....123 D7
Mere CI IP31 .....49 C5
Mere Gdns IP4 .....140 F4
Mere La IP28 .....46 A6
Mere Side CB7 .....28 C4
Meredith Rd IP1 .....134 E2
Meriton Rise IP7 .....149 F4
Merivale Rd 6 CO11 .....104 D2
Merlewood CO10 .....148 B5
Merlin Rd IP2 .....138 C3
Merriam CI 5 CO11 .....105 A3
Merrion Rd NR33 .....114 F3
Merrion CI CB9 .....132 C2
Merrylees NR34 .....114 C5
Mersey Rd IP3 .....139 F2
Merville 8 NR33 .....114 E3
Messenger CI NR35 .....110 E7
Metfield Rd IP20 .....23 D3
Metfield St IP20 .....23 C3
Mettersgate Hall Dr
    IP20 .....84 E1
Meynell Gdns 2 CB8 .....121 A5
Micawber Mews CB8 .....3 A4
Michaelhouse Way 12
    IP31 .....34 E4
Michaels Mount IP3 .....137 D5
Michaelstowe CI 1
    CO12 .....106 E1
Michigan CI IP5 .....141 B7
Mickfield Mews 16
    IP11 .....153 A4
Micklegate Rd IP12 .....152 E2
Micklesmere Dr 2 IP31 .....34 E1
Mid Suffolk Leisure Ctr
    IP14 .....124 B7
Middle Dro CB7 .....28 A4
Middle Gn CO6 .....101 B1
Middle La NR34 .....10 B5
Middle Rd
    Blo' Norton IP22 .....18 F2
    Earsham IP20 .....22 E5
Middle Way CO10 .....91 E8
Middle Wlk NR32 .....113 A6
Middlefield Dr 8 IP14 .....66 B4
Middlefield Rd 10 CO11 .....105 A3
Middleton CI IP2 .....138 D2
Middleton Prim Sch
    IP17 .....58 A6
Middleton Rd
    Sudbury CO10 .....148 B4
    Yoxford IP17 .....57 E7
Midhurst CI 3 IP22 .....123 D6
Midmeadow 4 NR34 .....111 B5
Mights Rd IP18 .....119 C6
Milano Ave IP5 .....98 B8
Milden CI 4 IP4 .....140 F5
Milden Rd
    Brent Eleigh CO10 .....79 A2
    Ipswich IP2 .....138 C5
    4 Redgrave IP22 .....21 A8
Mildenhall Airfield
    IP28 .....30 B7
Mildenhall Dro IP28 .....12 F3
Mildenhall Mus* IP28 .....116 C6
Mildenhall Rd
    Barton Mills IP28 .....116 C2
    Beck Row, Holywell
    Row & Kenny Hill IP28 .....13 E8
    8 Bury St Edmunds IP32 .....123 A8
    Fordham CB7 .....29 C1
    Icklingham IP28 .....31 A5
    Littleport CB7 .....12 A8

Mildenhall Stadium
    IP28 .....29 D8
Mildenhall Upper Sch
    IP28 .....116 E4
Mildmay Rd IP3 .....140 B1
Mile End IP27 .....14 E8
Mile End Rd CB7 .....12 A7
Miles Hawk Way IP28 .....116 A5
Miles Paddock IP14 .....52 A6
Military Rd CB7 .....28 C2
Military Way 5 IP12 .....146 D3
Mill Bank 1 NR32 .....112 F2
Mill Broadway IP12 .....131 C4
Mill Chase CB9 .....88 E3
Mill CI 3 Burwell CB5 .....44 B5
    Capel St. Mary IP9 .....150 C3
    Exning CB8 .....120 B8
    1 Felixstowe IP11 .....107 D8
    Felixstowe IP11 .....107 D8
    Kirby Row NR35 .....152 D4
    1 Walsham-le-willows
    IP31 .....35 C2
    Woolpit IP30 .....50 D1
Mill Cnr CB8 .....28 C3
Mill Croft 8 CB7 .....28 D3
Mill Drift IP26 .....5 A3
Mill Dro CB7 .....28 C3
Mill End La IP14 .....67 C7
Mill Field
    8 Aldeburgh IP15 .....130 E5
    Bramford IP8 .....134 B2
    Haverhill IP28 .....68 E6
Mill Fields IP31 .....51 D1
Mill Gdns
    Bedingham NR35 .....7 B8
    Elmswell IP30 .....50 F2
Mill Hill (Tumulus)*
    IP28 .....2 C8
Mill Hill Burgh IP13 .....83 F6
    Capel St. Mary IP9 .....150 C3
    Cotton IP14 .....52 A6
    Earl Soham IP13 .....54 C2
    Hadleigh IP7 .....94 B7
    Haverhill CB9 .....132 D5
    Lawford CO11 .....104 B2
    Leiston IP16 .....129 C2
    Manningtree CO11 .....104 E2
    Mettingham NR35 .....8 D5
    Newmarket CB8 .....121 A4
    Peasenhall IP17 .....56 F8
    Rattlesden IP30 .....65 D6
    Sudbury CO10 .....148 B5
    Wickham Market IP13 .....127 B7
Mill Hill Dr IP19 .....118 A4
Mill Hoo IP12 .....99 E4
Mill La
    All Saints & St Nicholas,
    South Elmham IP20 .....23 E5
    Barham IP24 .....16 B2
    Barrow IP29 .....47 A2
    Bayham IP6 .....81 F7
    Belham IP17 .....72 C8
    Boyton IP12 .....86 B2
    Bradfield CO11 .....105 B1
    Bramford IP8 .....134 A2
    Brandeston IP13 .....70 A7
    Bruisyard IP17 .....56 C5
    7 Burwell CB5 .....44 B5
    Buxley IP12 .....86 B6
    Campsey Ash IP13 .....127 C6
    Cavendish CO10 .....90 D8
    Chelmondiston IP9 .....100 E1
    Coddenham IP6 .....68 B1
    Combs IP14 .....124 B1
    Copdock & Washbrook
    IP8 .....138 A1
    Corton NR32 .....3 D4
    Cowlinge CB8 .....75 B8
    Creeting St Peter or
    West Creeting IP6 .....125 D8
    Dedham CO7 .....103 F4
    Dennington IP13 .....55 D5
    Ellingham NR35 .....8 D2
    Exning CB8 .....120 B8
    Felixstowe IP11 .....152 F4
    Fordham CB7 .....29 B1
    Garboldisham IP22 .....18 D3
    8 Great Blakenham IP6 .....82 A5
    Great Welham CO9 .....90 A2
    Hasketon IP13 .....146 A7
    Hoo IP13 .....70 D8
    Hopton IP22 .....18 C3
    Hundon CO10 .....75 D3
    Kersey IP7 .....94 A7
    Layham IP7 .....149 E2
    Leiston IP16 .....129 C2
    8 Manningtree CO11 .....104 E2
    Marlesford IP13 .....71 C5
    Metfield IP20 .....23 D3
    North Cove NR34 .....10 C4
    Polstead CO6 .....102 E8
    Pulham St Mary IP21 .....21 F8
    St John, Ilketshall NR34 .....8 E2
    Somersham IP8 .....81 C3
    Southwold IP18 .....119 C8
    Stetchworth CB8 .....59 F5
    Stoke Ash IP23 .....52 F8
    Stonham Earl IP14 .....67 D5
    Stradbroke IP21 .....39 C5
    Thelnetham IP22 .....35 B6
    Thetford IP26 .....4 D5
    Thurston IP31 .....49 A6
    Tunstall IP12 .....72 B1
    Weybread IP22 .....22 C3

Mill La continued
    Wickham Market IP13 .....127 C6
    2 Wilnesham IP6 .....83 A5
    Woodbridge IP12 .....147 A5
    Woolpit IP30 .....50 D1
    Wrentham NR34 .....26 F5
Mill Piece IP10 .....145 C6
Mill Rd (South) IP13 .....154 A1
Mill Rd
    Aldeby/Wheatacre/Burgh
    St Peter NR34 .....10 B8
    Ashley CB8 .....45 F1
    Badingham IP13 .....56 B6
    Barningham IP31 .....34 E7
    Battisford IP14 .....80 B8
    Beccles NR34 .....111 C2
    Birdbrook CO9 .....89 C5
    Botesdale IP22 .....36 B6
    Boxted CO4 .....102 F2
    Brockdish IP21 .....21 E3
    Brockley IP29 .....63 A1
    Burston & Shimpling IP22 .....20 E6
    Bury St Edmunds IP33 .....154 A2
    Buxhall IP14 .....65 F4
    Chevington IP29 .....62 C6
    Cockfield CO10 .....90 B8
    Coldfair Green IP17 .....129 A2
    Cotton IP14 .....52 A6
    East Bergholt CO7 .....151 E4
    Ellingham NR35 .....8 D7
    Foxearth CO10 .....91 B7
    Friston IP17 .....72 E6
    Gazeley CB8 .....46 B3
    Great Barton IP31 .....49 A6
    Halesworth IP19 .....118 E3
    Haverhill CB9 .....132 E5
    Hemley IP12 .....98 E5
    Hengrave IP28 .....48 A7
    Honington IP31 .....33 B1
    Hundon CO10 .....75 D4
    Ipswich IP3 .....140 E1
    Kedington IP28 .....133 E8
    Kirtling CB8 .....60 F3
    Lakenheath IP27 .....109 E6
    Laxfield IP13 .....40 B2
    Lowestoft NR33 .....115 C7
    Mendlesham IP14 .....52 D4
    Moulton CB8 .....46 A1
    Mutford NR34 .....10 B6
    Newbourne IP12 .....99 D5
    Occold IP23 .....37 F1
    Peasenhall IP17 .....56 E8
    Redlingfield IP23 .....38 C6
    Ridgewell CO9 .....89 D3
    Rumburgh IP19 .....24 B4
    Saxmundham IP17 .....128 C3
    Stambourne CO9 .....89 B2
    Swelling IP17 .....58 E1
    Thelnetham IP22 .....35 B6
    Westleton IP17 .....58 C7
    Weybread IP21 .....22 C4
    Winfarthing IP22 .....20 B1
    Wissett IP19 .....118 A5
    Worlingworth IP13 .....54 D7
    Wyverstone IP14 .....51 D6
Mill Rd S IP22 .....36 B6
Mill Reef CI CB8 .....120 D7
Mill Rise 8 Holbrook IP9 .....105 E7
    Saxmundham IP17 .....128 C2
Mill St Gislingham IP23 .....36 B2
    Isleham CB7 .....29 C5
    Mendlesham IP14 .....52 D5
    Mildenhall IP28 .....116 B3
    Nayland CO6 .....102 D5
    Stowupland IP14 .....67 A6
    Westleton IP17 .....58 C7
Mill Tye CO10 .....148 E2
Mill View CB8 .....46 B3
Mill View CI IP12 .....146 E5
Millbank CB8 .....120 F4
Millennium Grandstand
    CB8 .....120 C2
Millennium Way NR32 .....113 A4
Miller CI Elmswell IP30 .....50 F2
    Lowestoft NR33 .....115 B5
Millers Ct 8 IP5 .....82 A5
Millers Dr IP21 .....21 B5
Millfield IP11 .....117 B3
Millfield Ave IP14 .....124 C5
Millfield CI
    Ditchingham NR35 .....110 C8
    1 Saxmundham IP17 .....128 C2
Millfield Dr IP14 .....65 F4
Millfield Gdns IP14 .....140 A7
Millfield Rd
    2 Barningham IP31 .....34 F7
    Walberswick IP18 .....119 A2
Millfields
    2 Peasenhall IP17 .....56 F8
    Wangford NR34 .....26 B2
Millfields Way CB9 .....132 F6
Millmarsh Dro IP27 .....109 A7
Millside Dr NR32 .....3 D4
Mills La IP30 .....50 F2
Mills Mdw IP13 .....126 D3
Mills Rd CO10 .....148 E6
Mills The
    Framlingham IP13 .....126 C3
    Ipswich IP4 .....140 E8
Millside IP23 .....37 C4
Millway NR34 .....10 C4
Millway La
    Paignave IP22 .....20 A1
    Wortham IP22 .....19 F1

Millwood Rd CO6 ....94 A3
Milner Rd Chilton CO10 ...92 B4
Sudbury CO10 ....148 F6
Milnrow IP14 ....139 E6
Milton St IP4 ....138 C2
Milton N Rd ☑ IP14 .....124 D6
Milton Rd CO11 ....104 D1
Milton Rd E
Lowestoft NR32 ....113 D1
Stowmarket IP14 ....124 E6
Milton Rd S IP14 ....124 E6
Milton St IP4 ....140 B7
Minden Wlk NR32 ....113 B2
Minden Cl IP33 ....154 C2
Minden Dr
Bury St Edmunds IP33 ...122 D5
Leiston IP16 ....129 D5
Minden Rd
Lowestoft NR32 ....113 C2
Sudbury CO10 ....148 D5
Minerva Cl CB9 ....133 B4
Minos Rd NR33 ....113 C4
Minsmere House Hospl
IP4 ....140 C6
Minsmere Nature Reserve*
IP17 ....58 E6
Minsmere Rd IP17 ....58 F8
Minsmere Rise IP17 .....58 A6
Minsmere Way CO10 .....92 B3
Minster Rd CB9 ....132 D7
Mirbeck's Cl ☑ NR34 ....9 F4
Misburgh Way NR31 .....3 C6
Mission La CO7 ....104 C6
Mission Rd IP22 ....20 D2
Mistley Secret Bunker*
CO11 ....105 A2
Mistley Sta CO11 ......104 F2
Mistley Way IP12 ......146 F6
Mitchell Ave IP32 ......48 C5
Mitchery La IP14 ....65 E4
Mitford Cl IP1 ....135 A4
Mitford Rd IP17 ....72 B8
Mitre Cl ☑ IP30 ....50 D1
Mitre Way IP2 ....139 E4
Moat Farm Cl IP4 ......139 F8
Moat La
Alphamstone CO8 ....101 A6
Rushbrooke with Rougham
IP30 ....49 D1
Moat Rd Birdbrook CO9 ..89 B4
Theberton IP16 ....57 F4
Mobbs Way NR32 ....112 E3
Mockbeggars Hall*
IP8 ....134 C6
Moffat Ave IP14 ....136 B1
Moles La NR34 ....8 D1
Moll's La NR34 ....25 D5
Monarch Cl CB9 ....112 A6
Monarch Way IP6 ....142 D8
Monastery Hill IP17 ....43 B1
Monckton Ave NR32 ....112 C2
Monckton Cres NR32 ...112 F2
Monet Sq ☑ NR32 .....113 B5
Moneveden Rd IP13 .....70 A3
Moneyhole Cnr CO10 ....78 E5
Moneypiece Cl CB9 ....132 D7
Moneypot La IP22 ......19 B1
Monks Cl IP11 ....153 D6
Monks Eleigh CE VC Prim
Sch IP7 ....79 B2
Monks Gate IP8 ....138 A6
Monk's La CO7 ....103 E2
Monksgate IP24 ....16 B6
Monksfood Cl NR33 ...114 F2
Monmouth Cl IP30 ......49 D1
Montague Rd IP11 .....153 A4
Montana Rd IP5 ....141 A7
Montgomery Ave
NR32 ....
Montgomery Rd IP22 ..139 B1
Monton Rise IP22 .....138 D2
Montpelier Dr ☑ IP24 ..16 A5
Monument Farm Rd
IP10 ....141 B4
Moon Hall La CB9 .....132 E3
Moonhall Bsns Pk
CB9 ....132 E3
Moor Rd
Burston & Shimpling IP21 ..21 B6
Langham CO4 ....103 B2
Middleton IP17 ....57 F6
Moorbridge La IP14 ....66 B8
Moore Rd Ipswich IP1 ...134 F3
Rushbrooke with Rougham
IP30 ....49 B2
Mooreland Dr IP31 .....49 C6
Moore's Cl ☑ IP14 .....53 F2
Moorfield Rd IP12 ....146 E5
Moorhall Cswy IP23 ...117 C1
Moor's Way IP12 .....146 E5
Moorsfield CO10 .....148 F2
Moot Hall (Museum)*
IP15 ....130 F4
Moreton Hall Prep Sch
IP32 ....123 D5
Morgan Cl ☑ IP6 .....134 C8
Morgan Dr IP11 ......134 C1
Morgan Mdw IP24 .....12 A3
Morland Prim Sch
IP3 ....144 A8
Morland Rd ☑ IP3 ....144 A8
Morley Ave IP14 ......146 F4
Morley Cl ☑ IP28 .....30 B8
Morleys La IP23 ......36 D2
Mormor La IP21 ......21 F4

Mornington Ave ☑ IP1 .134 F1
Morris Way IP6 ....125 D4
Mors End ☑ CO7 .....103 E5
Morston Hall Rd IP11 ..98 B1
Mortimer La IP28 ......29 E3
Mortimer Pl ☑ CO10 ...76 A1
Morton Peto Cl NR32 ...2 D3
Morton Rd NR33 ......115 B4
Moss La IP6 ....135 F4
Mother Quy's IP24 .....15 C5
Mottram Cl ☑ IP8 ...138 C2
Moulton Ave CB8 .....46 A5
Moulton CE Prim Sch
CB8 ....45 F3
Moulton Packhorse Bridge*
CB8 ....45 F3
Moulton Rd
Cheveley CB8 ....121 D4
Gazeley CB8 ....46 B3
Moulton CB8 ....45 F1
Mount Cl IP30 ....64 F8
Mount Dr IP3 ....140 F1
Mount Pleasant
Framlingham IP13 .....126 B4
Halesworth IP19 ......118 B5
Lowestoft NR32 ......113 C3
Stowmarket IP14 ......56 F8
Southwold IP18 ......119 C8
Mount Rd
Bury St Edmunds IP32 ..123 D6
Haverhill CB9 ....132 E5
Rushbrooke with Rougham
IP30 ....49 A3
Mount St IP22 ....20 C3
Sudbury CO10 ....148 E2
Nelson Way
Beccles NR34 ....111 A4
Woodbridge IP12 ......146 F7
Nelson Wharf NR33 ...114 F7
Nelson's Pk** 88 F3
Neptune Sq ☑ IP4 .....17 C6
Neptune St NR33 .....115 C8
Ness Rd Arwarton IP9 ..106 D5
Burwell CB5 ....44 B7
Nether Hill CO9 ....90 E2
Nether Rd ☑ CO10 ....76 E1
Nethergate St
Bungay NR35 ....110 A5
Clare CO10 ....90 A7
Hopton IP22 ....48 B2
Netherhall Cl IP14 .....52 A1
Netley Cl IP2 ....142 F8
Netley Rd IP33 ....122 D3
Nettlestead Rd IP8 ....81 D4
Neve Gdns IP20 ....30 A6
New Cangle Prim Sch
CB9 ....132 D7
New Cardinal St IP1 ..155 A2
New Cheveley Rd CB8 ..121 C5
New Comm Rd IP22 ....35 B8
New Cut Bures CO8 ...101 C4
☑ Glemsford CO10 ....77 A2
Hadleigh IP7 ....149 E6
Halesworth IP19 ......118 B4
Saxmundham IP17 ....128 D3
New Cut W IP2 ....155 C1
New Dro
Beck Row, Holywell Row
& Kenny Hill IP28 .....12 E1
☑ Soham CB7 ....28 A4
New England Way ☑
IP24 ....
New Gn Ave ☑ IP31 ...49 E4
New Hampshire Way ☑
IP24 ....16 A5
New House La CO10 ...76 B3
New La IP9 ....105 F6
New Mkt NR34 ....111 B5
New Path ☑ CB7 .....29 A7
New Pleasurewood Hills
Leisure Pk* NR32 ....113 C8
New Queens Rd CO10 ..148 F7
New Rd Ampton IP31 ...33 A1
Aspall IP14 ....53 E4
Badingham IP13 ......56 B8
Barnby NR34 ....29 C5
Barrow IP29 ....47 B3
Beccles NR34 ....111 B7
Brettenham IP24 .....17 B6
☑ Burwell CB5 ....44 A6
Chevington IP29 ......62 C7
Dicklebergh & Rushall
IP21 ....21 A4
Elmswell IP30 ....50 E2
Exning CB8 ....120 B8
Felixstowe IP11 ......12 F4
Framlingham IP13 ....126 C5
Fritton & St Olaves NR31 ..2 B7
Gissing IP22 ....20 F8
Great Glemham IP17 ..71 E8
Helmingham IP14 ....69 A3
☑ Ixworth IP31 ....34 B1
Little Livermere IP31 ..33 A2
Long Melford CO10 ....91 D8
Manningtree CO11 ....104 E2
Marlesford IP13 ......72 C5
Melton IP12 ....84 D6
Mettingham NR35 ....110 F2
Nedging-with-naughton
IP7 ....80 C3
Rumburgh IP19 ......24 C4
Rushbrooke with Rougham
IP30 ....49 D1
St Cross, South Elmham
IP20 ....49 D1
Sibton IP17 ....41 D1
Thelnetham IP22 .....35 B7
Thrandeston IP21 ....37 C8
Timworth IP31 ....48 E8
Tivetshall St Mary NR15 ..21 B8

New Rd continued
Tostock IP30 ....50 B2
Troston IP31 ....33 D4
Worlingworth IP13 ....54 F8
New River Gn CB8 ....120 B8
New St Chippenham CB7 ..29 E1
Framlingham IP13 ....126 A4
Freessingfield IP21 ....39 D8
Glemsford CO10 ....77 A3
☑ Mildenhall IP28 ....116 C4
Stradbroke IP21 ......39 A4
Sudbury CO10 ....148 D6
☑ Woodbridge IP12 ..147 A5
New St Cl IP21 ....39 A4
New Way IP2 ....138 F6
New Wolsey Theatre*
IP1 ....155 A3
Newall Rd IP22 ....16 C2
Newark Cl IP2 ....138 F1
Newark Rd
☑ Lakenheath IP27 ....13 F2
Lowestoft NR33 ......115 B6
Newberry Rd ☑ IP7 ....79 F4
Newbourn Rd IP10 ....98 C4
Newbourne Gdns
IP11 ....152 D3
Newbourne Rd
Brightwell IP10 ....98 A6
Martlesham IP12 .....84 B1
Waldringfield IP12 ....97 E7
Newbury Rd IP4 ......140 C6
Newby Dr IP14 ....124 C6
Newcastle Cl ☑ IP27 ..13 F2
Newcombe Dr ☑ IP26 ..4 E5
Newcombe Rd NR32 ...113 E1
Newdelight Rd IP22 ...35 F2
Newell Rise IP6 ......134 C8
Newfen Gravel Dro
IP27 ....9 A8
Newgate Beccles NR34 .111 B5
Beccles NR34 ....111 B6
Kirby Row NR35 ....8 E7
Newgate La NR35 ......8 E7
Newhaven Way IP7 ...149 E7
Newland Ave NR34 ....11 B6
Newlands ☑ Elmsett IP7 .80 F1
Otley IP6 ....69 D2
Newlands Cl
☑ Harleston IP20 .....22 D6
Lowestoft NR33 ......114 F3
Newlands La CO6 ....102 D5
Newman's Rd CO10 ...148 B7
Newmarket Com Hospl
CB8 ....120 F5
Newmarket Lawn Tennis
Club CB8 ....120 E3
Newmarket Race Course
CB8 ....120 B1
Newmarket Rd
☑ Barton Mills IP28 ..116 D1
Burwell CB5 ....44 B5
Bury St Edmunds IP33 .122 D6
Cowlinge CB8 ....61 B2
Fordham CB7 ....44 E8
Moulton CB8 ....45 F3
Newmarket CB8 ......121 B8
Red Lodge IP28 ....30 C2
Risby IP28 ....47 C5
Snailwell CB8 ....45 A5
Newmarket Sports Ctr
CB8 ....121 A4
Newmarket Sta CB8 ...121 A5
Newmarket Swimming Pool
CB8 ....120 F4
Newmarket Upper Sch
CB8 ....120 F4
Newmill La CO10 .....105 A5
Newnham Ave IP12 ...146 D4
Newnham Cl ☑ IP28 ..116 D5
Newnham Ct IP22 ......21 B6
Newnham Dro CB5 ....44 A6
Newnham La ☑ CB5 ...44 A6
Newport Ave CB7 ......29 C1
Newport Cl ☑ IP27 ....13 F2
Newquay Cl IP5 ....140 F6
Newry Ave IP11 ....152 F4
Newson Ave NR34 .....10 C3
Newson St IP1 ....155 A4
Newsons' Mdw NR32 ...113 C2
Newthorpe IP20 ....49 C1
Newton Croft CO10 ..148 E5
Newton Rd
☑ Harwich CO12 .....107 A2
Ipswich IP3 ....140 A4
Stowupland IP14 .....124 D8
Sudbury CO10 ....148 D5
Newton St IP4 ....155 C3
Nicholas Dr IP12 .....147 A8
Nicholas Rd IP1 ......152 C4
Nicholls Cl ☑ IP13 ....84 F7
Nichols Cl ☑ CO11 ...104 D2
Nicholson Dr NR34 ...111 C2
Nicholson Sq ☑ NR33 .113 C4
Nicholsons Ct CO10 ...92 D3
Nick's La IP13 ....117 B6
Nidderdale ☑ NR33 ...114 E3
Nightall Rd CB7 ......28 D6
Nightingale Cl IP28 ...119 B7
Nightingale La
Bury St Edmunds IP33 ..154 A1
☑ Harwich CO12 .....106 F1
☑ Mildenhall IP28 ...116 D4
☑ Stowmarket IP14 ..124 C7
Nightingale Hill CO4 ..103 C3
Nightingale La
☑ Feltwell IP26 ....4 E5
☑ Feltwell IP26 ....4 E5

Nightingale Piece
IP12 ....131 C3
Nightingale Rd
Ipswich IP3 ....144 A8
Lowestoft NR33 ......115 B3
Nightingale Sq ☑ IP3 ..144 A8
Nimbus Way CB8 .....120 E8
Nine Acres IP7 ....138 D6
Ninfield Cl NR33 .....114 D2
Noahs Dr ☑ NR33 .....11 B1
Noaks Rd IP7 ....94 F1
Noel Cl NR31 ....3 B7
Noel Murless Dr CB8 ..120 F6
Noel Rd NR32 ....112 C1
Noel's Wlk NR34 .....111 B6
Noller's La IP19 ....26 F4
Nonsuch Mdw ☑ CO10 .148 E2
Norbury Rd IP4 ......140 B7
Nordalis The ☑ NR33 ..11 C1
Norfolk & Suffolk Aviation
Mus* NR35 ....
Norfolk Ave CB8 .....120 E5
Norfolk Cres ☑ IP13 ..126 C3
Norfolk Rd
Bury St Edmunds IP32 ..123 A8
☑ Honington IP31 .....33 D5
Ipswich IP4 ....155 C3
Thetford IP24 ....16 C5
Wangford NR34 ......26 B2
Wangford with Henham
NR34 ....
Norfolk St IP1 ....113 B1
Norgate La IP21 ......21 B2
Norman Cl
Felixstowe IP11 ......153 D6
Woodbridge IP12 .....147 A7
Norman Cres IP3 .....144 A2
Norman Rd
☑ Bury St Edmunds IP32 .48 C5
Bury St Edmunds IP32 ..
☑ Manningtree CO11 ..104 E2
Norman Way ☑ CO10 ..78 D4
Normandy Ave ☑ IP8 ..101 C4
Normandy Cl IP14 ....124 D3
Normandy Rd NR32 ...113 B4
Normanhurst Cl NR32 .113 A2
Normanston Dr ☑ NR32 .113 B2
Nornea La CB7 ....28 A8
Norse Ave IP29 ....64 A3
North Acres IP8 ......81 A6
North Ave CB9 ....132 C6
North Cl Bacton IP14 ..51 F5
Ipswich IP4 ....135 E1
☑ Stanton IP31 ......34 E4
North Cres CB9 ......88 D4
North Dr
Newmarket CB8 ......120 F5
☑ Soham CB7 ....28 D5
North End CB8 ......120 B8
North End Rd IP16 ....73 F6
North End Rd CO9 ....90 C2
North Entrance IP17 .128 D3
North Field Cl ☑ NR32 .112 F5
North Gn Rd
Cratfield IP19 ....40 C7
Pulham St Mary IP21 ..22 A8
North Hill IP12 ....146 F6
North Hill Gdns IP4 ..135 E4
North Hill Rd IP4 ....139 E6
North La IP14 ....140 B8
North Lopham Rd
NR16 ....19 A7
North Par
Lowestoft NR32 ......113 A4
Southwold IP18 ......119 E6
North Par Gdns IP18 ..119 E6
North Pl IP20 ....116 C4
North Rd
Great Yeldham CO9 ...90 A1
Lakenheath IP27 .....109 E4
Southwold IP18 ......119 D6
North Rise CO10 ....148 E4
North St Burwell CB5 ..44 A6
Freckenham IP28 ......29 E3
Hoxne CO10 ....75 D4
☑ Manningtree CO11 ..104 E2
Steeple Bumpstead CB9 ..88 D4
Sudbury CO10 ....148 C6
Wicken CB7 ....28 A1
North St Par ☑ CO10 .148 C5
North Terr IP28 ....116 C5
North Warren IP15 ...130 C8
Northacre ☑ NR33 ...11 B1
Northcroft ☑ CO10 ...148 F2
Northern Rd CO10 ...148 F7
Northern Way IP32 ...48 C5
Northfield Pk CB7 ....28 C5
Northfield Rd
Onehouse IP14 ....66 C6
☑ Soham CB7 ....28 C5
Northfield St Nicholas Sch
NR32 ....113 C3
Northgate
Beccles NR34 ....111 B6
☑ Harleston IP20 .....22 D5
Lowestoft NR32 ......113 B2
Northgate Ave IP32 ..154 B4
Northgate Cty High Sch
IP4 ....136 A2
Northgate Sports Ctr
IP4 ....136 A2
Northgate St
Bury St Edmunds IP33 ..154 C3
Ipswich IP4 ....155 B3
Northumberland Ave
IP32 ....122 E8
Northwood Cl NR33 ..114 F6

Norton CE Prim Sch
IP31 ....50 E6
Norton Rd
Haverhill CB9 ....132 C4
Hunston IP31 ....50 E5
11 Thurstow IP31 ....49 D4
Tostock IP30 ....50 C4
Norway Cres 2 CO12 ....106 F2
Norwich La
Bardwell IP31 ....34 C8
Coney Weston IP31 ....17 E2
Norwich Rd Barham IP6 ..82 A6
Claydon IP6 ....134 C8
Denton IP20 ....7 B3
5 Dickleburgh & Rushall
IP21 ....20 F1
Ditchingham NR35 ....110 A8
Earsham NR35 ....7 E5
Gillingham NR34 ....111 A8
Halesworth IP19 ....118 C5
Ipswich IP1 ....155 A3
5 Lakenheath IP27 ....26 D8
Lakenheath IP27 ....109 F1
Lowestoft NR32 ....113 C1
Bury St Mary IP21 ....21 F8
Scole IP21 ....21 B5
Stockton NR34 ....9 F8
Thetford IP24 ....16 C6
Thetford IP24 ....16 C6
Norwich Rd Sch IP24 ....16 C6
Norwood Rd IP27 ....14 E8
Notcutts CO7 ....151 E3
Notley Dr CB9 ....132 A7
Notley Ent Pk CO7 ....95 A2
Notley Rd NR32 ....113 C1
Nottidge Rd IP4 ....139 E6
Nova Scotia La
Bury St Edmunds IP33 ...123 C1
Norton IP30 ....63 E8
Noyes Ave IP33 ....40 B3
Nuffield Hospl (Private)
IP33 ....154 C1
Num Cl 1 IP22 ....84 A1
Nunnery Gn 2 CB8 ....61 E2
Nunn's Hill IP19 ....24 C3
Nunn's La IP21 ....23 E1
Nuns' Bridges Rd IP24 ...16 B5
Nuns Wlk CO9 ....89 F1
Nursery Cl NR34 ....29 B4
Nursery La IP26 ....5 A2
Nursery Rd CO10 ....148 F2
Nursery Wlk IP11 ....152 F4
Nursery Cl NR35 ....8 D7
Nuttery Vale IP23 ....38 B6

O

Oak Ave NR34 ....111 F5
Oak Cl
Bury St Edmunds IP28 ....48 C6
Felixstowe IP11 ....152 E4
4 Great Finborough IP14 ..66 B4
Oak Cres IP23 ....117 C3
Oak Dr 3 IP29 ....30 B8
Oak Eggar Chase IP8 ....142 D8
Oak Farm La IP14 ....52 D6
Oak Gn IP19 ....118 B2
Oak Gr
Framlingham St Martin IP31 ..48 D5
Sproughton IP8 ....138 A6
Oak Hill Cl NR34 ....26 E5
Oak Hill La IP22 ....139 B3
Oak La Beccles NR34 .....111 D2
Cheveley CB8 ....121 A3
Elmswell IP30 ....50 F3
Lakenheath IP27 ....13 F2
Rushbrooke with Rougham
IP30 ....64 D8
Woolpit IP30 ....65 E8
Oak Mdw Cl IP29 ....42 C6
Oak Rd 3 Sudbury CO10 ..92 B3
Sudbury CO10 ....148 F4
Oak Tree Way 8 IP20 .....22 D5
Oak Way IP19 ....118 A1
Oakdene IP22 ....98 D2
Oakes Cl IP32 ....122 E7
Oakes Rd IP32 ....122 E7
Oakey Field Rd 8 IP31 ...49 E4
Oakey Ley IP30 ....64 D6
Oakfield Bacton IP14 .....52 A6
Copdock & Washbrook
IP8 ....142 A6
Oakfield Wood Nature
Reserve* CO11 ....105 E3
Oaklands 3 CO12 ....107 B2
Oaklands CO10 ....102 B8
Oaklands Dr IP22 ....20 E3
Oakley Church La IP14 ...37 F8
Oakley Rd
11 Harwich CO12 ....106 C1
Ramsey & Parkeston
CO12 ....106 E1
Oaks Bsns Pk CB8 ....60 E7
Oaks Dr CB8 ....120 F7
Oaks La NR34 ....2 B1
Oaks The
7 Horringer IP29 ....63 A8
Martlesham Heath IP5 ...141 F6
Soham CB7 ....28 D3
Wattisfield IP22 ....35 C6
Woolpit IP30 ....65 F8
Oaksmere Gdns 8 IP22 ..139 A2
Oakwood Pk IP27 ....57 D7
Oakwood Rd NR33 ....114 F5
Oast Ct IP33 ....154 C1

Oatfields 6 IP21 ....39 D8
Oatlands Cl 4 NR33 .....114 F3
Oban St IP1 ....155 A4
Occold Prim Sch 37 F1
Occold Rd IP23 ....38 B2
Offton Rd Elmsett IP7 ....81 A2
Great Bricett IP7 ....80 F5
Ohio Cl 4 NR33 ....114 E3
Old Barn Rd CO8 ....101 C3
Old Barningham Rd 1
IP31 ....34 E4
Old Barrack Rd IP12 ....146 E4
Old Brandon Rd IP26 .....5 F1
Old Buckenham Hall Sch
IP7 ....79 B7
Old Bungay Rd NR35 ....10 C6
Old Bury Rd
Alpheton CO10 ....78 A6
Lackford IP28 ....31 F1
Palgrave IP22 ....37 A8
Stanton IP31 ....34 E4
Stuston IP21 ....20 D1
Wortham IP22 ....36 F8
Old Cattle Mkt IP1 ......155 B2
Old Church La
Bulmer CO10 ....91 C1
Westley IP33 ....122 A6
Old Church Rd NR31 .....3 B6
Old Clements La
CB9 ....132 D5
Old Convent Orch
IP33 ....154 B1
Old Dairy Bsns Pk IP31 ..49 B5
Old Farm Rd
Beccles NR34 ....111 C5
4 Lowestoft NR33 ......114 D5
Old Forge Cl IP22 ....36 D8
Old Foundry Pl IP16 ....129 C6
Old Foundry Rd IP4 ....155 C3
Old Gram La NR35 ....110 B3
Old Hall Cl 2 IP30 ....82 D6
Old Hall La Bentley IP9 ..95 F2
Bury St Edmunds IP33 ...48 D5
Cockfield IP30 ....64 E7
Westleton IP17 ....58 B8
Old Hall Mdw IP13 ....56 C8
Old Harleston Rd NR35 ...7 F3
Old Haverhill Rd CB9 ....74 F2
Old High Rd
Roydon IP22 ....20 B3
Yoxford IP17 ....57 D7
Old Homes Rd 7 IP16 ....57 A7
Old London Rd IP30 ....150 D1
Old Maids' La IP7 ....70 A7
Old Methwold Rd IP26 ....1 A1
Old Mill Dr IP21 ....21 F8
Old Mill La
Barton Mills IP28 ....116 F2
Beccles NR34 ....111 B4
Old Mill Terr 4 NR34 ....111 B6
Old Mkt 6 NR34 ....111 B6
Old Mkt Pl IP20 ....22 D6
Old Mkt Plain 8 NR32 ...113 E2
Old Mkt St IP14 ....52 E4
Old Nelson St 4 NR33 ...113 E1
Old Norwich CE Prim Sch
IP14 ....52 A1
Old Norwich Rd
Whitton IP1 ....134 D5
Yaxley IP23 ....117 C8
Old Orch IP7 ....149 F1
Old Orch Cl IP19 ....118 A2
Old Paper Mill La 8
IP30 ....34 C8
Old Post Office La
Blaxhall IP12 ....72 A4
Kirby Row NR35 ....8 E7
Sutton IP12 ....99 A8
Old Post Office Rd
IP20 ....62 C6
Old Priory Gdns NR34 ...26 B2
Old Rd The CO6 ....102 B8
Old Rectory Cl
6 Claydon IP6 ....82 B5
6 Roydon IP22 ....20 A3
Old Rectory Gdns 3
IP21 ....37 F1
Old Rectory La IP19 .....77 E6
Old Rectory Rd IP23 .....56 A6
Old Rly Rd Alburgh IP20 ..7 B3
Bungay NR35 ....110 A4
Old Rope Wlk CB9 ....132 C5
Old Sch Cl
5 Burwell CB5 ....44 B6
2 Soham CB7 ....28 D5
Old Sch La CB8 ....59 F1
Old Sch Rd IP29 ....30 B8
Old Sch The NR34 ....10 E1
Old School CI IP30 ....50 E2
Old St IP41 ....51 C1
Old Stoke The IP7 ......150 F3
Old Sta Rd
Halesworth IP19 ....118 B5
Mendlesham IP14 ....52 E1
Newmarket CB8 ....121 B4

Old Stores Cl IP13 ....54 E7
Old Stowmarket Rd
IP30 ....50 D1
Old Town La IP31 ....123 C1
Old Vicarage Dr 4 NR32 ..50 E7
Old Vicarage Dr 18
CO12 ....107 A2
Oldfield Rd IP6 ....138 B1
Oldhall Rd IP30 ....106 F6
Olding Rd IP33 ....122 D6
Olive Cl 2 IP27 ....14 D8
Olive Ct NR32 ....113 B3
Oliver Cl NR33 ....114 D2
Oliver Rd IP33 ....122 C6
Olivers Cl CO10 ....91 E8
Olympus Cl IP31 ....134 C2
One Eyed La IP21 ....22 D3
Onehouse La IP14 ....135 C1
Onehouse Rd IP14 ....124 B6
Onner's La IP16 ....58 C4
Ontario Rd NR33 ....115 C5
Opal Ave 5 Ipswich IP1 ..134 D1
Ipswich IP1 ....138 D8
Orch Way The 2 IP29 ....63 A8
Orchard Ave NR33 ......114 E6
Orchard Cl
2 Blundeston NR32 ......3 A4
Elmswell IP30 ....50 F3
Great Livermere IP31 ....33 C2
6 Haverhill CB9 ....132 D5
Lidgate CB8 ....61 C4
2 Ramsey & Parkeston
CO12 ....106 D1
Ridgewell CO9 ....89 D3
Risby IP28 ....122 A8
Rushbrooke with Rougham
IP30 ....64 D8
Woodbridge IP12 ....147 A2
Orchard Croft 2 NR33 ..114 E4
Orchard Ct IP14 ....66 F3
Orchard End 8 IP13 .....83 E5
Orchard Farm Barns 2
IP29 ....47 A2
Orchard Gate
Ipswich IP6 ....138 C5
7 Needham Market IP6 ..125 D7
Orchard Ave NR34 ......111 C4
Orchard Gr
Claydon IP6 ....134 C7
Ipswich IP4 ....141 A7
Orchard Pl
13 Bramford IP8 ....134 A2
Leiston IP16 ....129 C5
Orchard Rise
Badingham IP13 ....56 A7
Beccles NR34 ....111 F4
Carlton Row 28 E2
Orchard St
Bury St Edmunds IP33 ..154 B3
Ipswich IP4 ....155 C3
Orchard The 3
6 Ashley CB8 ....60 F8
Brandon IP27 ....5 F1
Felsham IP30 ....65 A4
Shadingfield NR34 ....25 B7
Orchard Valley IP19 ....118 D4
Orchard Way
Badwell Ash IP31 ....50 F7
12 Barrow IP29 ....47 A2
4 Burwell CB5 ....44 A6
Glemsford CO10 ....77 A2
Scole IP21 ....21 A2
Orchards The 11 IP23 ...40 B3
Orchid Cl
Halesworth IP19 ....118 C4
Ipswich IP2 ....138 E4
Orchid Way IP5 ....125 D3
Orchids Cl NR35 ....110 D3
Oregon Rd IP5 ....141 A6
Orford Castle & Visitor Ctr*
IP12 ....131 B2
Orford CE VA Prim Sch
IP12 ....131 B3
Orford Dr NR32 ....112 F3
Orford Ness National Nature
Reserve* IP12 ....131 C1
Orford Ness National Trust*
IP12 ....131 C1
Orford Rd
Bromeswell IP12 ....147 F7
Butley IP12 ....86 A6
Felixstowe IP11 ....152 E4
Haverhill CB9 ....132 D4
Tunstall IP12 ....71 F2
Orford St IP1 ....155 A4
Oriel Cl CO10 ....148 F4
Orkney Cl IP33 ....133 B5
Orkney Rd 4 IP4 ....136 A1
Orvis La CO7 ....151 A5
Orwell Ave IP7 ....44 E6
Orwell Dr 1 NR32 ....112 F3
Orwell Jun Sch IP3 ......139 F1
Orwell Pk Sch IP10 .....145 B3
Orwell Pl 4 IP4 ....155 C2
Orwell Rd
10 Harwich CO12 ....152 F3
Ipswich IP3 ....140 A4
Stowmarket IP14 ....124 D4
Orwell Ret Pk IP2 ......139 A5

Orwell Rise 10 IP9 ......106 C5
Orwell View Rd IP9 .....106 F6
Osborne Rd IP4 ....140 A4
Osborne St 4 NR32 .....113 E3
Osier Cl IP17 ....129 B4
Osier Rd IP33 ....154 B3
Osprey Rd IP2 ....133 A5
Oswyn Cl IP32 ....123 D4
Otley Coll IP6 ....69 C1
Otley Cl 8 IP11 ....152 D5
Otley Hall* IP6 ....69 C3
Otley Prim Sch IP6 ......69 C2
Otley Rd IP12 ....85 C2
Otten Rd CO10 ....90 D5
Oulton Broad N Sta
NR32 ....112 F1
Oulton Broad Prim Sch
NR32 ....112 C2
Oulton Broad S Sta
NR32 ....112 C2
Oulton Broad Water Sports
Ctr NR33 ....114 D7
Oulton Cl 6 CO10 ....148 F4
Oulton Rd Flixton NR32 ..112 F7
Ipswich IP3 ....139 F2
Lowestoft NR32 ....112 F5
Oulton St NR32 ....112 F7
Ousden Rd IP29 ....122 A8
Out Northgate IP33 .....154 B4
Out Risbygate IP33 .....122 C6
Out Westgate IP33 .....154 B1
Outney Rd NR35 ....110 A4
Overbury Hall Rd IP7 ...149 D1
Owell The NR31 ....49 E6
Oxer Cl IP30 ....150 F2
Oxford Cl
Mildenhall IP28 ....116 A4
Sudbury CO10 ....148 E4
Oxford Dr IP2 ....146 D3
Oxford Rd 2 Feltwell IP26 ..4 E5
Ipswich IP4 ....139 E5
Ipswich IP5 ....141 A7
Lowestoft NR32 ....113 D3
28 Manningtree CO11 ..104 E2
Oxford St CB8 ....120 B8

P

Packard Ave IP3 ....140 B2
Packard Pl IP3 ....134 B2
Packards La
Fordham CO6 ....102 A1
Wormingford CO6 ......101 F1
Packway La IP31 ....50 A5
Paddock Cl IP33 ....122 C5
Paddock Farm IP31 ......34 D8
Paddock Hill NR33 ......114 E7
Paddock Rd 8 IP20 .....22 D6
Paddock St CB7 ....28 D4
Paddock The 10 IP21 ....34 B1
Paddock Way
Chedburgh IP29 ....62 C4
Troston IP31 ....33 B4
Paddock Wood 8
NR33 ....114 C4
Paddocks Dr CB8 ....121 A2
Paddocks Rd NR34 ......111 F4
Paddocks Prim Sch
CB8 ....120 E4
Paddocks The
Ashen CO10 ....89 E5
3 Bures CO8 ....101 C4
12 Burwell CB5 ....44 A6
Halesworth IP19 ....118 B2
8 Martlesham Heath IP5 ..98 A4
Tuddenham St Martin
IP6 ....98 A4
Worlingham IP38 ....30 B4
Padstow Rd IP5 ....141 A6
Page Gdns IP5 ....141 E8
Pageant Pl IP11 ....126 E3
Page's Cl IP14 ....124 C6
Pages Hill Rd IP29 ......63 B6
Paget Cl IP31 ....125 C5
Paget Dr IP6 ....125 D2
Paget Rd IP1 ....155 A4
Pains Cl 2 NR14 ....7 A1
Pains Hill IP33 ....67 F6
Pakefield Mid Sch
IP33 ....115 A3
Pakefield Rd NR33 ......115 C5
Pakefield St NR33 ......115 C5
Pakenham St IP31 ....49 D6
Palace Cl IP33 ....122 C6
Palace St CB8 ....121 A3
Palgrave VC Prim Sch
IP22 ....20 C1
Palmcroft 10 IP31 ......135 A3
Palmer Cl NR32 ....135 A3
Palmer Cl NR32 ....113 B7
Palmer Dr IP27 ....109 C7
Palmer St IP31 ....35 C1
Palmer's La IP18 ....119 A2
Palmerston Rd IP3 .....139 E6
Palmerston St IP18 .....119 C6
Pamersvent Cl CO10 ....91 F8
Pamment's La IP28 ......29 F7
Pannells Cl 5 CO10 .....77 A2
Pannells La IP12 ....44 A6
Papeley Mdw IP27 ......87 B2
Paper Mill La IP8 ....134 B4
Parade Ave IP4 ....139 F7
Parade Rd N 08 NR33 ..115 B7
Parade Rd S NR33 ......115 C7
Paradise PI IP16 ....129 D5
Pardoe PI IP4 ....140 C5
Parish Barn Dro CB7 ....12 A1

Park Ave
Felixstowe IP11 ....153 B5
3 Fornham St Martin IP28 ..48 C6
Newmarket CB8 ....121 B3
Saxmundham IP17 ......128 C3
Park Cl
2 Bentwaters Airfield
IP12 ....85 D8
1 Lowestoft NR33 ......114 D4
5 Martlesham Heath IP5 ..98 A8
4 Moulton CB8 ....45 F3
Sudbury CO10 ....148 E6
Park Cotts CB8 ....121 B2
Park Dr NR34 ....111 E4
Park End IP17 ....128 C2
Park Farm Dr
Barton Mills IP28 ....30 C2
Stanton IP31 ....34 E3
Park Farm La
Euston IP24 ....33 E8
Hoxne IP21 ....117 A6
Park Hill IP16 ....129 C6
Park La Aldeburgh IP15 ..130 E4
Bulmer CO10 ....91 C2
Charsfield IP13 ....70 C3
Eye IP23 ....117 D1
Glemsford CO10 ....77 B2
Hawstead IP29 ....63 D7
Kirton IP10 ....98 E3
Langham CO4 ....103 C2
Newmarket CB8 ....121 B3
Southwold IP18 ....119 D4
Thornham Parva IP23 ...37 A3
Park Mews NR32 ....112 F6
Park N IP1 ....139 D8
Park PI IP17 ....57 D7
Park Rd
Aldeburgh IP15 ....130 D4
Benhall IP17 ....72 A4
Burwell CB5 ....44 A5
Bury St Edmunds IP33 ..154 C1
Combs IP14 ....124 B2
Diss IP22 ....20 C2
Drinkstone IP30 ....50 B1
East Bergholt CO7 ......104 D5
Great Horkesley CO6 ...102 D4
Grundisburgh IP13 ....83 E5
Halesworth IP19 ....118 A5
2 Harwich CO12 ....107 B2
Haverhill CB9 ....132 B7
Ipswich IP1 ....139 C8
Lavenham CO10 ....78 D4
Letheringham IP13 ......70 D4
Lowestoft NR32 ....113 D3
Needham Market IP6 ...125 D4
St Cross, South Elmham
IP29 ....23 C7
Southwold IP18 ....54 A8
Stoke-by-nayland CO6 ..102 F6
Sudbury CO10 ....148 E6
Wetherden IP14 ....65 F8
Park St CO6 ....102 E7
Park The IP31 ....49 A5
Park View
Botesdale IP22 ....36 B7
Weeting IP27 ....5 B3
Wetherden IP14 ....51 A1
Park View Rd IP1 ....135 B1
Park Wlk IP19 ....118 E5
Parker Ave IP21 ....152 B4
Parker Dro 8 IP29 ......29 F6
Parkers PI 8 IP31 ....98 A8
Parker's Rd IP14 ....52 A6
Parker's Way CO6 ......102 D5
Parkers Wlk CB8 ....120 D5
Parkeston Rd
Felixstowe IP11 ....152 D4
Harwich CO12 ....107 A4
Parkhill NR32 ....112 F5
Parkington Wlk IP22 ....122 D7
Parklands 8 IP13 ....84 F7
Parklands Cl 7 CO10 ....77 B3
Parklands Gn 2 IP28 ....48 C6
Parklands Rd NR34 .....114 D4
Parklands Way 11 IP20 ..22 D6
Parkside
Chippenham CB7 ....45 C8
Mildenhall IP28 ....30 C8
Parkside Ave IP4 ....154 E4
Parkside Ave NR32 .....113 A2
Parkway
Bury St Edmunds IP33 ..154 A2
Ipswich IP14 ....127 C7
Parkway Mid Sch IP33 ..132 B6
Parkwood Dr CO10 .....148 C8
Parliament Rd IP4 ......140 B5
Parmenter Dr 10 CO10 ..92 B3
Parnell Cl IP1 ....50 D3
Parnell La IP30 ....134 F3
Parnham PI 2 IP4 ....140 B5
Parr Rd CB9 ....132 B4
Parrington Way 26
CO11 ....104 D2
Parsonage Cl
5 Burwell CB5 ....44 B6
Felixstowe IP11 ....152 D4
Parsonage Farm La
CB8 ....60 C5
Parsonage Gr 7 CO8 ....101 C4
Parsonage La
Burwell CB5 ....44 A5
Chelsworth IP7 ....79 E3

Parsons Ct IP3 ....122 A6
Parsons Field 4 IP15 ....130 E5
Parson's Field CO7 ....104 A2
Parsons Hill IP12 ....99 F7
Parson's La IP4 ....125 B2
Parsons Yd 2 CO11 ....104 E2
Partridge Cl 12 IP31 ....49 D4
Partridge Rd IP2 ....138 D3
Pashford Cl IP27 ....109 D6
Paske Ave C89 ....132 D5
Pastures The
  Ipswich IP4 ....140 F5
  Oulton NR32 ....112 F6
Patricia Cl NR32 ....112 D2
Patrick Stead Hospl
  IP19 ....118 C5
Patten La NR15 ....21 B7
Patterdale Gdns 3
  NR32 ....113 A4
Pattern Bush Cl 1
  CO11 ....104 E4
Patteson Rd IP2 ....139 E4
Patticrofit 7 CO10 ....77 A3
Pauline St IP2 ....155 B1
Paul's Rd IP2 ....138 F5
Pavilion Cl C89 ....132 F5
Paxton Chadwick Cl 1
  IP16 ....129 D5
Payne St NR33 ....115 C7
Payne's La IP26 ....4 E5
Peacock Cl
  Hockwold cum Wilton IP26 .....4 F3
  5 Ipswich IP8 ....138 C2
  Lowestoft NR33 ....114 C2
Peacock Rise 12 IP31 ......34 B1
Peacock St IP5 ....141 E7
Peacocks Cl 11 CO10 ....76 E1
Peacock's Pyghtle
  IP12 ....131 C3
Peacocks Rd CO10 ....76 E2
Peak Dale NR33 ....114 E3
Pear Cl 2 IP23 ....36 D2
Pearce Rd IP3 ....140 A4
Pearce's Cl 2 IP26 ....5 A3
Pearcroft Rd IP3 ....135 B3
Pearl Rd IP3 ....138 D8
Pearse Way IP3 ....140 E1
Pearson Rd IP4 ....140 C6
Parsons Way IP8 ....95 F5
Peartree Cl IP17 ....128 C6
Peartree Hill C08 ....101 D2
Peasecroft Rd 2 IP31 ....34 B1
Pebble Cl NR32 ....113 A3
Pebble View Wlk 8 NR31 ....32 C6
Peckham St IP33 ....154 B3
Pecockes Cl 10 CO10 ....92 B3
Peddars Cl 1 IP31 ....34 B1
Peddars La NR34 ....111 B4
Peddars Way NR32 ....113 B4
Peel St IP1 ....155 B3
Peel Yd 2 IP5 ....98 A8
Peewit Rd IP11 ....156 D3
Peewit Rd IP2 ....138 C3
Pegasus Mews 1 NR32 .....112 D1
Pegg's Hill IP20 ....22 F2
Pelham Cl 2 CO12 ....106 F1
Pelican Cl IP2 ....138 C3
Pemberton Rd 6 IP20 ....22 D5
Pembroke Ave IP12 ....146 E4
Pembroke Cl
  Ipswich IP2 ....139 B3
  Mildenhall IP28 ....12 B5
  Newmarket C88 ....121 B2
Pembroke Pl CO10 ....148 B8
Pembroke Way 1
  NR32 ....113 A3
Pendleton Rd IP2 ....138 D1
Penfold Rd IP11 ....154 D3
Penn Cl IP9 ....150 F4
Pennine Way NR32 ....112 E2
Penny La Ipswich IP3 ......140 F1
  Lowestoft NR33 ....112 E3
Penny Mdw 3 IP9 ....150 E3
Pennyfields NR35 ....110 B2
Pennygate Dr IP18 ....114 C6
Pennyroyal Gdns IP2 ....18 C3
Penryn Rd IP5 ....141 A7
Penshurst Rd IP3 ....140 D4
Pentland Wlk 9 NR32 ....113 A4
Pentlow Dr CO10 ....76 F1
Pentlow Hawke Cl
  C89 ....133 A5
Pentlow Hill CO10 ....91 A8
Penzance Rd IP5 ....141 A6
Pepper La IP31 ....49 E3
Peppercorn Way 2 IP2 ...139 C3
Peppers Cl IP27 ....5 E3
Pepper's Rd C04 ....102 F1
Peppers Wash IP13 ....126 B6
Pepys Ave 1 NR34 ....9 F4
Peregrine Way 6 NR33 ...11 C1
Periwinkle Cl 8 NR33 ......114 C5
Perkins Rd IP30 ....114 C5
Perkins Way
  Ipswich IP3 ....139 F1
  Tostock IP30 ....50 C3
Perry La C04 ....103 D2
Perrydown La IP30 ....64 C1

Persimmon Wlk C88 ....120 E7
Pesthouse La IP6 ....82 A6
Petch Cl IP33 ....154 B3
Peterhouse Cl IP2 ....139 B3
Peterhouse Cres IP12 ......146 D4
Peterhouse Dr C88 ....121 A2
Peter's Gr 4 IP5 ....150 E2
Petingo Cl C88 ....120 D7
Petit Couronne Way
  NR34 ....111 D3
Peto Way NR32 ....113 A1
Pettaugh La IP6 ....68 E2
Petticoat La
  9 Barrow IP29 ....47 A2
  Bury St Edmunds IP33 ....154 A1
Pettits La IP21 ....20 F3
Pheasant Cl 4 IP11 ....49 D4
Pheasant Rd IP2 ....138 E3
Pheasant Rise IP8 ....95 F4
Pheasants Wlk NR35 ....7 E4
Philip Ave IP11 ....152 E3
Philip Rd
  Bury St Edmunds IP32 ....122 F8
  Ipswich IP2 ....138 D3
Phillips Cl C88 ....120 D4
Phillips Rd 3 IP6 ....82 B5
Phillips Cres IP6 ....125 E4
Phillips Field Rd CO10 .....148 E3
Phoenix Day Hospl
  IP33 ....154 A1
Phoenix Rd IP4 ....140 A7
Picketts Rd IP1 ....153 C5
Pickwick Dr 6 NR32 ....3 A4
Pickwick Rd IP2 ....138 C6
Picton Ave 6 IP1 ....135 D1
Pier Ave IP18 ....119 D6
Pier Terr NR33 ....115 D8
Pigeon La IP28 ....46 B6
Pigeon's La 1 IP6 ....138 A3
Pightle Cl IP30 ....50 E2
Pightle The
  Capel St Mary IP9 ....150 F4
  Haverhill C89 ....132 E6
  4 Needham Market IP6 ...125 D5
  North Cove NR34 ....10 B4
Pilgrims Way
  Bungay NR35 ....110 C3
  8 Great Finborough IP14 ...66 B4
Pilgrim's Way 7 IP20 ....22 D6
Pilgrims Way 1 IP16 ....73 F6
Pimpernel Rd IP2 ....138 F3
Pin Mill Cl IP8 ....138 C1
Pin Mill Cliff National Trust*
  IP9 ....106 C8
Pinbush Cl NR33 ....114 F2
Pinbush Rd NR33 ....114 F2
Pine Ave IP1 ....135 B1
Pine Bank IP5 ....141 F6
Pine Cl
  1 Brantham CO11 ....104 E4
  Eye IP23 ....117 D3
  4 Harleston IP20 ....22 D5
  Haverhill IP27 ....13 F2
Pine Gr 14 IP13 ....83 E5
Pine Leys IP32 ....122 E8
Pine Sq IP7 ....80 D6
Pine Tree Cl NR34 ....111 F4
Pine Trees Ave IP28 ....116 E4
Pine View CO10 ....92 D1
Pine View Rd IP1 ....139 B8
Pinecroft Rd IP1 ....135 A2
Pinecroft Rise CO10 ....148 B3
Pinecroft Way CO10 ....125 E4
Pines The IP11 ....153 E6
Pinetree Cl IP5 ....140 F7
Pinetrees NR31 ....2 B7
Pineview Cir IP14 ....124 D5
Pineway Cl 8 IP27 ....63 A1
Pinewood IP12 ....146 E3
Pinewood Ave NR33 ....114 F6
Pinewood Dr IP27 ....14 C5
Pinewood Gdns NR34 ....10 B4
Pinewood Nature Reserve*
  IP9 ....142 E7
Pinkney's La 10 IP18 ....119 D5
Pinkuah La CO10 ....90 F7
Pinmill Rd IP9 ....106 C8
Pinners La IP13 ....146 B7
Pinners Way IP33 ....122 E4
Pintail Cl IP2 ....138 E3
Pintza Cl C88 ....120 D4
Piperell Way C89 ....132 E3
Pipers Cl C89 ....133 A4
Pipers Mdw IP13 ....54 E2
Pipney Hill IP17 ....56 F4
Pippin Cl 2 IP22 ....123 E6
Pippin Post Cl CO10 ....76 C6
Pippins The
  Blundeston NR32 ....3 A4
  Glemsford CO10 ....92 D3
Plampin Cl CO10 ....92 D3
Plantation Cl IP15 ....130 D5
Plantation Way IP14 ....66 C1
Planters Gn 8 NR33 ....114 F7
Plash Rd IP23 ....53 F7

Plashwood Rd IP14 ....51 B1
Platters Wlk IP16 ....129 C5
Platten Cl IP6 ....125 C5
Platters Cl IP3 ....144 A7
Platters Rd IP11 ....152 E2
Playfield Rd IP9 ....150 F3
Playford Cl IP11 ....137 A4
Playford Hall* IP6 ....137 C6
Playford La IP6 ....136 E2
Playford Rd
  Ipswich IP5 ....140 E8
  Playford IP5 ....137 B2
Pleasant Pl NR34 ....111 B3
Pleasant Row IP4 ....155 C2
Pleasurewood Cl 5
  NR32 ....113 B5
Pleasurewood Hill
  NR32 ....113 A7
Plough Cl CO10 ....76 C7
Plough La
  Leavenheath CO6 ....102 D6
  Sudbury CO10 ....148 B5
Plough Rd
  Capel St. Mary IP9 ....150 D3
  Woolpit IP30 ....50 D1
Plough St IP3 ....139 E4
Ploughman's Dro IP28 ....7 D5
Plover Cl 4 IP28 ....13 B1
Plover Rd IP2 ....138 E2
Plovers Way
  Bury St Edmunds IP33 .....123 C1
  Hockwold cum Wilton IP26 ...4 F3
  Lowestoft NR33 ....114 D5
Plum St CO10 ....77 A3
Plum Tree Rise 3 IP7 ....80 D6
Plummer Cl 2 IP31 ....34 B1
Plummers Dell 10 IP6 ....82 A5
Plumpton Ave IP28 ....116 C5
Plumtrees 8 NR32 ....112 D2
Plymouth Rd
  Felixstowe IP11 ....152 F6
  4 Troston IP31 ....33 D5
Pole Hill (Tumulus)*
  IP10 ....141 F5
Police Sta Rd 6 NR34 ....111 B4
Pollards La IP28 ....29 F7
Polls La NR34 ....9 C2
Polstead Cl IP14 ....124 F4
Polstead Hill CO6 ....102 E6
Polstead St CO6 ....102 E7
Pond Cl IP11 ....152 D5
Pond Gn C87 ....28 A1
Pond Gr C87 ....28 A2
Pond Hall Rd IP7 ....149 F5
Pond Piece IP13 ....70 A7
Ponds End La IP22 ....35 A8
Poole Cl IP3 ....140 D3
Poole St CO10 ....76 E1
Pooley St IP22 ....19 C3
Popes Cl CO9 ....133 C3
Pope's Gn La IP7 ....94 D8
Poplar Cl 1 Barrow IP29 ....47 A2
  4 Claydon IP6 ....134 C8
Poplar Farm Rd IP12 ....92 F7
Poplar Hill IP14 ....124 E4
Poplar La IP8 ....138 B3
Poplar Rd
  Lowestoft NR33 ....114 D3
  Sudbury CO10 ....148 C5
Poplars Cl 1 IP5 ....44 A5
Poplars CP Sch NR32 ......113 C3
Poplars The
  Beck Row, Holywell Row
    & Kenny Hill IP28 ....13 D1
  8 Brantham CO11 ....104 E5
  Spexhall IP19 ....24 C5
Poppy Cl
  Bury St Edmunds IP32 ....123 E5
  Ditchingham NR35 ....110 B7
  Ipswich IP2 ....138 F5
  Worlingham NR34 ....111 F3
Poppy Fields 9 C87 ....28 D5
Popson St NR34 ....110 A4
Port La IP23 ....37 C3
Port of Felixstowe
  IP11 ....152 C3
Portal Ave IP5 ....84 A1
Portal Cl 4 Barnham IP24 ..16 C2
  2 Felixstowe IP11 ....152 E3
Porter Rd IP3 ....140 F1
Porthole Cl NR33 ....114 B4
Portland Ave 4 CO12 ....107 B2
Portland Cl IP27 ....13 F1
Portland Cres 4 IP12 ....146 E4
Portland Pl 3 IP2 ....24 A5
Portland Rd C88 ....120 E3
Portland St 9 CO11 ....105 A2
Portman Rd IP1 ....155 A2
Portman's Wlk IP1 ....139 A5
Portsch Rd NR33 ....114 E3
Portsmouth Cl IP4 ....73 F2
Portsmouth Rd 18 IP27 ......13 F7
Post Mill Cl IP13 ....83 E5
Post Mill Cres IP13 ....83 E5
Post Mill Gdns 10 IP13 ....83 E5
Post Office La
  Glemsford CO10 ....77 A3
  Martlesham IP12 ....146 C1
Post Office Rd IP17 ....129 A3
Posters La IP31 ....35 A2
Pot Kiln Chase CO9 ....90 F1
Pot Kiln Prim Sch
  CO10 ....148 E4
Pot Kiln Rd CO10 ....148 F4
Pot Kiln Wlk CO10 ....92 B3
Potash La Bentley IP9 ....104 F8
Potash La
  Eye IP23 ....117 B5

Potash La continued
  Polstead CO6 ....93 F4
Wyverstone IP14 ....51 D7
Potkins La IP12 ....131 B3
Potland La 15 CO10 ....78 D4
Pott Hall Rd IP28 ....30 A6
Potters Dr NR31 ....3 B7
Potter's La
  Rickinghall Superior IP22 ...36 B5
  Stanton IP31 ....34 E4
Potter's St IP28 ....58 C4
Potters Vale IP22 ....35 C7
Pouch Mill IP11 ....152 E8
Poulter's La IP29 ....62 F6
Poultry Rd IP27 ....13 A7
Pound Cl 8 Burwell CB5 .....44 A5
Pound Cl 1 IP2 ....56 C7
Pound La Bacton IP14 ....51 F6
  Dallingham IP13 ....70 C1
Pound Hill Cl IP14 ....41 A5
Pound La
  Blundeston NR32 ....3 A4
  Bramford IP8 ....81 F3
  Capel St Mary IP9 ....150 D1
  Dallingham IP13 ....70 C1
  Ditchingham NR35 ....7 E6
  Hadleigh IP7 ....149 C6
  Isleham CB7 ....29 C5
  Stowmarket IP14 ....98 E2
Pound Mdw 8 IP28 ....48 B6
Pound Pl 4 NR34 ....111 B6
Pound Rd
  8 Beccles NR34 ....111 B4
  Creeting St Peter or West
    Creeting IP6 ....67 B4
  Sotterley NR34 ....26 A7
Pouy St IP17 ....41 B1
Powling Rd IP3 ....140 A2
Pownsy St IP7 ....93 B8
Pratt St C87 ....28 D4
Pratt's La IP9 ....144 A2
Prentice Rd IP14 ....84 D4
Prentice St 8 CO10 ....78 D4
Prenticas La IP13 ....146 D6
Prescott Dr 11 IP30 ....50 F2
Presmere Rd IP13 ....127 A4
Preston Dr IP1 ....134 F2
Preston Rd CO10 ....78 D4
Prestwick Ave 2 IP11 ......153 D6
Pretty Dr IP21 ....21 A2
Pretty Rd IP16 ....58 A4
Pretyman Ave IP14 ....51 F6
Pretyman Rd
  Felixstowe IP11 ....152 E1
  4 Harwich CO12 ....107 A2
  Lowestoft NR32 ....113 C2
Priestley Dr IP6 ....125 D4
Primes La Blyford IP19 ....42 B8
  Holton IP19 ....118 F5
Primrose Alley IP18 ....119 D4
Primrose Cl NR33 ....114 F2
Primrose Rd
  Haverhill C89 ....132 D5
  Ipswich IP2 ....138 F4
  Royal Hospital School
    IP9 ....105 E6
Primrose La
  Frostenden NR34 ....26 B4
  Ramsey & Parkeston
    CO12 ....106 A1
  10 Soham CB7 ....28 D5
Primrose Rise IP14 ....111 E3
Primrose Way CO10 ....92 E3
Prince Charles Ave 17
  IP2 ....48 C5
Prince Charles Cl
  CO10 ....148 D6
Prince of Wales Cl
  IP33 ....122 E5
Prince of Wales Dr 9
  IP2 ....139 A2
Prince St CO10 ....148 C6
Princedale Cl IP1 ....135 A1
Princess La C07 ....105 D1
Princes Gdns IP14 ....152 F4
Princes' Gdns 5 IP8 ....81 A3
Princes Gn IP11 ....118 A2
Prince's Rd NR35 ....110 D3
Princes Rd
  Felixstowe IP11 ....152 F4
  18 Harwich CO12 ....107 A2
  Lowestoft NR32 ....113 C2
Princes St
  Bury St Edmunds IP33 .....154 A2
  Ipswich IP1 ....155 A1
Princes Wlk IP2 ....113 A2
Princess Rd 8 IP28 ....119 C8
Princess Way
  4 Earsham NR35 ....10 A2
  Haverhill C89 ....132 B6
  Newmarket C88 ....121 B3
  Southwold IP18 ....119 C5
Princethorpe Rd IP3 ....144 C4
Printing Mus* NR34 ....111 B6
Prior's Ave IP33 ....122 E4
Priors Cl
  Lowestoft NR32 ....113 C5
  Rushbrooke with Rougham
    IP30 ....24 D8

Priors' Hill Rd IP15 ....130 D6
Priors Way IP15 ....130 E5
Priory Ave 8 C89 ....132 D6
Priory Cl 7 Burwell CB5 .....44 A5
  Ingham IP31 ....30 E7
  Palgrave IP22 ....20 C8
  Snape IP17 ....39 D2
Priory Cres IP11 ....39 D6
Priory Ct IP21 ....39 A1
Priory La Bungay NR35 .....110 B3
  Carlton Colville NR33 ....114 A4
  Darsham IP17 ....42 E4
  Debenham IP14 ....72 C7
Priory Rd Beccles NR34 ...111 B3
  Blythburgh IP17 ....42 E4
  Felixstowe IP11 ....153 C7
  Fressingfield IP21 ....39 D6
  Fritton & St Olaves NR31 ....2 A4
  Palgrave IP22 ....20 C8
  Snape IP17 ....39 D2
  Sudbury CO10 ....148 B8
  Wrentham NR34 ....26 E3
Priory Stadium CO10 ....148 C8
Priory Wlk CO10 ....148 C6
Prittlewell Cl IP2 ....138 F7
Private Rd Earsham NR35 ....7 D5
  Mutford NR34 ....10 B8
Privet Gn NR33 ....115 A4
Progress Way IP23 ....117 B8
Promenade
  Harwich CO12 ....107 A3
  Southwold IP18 ....119 D5
Prospect Hill CO10 ....92 B3
Prospect La
  Leiston IP16 ....129 D6
  Lowestoft NR33 ....115 B1
Prospect Rd
  Ipswich IP1 ....139 A6
  Lowestoft NR32 ....112 C1
  Norton IP31 ....52 A6
Prospect Row IP33 ....154 B3
Providence La 1 IP1 ....139 A4
Providence Stree IP1 ....155 B2
Provost Rd IP26 ....4 D7
Prussia La IP14 ....54 A3
Puddingmoor NR34 ....111 A5
Puddleduck La NR34 ....111 F2
Pug St IP21 ....21 A4
Pulham Cl IP21 ....21 D6
Pulham Rd IP21 ....21 D6
Pump Cl IP13 ....73 D4
Pump Ct 1 IP3 ....138 D6
Pump House La IP17 ....57 A4
Pump La IP7 ....94 C2
Pump St
  Needham Market IP6 ....125 C6
  Orford IP12 ....131 C2
Punchard Way IP11 ....124 B8
Purcell Rd IP14 ....124 B8
Purdis Ave IP3 ....140 F2
Purdis Farm La
  Foxhall IP10 ....141 C2
  Ipswich IP3 ....140 F2
Purdis Farm La IP10 ....141 D2
Purdis Rd IP3 ....141 D2
Purplett St IP2 ....155 C2
Putney Cl IP27 ....14 E8
Puttick La C07 ....151 E5
Pyes Mdw 1 IP30 ....50 F2
Pykenham Way IP7 ....149 D6
Pytches Cl 2 IP12 ....147 B6
Pytches Rd IP12 ....147 A6

Q

Quadling St IP1 ....155 B2
Quaker La Bardwell IP31 .....34 C4
  Beyton IP30 ....49 F1
Quaker's La 2 C89 ....132 E5
Quakers' Rd IP28 ....116 F5
Quakers Way
  4 Leiston IP16 ....129 D5
  3 Leiston IP16 ....129 D5
Quantock Cl IP5 ....140 F7
Quarries Cross IP14 ....66 C8
Quaves La NR35 ....110 B4
Quay La Reydon IP18 ....26 D3
  Sudbury CO10 ....148 C6
Quay Side IP12 ....147 A4
Quay St
  Halesworth IP19 ....118 A4
  18 Manningtree CO11 ....104 E2
  Orford IP12 ....131 C2
  Woodbridge IP12 ....147 A4
Quay The 12 CO12 ....107 B3
Quay's Rd IP28 ....12 D5
Quayside IP27 ....09 C7
Quebec Dr IP5 ....141 B8
Queech La IP9 ....105 B4
Queech The IP9 ....150 F4
Queen Edith Dr
  NR34 ....111 D3
Queen St 5 Cowlinge C88 ...61 B3
  Felixstowe IP11 ....152 E5
  6 Hadleigh IP7 ....149 C6
  Haverhill C89 ....132 B6
  Ipswich IP1 ....155 B2
  Newmarket C88 ....121 B3
  Southwold IP18 ....119 D5
  Stradbroke IP21 ....39 B4
Queens Ave 5 IP12 ....146 E4
Queen's Ct IP33 ....122 E5
Queens Cl
  Halesworth IP19 ....118 A3
  Lowestoft NR32 ....148 C6
Queens Dr IP28 ....118 A3
Queen's Dr IP28 ....116 B6

ueen's Head La IP12 ..146 F5
ueen's Head Rd CO4 ..102 F1
ueen's Highway
 NR32 ....112 C2
ueens La IP29 ....62 D5
ueen's Oak* IP19 ....41 A5
ueen's Rd
 Beccles NR34 ....111 B6
 Bungay NR35 ....111 A3
 Bury St Edmunds IP33 ..154 A2
 Felixstowe IP11 ....153 A3
 4 Harwich CO12 ....107 A1
 Lowestoft NR32 ....113 D3
 Southwold IP18 ....119 D8
ueens Rd Brandon IP27 ..4 E8
 1 Southwold IP18 ......119 C8
ueens St CO10 ....148 C6
ueen's View CO88 ......74 B2
ueen's Way 4 IP13 ....140 B2
ueensberry Rd
 4 Ipswich IP3 ....144 B8
ueenscliffe Rd IP2 ....139 A3
ueensdale Cl IP1 ......135 B1
ueensdale Rd IP1 ....135 B1
ueensgate Dr IP14 ....124 D6
ueensland IP9 ....106 F5
ueensway 4 Acton CO10 ..8 D7
 7 Earsham NR35 ....7 F4
 oning CB8 ....120 B8
 averhill CB9 ....132 C6
 1 Manningtree CO11 ..104 C2
 1 Mildenhall IP28 ....116 B4
 3 Soham CB7 ....28 D4
 udbury CO10 ....148 F3
 hetford IP24 ....16 B5
ueensway Mid Sch
 ....16 B5

R

ackham Cl 1 NR31 ......3 B7
adcliffe Dr IP2 ....138 D2
adcliffe Rd 8 IP27 ......14 A2
adiator Rd CO11 ....81 C8
adleys La CO6 ....102 B6
adnor Cl IP32 ....123 E6
aeburn Rd IP3 ....139 F1
edwald Dr IP32 ....123 D5
aglan Rd 2 NR32 ......113 D1
aglan St IP1 ....155 B3
agyll La IP30 ....50 D1
aile Wlk CO10 ....91 E8
ailway App 1 CO11 ....153 A3
ailway Hill IP20 ....22 C6
ailway St 10 CO11 ....104 E2
aine Ave CB9 ....132 B6
ainey Ct 7 IP20 ....22 D6
aingate St IP33 ....154 C1
andall Cl
 2 Hopton on Sea NR31 ..3 B7
 Ipswich IP5 ....141 E7
ands Rd IP7 ....149 B1
ands Way IP30 ....63 D6
andwell Cl IP4 ....140 B5
andleigh Prim Sch
 IP2 ....138 F5
anelagh Rd
 Felixstowe IP11 ......153 A4
 Ipswich IP2 ....155 A1
ansom Rd IP21 ....146 E6
ansome Ave IP27 ......21 A2
ansome Rd IP8 ....138 A4
ansome Cres IP3 ......140 B2
ansomes Europark
 IP10 ....138 F5
ansomes Way IP3 ....140 D1
apier Rd CO6 ....125 C4
anville NR33 ....114 E3
aworth Ave NR33 ....114 C3
apier St 6 IP1 ....139 C3
are Breeds Farm*
 CO7 ....151 A1
attla Cnr IP15 ....58 C5
atterlow Hill IP21 ....39 B6
aven Cl IP28 ....5 F1
attlesden CE Prim Sch
 IP30 ....65 D6
attlesden Cl IP14 ....124 D3
attlesden Rd IP30 ....65 C6
aven Cl IP28 ....116 D3

Raven Rd IP33 ....123 C1
Raven Way IP7 ....149 D4
Raveningham Rd NR34 ..9 C8
Ravens La IP8 ....134 A2
Ravens Way 6 IP12 ....84 A1
Ravensfield Rd IP1 ....134 E1
Ravensmere NR34 ....111 B6
Ravensmere E NR34 ..111 B6
Ravenswood Ave IP3 ..144 B8
Ravenswood Com Prim Sch
 IP3 ....144 C8
Ravenwood Mews
 NR33 ....115 A5
Raven's La IP29 ....113 E3
Rawlings Way IP21 ......4 E5
Ray Ave CO12 ....107 A2
Ray La 1 CO12 ....106 F3
Raydon Cl IP14 ....124 F3
Raydon La IP12 ....131 D3
Raydon Rd CO10 ....92 B3
Rayes La CO88 ....121 A4
Rayleigh Rd IP1 ....134 E1
Rayment Drift 5 IP5 ..141 C7
Rayner's La NR35 ....8 D8
Raynham Rd IP32 ......154 A4
Raynsford Rd IP30 ......63 F7
Reach Ct CB5 ....44 A5
Reade Rd 5 IP9 ....105 E7
Reading Gn IP21 ....38 D4
Reading Rd IP4 ....140 B7
Reading's La IP31 ......35 A2
Rebow Rd 9 CO12 ......107 A1
Reckford Rd IP17 ......58 B6
Recreation Cl IP14 ....132 D5
Recreation La IP11 ....152 F6
Recreation Rd
 Haverhill CB9 ....132 C5
 Stowmarket IP14 ....124 C6
Recreation Way
 Ipswich IP3 ....140 C2
 Mildenhall IP28 ......116 C4
Recreation Wlk CO10 ..148 F3
Rectory Cl
 Beccles NR34 ....111 F4
 3 Glemsford CO10 ....77 A3
 Ousden CB8 ....61 E6
 Raydon IP7 ....94 F1
Rectory Field IP7 ......106 C8
Rectory Gdns IP30 ......49 F1
Rectory Gr IP29 ....63 B5
Rectory Hill
 Botesdale IP22 ....35 F6
 East Bergholt CO7 ....151 C3
 Polstead CO6 ....102 E8
 Rickinghall Superior IP22 ..36 A5
Rectory La Beccles NR34 ..9 F4
 Brantham CO11 ....104 F5
 Hedenham NR35 ....7 D8
 Hintlesham IP8 ....95 C6
 Liebenston IP7 ....79 B5
 Kirton IP10 ....98 D2
 Mettingham NR35 ......8 A1
 4 Ramsey & Parkeston
  CO12 ....106 D1
 Scole IP21 ....21 A2
 Stuston IP21 ....37 D8
 Whatfield IP7 ....80 D1
 3 Woolpit IP30 ....50 D1
Rectory Mdw IP28 ......48 B6
Rectory Pk 3 CO10 ....93 C3
Rectory St 10 CO11 ....99 F2
Rectory Way
 IP16 ....138 F5

Red Rose Cl IP12 ....99 E4
Red Sleeve IP9 ....150 D3
Redan St IP1 ....155 A4
Redbarn La IP17 ....72 D7
Redcastle Furze Prim Sch
 IP24 ....16 B5
Rede La IP29 ....134 F8
Rede Rd IP29 ....62 F4
Rede Way CO10 ....92 B3
Redenhall Rd IP20 ......22 D6
Redgate IP4 ....16 C6
Redgate La IP9 ....143 D5
Redgrave & Lopham Fen
 Nature Reserve*
 IP22 ....19 B2
Redgrave & Lopham Fen
 Visitor Ctr* IP22 ......19 C3
Redgrave Rd IP22 ....19 B3
Redhouse Gdns 5 CB7 ..28 D3
Redhouse La
 Bawdsey IP12 ....99 E3
 Boxted CO4 ....102 E1
 5 Sudbury CO10 ......148 C5
Redhouse Rd IP13 ......56 B8
Redisham Cl NR32 ......113 A5
Redisham Rd
 Brampton with Stoven
  NR34 ....25 B6
 Weston NR34 ....9 C1
Redlingfield Rd
 Horham IP21 ....38 D2
 Occold IP23 ....37 F2
Redshank Cl CB9 ......133 A5
Redshank La CB9 ......133 A5
Redwald Rd IP32 ......85 E8
Redwing Cl IP2 ....138 D3
Redwing Rd IP33 ......123 C1
Redwings Visitor Ctr*
 ....2 C8
Redwold Cl IP12 ......124 C6
Redwood Gdns IP3 ....154 C2
Redwood La 23 IP27 ..13 F2
Reedland Way IP11 ....152 D5
Reed's Bldgs IP3 ......154 C3
Reeds La CB9 ....132 C6
Reet 1 NR32 ....115 D8
Reeve 1 NR32 ....115 D8
Reeve Cl
 5 Bury St Edmunds IP32 ..48 C5
 Scole IP21 ....21 A2
Reeve Gdns IP5 ....141 C8
Reeve's Cl NR33 ......110 C3
Reeves La IP26 ....75 A3
Refinery Rd CO12 ......106 F3
Regal Cl 4 CB7 ....28 E3
Regal La CB7 ....28 E3
Regent Rd 8 CB7 ....28 D3
Regent Rd NR32 ......113 D1
Regent St
 20 Manningtree CO11 ..104 E2
 Stowmarket IP14 ......124 D7
Regiment Way 6
 CO12 ....106 E1
Regimental Mus*
 CO12 ....122 C6
Regina Cl IP4 ....140 B5
Reigate Cl IP3 ....140 B3
Rembrandt Cl 3 NR32 ..113 C6
Rembrandt Gdns IP3 ..122 F3
Rembrandt Rd IP3 ......123 A3
Remembrance Rd
 IP16 ....73 F6
Remercie Rd 7 CO11 ..105 A2
Rendall La IP14 ....67 A8
Rendham Hall IP17 ......56 F7
Rendham Rd
 Bruisyard IP17 ....56 D4
 Kelsale cum Carlton
  IP17 ....128 A6
 Peasenhall IP17 ......56 F7
Rendlesham Rd
 8 Felixstowe IP11 ....152 D5
 Ipswich IP1 ....139 A7
Renfrew Way IP31 ......136 B1
Renoir Pl 2 NR32 ......113 B5
Renson Cl IP30 ....64 F8
Richard Burn Way
 CO10 ....148 C8
Richard Crampton Rd
 NR34 ....111 B3
Richards Dr IP31 ......137 D7
Richardson Rd CO7 ....151 D5
Richardsons La IP9 ..106 B8
Richard's Cl NR31 ......114 E6
Richer Cl IP31 ....50 E7
Richer Rd IP31 ....50 F7
Richmond Cres 8 CO12 ..107 A1
Richmond Rd
 Ipswich IP1 ....138 F7
 Lowestoft NR33 ......115 C6
Riddlesworth Hall La
 IP22 ....17 F4
Rider Haggard La 7
 NR33 ....11 C1

Rider Haggard Way
 NR35 ....110 C7
Ridgeville 6 IP20 ......114 F3
Ridgeway IP14 ....124 B6
Ridgeway The 10 CO12 ..107 A2
Ridgeways The NR33 ..114 D5
Ridgewell Rd
 Ashen CO10 ....89 D5
 Birdbrook CO9 ....89 C5
Ridings The
 3 Beccles NR34 ......111 F4
 Leavenheath CO6 ....102 B8
Ridley Rd IP33 ....122 C6
Rigbourne Hill NR34 ..111 C3
Rigbourne Hill La 6
 NR34 ....111 C2
Rigg's Cl IP18 ....119 B8
Rightup Dro IP27 ......105 A2
Riley Cl IP1 ....134 C1
Ringham Rd IP4 ....140 A6
Ringsfield CE Prim Sch
 NR34 ....9 B1
Ringsfield Rd
 Beccles NR34 ....111 A4
 6 Lowestoft NR32 ....113 A3
 Ringsfield NR34 ......9 A1
Ringshall Prim Sch
 IP14 ....80 F6
Rio Cl 2 NR33 ....114 C5
Rishangles Rd IP23 ....38 D8
Risby CEVC Prim Sch
 IP28 ....47 D5
Risby Cl IP4 ....140 B6
Risbygate St IP33 ......154 B2
Riseway Cl IP23 ....38 C8
Rishton Rd 7 NR32 ....113 D1
Rising Sun Hill IP30 ..65 D5
Rissemere La E IP18 ..119 C8
Rissemere Rd IP22 ....138 E1
Rivendale 4 NR33 ....114 D3
River La Fordham CB7 ..29 A1
 Halesworth IP19 ......118 B3
River View Rd 1 IP9 ..106 A5
Riverbank Cl CO10 ......90 B8
Rivers St IP9 ....139 F7
Riverside
 2 Framlingham IP13 ..126 C3
 Haskelton IP13 ......146 A7
 Palgrave IP22 ....20 B2
Riverside Ave E 6
 CO11 ....104 E3
Riverside Ave W 4
 CO11 ....104 E3
Riverside Bsns Ctr
 NR33 ....115 C8
Riverside Bsns Pk
 NR33 ....115 B8
Riverside Ct IP28 ......116 B4
Riverside Ct IP32 ......123 A8
Riverside Ind Est IP33 ..127 C7
Riverside Ind Pk IP2 ..139 D3
Riverside Mid Sch
 IP28 ....116 B4
Riverside Rd
 Ipswich IP1 ....138 F7
 Lowestoft NR33 ......115 B8
Riverside View IP13 ..127 C8
Riverview IP12 ....147 C7
Rivish La CO10 ....91 E8
Rixon Cres 3 IP22 ....84 E6
Roamwood Gn La IP31 ..53 E3
Robeck Rd IP1 ....139 E1
Robert Boby Way
 IP33 ....154 B2
Robert's Hill CO8 ......101 C2
Robert's Rd IP16 ......129 D6
Robertsbridge Wlk 6
 NR33 ....114 D4
Robin Cl Haverhill CB9 ..133 A5
 Mildenhall IP28 ......116 D4
 8 Thurstow IP31 ......49 D4
Robin Dr IP2 ....138 D3
Robin Rd IP33 ....113 A2
Robin Way CO10 ......148 A3
Robins Cl 10 CB7 ......28 E3
Robinson Cl IP31 ......122 D6
Robinson Rd 7 IP21 ..20 F1
Robletts IP13 ....84 D7
Robletts Way 1 CO6 ..106 E1
Rochdale IP18 ....26 D1
Rochester Rd 1 NR34 ..115 B4
Rochester Way CO10 ..148 B8
Rochfort Ave CB8 ......120 E5
Rock Rd NR32 ....113 D2
Rockall CB8 ....61 E6
Rockall Cl CO6 ....93 F1
Rockingham Rd IP33 ..123 B1
Rockstone La IP9 ......41 C7
Rodber Way NR32 ......113 A6
Rodbridge Hill CO10 ..91 D6
Rodney Cl IP12 ....146 F7
Roebuck Dr IP27 ......109 E4
Rogeron Cl CO10 ......75 D3
Rogers Cl IP11 ....152 F6
Roger's La CO10 ....92 F4
Rogue's La IP13 ......127 C5
Rokewood Pl IP29 ......63 B5
Roman Cl 3 CB5 ......44 A5
Roman Rd NR32 ......113 C1
Roman Way
 Felixstowe IP11 ......153 D6

Roman Way continued
 Halesworth IP19 ......118 A3
 Haverhill CB9 ....133 B4
 Long Melford CO10 ....91 E7
Romany La NR33 ....11 B3
Romany Rd NR32 ......114 C8
Romany Way IP33 ......123 D3
Romney Pl 6 NR32 ....113 B6
Romney Rd IP3 ....140 A1
Romsey Rd IP33 ......122 B3
Ronald La IP17 ....128 D5
Ronden Cl NR34 ......111 B2
Rookery Chase CO7 ..103 F1
Rookery Cl IP27 ......109 E4
Rookery Dro 3 IP26 ..13 B1
Rookery La IP19 ....23 F4
Rookery Rd Elmsett IP7 ..80 E2
 Moneweden IP13 ......69 F5
Rookery The
 Brandon IP27 ....5 D1
 Eye IP23 ....117 D2
 4 Manningtree CO11 ..104 E2
Rookery Way IP14 ......51 F1
Rook's La 7 NR34 ....111 B5
Rookwood La CO10 ....78 F6
Rookwood Way CO9 ..133 C8
Roosevelt Wlk 3 NR33 ..114 C5
Rope Wlk IP4 ....155 C2
Roper's Ct 3 CO10 ....78 D4
Ropers La CO10 ....91 D7
Ropes Dr IP5 ....141 B8
Rosbrook Cl 1 NR32 ..113 A2
Rose Acre CO7 ....103 F7
Rose Ave IP22 ....20 A3
Rose Ct Lowestoft NR32 ..113 C2
 Shotley IP9 ....106 F6
Rose Gn CO10 ....101 F8
Rose Gn La 4 IP28 ....30 B8
Rose Hall Gdns NR35 ..110 B3
Rose Hill
 Grundisburgh IP13 ....83 E5
 Withersfield CB9 ......74 B3
 Witnesham IP6 ....135 F7
Rose Hill Prim Sch
 IP3 ....140 A4
Rose La Botesdale IP22 ..36 A7
 Bungay NR35 ....110 B3
 Diss IP22 ....20 D1
 Elmswell IP30 ....50 E2
 Spexhall IP19 ....155 B2
 Wickham Skeith IP23 ..52 D8
Rose La Cl IP22 ....20 C1
Rose Wlk IP6 ....125 D3
Rosebay Gdns 11 CB7 ..28 E4
Rosebery Rd
 Felixstowe IP11 ......153 B4
 Ipswich IP4 ....139 F5
Rosebery Way CB8 ....120 E5
Rosedale Gdns 4 NR33 ..114 E4
Rosefinch Cl CB9 ......133 A5
Rosehill Cres IP3 ......139 F4
Rosehill Rd IP3 ....139 F4
Rosemary Ave IP11 ..153 B5
Rosemary Cl 2 IP28 ..30 C1
Rosemary Gdns CO10 ..148 C8
Rosemary La
 Ipswich IP4 ....155 B2
 Kelsale cum Carlton
  IP17 ....128 C6
Rosemary Musker Cty High
 Sch IP24 ....16 C7
Rosemary Rd 5 IP32 ..137 F6
Rosery La IP13 ....83 A4
Rosewood Cl IP27 ......13 C5
Ross Cl CB9 ....133 B5
Ross Peers Sports Ctr The
 CO10 ....28 B3
Ross Rd IP4 ....136 B1
Rosyth Rd 5 IP31 ......33 D5
Rotheram Rd 8 IP27 ..79 F4
Rotten Row CO10 ......92 D2
Rotterdam Rd NR32 ..113 B1
Rougham CE Prim Sch
 IP30 ....49 D1
Rougham Hill IP33 ....123 C3
Rougham Rd
 Bradfield St George IP30 ..64 D7
 Bury St Edmunds IP33 ..123 C3
Roughlands IP27 ......109 D6
Roundridge Rd IP30 ..150 F4
Roundwood Rd IP4 ..140 A7
Rous Rd CB8 ....121 B3
Rousies Cl 6 IP7 ......149 E6
Routh Ave IP3 ....140 F1
Row The CO7 ....103 F5
Rowan Dr Brandon IP27 ..14 F8
 Bury St Edmunds IP32 ..123 F6
Rowan Gn 7 IP30 ......50 F2
Rowan Way
 Beccles NR34 ....111 C3
 Lowestoft NR33 ......114 D6
 5 Thurstow IP31 ......49 D4
Rowanhayes Cl IP2 ..139 B3
Rowans Way 1 CO6 ..102 E7
Rowarth Ave IP5 ......141 C7
Rowell Cl CB8 ....132 E8
Rowell's La IP14 ......51 D4
Rowley Cl 1 IP11 ......40 C2
Rowley Cl 7 CO11 ....104 E4
Rowley Ct CB8 ....133 C3
Rowley Dr CB8 ....133 B3
Rowley Rd CB9 ....133 B3
Rows The CB8 ....120 E3

Roxburgh Rd IP4 . . . . 136 B1
Roy Ave IP4 . . . . 140 B5
Roy Cl IP5 . . . . 141 B7
Royal Ave NR32 . . . . 113 D3
Royal Hospl Sch IP9 . . . . . . 105 E6
Royal Norfolk & Suffolk
  Yacht Club NR33 . . . . 115 D8
Royal Nrl Cl IP8 . . . . 128 D7
Royal Terr NR33 . . . . 115 D7
Roydon Fen IP22 . . . . 20 B2
Roydon Prim Sch IP22 . . . . . 20 B3
Roydon Rd IP22 . . . . 20 C3
Roylands La CO10 . . . . 93 D3
Royston Dr IP2 . . . . 138 D2
Rozlyne Cl 8 NR33 . . . . 114 E4
Rubens Rd IP3 . . . . 140 A1
Rubens Wlk CO10 . . . . 148 E8
Ruby Cl 9 NR32 . . . . 3 D4
Rudlands IP8 . . . . 138 C1
Rudlands Cl 6 CB7 . . . . 29 C5
Rue's La IP11 . . . . 153 C8
Rugby Rd CO10 . . . . 148 F2
Rumburgh La NR35 . . . . 24 D6
Rumburgh Priory*
  IP19 . . . . 24 B4
Rumburgh Rd
  Lowestoft NR32 . . . . 113 B5
  Rumburgh IP19 . . . . 24 B3
Run Mdw NR33 . . . . 114 C6
Run The NR34 . . . . 26 A7
Runce's La NR33 . . . . 114 C3
Runnacles Way IP11 . . . . . . 152 D5
Runnymede Gn IP33 . . . . . . 123 A3
Rushall Rd IP20 . . . . 22 B6
Rushbrooke La IP33 . . . . . . 123 D3
Rushbury Cl IP4 . . . . 140 B8
Rushford Rd
  Coney Weston IP31 . . . . 17 E1
  Euston IP24 . . . . 16 E2
Rushlake Way 7 NR33 . . . . . 114 D4
Rushmeadow Way 1
  IP4 . . . . 153 D7
Rushmere Hall Prim Sch
  IP4 . . . . 136 A1
Rushmere Pl CB9 . . . . 132 F6
Rushmere Rd
  Gisleham NR33 . . . . 114 B1
  Ipswich IP4 . . . . 140 D7
  Rushmere NR33 . . . . 10 F3
Rushmere St IP5 . . . . 136 E1
Ruskin Cl 3 IP14 . . . . 124 E8
Russ Rd IP4 . . . . 139 F5
Russell Baron Rd IP11 . . . . . 48 D5
Russell Rd
  Felixstowe IP11 . . . . 152 F2
  Ipswich IP1 . . . . 155 A2
Russell's Gn NR34 . . . . 9 C2
Russet Cl
  1 Beccles NR34 . . . . 111 C3
  Great Barton IP32 . . . . . . 123 E7
Russett Cl IP4 . . . . 132 A6
Rydal Ave IP11 . . . . 153 D7
Rydal Cl IP14 . . . . 124 B6
Rydal Wlk IP3 . . . . 140 C2
Ryders Way 7 IP22 . . . . 36 A6
Rye Cl Ipswich IP3 . . . . 140 D4
  1 Lowestoft NR33 . . . . . . 114 C6
Ryeburn Cl 1 NR33 . . . . 11 B1
Ryedale 1 NR33 . . . . 114 F3
Ryefields 3 IP31 . . . . 49 E4
Ryes La CO10 . . . . 91 F6
Rylands IP9 . . . . 150 E4
Rylands Cl 1 IP31 . . . . 49 E4

S

Sackville St CB8 . . . . 121 B4
Sackvylle St IP14 . . . . 53 E1
Saddlemakers La
  IP12 . . . . 147 C8
Saddlers Mdw 2 IP13 . . . . . . 83 E5
Saddlers Pl IP15 . . . . 98 A8
Saddlers Yd 17 IP35 . . . . 34 B1
Saffron Sq NR33 . . . . 115 A3
Saffrons Cl IP30 . . . . 50 D1
Sages Ead Rd CB9 . . . . 88 A4
St Agnes Way IP5 . . . . 140 F6
St Albans CB8 . . . . 121 A6
St Albans Cath High Sch
  IP4 . . . . 140 D7
St Andrew St 1 NR31 . . . . 3 C7
St Andrews CE VA Prim Sch
  IP22 . . . . 19 A5
St Andrew's Church Cl
  IP5 . . . . 136 D1
St Andrew's Cl
  2 Barningham IP31 . . . . . . 34 E7
  3 Great Finborough IP14 . . . 66 B4
  Ipswich IP1 . . . . 140 D5
  3 Isleham CB7 . . . . 29 C5
St Andrew's Ct 8 IP33 . . . . . 154 B2
St Andrew's Dr 3 IP9 . . . . . 106 C8
St Andrews Dr IP28 . . . . 48 C6
St Andrews Mead IP4 . . . . . . 68 B8
St Andrew's Pl IP12 . . . . . . 147 D8
St Andrew's Rd
  Beccles NR34 . . . . 111 C2
  Goldfair Green IP17 . . . . . 129 B2
  Felixstowe IP11 . . . . 153 A5
St Andrews Rd
  Scole IP21 . . . . 21 A1

St Andrews Rd continued
  Sudbury CO10 . . . . 148 E4
St Andrew's St 2 IP28 . . . . . 116 C4
St Andrew's St N IP33 . . . . 154 B2
St Andrew's St S IP33 . . . . 154 B2
St Anne's Cl NR34 . . . . 111 C4
St Annes Cl IP12 . . . . 146 D3
St Anne's Rd NR34 . . . . 111 C4
St Anns Dr IP28 . . . . 116 B4
St Aubyn's Rd 6 NR33 . . . . . 115 C6
St Aubyns Rd IP4 . . . . 140 A5
St Audrys Pk Rd 5 IP12 . . . . 84 E6
St Audrys Rd IP12 . . . . 84 E6
St Augustine Rd IP4 . . . . . . 140 D4
St Augustine's Gdns
  IP3 . . . . 140 C3
St Austell Cl IP5 . . . . 141 A6
St Austin's La 1 CO12 . . . . 107 C3
St Bartholomews La
  CO10 . . . . 148 B7
St Benedicts RC Sch
  IP32 . . . . 122 E8
St Benedict's Rd NR34 . . . . 111 B6
St Benedicts Rd IP27 . . . . . . 6 A1
St Benet's Dr NR34 . . . . . . 111 C3
St Benet's RC Minst
  NR34 . . . . 111 A4
St Benets Rd Brundish . . . .
St Botolph's La IP33 . . . . . 154 C1
St Botolphs Prim Sch
  IP22 . . . . 23 B8
St Botolph's Way CB9 . . . . . 132 D6
St Catherine's Cl
  NR33 . . . . 114 E4
St Catherines Cl IP28 . . . . . 116 D6
St Catherine's Ct 2 IP38 . . . 138 E1
St Catherine's Rd 11
  CO10 . . . . 91 E8
St Clare Ct 15 NR31 . . . . 3 B7
St Clement Mews 13 NR31 . . 3 B7
St Clement's Hospl
  IP3 . . . . 140 C4
St Cross Rd IP20 . . . . 23 B8
St David's Cl 8 NR34 . . . . . 111 C2
St Denis Cl 11 CO12 . . . . . . 107 A1
St Domonic's Dr IP27 . . . . . . 6 A1
St Edmund Cl IP31 . . . . 34 B1
St Edmund Rd IP27 . . . . 5 E4
St Edmund's Cl 1 IP33 . . . . . 85 C5
St Edmunds Cl
  2 Beccles NR34 . . . . 111 C2
  6 Harwich CO12 . . . . 107 A1
  Stowmarket IP14 . . . . 124 C8
  4 Woodbridge IP12 . . . . . 146 E4
St Edmunds Cres 1
  NR33 . . . . 111 C1
St Edmund's Dr IP30 . . . . . . 50 F3
St Edmunds Gate 1
  IP31 . . . . 33 D5
St Edmund's Hill CO10 . . . . 101 B7
St Edmunds La CO10 . . . . . 101 D5
St Edmund's Pl IP11 . . . . . . 139 C8
St Edmunds Prim Sch
  IP31 . . . . 38 C6
St Edmunds RC Prim Sch
  NR35 . . . . 110 B4
St Edmunds RCVA Prim Sch
  IP33 . . . . 154 B1
St Edmund's Rd
  Felixstowe IP11 . . . . 152 E2
  Ipswich IP1 . . . . 139 B8
  Southwold IP18 . . . . 119 D6
St Edmunds Rd IP14 . . . . . 124 C7
St Edmunds Sq IP33 . . . . . 154 B2
St Edmundsbury Cath*
  IP33 . . . . 154 C2
St Edmundsbury CE Prim Sch
  IP33 . . . . 154 A3
St Edmundsbury Ret Pk
  IP32 . . . . 123 E4
St Etienne IP14 . . . . 69 B6
St Fabians Cl CB8 . . . . 120 F5
St Felix CEVE Mid Sch
  CB8 . . . . 120 F6
St Felix Cl 2 CB7 . . . . 28 D5
St Felix Sch IP18 . . . . 119 A6
St George's Ave 2
  CO12 . . . . 107 B1
St George's Rd
  Beccles NR34 . . . . 111 B4
  Felixstowe IP11 . . . . 153 C6
  Lowestoft NR33 . . . . 115 A4
  Stowlangtoft IP31 . . . . 50 B7
Saint Georges Sch
  IP18 . . . . 119 A7
St George's St IP1 . . . . 155 B3
St Gotthards Ave IP12 . . . . . 98 B8
St Gregorys Cl 1 IP21 . . . . . 85 E8
St Gregory's Ct CO10 . . . . . 148 B6
St Gregorys Prim Sch
  CO10 . . . . 148 B5
St Helena Wlk IP28 . . . . . . 116 C6
St Helens Prim Sch
  IP4 . . . . 139 E6
St Helen's St 1 IP4 . . . . . . 155 C3
Saint Helens Way IP4 . . . . . . 16 B7
Saint Isidores IP5 . . . . 141 E7
St Ives Cl IP5 . . . . 141 A6
St James' Gn 3 IP33 . . . . . . 119 D5
St James' La
  Chediston IP19 . . . . 24 A3
  St James South Elmham
    IP19 . . . . 23 F4
St James Rd
  IP33 . . . . 123 C5

St James Rd
  All Saints & St Nicholas,
    South Elmham IP19 . . . . 24 A5
  St James, South Elmham
    IP19 . . . . 23 F4
St James's St 1 IP17 . . . . . . 43 B1
St Johns Ave CB8 . . . . 121 A1
St John's CE Prim Sch
  IP4 . . . . 140 A7
St John's Cl IP28 . . . . 116 D6
St John's Hill
  Bungay NR35 . . . . 110 C2
  4 Woodbridge IP12 . . . . . 147 A5
St Johns Mdw IP20 . . . . 23 C3
St John's Pl IP33 . . . . 154 B3
St John's Rd
  Bungay NR35 . . . . 110 B3
  Ipswich IP4 . . . . 140 A6
  Lowestoft NR33 . . . . 115 D7
  Saxmundham IP17 . . . . . . 128 C3
St John's St
  Beck Row, Holywell Row
    & Kenny Hill IP28 . . . . . 30 C8
  Bury St Edmunds IP33 . . . 154 B3
  Woodbridge IP12 . . . . . . 147 A5
  St John's St IP12 . . . . 147 A5
St John's Way
  1 Feltwell IP26 . . . . 4 E5
  Thetford IP24 . . . . 16 A5
St Josephs Coll IP2 . . . . . . 139 A3
St Joseph's RC Prim Sch
  CO10 . . . . 148 D5
St Lawrence Cl NR34 . . . . . 111 C2
St Lawrence Prim Sch . . . .
St Lawrence Rd NR33 . . . . . 115 B3
St Lawrence Way IP5 . . . . . 141 A6
St Leonards Cl IP21 . . . . 21 A1
St Leonards Hospl
  CO10 . . . . 148 D5
St Leonards Rd 2 IP33 . . . . 140 B3
St Leonard's Rd NR33 . . . . . 115 C6
St Leonards St CB8 . . . . 6 B8
St Louis Cath Mid Sch
  IP33 . . . . 154 B1
St Louis Rd IP4 . . . .
  CB8 . . . . 121 A4
St Margaret's Cres
  IP16 . . . . 129 B6
St Margaret's Pl CB8 . . . . . . 75 F7
St Margarets Prim Sch
  NR32 . . . . 113 C3
St Margaret's Rd
  Bungay NR35 . . . . 110 B3
  1 Lowestoft NR32 . . . . . . 113 C3
St Margaret's St 4 NR34 . . . 155 C3
St Margaret's Way 3
  NR31 . . . . 3 B7
St Marks RC Prim Sch
  IP2 . . . . 138 F3
St Martin's Cl IP28 . . . . . . 120 C7
St Martins Ct IP5 . . . . 141 E7
St Martin's Gn 14 IP11 . . . 107 D8
St Martin's La IP14 . . . . 16 B2
St Martin's St 4 NR33 . . . . . 115 B3
St Mary's Ave CB8 . . . . 51 C1
St Marys Cath Prim Sch
  IP4 . . . . 139 F6
St Mary's Cl
  Benhall IP17 . . . . 72 C8
  Mildenhall IP28 . . . . 116 C5
  Woodbridge IP12 . . . . . . 146 F5
St Mary's Cl Bacton IP14 . . . 51 F6
  Bramford IP8 . . . . 134 B1
  Felixstowe IP11 . . . . 152 B7
  Flixton NR35 . . . . 7 E1
  Harleston IP20 . . . . 22 E6
  Horham IP21 . . . . 38 F3
  Sudbury CO10 . . . . 148 F8
St Mary's Ct IP23 . . . . 36 D2
St Mary's Cres
  Badwell Ash IP31 . . . . 50 E7
  Felixstowe IP11 . . . . 152 F6
St Mary's Gdns IP6 . . . . . . 125 E6
St Marys Pk IP10 . . . . 98 A4
St Marys Prim Sch
  IP7 . . . . 149 E6
  NR33 . . . . 115 C5
St Mary's Rd
  Aldeby NR34 . . . . 10 A7
  Beccles NR34 . . . . 111 A5
  Ipswich IP4 . . . . 140 B6
  Sandhurst Ave IP3 . . . . . . 140 C8
  Stowmarket IP14 . . . . 124 B7
St Mary's Sq IP33 . . . . 154 C1
St Mary's St NR35 . . . . 110 B4
St Marys View IP21 . . . . 49 E6
St Mary's Wlk IP1 . . . . 135 F4
St Mary's Wlk 5 CB7 . . . . . . 88 D3
St Matthew's Ave 3
  IP1 . . . . 155 A3
St Matthews CE Prim Sch
  IP1 . . . . 155 A3
St Michaels CE Prim Sch
  NR34 . . . . 9 B6
St Michael's Cl
  1 Beccles NR34 . . . . 111 C2
  Ipswich NR32 . . . . 141 A6
  Lowestoft NR32 . . . . 112 C1
St Michael's Rd 10 CO11 . . . 107 B1
St Michael's CE 4 CO12 . . . 107 B1
St Michael's Way 1 IP19 . . . 42 C6
St Nicholas
  Bury St Edmunds IP32 . . . 123 C6
  Rattlesden IP30 . . . . 65 D5

St Nicholas Dr IP26 . . . . 4 E6
St Nicholas St IP1 . . . . 155 B2
St Olaves Rd
  Bury St Edmunds IP32 . . . 122 E8
  Ipswich IP5 . . . . 141 C8
St Osyth Cl IP2 . . . . 142 F8
St Pancras Cath Prim Sch
  IP1 . . . . 134 F2
St Paul's Cl
  4 Beccles NR34 . . . . 111 C2
  Brockdish IP21 . . . . 21 F2
St Pauls Cl IP15 . . . . 130 E5
St Peter & Paul Ceva Prim
  Sch IP23 . . . . 117 D2
St Peter's Ave
  13 Claydon IP6 . . . . 82 A5
  Claydon IP6 . . . . 134 C8
St Peters Ave CB8 . . . . 45 F7
St Peter's Cl
  Brockdish IP21 . . . . 21 F2
  6 Claydon IP6 . . . . 82 A5
  Stowmarket IP14 . . . . 128 B6
  Woodbridge IP12 . . . . . . 146 D4
St Peters Cl
  Charsfield IP13 . . . . 70 B3
  6 Moulton CB8 . . . . 45 F3
St Peters Ct 9 IP33 . . . . 154 B1
St Peter's Hall* NR35 . . . . 24 A8
St Peters Pl CB7 . . . . 29 B1
St Peters Rd
  Aldeburgh IP15 . . . . 130 E5
  Lowestoft NR33 . . . . 115 C6
St Peter's Rd
  Lowestoft NR33 . . . . 115 C6
  Stowmarket IP14 . . . . 124 B6
St Peter's St
  Ipswich IP1 . . . . 155 B2
  Lowestoft NR32 . . . . 113 C2
  4 Lowestoft NR32 . . . . . . 113 D2
  10 Lowestoft NR32 . . . . . 113 D2
St Peters Way 11 NR31 . . . . . 49 E4
St Peter's Wlk IP26 . . . . 4 F3
St Philips Rd CB8 . . . . 120 F5
St Quinton's Ct NR34 . . . . . 155 B3
St Stephens Cl IP33 . . . . . 123 A3
St Stephens La IP1 . . . . . . 155 B2
St Vincent Wlk 14 NR31 . . . . 3 B7
St Wendred's Way
  CB8 . . . . 120 B7
Salehurst Rd IP3 . . . . 140 E3
Salisbury Gn IP33 . . . . 123 B3
Salisbury Rd
  Ipswich IP4 . . . . 140 A3
  Lowestoft NR33 . . . . 115 C7
  1 Southwold IP18 . . . . . . 119 D5
Sallows Cl IP1 . . . . 138 F7
Sally Wood's La IP6 . . . . . 125 F6
Salmond Dr 8 IP24 . . . . 16 C2
Salter Cl IP22 . . . . 123 E4
Salters Gdns 4 IP13 . . . . . . 83 E5
Saltgate 5 IP33 . . . . 111 B6
Salthouse La IP4 . . . . 155 C2
Saltwater Way NR33 . . . . . . 114 E8
Samford Cl IP9 . . . . 105 E8
Samford Ct 5 NR34 . . . . . . 111 F4
Samford Rd IP8 . . . . 138 B6
Sampson Dr 8 CO10 . . . . . . 91 E8
Samson Cl 1 IP32 . . . . 48 C5
Samson's La IP22 . . . . 19 F4
Samuel Cl IP4 . . . . 140 E5
Samuel Vince Rd 2
  IP21 . . . . 39 D8
Samuel Ward Sch
  CB9 . . . . 132 F7
San Francisco Wlk 3
  IP33 . . . . 114 C5
Sancroft Way
  5 Fressingfield IP21 . . . . . 39 D8
  Wortwell IP20 . . . . 23 A7
Sanctuary Gdns 4
  IP16 . . . .
Sanctuary The IP16 . . . . 73 F6
Sanctuary Way 9 NR33 . . . . . 11 B1
Sand Acre Cl IP28 . . . . 116 D5
Sand Hill CO10 . . . . 93 C3
Sand St CB7 . . . . 29 B1
Sandbank Rd 1 NR33 . . . . . 114 E4
Sanderling Cl 3 IP28 . . . . . 116 D4
Sanders Cl 2 NR32 . . . . . . 112 F4
Sandford Rd IP14 . . . . 52 A1
Sandgalls Rd IP27 . . . . 109 D6
Sandholme Cl IP33 . . . . 123 B2
Sandhurst Ave IP3 . . . . 140 C8
Sandling Cres IP4 . . . . 140 E5
Sandlings Prim Sch
  IP4 . . . . 85 C5
Sandlings The
  Aldeburgh IP15 . . . . 130 C6
  Ipswich IP3 . . . . 140 D1
Sandown Cl 3 IP11 . . . . . . 153 A3
Sandown Rd IP1 . . . . 135 A3
Sandpath 5 IP21 . . . . 39 E8
Sandpiper Cl CB9 . . . . 133 A6
Sandpiper Rd
  Bury St Edmunds IP33 . . . 123 C2
  Ipswich IP2 . . . . 138 E2
Sandpit Cl IP4 . . . . 140 F5
Sandpit Dr 3 IP31 . . . . 49 E4
Sandpit Hill IP20 . . . . 23 B3
Sandpit La
  Thurston IP31 . . . . 49 E4
  Worlingham NR34 . . . . 9 F4
Sandringham Cl IP2 . . . . . 138 F2
Sandringham Rd
  NR32 . . . . 113 C1
Sands Cl 9 NR31 . . . . 3 C6
Sands La NR32 . . . . 112 D2
Sandy Cl 9 IP11 . . . . 107 D8

Sandy Dro IP28 . . . . 30 F7
Sandy Hill Barham IP6 . . . . 82 B1
  Wormingford CO6 . . . . . . 101 E7
Sandy La Barham IP6 . . . . . 82 A4
  Barningham IP31 . . . . 34 E8
  Barsham NR34 . . . . 9 A4
  2 Bromeswell IP12 . . . . . . 85 A8
  Bulmer CO10 . . . . 91 D7
  Diss IP22 . . . . 20 D5
  Gisleham NR33 . . . . 11 A1
  Holton IP19 . . . . 118 E2
  Hoo IP13 . . . . 71 B4
  Ixen IP12 . . . . 72 F7
  Little Bealings IP13 . . . . . 137 D5
  Marlesford IP13 . . . . 71 F6
  Rendham IP17 . . . . 56 F7
  Ringshall IP14 . . . . 66 E7
  St Mary, South Elmham
    Otherwise Homersfield
    IP20 . . . . 23 B8
  Sternfield IP17 . . . . 72 C6
  Stowlangtoft IP31 . . . . 50 A8
  Sudbury CO10 . . . . 148 A6
  Sutton IP12 . . . . 99 B6
  Waldingfield IP12 . . . . 98 E6
  Wickham Market IP13 . . . 127 D1
  Witnesham IP6 . . . . 136 B8
  Woodbridge IP12 . . . . . . 146 D2
Sandyhill La IP13 . . . . 139 E5
Sapiston Rd IP31 . . . . 33 F7
Sapling Pl IP4 . . . . 140 F7
Sarsen Cl IP19 . . . . 118 C7
Saturn Cl NR32 . . . . 113 D1
Sawmill La IP10 . . . . 98 A6
Sawmills Rd IP22 . . . . 20 E2
Sawston Cl 10 IP2 . . . . 139 F7
Sawyers 2 . . . . 80 F1
Sawyers Cl IP9 . . . . 150 E1
Saxham Bsns Pk IP29 . . . . . 47 E6
Saxmundham Mid Sch
  IP17 . . . . 128 C2
Saxmundham Prim Sch . . . .
Saxmundham Rd
  Aldeburgh IP15 . . . . 130 C3
  Framlingham IP13 . . . . . . 126 E4
  Friston IP17 . . . . 72 E1
  Knodishall IP17 . . . . 57 F7
  Theberton IP16 . . . . 73 C7
Saxmundham Sports Club
  IP17 . . . . 128 C2
Saxmundham Sta
  IP17 . . . . 128 C2
Saxon Cl Exning CB8 . . . . . 120 D7
  11 Felixstowe IP11 . . . . . . 153 C6
  Felixstowe IP11 . . . . 33 D7
  Saxon Dr 2 CB5 . . . . 44 A8
  Saxon La IP6 . . . . 95 E6
Saxon Pl IP27 . . . . 5 E7
Saxon Rd
  Lowestoft NR33 . . . . 115 B3
  Saxmundham IP17 . . . . . . 128 B2
Saxon Rise IP33 . . . . 122 E2
Saxon St Rd CB8 . . . . 60 E6
Saxon Way IP2 . . . . 147 A1
Saxonfields IP17 . . . . 72 D9
Saxons Way IP19 . . . . 118 B4
Saxtead Rd
  Dennington IP13 . . . . 55 D1
  Framlingham IP13 . . . . . . 126 A3
Scales St NR33 . . . . 15 C3
Scalesbrook La IP19 . . . . . 118 E1
Scaltback Mid Sch
  CB8 . . . . 120 E5
Scama La IP29 . . . . 36 C6
Scarlin Rd IP33 . . . . 122 C2
Schneider Rd 3 IP11 . . . . . 153 H1
Scholars Wlk IP22 . . . . 20 C3
School Ave IP30 . . . . 50 E2
School Cl
  1 Capel St. Mary IP9 . . . . 150 E3
  Cheveley CB8 . . . . 60 E8
  Hadleigh IP7 . . . . 149 E5
  Kenninghall NR16 . . . . 19 A8
  North Cove NR34 . . . . 10 C4
  Norton IP31 . . . . 50 B4
  20 Stanton IP31 . . . . 34 E4
School Cres CB9 . . . . 133 E8
School Farm La CO10 . . . . . . 78 C2
School Hill
  Boxford CO10 . . . . 93 C3
  Copdock & Washbrook
    IP8 . . . . 150 E1
  Kettleburgh IP13 . . . . 70 C2
School La Bardwell IP31 . . . 34 A5
  Bawdsey IP12 . . . . 99 B3
  Benhall IP17 . . . . 72 C8
  5 Brantham CO11 . . . . . . 104 E9
  6 Burwell CB5 . . . . 44 A8
  Dedham CO7 . . . . 103 F4
  East Bergholt CO7 . . . . . . 151 B5
  Easton IP13 . . . . 70 E1
  Fornham St Martin IP31 . . . 48 D6
  Great Barton IP31 . . . . 49 B8
  Great Horkesley CO6 . . . . 102 C5
  Halesworth IP19 . . . . 118 A4
  17 Harleston IP20 . . . . 22 D6
  Haverhill CB9 . . . . 132 B8
  Hollesley IP12 . . . . 99 F4
  Little Horkesley CO6 . . . . 102 B8
  Long Melford CO10 . . . . . . 77 F7
  Manningtree CO11 . . . . . 104 E3
  Martlesham IP12 . . . . 146 C2
  Metfield IP20 . . . . 23 D2
  4 Mistley CO11 . . . . 104 F7
  Reydon IP18 . . . . 26 E7

School La continued
Stratford St Mary CO7 ...... 103 E5
Thelnetham IP22 ....18 E1
Thurston IP31 ....49 E4
Ufford IP13 ....84 F7
School Mdw
1 Stowmarket IP14 ....124 E2
4 Wetheringsett IP14 ....51 A1
School Rd Alburgh IP20 ......7 A1
Bedingham NR35 ....7 B7
Blaxhall IP12 ....72 A3
Bressingham IP22 ....19 E4
Coddenham IP6 ....68 B1
Coldfair Green IP17 ....129 A3
Earsham NR35 ....7 F7
Elmswell IP30 ....50 E2
Great Ashfield IP31 ....50 F6
Great Barton IP31 ....49 B6
Great Wratting CB9 ....74 F3
Hinderclay IP22 ....35 E7
Hollesley IP12 ....99 F7
Kedington CB9 ....133 E8
Kirby Cane NR35 ....8 E8
Knodishall IP17 ....73 A8
Langham CO4 ....103 C2
Little Yeldham CO9 ....102 B2
Lowestoft NR33 ....114 F8
Monk Soham IP31 ....54 D4
Pentlow CO10 ....90 F7
Ringsfield NR34 ....9 B1
Risby IP28 ....48 E3
St Andrew, Ilketshall
NR34 ....8 E2
9 Shotley Gate IP9 ....107 A4
Subbourne IP12 ....87 A8
Tattingstone IP9 ....142 D1
Thurston IP31 ....49 E4
Tunstall IP12 ....71 F2
Waldringfield IP12 ....98 D7
Woodditton CB8 ....60 D6
School La Foxearth CO10 ...91 B7
Needham Market IP6 ....125 D4
Stoke-by-Nayland CO6 ....102 E7
Sudbury CO10 ....148 E8
School View NR34 ....24 F5
Schoolhall La IP33 ....154 B3
Schreiber Rd IP4 ....140 B7
Scofield Ct CO10 ....148 E8
Scole Comm IP21 ....20 F3
Scole Comm Sch IP21 ....21 A2
Scole Prim Sch IP21 ....21 A2
Scole End IP21 ....21 F2
Sconch Beck Rd IP19 ....42 C4
Scopes Rd IP5 ....141 C8
Scotland End CB7 ....29 E1
Scotland Pl* CO6 ....102 F7
Scotland St CO6 ....103 A7
Scotred Ct CB5 ....44 B8
Scott Ave IP28 ....116 C5
Scott La 2 IP12 ....84 E6
Scott Rd Ipswich IP3 ....140 B1
1 Ixworth IP31 ....34 B1
Scotts Cl NR33 ....11 B1
Scott's Hill CO6 ....68 B6
Scott's La IP13 ....84 C7
Scrivener Dr IP8 ....138 B2
Scuffin's La IP14 ....52 A6
Sea La NR32 ....114 E8
Sea Rd IP11 ....152 F2
Sea View NR33 ....11 C1
Sea View Rise NR31 ....3 C6
Seabreeze Rd IP14 ....124 D5
Seafield Ave 5 CO11 ....105 A2
Seafield Rd 6 CO12 ....107 A1
Seago St NR32 ....113 D1
Sealodes Rd CB7 ....28 A5
Seaman Ave IP17 ....128 B2
Seaton Cl 11 CO11 ....104 D2
Seaton Rd IP11 ....152 E5
Seavert Cl 3 NR33 ....114 E3
Seaward Ave 3 IP16 ....129 D5
Sebert Rd IP32 ....123 F2
Sebert Wood Cty Prim Sch
IP32 ....123 E5
Seckford Cl 11 IP4 ....140 F5
Seckford Hall Rd
IP12 ....146 D3
Seckford St IP12 ....146 F5
Second Ave
Felixstowe IP11 ....152 B7
2 Glemsford CO10 ....77 B3
Sudbury CO10 ....148 E2
Second Dro IP27 ....13 C2
Sedan Wlk IP4 ....155 A2
Sedgefen Rd IP27 ....12 F7
Sedlescombe Ave 8
NR33 ....114 C5
Sefton Way CB8 ....120 D5
Selby St NR32 ....113 D1
Self's La IP22 ....18 F3
Selkirk Rd IP4 ....136 C1
Selvale Way IP14 ....152 E4
Selwyn Cl Ipswich IP2 ....155 B1
Mildenhall IP28 ....116 C6
Semer Cl IP14 ....124 E3
Semere La IP21 ....21 D8
Serpentine Rd IP4 ....140 B2
Seven Cotts La IP5 ....136 C1
Seven Gdns Rd IP13 ....83 F6
Seven Hills (Barrow
Cemetery)*
Brettenham IP24 ....16 F4
Little Livermere IP31 ....33 A4
Sevenhills La IP31 ....33 A4
Several Rd IP11 ....55 B3

Severalls La IP13 ....55 D6
Severn Rd
Bury St Edmunds IP32 ....48 C5
Ipswich IP3 ....139 F3
Sewell Wontner Cl
IP5 ....141 C8
Sewell's La CO10 ....90 D5
Sexton Rd NR35 ....7 D6
Sextons Manor Prim Sch
IP33 ....122 C6
Sextons Md IP33 ....154 C1
Sextons Mdw IP33 ....123 B3
Seymore Dr CB9 ....132 B5
Seymour Ave IP27 ....14 D8
Seymour Cl CB8 ....121 C3
Seymour Rd IP12 ....155 B1
Shackleton Cl 20 CO12 ......106 F1
Shackleton Rd 3 IP33 ....140 B3
Shackleton Sq 3 IP33 ....140 B3
Shaddick Rd IP14 ....119 B8
Shade The CB7 ....28 C5
Shadingfield Cl NR32 ....113 A5
Shadowbush Cl CB9 ....132 D7
Shadwell Cl IP27 ....75 E1
Shaftesbury Ave 4
CO12 ....107 A2
Shafto Rd IP11 ....134 E1
Shaker's La IP13 ....123 C5
Shaker's Rd IP29 ....47 B4
Shakers' Rd
Brandon IP27 ....15 A5
Wangford IP27 ....14 E4
Shakespeare Rd
Ipswich IP4 ....134 E3
Stowmarket IP14 ....124 B8
Shamrock Ave IP2 ....138 E4
Shannon Cl CB9 ....133 B5
Shannon Rd 3 IP3 ....144 A8
Shardlow Cl CB9 ....132 A7
Sharman's Rd CB7 ....29 A1
Sharon Dr NR32 ....113 A3
Sharon Rd IP33 ....122 D5
Sharp Rd IP33 ....122 F2
Sharper's Cnr IP27 ....109 B8
Sharpes Cnr IP27 ....109 C7
Sharpe's Hill IP29 ....47 B2
Sharpe's Row IP30 ....63 A7
Sharp's Gn 11 IP29 ....63 A8
Shaw Ave NR33 ....11 A3
Shaw Rd CO10 ....91 E8
Shaw Valley Rd 7 IP12 ....84 A1
Shawlands Ave CO10 ....148 F5
Shavegate Vinery*
IP13 ....126 F6
Shearman Rd IP2 ....149 F5
Sheepdrift Rd IP2 ....85 B5
Sheepgate La
Badwell Ash IP31 ....51 B7
Fakenham IP21 ....98 F1
Sheepshead La 2 CO10 ......102 B3
Sheepwash La IP7 ....58 E6
Sheerwater IP30 ....123 F6
Sheldrake Dr IP2 ....138 D1
Sheldrake Dr 2 IP32 ....138 E1
Sheldrick's Rd CB7 ....29 D5
Shelley Cl IP14 ....148 F4
Shelley Cl IP14 ....124 F3
Shelley Rd
5 Bury St Edmunds IP32 ....48 C5
Layham IP7 ....149 E1
Shelley St IP2 ....155 B1
Shelley Way
Bacton IP14 ....51 E5
Thetford IP24 ....16 C7
Shelterhouse Cnr IP24 ....32 C8
Shelton Hill IP21 ....9 B5
Shelton Rd 8 NR33 ....114 E5
Shenley Rd IP1 ....140 B1
Shenstone Dr IP14 ....135 A3
Shepherd Dr IP8 ....138 A2
Shepherds Dr 1 IP29 ....63 D1
Shepherds Gr Ind Est
IP22 ....35 B4
Shepherds La
Burgate IP22 ....36 D7
Glemsford CO10 ....77 A3
Onehouse IP14 ....124 A8
Sheppards Way 8 IP5 ....141 D7
Sherborne Ave IP4 ....136 A2
Sherborne Rd IP33 ....122 D3
Sherbourne St CO10 ....63 A8
Sheridan Wlk NR34 ....111 E4
Sheriffs Ct CB8 ....59 F2
Sherrington Rd IP1 ....139 A8
Sherwood Fields 4 IP5 ....141 C7
Shetland Cl
3 Ipswich IP4 ....136 A1
Ipswich IP4 ....140 A8
Shetland Rd CB9 ....133 B5
Shetlands 8 IP31 ....34 E4
Shickle Pl IP27 ....18 C2
Shilling St 14 CO10 ....79 B8
Shillitoe Cl IP33 ....154 A2
Shimpling Cl 1 IP14 ....124 E3
Shimpling Rd IP21 ....51 A3
Shingle Hill IP31 ....38 C4
Ship Gdns IP28 ....116 B3
Ship Launch Rd IP3 ....105 C2
Ship Rd NR33 ....113 A3
Shippea Hill Sta CB7 ....12 C7
Shire Hall Yd IP4 ....155 C2
Shires The NR32 ....113 B8
Shirley Cl 3 IP1 ....135 A3
Shi-tennoji Sch IP28 ....30 D1
Shoals Wlk NR33 ....114 E6

Shoe Devil La NR35 ....24 C8
Shoebridge's Hill CO7 ....103 F3
Shop Hill CB8 ....61 E1
Shop La IP13 ....71 E5
Shop Rd IP13 ....69 E1
Shop St IP13 ....54 D7
Shore La
Bradfield CO11 ....105 C2
Harkstead IP9 ....106 A5
Mistley IP9 ....145 B3
Shores Cl IP28 ....29 F6
Short Beck 10 IP26 ....4 E5
Short Brackland IP33 ....154 B2
Short La Feltwell IP26 ....4 A5
Lowestoft NR33 ....114 C2
Walberswick IP18 ....43 C5
Short Rd
Belton with Browston NR31 ...2 D8
Blundeston NR32 ....3 A4
Snailwell CB8 ....45 A5
Short St 2 NR33 ....115 B4
Shortlands IP11 ....138 D1
Shotford Rd IP20 ....22 D5
Shotley Cl
Felixstowe IP11 ....152 D4
Ipswich IP8 ....138 C2
Shotley Mews 8 IP12 ....85 B3
Shotley Prim Sch IP9 ....106 F5
Shotley Wlk IP9 ....106 F7
Shrub House Cl 1 IP28 ....30 B8
Shrubberies The CB8 ....121 D1
Shrubbery Rd IP13 ....146 B7
Shrubland Ave IP1 ....134 E1
Shrubland Dr IP4 ....140 F5
Shrubland 11 CO11 ....105 A2
Shrublands 2 IP28 ....116 C4
Siam Hall La CO10 ....92 F3
Sicklesmere Rd
Bury St Edmunds IP33 ....123 D2
Newton IP30 ....63 E8
Sidegate La IP4 ....140 A8
Sidegate La IP4 ....136 A1
Sidegate La W IP4 ....135 F1
Sidegate Prim Sch
IP4 ....140 A8
Siding Rd IP3 ....3 A8
Silent St 1 IP1 ....155 B2
Silhalls Cl 17 CB8 ....60 F8
Silk Mill Cl 2 IP7 ....149 D5
Silver Dr 7 IP15 ....130 C6
Silver Hill IP8 ....95 D6
Silver Leys IP9 ....104 F3
Silver St Burwell CB5 ....44 A6
Kedington CB9 ....133 F7
Old Newton with Dagworth
IP14 ....125 A5
South Lopham IP22 ....19 C3
Wittersfield CB9 ....74 A2
Silverdale Ave IP4 ....124 C7
Silverdale Cl IP3 ....135 A1
Silverley Way 6 CB8 ....60 E8
Silverwood Cl NR33 ....114 C6
Simon's Cross IP13 ....127 B7
Simons Rd IP12 ....147 A7
Simper's Drift IP17 ....56 D1
Simpson Cl IP9 ....139 F1
Sim's La CB9 ....133 F7
Sinclair Dr IP2 ....139 C3
Singleton Ct CO10 ....148 E3
Sir John Leman High Sch
NR34 ....111 D2
Sir John Leman Rd
NR34 ....111 D2
Sir Robert Hitchams CE Prim
Sch IP13 ....126 C4
Sir Robert Hitchams Sch
IP13 ....53 F2
Sirdar Rd IP1 ....139 A6
Siskin Cl 1 NR33 ....114 F5
Sitwell Cl 3 CO11 ....104 D2
Sitwell Gdns 4 IP13 ....126 C5
Sizewell Gap IP16 ....58 F1
Sizewell Power Sta
IP16 ....58 F2
Sizewell Rd IP16 ....129 D5
Sizewell Visitor Ctr*
IP16 ....58 F2
Skamacre Heath NR32 ....113 A2
Skate's Hill CO10 ....77 A2
Skelton Cl 9 CO11 ....104 E2
Skelton Rd IP22 ....20 D2
Skelton's Dro IP28 ....13 A2
Skinner St IP2 ....154 B2
Skinner's La
Metfield IP20 ....23 C3
Starston IP20 ....22 B8
Skipper Cl IP8 ....142 E8
Skipper Rd IP13 ....138 D1
Skipper's La CB9 ....74 A3
Skoulding Cl 1 NR33 ....114 F7
Sky Hall Hill CO4 ....103 B4
Skylark La IP8 ....138 C2
Slade La IP30 ....19 E2
Slade St NR33 ....115 C2
Slade The IP6 ....134 D8
Slades Cl 1 IP30 ....77 B3
Slaughden Rd IP15 ....130 D4
Sleaford Cl IP2 ....139 A3
Sloe La IP17 ....128 A4
Slough Hill IP29 ....77 F7
Slough La Acton CO10 ....78 C1
Horringer IP29 ....122 A2
Slough Rd
Botesdale IP22 ....36 C5
Brantham CO11 ....104 E5

Sir Alf Ramsey Way
IP1 ....155 A2
Slugs La NR32 ....3 C2
Sluice Dro IP26 ....4 E3
Slushy La IP14 ....106 A6
Smaley La 1 CO10 ....91 E8
Smallbridge Entry
CO8 ....101 E4
Smallbridge Hall*
CO8 ....101 E4
Smallgate 6 NR34 ....111 B6
Smallworth La IP22 ....18 B3
Smart St IP4 ....155 C2
Smear La 11 IP18 ....26 D2
Smear La E IP18 ....26 F1
Smeetham Hall La
CO10 ....91 C3
Smith Cres 19 NR33 ....11 B1
Smithbrook La IP29 ....77 A8
Smithers Cl 2 IP9 ....106 F5
Smithfield IP12 ....147 B6
Smiths Dr IP21 ....21 B5
Smiths Pl 9 IP5 ....141 D7
Smith's Wlk NR33 ....114 C6
Smithy Cl
Bradfield Combust with
Stanningfield IP29 ....64 A3
Rushbrooke with Rougham
IP30 ....64 D8
Smock Mdw 8 IP7 ....79 F4
Snab Hill NR33 ....11 A1
Snailwell Rd
Fordham CB8 ....44 F7
Newmarket CB8 ....121 B7
Snailwell Short Rd CB8 ....44 F5
Snake's La Lound NR32 ....2 F6
Topcroft NR35 ....7 A8
Snape Com Prim Sch
IP17 ....72 D5
Snape Dr NR33 ....113 A4
Snape Hill IP22 ....35 F6
Snape Rd Friston IP17 ....129 A2
Saxmundham IP17 ....131 A7
Tunstall IP12 ....72 A2
Snare Hill IP24 ....8 A4
Snipe Farm Rd IP13 ....69 E1
Snow Hill CO10 ....148 A6
Snow Hill La CB8 ....103 B7
Snowberry Way 6 CB7 ....28 C5
Snowcroft IP9 ....150 E3
Snowdens Yd 14 IP18 ....119 D5
Snowdon Hill IP13 ....127 C7
Snowdon Rd IP2 ....139 B2
Snowdrop Cl IP32 ....123 F5
Soft Rd CO10 ....90 F3
Soham Town Cnr IP18 ....75 C8
Soane St 1 IP4 ....155 B3
Soft Rd CO10 ....90 F3
Soham Cl IP14 ....124 C7
Soham Ely CB7 ....28 A8
Fordham CB8 ....28 F2
Soham Town Dr IP18 ....75 C8
Soham Wlk 1 IP14 ....124 C7
Soham Rd IP33 ....11 C1
Somerleyton Hall & Gdns*
NR32 ....2 E4
Somerleyton Prim Sch
NR32 ....2 D4
Somerleyton Rd NR32 ....112 F4
Somerleyton Sta NR32 ....2 C3
Somerset Rd IP4 ....139 F8
Somersham Prim Sch
IP8 ....81 C3
Somersham Rd IP8 ....81 F2
Somerton Ave NR32 ....113 C3
Somerton Rd IP29 ....77 A7
Somerville Lea 2 IP15 ....130 C5
Sorrel Cl IP2 ....138 F3
Sotterby Rd
6 Lowestoft NR33 ....112 F4
Sotterley NR34 ....10 C1
Willingham St Mary NR34 ....25 F7
Sound The NR33 ....114 C5
South Cl Beccles NR34 ....111 A3
Bury St Edmunds IP33 ....154 B3
Ipswich IP4 ....139 E8
Leiston IP16 ....129 C8
South Elmham Terr
NR33 ....114 C8
South Entrance IP7 ....128 D2
South Hill IP11 ....152 F3
South Lee Sch IP33 ....123 C2
South Leet 4 NR32 ....112 E4
South Lodge Dr 1 IP28 ....48 C6
South Lowestoft Ind Est
NR33 ....115 C5
South Pk CB7 ....120 F4
South Pk 3 Beccles NR34 ....111 A3
Lakenheath IP27 ....109 C3
South St
Hockwold cum Wilton IP26 ....4 F2
Ipswich IP1 ....155 A4
12 Manningtree CO11 ....104 E2
Risby IP28 ....48 F6
South Strand 11 CO11 ....104 E2
Southern La IP22 ....19 A1
Southery Rd IP26 ....4 A6
Southfield Dr IP16 ....129 C5
Southfield Gdns NR33 ....114 F4
Southfields CO7 ....103 F3
Southfields Cl CB8 ....120 F4
Southgate 17 IP28 ....22 D5
Southgate Ave IP28 ....116 B7
Southgate Gdns
Bury St Edmunds IP33 ....123 C3
3 Long Melford CO10 ....91 E7

Southgate St IP8 ....138 B1
Southgate St
Bury St Edmunds IP33 ....154 C1
4 Long Melford CO10 ....91 E7
Southolt Rd
Athelington IP21 ....38 F1
Bedfield IP13 ....54 D6
Southwald & District Hospl
IP18 ....119 C6
Southwell La IP33 ....36 A6
Southwell Rd NR33 ....115 B7
Southwold Mus*
IP18 ....119 D5
Southwold Prim Sch
IP18 ....119 D5
Southwold Rd
Blyford IP19 ....42 B8
Brampton with Stoven
NR34 ....25 E5
Holton IP19 ....118 F3
Wrentham NR34 ....26 E5
Southwood Cl IP17 ....128 C2
Spalding's Chair Hill
IP24 ....17 B3
Spanbies Rd 5 CO7 ....103 E5
Sparhawk St CO10 ....154 C1
Sparkes Cl 5 CB7 ....29 C5
Sparks La CO9 ....99 D3
Sparrow Ct 11 IP14 ....53 F2
Sparrow Rd CO10 ....148 F4
Sparrowhawk Rd
IP2 ....118 C7
Sparrows Croft Rd 8
IP12 ....85 B3
Spashett Rd 8 NR32 ....113 B4
Speed La CB7 ....28 D4
Speedwell Cl 7 NR33 ....115 A3
Speedwell Rd IP2 ....138 F4
Speedwell Way 16 IP20 ....22 D5
Spencer Dr NR32 ....113 B6
Spencer Dro CB7 ....28 C4
Spencer Rd 4 IP14 ....85 E8
Spencer Way 4 IP14 ....124 B7
Spenhall Mnr NR34 ....13 E3
Spexhall Way NR32 ....113 B5
Spicers La 8 CO10 ....91 E8
Spiers Way IP22 ....20 B2
Spike's La IP14 ....66 F2
Spindle Rd CB9 ....132 B7
Spinks' La NR35 ....7 D6
Spinnel's Hill CO11 ....105 D1
Spinnel's La CO11 ....105 E1
Spinner Cl IP2 ....138 D8
Spinney La 3 IP18 ....119 D5
Spinney Ct NR34 ....10 B4
Spinney Rd IP31 ....33 B3
Spinney The
Beccles NR34 ....111 D4
Ipswich IP4 ....140 F4
Spire Chase CO10 ....148 E8
Spirkett's La IP20 ....22 D5
Spitfire Cl IP3 ....140 B1
Spong La IP30 ....50 E2
Spong The IP20 ....23 C3
Spooners Cl CB8 ....59 F4
Spout La CO10 ....91 D6
Spoutman's Cl 5 IP27 ....149 D6
Spout La CO10 ....101 B8
Spring Cl
8 Bentwaters Airfield
IP12 ....85 D8
Burwell CB5 ....44 A5
Spring La
Bury St Edmunds IP33 ....154 A3
Crowfield IP6 ....68 B3
Dennington IP13 ....55 B5
5 Lavenham CO10 ....78 D4
Polstead CO6 ....93 D2
Ufford IP13 ....127 B1
Wickham Market IP13 ....127 D7
Spring Mdw
1 Playford CO10 ....77 A3
Playford IP6 ....137 B4
Spring Pk IP6 ....69 C2
Spring Rd Bardwell IP31 ....34 C5
Copdock & Washbrook
IP8 ....95 E5
Ipswich IP4 ....139 F6
Spring Row IP27 ....124 D7
Spring St 6 CO10 ....78 D4
Springbank Ave IP2
CO11 ....104 D2
Springett's Hill CO8 ....101 B5
Springfield IP18 ....119 A7
Springfield Ave
Bury St Edmunds IP33 ....154 A3
Felixstowe IP11 ....153 A5
Springfield Dr IP27 ....109 D6
Springfield Gdns
NR33 ....114 F5
Springfield Jun Sch
IP1 ....138 F8
Springfield La IP18 ....119 A7
Springfield Rd
Aldeburgh IP15 ....130 C5
Bury St Edmunds IP33 ....154 A3
4 Somersham IP8 ....81 C3
Sudbury CO10 ....148 C7
Springfield St IP4 ....139 F6
Springland Cl IP4 ....140 A8
Springlands Way
CO10 ....148 D8
Sprites End IP11 ....152 D7
Sprites Jun Sch IP2 ....138 C2

Sprites La IP8 . . . . .138 C1
Spriteshall La IP11 . . . . .152 D7
Sproughton Bsns Pk
 IP1 .138 D7
Sproughton CE Prim Sch
 IP8 .138 B6
Sproughton Rd IP8 . . . . .138 C7
Spruce Cl [14] IP27 . . . . . .13 F2
Spur End IP12 . . . . .147 C7
Spurgeon Score [12]
 NR32 . . . . .113 E2
Spurling Cl [2] C8B 60 E7
Square The IP14 . . . . .124 E4
Squires La [4] IP5 . . . . .98 A8
Squires Wlk NR32 . . . . . .113 C5
Squirrels Mill Rd [3] IP7 . .79 F4
Squirrels The IP9 . . . . . . .150 E4
Stackwood Rd CO6 . . . . . .93 F3
Stafford Ct NR32 . . . . . . .112 E4
Staithe Cl NR35 . . . . .110 B4
Staithe Rd
 Bungay NR35 . . . . .110 B4
 Bungay NR35 . . . . .110 A4
 Burgh St Peter NR34 . . . .110 C7
Staithe The NR33 . . . . . . .114 E6
Stambourne Rd CO9 . . . . .89 E2
Stamford Cl IP2 . . . . .142 F8
Stamford St C88 . . . . .121 B2
Stammers Pl IP5 . . . . .141 E8
Stanford St [3] NR32 . . . . .113 C1
Stanhope Cl IP17 . . . . .72 D5
Stanley Ave IP3 . . . . .140 A4
Stanley Rd Diss IP22 . . . . .20 B2
 Felixstowe IP11 . . . . .153 A3
 Lowestoft NR33 . . . . .114 E7
 Newmarket C88 . . . . .121 C3
 Sudbury CO10 . . . . .148 C6
Stanley St NR32 . . . . .113 D1
Stanley Wood Ave
 CO10 . . . . .148 D7
Stannard Way CO10 . . . . .148 E4
Stanningfield Rd IP30 . . . . .63 F5
Stansfield Cl IP14 . . . . . . .134 E6
Stanton Cl
 Beccles NR34 . . . . .111 C3
 Lowestoft NR32 . . . . .113 C4
Stanton Hughes Way [10]
 CO11 . . . . .104 D2
Stanton Prim Sch IP31 . . .34 E4
Stanton Rd IP31 . . . . .34 C4
Stanway Cl CO10 . . . . .77 B3
Staple Cl IP31 . . . . .35 C1
Staplehurst Rd [7] NR33 . .114 C4
Staples La IP7 . . . . .28 D3
Star La IP4 . . . . .155 C2
Starfield Cl IP4 . . . . .140 B6
Starhouse La IP14 . . . . . . .66 C5
Starre Rd IP33 . . . . .122 C5
Starston La IP20 . . . . .22 C2
Station App
 Newmarket C88 . . . . .121 A2
 Saxmundham IP17 . . . . . .128 D3
Station Hill
 [1] Bures CO8 . . . . .101 C4
 Bury St Edmunds IP33 . . .154 B4
 Harleston IP20 . . . . .22 D6
 Little Whelnetham IP30 . . .64 D6
 Thurston IP31 . . . . .49 D4
Station La [6] CO12 . . . . .107 B2
Station Rd Alburgh IP20 . . .7 A1
 Bacton IP14 . . . . .52 A6
 Barnham IP24 . . . . .16 B2
 Beccles NR34 . . . . .111 B5
 Bentley IP9 . . . . .104 E7
 Birdbrook CO9 . . . . .89 B4
 Blaxhall IP12 . . . . .71 E3
 Bradfield CO11 . . . . .105 B2
 Brampton with Stoven
  NR34 . . . . .25 C5
 Burston & Shimpling IP21 . .20 F6
 Clare CO10 . . . . .90 B8
 Claydon IP6 . . . . .134 B8
 [2] Corton NR32 . . . . .3 D4
 Corton NR32 . . . . .113 C8
 Diss IP22 . . . . .20 D2
 Ditchingham NR35 . . . . . .110 C6
 Elmham C88 . . . . .59 E5
 [2] Earsham NR35 . . . . .7 F4
 Ellingham NR35 . . . . .8 D7
 Elmswell IP30 . . . . .50 F2
 Felixstowe IP11 . . . . .152 C7
 Fordham C87 . . . . .29 A1
 Framlingham IP13 . . . . . . .126 C2
 Geldeston NR34 . . . . .8 F6
 Haddiscoe NR31 . . . . .2 A5
 Hadleigh IP7 . . . . .149 E5
 Halesworth IP19 . . . . .118 B4
 Harleston IP20 . . . . .22 D6
 [1] Harwich CO12 . . . . . . .106 F3
 [8] Harwich CO12 . . . . . . .107 B2
 Haughley IP14 . . . . .66 C3
 [4] Haverhill CB9 . . . . . . .132 E6
 Hopton on Sea NR31 . . . . . .3 B6
 Isleham C88 . . . . .29 C4
 Kennett C88 . . . . .45 F7
 Lakenheath IP27 . . . . .109 C7
 Larfield IP13 . . . . .39 F4
 Leiston IP16 . . . . .129 C6
 Long Melford CO10 . . . . . . .91 E7
 Lowestoft NR32 . . . . .113 D4
 Manningtree CO11 . . . . . .104 E3
 Mildenhall IP28 . . . . .116 B3
 Pulham Market IP21 . . . . . .21 E8
 Pulham St Mary IP21 . . . . .22 A8
 Soham C87 . . . . .28 C4

Station Rd continued
Somerleyton, Ashby &
 Herringfleet NR32 . . . . .2 C3
Southwold IP18 . . . . .119 C6
Sudbury CO10 . . . . .148 C5
Tattingstone IP9 . . . . .105 A7
Thetford IP24 . . . . .16 B6
Wetheringsett-cum-brockford
 IP14 . . . . .53 B4
Woodbridge IP12 . . . . .147 A4
Wrabness CO11 . . . . .105 F2
Station Rd E IP14 . . . . . . .124 E6
Station Rd W IP14 . . . . . . .124 D6
Station Rd CO12 . . . . .106 F3
Station Sq
 Lowestoft NR32 . . . . .115 D8
 [1] Lowestoft NR32 . . . . . .115 D8
Station St IP2 . . . . .139 C3
Station Terr IP11 . . . . . . .126 C2
Station Yd
 Mildenhall IP28 . . . . .116 B3
 Needham Market IP6 . . . . .125 E4
Staverton Cl IP2 . . . . .85 B6
Stayngate Wlk [7] NR32 . .112 E4
Stearn Dr IP14 . . . . .66 C6
Stearn's La IP14 . . . . .67 D6
Stebbings La IP12 . . . . .99 E7
Steds Mdw [7] CO10 . . . . . .91 E8
Steeples Rd IP30 . . . . .50 D1
Steeple Bumpstead Pottery*
 . . . . .88 D3
Steeple Bumpstead Sch
 CB9 .88 B4
Steeple End IP19 . . . . .118 B3
Steeplechase CO10 . . . . . . .75 C4
Steggall Cl IP6 . . . . .125 C6
Stella Maris IP2 . . . . .138 D5
Stennetts Cl IP11 . . . . . . .152 B8
Stephen Cl
 Haverhill CB9 . . . . .132 D6
 Long Melford CO10 . . . . . . .91 D7
Stephen Rd IP5 . . . . .141 E8
Stepping Hill [8] NR34 . . . .111 B5
Stetchworth Rd
 Dullingham C88 . . . . .59 F4
 Stetchworth CB8 . . . . .60 B4
Stevens St NR32 . . . . .113 C1
Stevenson Rd IP1 . . . . . . .155 A2
Steward Rd IP23 . . . . .123 C2
Stewart Young Gr
 IP5 . . . . .141 D7
Stimpson Cl [3] NR32 . . . .113 A6
Stirling Cl
 Lowestoft NR32 . . . . .112 F4
 [7] Thistley Green IP28 . . . .29 F6
Stirling Dr CB9 . . . . .132 C6
Stirling Gdns C88 . . . . . . .120 E4
Stirrups La NR32 . . . . .3 C5
Stobart Cl NR34 . . . . .111 D3
Stockley Cl CB9 . . . . .133 A5
Stockmers End [8] IP9 . . .150 E3
Stockton Cl IP27 . . . . .149 F4
Stockton Rd NR34 . . . . .9 A7
Stoke Ash Prim Sch
 IP23 . . . . .52 F8
Stoke Coll CO10 . . . . .89 E6
Stoke City High Sch
 IP2 . . . . .139 C3
Stoke Hall Rd IP2 . . . . . . .155 B1
Stoke Pk Dr IP2 . . . . .139 A1
Stoke Rd IP12 . . . . .155 C1
Stoke Rd Clare CO10 . . . . .90 A7
 Layham IP7 . . . . .149 C1
 Leavenheath CO6 . . . . . . .102 B8
 Nayland-with-wissington
  CO6 . . . . .102 D5
 Stoke Ash IP23 . . . . .37 D1
 Stoke-by-clare CO10 . . . . .89 F7
Stoke St IP7 . . . . .155 B1
Stoke-by-Nayland CEVC
 Prim Sch CO6 . . . . .102 E7
Stoke-by-Nayland Mid Sch
 CO6 . . . . .102 E7
Stollery Cl IP5 . . . . .141 B7
Stonalls IP30 . . . . .50 C1
Stone Hall Rd IP23 . . . . . . .36 D5
Stone La
 Bressingham IP22 . . . . .19 F6
 Wrabness CO11 . . . . .105 F2
Stone Lodge La W IP2 . . .139 A3
Stone Lodge La W
 IP2 . . . . .138 F3
Stone Lodge Wlk IP2 . . . .139 B3
Stone St Boxford CO6 . . . . .93 C3
 Crowfield IP6 . . . . .68 C3
 Hadleigh IP7 . . . . .149 B8
 Spexhall IP19 . . . . .118 C8
Stone St Rd [2] CO10 . . . . .93 C3
Stonebridge Ave IP33 . . . .122 F3
Stonebridge La IP14 . . . . . .67 A8
Stonechat Rd IP2 . . . . .138 C3
Stonegrove Rd IP11 . . . . .152 D1
Stonehouse Rd IP7 . . . . . .149 D6
Stonewell Hill IP6 . . . . .68 D1
Stoney La Barrow IP29 . . . .47 B2
 Thurston IP31 . . . . .49 F4
Stoney Rd IP13 . . . . .83 D6
Stonham Aspal CE Prim Sch
 IP14 . . . . .68 B6
Stonham Rd IP14 . . . . .52 B4
Stony La
 [2] Aldringham cum Thorpe
  IP16 . . . . .73 F6
 Debenham IP14 . . . . .53 D2
 Wortwell IP20 . . . . .22 F8
Stopford Ct [8] IP1 . . . . . .139 C7
Stour Ave IP11 . . . . .152 E3

Stour Cl Glemsford CO10 . .77 B1
 [4] Harwich CO12 . . . . . . .106 E1
Stour Gdns CO10 . . . . . . .148 E2
Stour Rd CO12 . . . . .107 B3
Stour St Cavendish CO10 . .90 D8
 [7] Manningtree CO11 . . . .104 E2
 Sudbury CO10 . . . . .148 B5
Stour Vale CO9 . . . . .89 B5
Stour Valley Rd CB9 . . . . .132 F5
Stourdale Cl CO11 . . . . . . .104 D2
Stourmead Cl CB9 . . . . . . .133 E8
Stourview Ave [4] CO11 . . .105 A2
Stourview Cl CO11 . . . . . .105 A2
Stoven Cl NR32 . . . . .113 B5
Stoven Rd NR34 . . . . .25 F3
Stow La IP31 . . . . .50 A8
Stow Rd IP31 . . . . .34 B1
Stowmarket High Sch
 IP14 . . . . .124 B7
Stowmarket Mid Sch
 IP14 . . . . .124 C6
Stowmarket Rd
 Badley IP6 . . . . .125 A8
 Great Blakenham IP6 . . . . .81 F6
 Old Newton with Dagworth
  IP14 . . . . .51 E1
 Rattlesden IP30 . . . . .65 E6
 Stonham Aspal IP14 . . . . . .68 A6
 Wetherden IP14 . . . . .51 A1
Stowmarket Sta IP14 . . . .124 E6
Stowmarket Town FC
 IP14 . . . . .124 D8
Stowupland Rd IP14 . . . . .124 F7
Stowupland St IP14 . . . . . .124 D6
Stradbroke CE Prim Sch
 IP21 . . . . .39 A5
Stradbroke High Sch
 IP21 . . . . .39 B4
Stradbroke Rd
 Fressingfield IP21 . . . . .39 D7
 Ipswich IP4 . . . . .140 A7
 Lowestoft NR33 . . . . .115 A4
 Southwold IP18 . . . . .119 D5
Stradishall Rd CO10 . . . . . .75 E5
Straight La [10] IP20 . . . . . .22 D6
Straight Rd
 Bradfield IP14 . . . . .66 D1
 Boxted CO4 . . . . .102 F1
 Bradfield CO11 . . . . .105 B1
 Foxhall IP10 . . . . .141 C1
 Polstead CO6 . . . . .93 F3
 Whepstead IP29 . . . . .63 C4
Strand The IP7 . . . . .143 C8
Stratford Rd
 Dedham CO7 . . . . .103 E4
 Ipswich IP1 . . . . .134 F2
Stratford St Mary Prim Sch
 CO7 . . . . .103 E5
Strattonhall Drift
 IP10 . . . . .145 F2
Straw La CO10 . . . . .148 B5
Strawberry Fields
 CB9 . . . . .132 B5
Strawberry La IP19 . . . . . .25 D3
Street Farm La [4] IP31 . . .34 B1
Street Farm Rd IP17 . . . . .128 D3
Street The Aldeby NR34 . . . .9 F8
 Alderton IP12 . . . . .99 E3
 Aldham IP7 . . . . .94 E8
 Ashen CO10 . . . . .89 B5
 Ashfield cum Thorpe IP14 . .54 C1
 Bacton IP14 . . . . .51 E5
 Badwell Ash IP31 . . . . .50 E7
 Barnham IP24 . . . . .16 B2
 Barrow IP29 . . . . .47 A2
 Barton Mills IP28 . . . . .116 E2
 Bawdsey IP12 . . . . .99 E3
 Beck Row, Holywell Row
  IP28 . . . . .30 C8
 Belchamp Otten CO10 . . . . .90 E4
 Belstead IP8 . . . . .142 C6
 Benacre NR34 . . . . .27 A7
 Birdbrook CO9 . . . . .89 A3
 Blo' Norton IP22 . . . . .18 E2
 Blundeston NR32 . . . . .3 A4
 Botesdale IP22 . . . . .36 A6
 Boxted IP29 . . . . .77 A6
 Bradfield CO11 . . . . .105 C1
 Bradfield Combust with
  Stanningfield IP30 . . . . . . .64 B4
 Bramfield IP19 . . . . .41 F5
 Bramford IP8 . . . . .134 A2
 Brampton with Stoven
  NR34 . . . . .25 E4
 Brandon IP27 . . . . .5 E1
 Brantham CO11 . . . . .105 A5
 Bredfield IP13 . . . . .84 C8
 Bressingham IP22 . . . . .19 D6
 Brettenham IP7 . . . . .65 C1
 Bridgham NR16 . . . . .17 E8
 Brockdish IP21 . . . . .21 E2
 Brome & Oakley IP23 . . . . .117 D8
 Bruisyard IP17 . . . . .56 B4
 Brundish IP13 . . . . .39 D1
 Bulmer CO10 . . . . .91 C3
 Burrough Green CB8 . . . . . .59 E3
 [12] Bury St Edmunds IP28 . .48 C6
 Butley IP12 . . . . .86 A6
 Capel St. Mary IP9 . . . . . . .150 D3
 Cavenham IP28 . . . . .47 A8
 Charsfield IP13 . . . . .70 B3
 Charsfield IP13 . . . . .70 C3
 Chattisham IP8 . . . . .95 C4
 Chedburgh IP29 . . . . .62 C4
 Chelsworth IP7 . . . . .79 D3
 Coney Weston IP31 . . . . . .17 E1

Street The continued
Copdock & Washbrook
 IP8 .95 F5
 [2] Corton NR32 . . . . .3 D4
 Cranfield IP19 . . . . .40 D5
 Cretingham IP13 . . . . .69 E7
 Culford IP28 . . . . .48 B8
 Dalham C88 . . . . .61 B8
 Dalham C88 . . . . .61 C8
 Darsham IP17 . . . . .42 B1
 Dennington IP13 . . . . .55 E6
 Dickleburgh IP21 . . . . .21 B5
 Drinkstone IP30 . . . . .65 B8
 Earl Soham IP13 . . . . .54 F2
 Earsham NR35 . . . . .7 F4
 East Bergholt CO7 . . . . . . .151 B4
 Easton IP13 . . . . .70 E5
 Elmsett IP7 . . . . .80 F1
 Eriswell IP27 . . . . .13 F1
 Eye IP21 . . . . .38 B4
 Eyke IP12 . . . . .85 B6
 Farnham IP17 . . . . .72 F2
 Flixton NR35 . . . . .7 E2
 Foxearth CO10 . . . . .91 B7
 Framsden IP14 . . . . .69 B6
 Freckenham IP28 . . . . .29 E3
 Gazeley C88 . . . . .46 B3
 Geldeston NR34 . . . . .8 F6
 Great Barton IP31 . . . . .49 B5
 Great Bricett IP7 . . . . .80 D5
 Great Livermere IP31 . . . . .33 C2
 Great Waldingfield CO10 . . .92 D6
 Great Wratting C89 . . . . . . .74 F3
 Grundisburgh IP13 . . . . . . .83 E5
 Hacheston IP13 . . . . .71 A6
 Halesworth IP19 . . . . .118 E3
 Harkstead IP9 . . . . .106 A5
 Hessett IP30 . . . . .64 F8
 Hinderclay IP22 . . . . .35 E7
 Holbrook IP9 . . . . .105 E7
 Hollesley IP12 . . . . .99 F7
 Horham IP21 . . . . .38 E3
 Horringer IP29 . . . . .122 B1
 Huntingfield IP19 . . . . .41 A4
 Icklingham IP28 . . . . .31 D4
 Kersey IP7 . . . . .93 F7
 Kettleburgh IP13 . . . . .70 C7
 Kirtling C88 . . . . .60 E3
 Lawshall IP29 . . . . .63 E1
 Layham IP7 . . . . .149 E2
 Letheringham IP13 . . . . . . .70 D4
 Lidgate C88 . . . . .61 B4
 Little Bealings IP13 . . . . . .137 D4
 Little Glemham IP13 . . . . . .72 D5
 Little Waldingfield CO10 . . .92 E8
 Lound NR32 . . . . .2 F6
 Lowestoft NR32 . . . . .113 D8
 Lowestoft NR33 . . . . .114 C2
 Market Weston IP22 . . . . . .35 A8
 Martlesham IP12 . . . . .146 C1
 Middleton CO10 . . . . .148 C1
 Mildenhall IP28 . . . . .30 B8
 Monks Eleigh IP7 . . . . .79 C2
 Moulton C88 . . . . .45 F2
 Nacton IP10 . . . . .145 C5
 Newbourne IP12 . . . . .98 D6
 North Cove NR34 . . . . .10 B4
 North Lopham IP22 . . . . . . .19 A6
 Norton IP31 . . . . .50 B4
 Occold IP23 . . . . .37 F1
 Pakenham IP31 . . . . .49 E6
 Parham IP13 . . . . .71 A7
 Peasenhall IP17 . . . . .56 F8
 Pettistree IP12 . . . . .127 C4
 Poslingford CO10 . . . . .76 D4
 Preston St Mary CO10 . . . .79 A5
 Pulham St Mary IP21 . . . . .22 A7
 Ramsey & Parkeston
  CO12 . . . . .106 D1
 Raydon IP7 . . . . .94 E1
 Redenhall with Harleston
  IP20 . . . . .22 F5
 [1] Redgrave IP22 . . . . . . .36 A8
 Riddlesworth IP22 . . . . . . .18 A3
 Rumburgh IP19 . . . . .24 C4
 Rushmere NR33 . . . . .10 E1
 St James South Elmham
  IP19 . . . . .23 F4
 Shotley IP9 . . . . .106 F6
 Shottisham IP12 . . . . .99 B7
 Snailwell C88 . . . . .45 A6
 Somerleyton, Ashby &
  Herringfleet NR32 . . . . . . .2 D4
 Somerleyton, Ashby &
  Herringfleet NR32 . . . . . . .2 D4
 South Lopham IP22 . . . . . .19 D4
 Southolt IP23 . . . . .54 B7
 Stanton IP31 . . . . .34 E4
 Starston IP20 . . . . .22 C7
 Sternfield IP17 . . . . .72 D8
 Stoke Ash IP23 . . . . .52 F8
 Stoke-by-clare CO10 . . . . .89 D6
 Stonham Aspal IP14 . . . . . .68 B6
 Stowlangtoft IP31 . . . . .50 B6
 Stradishall C88 . . . . .75 C6
 Stratford St Mary CO7 . . . .103 E4
 Thorndon IP23 . . . . .53 B8
 Thornham Magna IP23 . . . .37 A2
 Troston IP31 . . . . .33 D3
 Tuddenham St Martin
  IP6 . . . . .136 C5
 Ubbeston IP19 . . . . .40 F3
 Walberswick IP18 . . . . . . .119 A2
 Wattisfield IP22 . . . . .35 C6
 Weston IP17 . . . . .58 C7
 Westleton IP17 . . . . .58 C7

Street The continued
Wetheringsett-cum-brockford
 IP14 . . . . .52 F6
Weybread IP21 . . . . .22 D2
Whatfield IP7 . . . . .80 C1
Wherstead IP9 . . . . .143 A6
Winfarthing IP22 . . . . .20 B8
Wingfield IP21 . . . . .39 E3
Winston IP14 . . . . .54 C2
Witnesham IP6 . . . . .136 A8
Woodbridge IP12 . . . . .147 C7
Woodditton C88 . . . . .60 D5
Woodditton C88 . . . . .60 D6
Woolpit IP30 . . . . .50 D2
Worlington IP28 . . . . .30 B4
Streetfield Cl IP29 . . . . . . .77 F7
Stretham Rd C87 . . . . .28 A2
Stretton Ave C88 . . . . .121 B2
Strickland Manor Hill
 IP17 . . . . .57 C8
Strickland Pl [18] IP18 . . . .119 D5
Stricklands Rd [1] IP14 . . .124 E5
Strickmere CO7 . . . . .103 E5
Strollers Way C88 . . . . .60 A5
Strowger's Way [6] NR33 . .11 C1
Struggler's La IP14 . . . . . .136 A8
Stuart Cl
 [8] Felixstowe IP11 . . . . . .153 D7
 Ipswich IP4 . . . . .139 F7
Stuart Dr NR34 . . . . .111 C4
Stubbing's La IP21 . . . . . . .22 E3
Stubbin's La C88 . . . . .46 B3
Stubbs Cl Ipswich IP3 . . . .140 A1
 [8] Manningtree CO11 . . . .104 D2
Stubbs Wood NR32 . . . . . .113 B6
Studio Cl IP17 . . . . .58 C8
Studlands Pk Ave
 C88 . . . . .120 D6
Stump St IP13 . . . . .127 A3
Stump's Cross CO9 . . . . . . .89 D1
Sturdee Ave IP3 . . . . .140 B3
Sturgeon Way [2] IP31 . . . .34 E4
Sturmer End Ind Est
 C89 . . . . .133 A3
Sturmer Rd C89 . . . . .133 D5
Sturston La IP21 . . . . .117 B8
Stuston Rd IP21 . . . . .20 D1
Stutton CE Prim Sch
 IP9 . . . . .105 D5
Stutton Gn IP9 . . . . .105 C5
Stutton Gn IP9 . . . . .105 E5
Stutton Hall* IP9 . . . . .105 C4
Stutton La IP9 . . . . .105 C5
Stutton Rd CO11 . . . . .105 A5
Sub-station Rd IP11 . . . . .152 D2
Sudbourne Rd
 [14] Felixstowe IP11 . . . . .152 D5
 Orford IP12 . . . . .131 B5
Sudbury Rd Acton CO10 . . .92 B7
 Bulmer CO10 . . . . .91 C3
 Bures St Mary C08 . . . . . .101 C5
 [3] Felixstowe IP11 . . . . . .152 C4
 Gestingthorpe CO9 . . . . . . .90 F1
 Great Whelnetham IP30 . . .64 A6
 Lavenham CO10 . . . . .78 D3
 Long Melford CO10 . . . . . . .91 D6
 Newton CO10 . . . . .92 C4
 Stoke-by-nayland CO6 . . . .102 D7
Sudbury Rugby Union FC
 CO10 . . . . .148 E2
Sudbury Sta CO10 . . . . . .148 D5
Sudbury Upper Sch
 CO10 . . . . .148 D7
Sue Ryder Foundation Mus*
 CO10 . . . . .76 C1
Suffolk Ave IP31 . . . . .33 D5
Suffolk Bsns Pk IP30 . . . .123 F4
Suffolk CI IP28 . . . . .85 D8
Suffolk Horse Mus*
 IP12 . . . . .147 A5
Suffolk Nuffield Hospl
 IP1 . . . . .141 A4
Suffolk Owl Sanctuary*
 IP14 . . . . .68 C6
Suffolk Rd
 [8] Bury St Edmunds IP32 . .48 C5
 [3] Bury St Edmunds IP32 . .122 E8
 Ipswich IP4 . . . . .115 D8
 Lowestoft NR32 . . . . .115 D8
 Sudbury CO10 . . . . .148 C6
Suffolk Ret Pk IP1 . . . . . . .139 A6
Suffolk Ski Ctr* IP2 . . . . . .143 B7
Suffolk Way C88 . . . . .120 F7
 NR33 . . . . .11 B1
Suffolk Wr Pk* IP8 . . . . . .134 A5
Sulleys Hill IP7 . . . . .103 D8
Sullivan Pl IP12 . . . . .98 D7
Summer La IP22 . . . . .85 A6
Summer Rd [8] NR32 . . . .113 D1
Summercliff CI IP4 . . . . . .140 D8
Summerfield Gdns
 NR33 . . . . .115 A6
Summerhill Sch IP16 . . . . .129 C2
Summers Rd IP22 . . . . . . .122 E8
Summer Rd IP22 . . . . .35 B4
Sun La IP12 . . . . .147 A5
Sun Rd NR35 . . . . .110 D8
Sun St [4] C87 . . . . .29 C5
Sunderland Rd [2]
 IP1 . . . . .153 H11
Sunfield Cl IP14 . . . . .140 B6
Sunley Cl NR35 . . . . .110 E8
Sunningdale Ave
 Ipswich IP4 . . . . .140 D5
 Lowestoft NR33 . . . . .115 B4
 Mildenhall IP28 . . . . .116 B4
Sunningdale Dr IP11 . . . . .153 B6
Sunnyfields NR33 . . . . . . .115 A7

Sunnyhill IP12 .... 98 D7
Sunnyside
  Bedingham NR35 .... 7 C8
  Diss IP22 .... 20 C3
Sunray Ave IP11 .... 153 B6
Surbiton Rd IP1 .... 138 F7
Surrey Cl ⑥ IP13 .... 126 C3
Surrey Rd
  Felixstowe IP11 .... 152 F4
  Ipswich IP1 .... 139 A6
Surrey St
  ⑤ Lowestoft NR32 .... 113 D1
  Lowestoft NR32 .... 115 D8
Sussex Crof ⑨ IP32 .... 48 B3
Sussex Rd NR32 .... 113 D3
Sutherland Dr NR32 .... 113 B5
Sutton Cl
  Bury St Edmunds IP32 .... 123 E5
  Woodbridge IP12 .... 147 B5
Sutton Hoo National Trust*
  IP12 .... 147 D5
Swaffham Heath Rd
  CB8 .... 59 A7
Swaffham Rd
  Burwell CB5 .... 44 A3
  Mundford IP26 .... 6 B8
Swainston Way IP13 .... 55 D5
Swallow Cl
  Felixstowe IP11 .... 153 C7
  ■ Harwich CO12 .... 106 F1
  Swallow Dr Brandon IP27 .... 6 A1
  ■ Stowmarket IP14 .... 67 A5
Swallow Rd IP2 .... 138 C3
Swallowfields NR33 .... 114 E3
Swallowtail Cl IP8 .... 142 E8
Swamp La IP22 .... 20 A3
Swan Cl
  Halesworth IP19 .... 118 B3
  ⑳ Martlesham Heath IP5 .... 98 A8
  Stowmarket IP14 .... 124 A6
Swan Ct ② CO11 .... 105 A2
Swan Gn La IP19 .... 40 C5
Swan Gr CB8 .... 120 B8
Swan Hill IP8 .... 138 A2
Swan La
  Bury St Edmunds IP33 .... 154 C1
  Coney Weston IP31 .... 34 D8
  Cretingham IP13 .... 69 E8
  Exning CB8 .... 120 B8
  Haverhill CB9 .... 132 E6
  ⑧ Long Melford CO10 .... 91 E8
  North Cove NR34 .... 10 C1
  Redenhall with Harleston
    IP20 .... 22 D6
  Westerfield IP6 .... 135 E4
Swan Mdw CO7 .... 103 E5
Swan Rd IP13 .... 54 E7
Swan St CO10 .... 93 B3
Swanfield CO10 .... 91 E8
Swansea Ave IP2 .... 139 B1
Swatchway Cl ③ IP3 .... 144 A8
Swaynes ■ CO7 .... 103 E5
Sweden Cl ⑧ CO12 .... 106 F2
Swift Cl NR33 .... 114 D3
Swiltlub La IP14 .... 52 A4
Swinburne Rd IP1 .... 134 E3
Swine's Gn NR34 .... 111 C4
Swington Dr IP7 .... 79 C2
Swinton Cl IP7 .... 138 D1
Swonnell's Wlk
  ② Lowestoft NR32 .... 112 D1
  Lowestoft NR32 .... 114 D8
Sycamore Ave NR33 .... 114 D7
Sycamore Cl
  Beccles NR34 .... 111 E3
  ⑦ Great Bricett IP7 .... 80 D6
  Ipswich IP8 .... 138 C1
  Leiston IP16 .... 129 C5
Sycamore Dr
  ⑧ Beck Row, Holywell
    Row & Kenny Hill IP28 .... 13 B1
  ⑤ Mildenhall IP28 .... 30 A8
Sycamore Way
  Brantham CO11 .... 104 E5
  Diss IP22 .... 20 D3
Sycamore Wlk ⑳ IP27 .... 13 F2
Syleham Hall La IP21 .... 22 C1
Syleham Rd
  Brockdish IP21 .... 22 A2
  Syleham IP21 .... 38 D8
Sylvester Rd IP16 .... 129 D5
Symonds Rd IP23 .... 123 C4

Tanns La IP22 .... 19 A6
Tansy Cl ⑤ NR33 .... 114 F3
Tansy Mdw ③ IP20 .... 39 D8
Target Hill IP20 .... 23 B6
Tarn Hows Cl ■ IP11 .... 153 D6
Tasman Rd CB9 .... 133 A5
Tasmania Rd IP4 .... 140 D6
Tassel Rd IP32 .... 123 F6
Tattingstone CE Prim Sch
  IP9 .... 105 B8
Taunton Cl IP1 .... 135 B4
Taunton Rd IP1 .... 152 F5
Tavern Cl Ipswich IP1 .... 155 B3
Tavern St Ipswich IP1 .... 155 B3
Tawneys Rdg ② CO8 .... 101 D4
Tayfen Rd IP33 .... 154 B3
Tayfen Terr IP33 .... 154 B4
Taylor Cl ■ IP7 .... 149 D5
Taylor Rd IP7 .... 149 E5
Taylor Dr ⑧ CO11 .... 104 E2
Taylor Rd IP22 .... 20 B2
Taylors Farm La IP14 .... 66 C1
Taylors Field CB8 .... 59 F4
Tea Kettle La CB8 .... 59 F4
Teal Cl IP2 .... 138 D3
Tedder Cl ③ IP24 .... 16 C2
Tedder Rd NR32 .... 113 B4
Teesdale NR33 .... 114 B4
Telesia Cl NR32 .... 113 B4
Temperance Pl ⑥ NR34 .... 111 B5
Temple Cl IP28 .... 31 C4
Temple End CB8 .... 74 C5
Temple Pattle ■ CO11 .... 104 E4
Temple Rd Ipswich IP1 .... 140 C4
  Isleham CB7 .... 29 B4
  Stowmarket IP14 .... 124 D5
Ten Bell La ■ CB7 .... 28 D4
Tenby Rd IP2 .... 139 B1
Tennyson Cl IP12 .... 146 E6
Tennyson Rd
  ■ Bury St Edmunds IP32 .... 48 C5
  Lowestoft NR32 .... 113 D2
Tennyson Way IP24 .... 16 C7
Tenter Field ④ CO7 .... 103 E5
Tenter Piece ⑥ CO10 .... 78 D4
Tenterden Cl ⑧ NR33 .... 114 D5
Tenth Rd IP10 .... 98 A3
Tentree Rd CO10 .... 92 C7
Terence Airey Ct ⑳ IP22 .... 20 D6
Tern Cl CB9 .... 133 A5
Tern Rd IP2 .... 138 E2
Terr The
  Aldeburgh IP15 .... 130 E4
  Snape IP17 .... 72 D5
Terrace The CB8 .... 121 A3
Tewkesbury Rd IP1 .... 149 A5
Thackeray Gr IP14 .... 124 B7
Thackeray Rd IP1 .... 134 E3
Thanet Rd IP4 .... 140 B6
Tharp Way CB7 .... 29 A6
Theatre Royal* IP33 .... 154 C1
Theatre St IP12 .... 146 F5
Theberton Rd IP13 .... 140 B1
Thedwastre Cl ⑱ IP30 .... 50 F2
Thedwastre Rd IP31 .... 49 E3
Thellusson Rd ③ IP22 .... 85 E8
Thelnetham Rd IP22 .... 18 E2
Thelnetham Windmill*
  IP22 .... 18 E1
Theobald Cl ⑧ IP6 .... 125 D4
Thetford Cl ⑱ IP27 .... 13 F2
Thetford Cottage Hospl
  IP24 .... 16 C6
Thetford Gram Sch
  IP24 .... 16 B6
Thetford Mus* IP24 .... 16 C6
Thetford Rd Brandon IP27 .... 5 F1
  Coney Weston IP31 .... 34 D8
  Fakenham Magna IP24 .... 33 E8
  Fornham St Martin IP31 .... 48 D5
  Garboldisham IP22 .... 18 C4
  ② Ipswich IP1 .... 139 A7
  Ixworth IP31 .... 34 A2
  Ixworth Thorpe IP31 .... 33 F3
  Mildenhall IP28 .... 116 C4
  Santon Downham IP27 .... 6 B1
  South Lopham IP22 .... 19 A4
  Thetford Star IP24 .... 16 B6
Thieves La IP31 .... 49 F8
Thingoe Hill IP32 .... 154 B4
Third Ave CO10 .... 77 B3
Thirlmere Dr IP14 .... 124 B8
Thirlmere Wlk NR32 .... 113 A4
Thirwall Dr CB7 .... 29 C1
Thistle Cl IP2 .... 138 F4
Thistledown Dr IP14 .... 124 D4
Thistledown Rd IP22 .... 34 B2
Thomas Arne Cl IP14 .... 124 C8
Thomas Ave IP21 .... 152 C8
Thomas Bardwell Dr ④
  NR35 .... 110 C2
Thomas Bole Cl ⑥ NR34 .... 110 C8
Thomas Cl ⑳ IP31 .... 34 B1
Thomas La IP31 .... 154 B1
Thomas Mills High Sch
  IP13 .... 126 A5
Thomas Walls Cl ■ IP13 .... 83 E5
Thomas Young Cl
  IP14 .... 124 D3
Thompson La IP31 .... 51 D1
Thompson Rd IP1 .... 138 D1
Thomsons La IP6 .... 69 A2
Thong Hall Rd IP12 .... 117 A5
Thorington Rd IP19 .... 42 A5
Thorn Cl CB7 .... 28 C5
Thorn Way IP11 .... 152 E4
Thorn Wlk IP12 .... 85 C2

Thornbush La IP8 .... 138 A8
Thornden CE Prim Sch
  IP23 .... 53 C8
Thorney Gn Rd IP14 .... 67 A6
Thorney Rd IP9 .... 150 E4
Thornham Rd IP23 .... 114 F4
Thornham Rd IP23 .... 36 C1
Thornhayes Cl IP2 .... 139 A3
Thornhill Rd IP6 .... 82 B5
Thornley Dr IP4 .... 140 C8
Thornley Rd IP11 .... 153 C4
Thorns Cl CB8 .... 61 E2
Thornton Cl ⑮ IP27 .... 13 F2
Thornton Rd IP33 .... 122 E2
Thoroughfare IP19 .... 118 B3
Thoroughfare The
  Brundish NR13 .... 55 C8
  Harleston IP20 .... 22 D6
  Wilby IP21 .... 39 D1
  ⑩ Woodbridge IP12 .... 147 A5
Thorpe Abbotts Rd
  IP21 .... 21 D4
Thorpe Hall Rd IP11 .... 38 F4
Thorpe La
  Ashfield cum Thorpe IP14 .... 69 C8
  Debenham IP14 .... 53 F1
  Trimley St Martin IP11 .... 107 C8
Thorpe Rd IP16 .... 130 F6
Thorpe's Hill IP9 .... 95 E6
Threadneedle St
  Dedham CO7 .... 103 F4
  ■ Hadleigh IP7 .... 149 D6
Three Marsh La IP19 .... 119 B6
Throckmorton Rd
  NR35 .... 110 D3
Through Duncans
  IP12 .... 146 E3
Through Jollys IP5 .... 141 D8
Thurleston Cty High Sch
  IP1 .... 135 A4
Thurleston La IP1 .... 134 F5
Thurlow CE Prim Sch
  CB9 .... 74 D6
Thurlow Cl ② IP14 .... 124 D6
Thurlow Rd CB9 .... 74 D7
Thurmans La IP11 .... 152 B8
Thurne Rd NR33 .... 114 F5
Thurston CE Prim Sch
  IP31 .... 49 E4
Thurston Cl ⑧ IP14 .... 152 C4
Thurston Rd CO10 .... 76 C7
Thurston Sta ■ IP31 .... 49 D3
Thwaite Rd
  Ditchingham NR35 .... 110 C7
  Thornden IP23 .... 53 B8
  Wickham Skeith IP23 .... 52 D7
Tibbenham's Score ⑥
  NR32 .... 3 D4
Tiberius Cl ⑨ IP30 .... 133 B5
Tide Mill* IP12 .... 147 B4
Tide Mill Way IP12 .... 147 A4
Tideway NR33 .... 114 E8
Tiggins La IP7 .... 128 D8
Tilbury Rd
  Great Yeldham CO9 .... 90 A2
  Ridgewell CO9 .... 89 E4
Tile Barn La CO11 .... 104 B1
Tilbrooks Hill CB8 .... 61 B1
Timperley Cl IP7 .... 149 D7
Timperley Rd IP7 .... 149 E7
Timperleys IP8 .... 95 C6
Tinabrook Cl IP2 .... 138 E2
Tinker Brook IP13 .... 71 F5
Tinker's La IP7 .... 149 D5
Tinkers La NR34 .... 10 D1
Tinker's La NR15 .... 21 C8
Tinker's Cl ⑥ IP22 .... 139 A2
Tippet Ave IP14 .... 124 C8
Titlow Rd ⑳ IP20 .... 22 D6
Toad Row NR34 .... 10 F1
Todhunter Ave IP4 .... 9 B6
Tog La CO6 .... 102 D2
Tokio Rd IP4 .... 140 A6
Toll Gate Rd IP9 .... 150 E3
Tollemache Bsns Pk
  IP7 .... 80 E4
Toller Cl IP12 .... 131 C3
Toller Rd IP3 .... 139 E3
Tollgate La ■ IP32 .... 123 A8
Tollgate Prim Sch
  IP32 .... 122 F8
Tolworth Rd IP4 .... 140 A6
Tom Jennings Cl CB8 .... 120 F5
Tomline Rd
  Felixstowe IP11 .... 153 A3
  Ipswich IP3 .... 140 A5
Tomo Bsns Pk IP14 .... 124 F6
Tomtit's La IP14 .... 51 B2
Tonning St ② NR32 .... 113 C1
Tooks Comm La NR34 .... 9 F1
Top Rd Hasketon IP13 .... 146 B8
  Rattlesden IP30 .... 65 D5
  St Andrew, Ilketshall
  ... NR34 ....
  Wingfield IP21 .... 39 A7
Top St IP12 .... 146 C2

Toper La IP33 .... 154 C1
Toppesfield Cl ■ IP7 .... 149 D5
Tortoiseshell Cl IP9 .... 142 E8
Tostock Rd IP30 .... 49 F2
Tot Hill IP14 .... 66 C8
Tottington La IP22 .... 20 B2
Tovells ■ IP13 .... 126 C3
Towell's Rd IP14 .... 139 F6
Tower Field Rd IP12 .... 85 B7
Tower Hill IP11 .... 153 B4
Tower Mill La ■ IP7 .... 149 E6
Tower Mill Rd
  Bungay NR35 .... 110 B3
  Ipswich IP1 .... 138 F7
Tower Ramparts IP1 .... 155 B3
Tower Rd
  Felixstowe IP11 .... 152 F4
  Lowestoft NR33 .... 115 A2
Tower St IP1 .... 155 B3
Town Farm Cl IP20 .... 23 C3
Town Farm Est IP22 .... 131 B3
Town Gn IP14 .... 124 C6
Town House Cnr IP14 .... 68 F7
Town House La IP22 .... 35 D6
Town La IP12 .... 53 A3
Townhouse Rd IP33 .... 35 C1
Townlands Dr NR34 .... 111 B3
Townlane Rd IP33 .... 123 B1
Townsend CB7 .... 28 C5
Toyse Cl ■ CB5 .... 44 B6
Toyse La CB5 .... 44 A6
Trafalgar Cl IP14 .... 139 F6
Trafalgar Rd CO10 .... 148 E7
Trafalgar St
  ④ Lowestoft NR32 .... 113 C1
  Lowestoft NR32 .... 115 C8
Trafford Cl ② IP14 .... 51 E1
Tranmere Gr IP1 .... 134 F2
Traveller's Hill (Tumuli)*
  IP28 .... 14 B7
Travellers Field IP13 .... 69 E5
Treeline IP3 .... 144 B6
Treetops IP12 .... 154 B2
Treeview IP14 .... 124 B6
Trefoil Cl IP2 .... 138 F4
Trenchard Sq ⑧ IP22 .... 4 D5
Trent Rd
  ■ Bury St Edmunds IP32 .... 48 C5
  Ipswich IP3 .... 139 F2
Trevethan Cl IP32 .... 122 E7
Triangle Yd ⑨ NR32 .... 113 E2
Trimley St Martin Prim Sch
  IP11 .... 98 D1
Trimley St Mary Prim Sch
  IP11 .... 152 C8
Trimley Sta ■ IP11 .... 152 C7
Trinity Ave
  Felixstowe IP11 .... 152 B3
  Felixstowe IP11 .... 152 B3
  Mildenhall IP28 .... 116 D5
Trinity Cl Farnham CB7 .... 29 B1
  Ipswich IP5 .... 140 F7
  ⑳ Manningtree CO11 .... 104 E2
  ■ Southwold IP18 .... 119 D5
  Woodbridge IP12 .... 146 D2
Trinity Dr CB8 .... 121 B2
Trinity Gdns NR35 .... 110 B4
Trinity Gild ⑦ CO10 .... 78 D4
Trinity Link CB9 .... 132 E7
Trinity Mews IP14 .... 154 A3
Trinity Rd
  Lowestoft NR32 .... 113 E1
  Manningtree CO11 .... 104 E2
Trinity St ■ Bungay NR35 .... 110 B4
  ■ Southwold IP18 .... 119 D5
Trinity Wlk IP14 .... 67 A7
Triple Plea La NR35 .... 7 B8
Triple Plea Rd NR35 .... 7 B8
Troon Gdns ⑧ IP4 .... 136 B1
Trossachs The ■ NR32 .... 112 D2
Troston Mount (Tumulus)*
  IP31 .... 33 D5
Troston Rd IP31 .... 34 A6
Trotting Horse La CB8 .... 75 A8
Trott's La CO10 .... 92 F3
Trunch Hill IP20 .... 7 A3
Trunch Rd IP20 .... 7 B2
Tuddenham Ave IP4 .... 139 E7
Tuddenham CE Prim Sch
  IP28 .... 30 F2
Tuddenham Cnr IP28 .... 46 E6
Tuddenham La IP5 .... 136 B2
Tuddenham Rd
  Barton Mills IP28 .... 116 F2
  Ipswich IP4 .... 155 C4
  ■ Westerfield IP4 .... 136 A4
Tudor Ave IP21 .... 20 B3
Tudor CE Prim Sch
  CO10 .... 148 D7
Tudor Cl
  Chedburgh IP29 .... 62 D5
  ⑦ Framlingham IP13 .... 126 C3
  ⑧ Shotley Gate IP9 .... 107 A5
  Sudbury CO10 .... 148 C7
Tudor Ct ■ IP23 .... 37 F1
Tudor Gn CO10 .... 148 C8
Tudor Rd CO10 .... 148 C7
Tudor Wlk
  ⑧ Honington IP31 .... 33 D5
  ■ Lowestoft NR33 .... 114 E4
Tuffen La IP22 .... 35 D8
Tuffields Rd IP29 .... 63 B3
Tumbril La IP29 .... 25 D8
Tunbeck Cl IP20 .... 23 A7
Tunbeck Rd IP20 .... 23 A8
Tunbridge Cl ④ CB5 .... 44 A5

Tunneys La NR35 .... 110 C8
Tuns La IP33 .... 154 C1
Tunstall Dr NR32 .... 112 F4
Tunstall Gn IP12 .... 71 F2
Turin St IP2 .... 155 B1
Turin Way ② NR33 .... 114 F4
Turino Ave IP12 .... 98 B8
Turkentine Cl ⑩ CO10 .... 92 B3
Turkeyhall La IP14 .... 66 D6
Turnberry Cl ⑧ NR33 .... 114 F4
Turnberry Dr IP28 .... 48 C6
Turner Ave ■ CO11 .... 104 D2
Turner Cl
  Ditchingham NR35 .... 110 C7
  Haverhill CB9 .... 132 B7
  ④ Lowestoft NR32 .... 113 C6
  Sudbury CO10 .... 148 E8
Turner Gdns IP14 .... 146 D3
Turner Gr IP5 .... 141 D8
Turner La ④ IP14 .... 51 C1
Turner Rd Ipswich IP3 .... 144 A8
Turnpike Hill IP24 .... 124 B7
Turnpike Hill IP30 .... 74 B2
Turnpike Rd
  Chippenham CB8 .... 45 F8
  Red Lodge IP28 .... 30 B1
  Woodbridge IP12 .... 84 C8
Turnstone Cl ⑧ IP28 .... 116 D4
Turret La IP4 .... 155 B2
Tut Hill IP28 .... 48 B5
Tutelina Rd IP30 .... 64 A6
Tutt Hill (Tumulus)*
  IP24 .... 16 D4
Tuyar Wlk CB8 .... 120 E8
Tweed Cl CB8 .... 45 F3
Twelve Acre App IP5 .... 141 B7
Twin Oak Dr IP13 .... 56 B7
Twinnings The IP14 .... 124 C3
Twiss Cl ⑤ IP22 .... 20 A3
Two Acres IP9 .... 150 F4
Two House Cl ⑬ IP23 .... 127 C7
Two Pole Dro CB7 .... 28 A7
Tydemans Ct ■ IP14 .... 124 D6
Tye Cl ⑦ IP6 .... 106 F3
Tye La IP6 .... 111 B3
Tyler St ⑧ Harwich CO12 .... 106 F3
  Ipswich IP2 .... 155 B1
Tylers Gn IP14 .... 152 C7
Tylers Way IP14 .... 124 D3
Tymmes Pl IP13 .... 146 C8
Tyrone Cl IP1 .... 134 D2

Ubbeston Way NR33 .... 114 F4
Ufford Pl ⑧ IP13 .... 84 F7
Ufford Rd Bredfield IP13 .... 84 D7
  Eyke IP12 .... 85 B6
Uggeshall Cl NR32 .... 113 A5
Ullswater Ave ④ IP1 .... 153 D7
Ullswater Rd IP12 .... 71 C2
Ulster Ave IP1 .... 134 D1
Una Rd CO12 .... 106 F2
Uncle's La IP19 .... 24 B6
Undercliff Rd E IP1 .... 153 C4
Undercliff Rd W IP11 .... 153 A3
Underhill IP14 .... 124 D5
Undley Rd IP27 .... 109 B4
Unicorn Pl IP33 .... 123 C6
Union Hill IP7 .... 94 A8
Union La
  Lowestoft NR32 .... 112 F5
  Wortham IP22 .... 20 A1
Union Pl NR33 .... 115 C7
Union Rd
  Lowestoft NR32 .... 113 C1
  Onehouse IP14 .... 66 C6
  Stowmarket IP14 .... 124 A7
Union St IP4 .... 155 C3
Union St E IP14 .... 124 D6
Union St W IP14 .... 124 D6
Unitarian Meeting House*
  IP1 .... 155 B2
Unity Rd IP14 .... 124 D5
Unity St IP3 .... 139 E4
Univ Coll Suffolk IP4 .... 139 E5
Up St IP31 .... 34 C4
Upland Rd IP4 .... 140 A6
Uplands Cl NR33 .... 114 D4
Uplands Cres CO10 .... 148 C2
Uplands Mid Sch
  CO10 .... 148 D7
Uplands Rd N NR33 .... 114 D5
Uplands Rd S NR33 .... 114 C3
Uplands The
  Aldringham cum Thorpe
    IP16 .... 73 E6
  Beccles NR34 .... 111 D4
Uplands Way Diss IP22 .... 20 C3
  Ipswich IP4 .... 139 B5
Upper Ave IP19 .... 118 B5
Upper Barclay St IP4 .... 155 C2
Upper Brook La IP20 .... 22 B4
Upper Brook St IP4 .... 155 B3
Upper Broadlands La
  IP20 .... 22 A5
Upper Cavendish St
  IP3 .... 140 A5
Upper E St CO10 .... 148 D6
Upper Farm Rd CO10 .... 89 C4

Upper Grange Rd NR34 ...111 A4
Upper Harmans La IP20 ...22 B5
Upper High St IP1 ...155 B4
Upper Melton Terr IP12 ...84 E6
Upper Moorfield Rd IP12 ...146 F6
Upper Oakley IP23 ...117 F8
Upper Olland St NR35 ...110 B3
Upper Orwell St IP4 ...155 C2
Upper Rd CO10 ...101 C8
Upper Rose La IP22 ...20 C1
Upper St Gissing IP22 ...20 F8
  Layham IP7 ...149 F1
  Stansfield CO10 ...76 C6
  Stanstead CO10 ...77 C4
  Stratford St Mary CO7 ...103 E5
Upper Tumbril La IP20 ...22 A4
Upperfield Dr IP11 ...153 C6
Upsons Way IP5 ...141 E8
Upthorpe Rd IP31 ...34 F4
Upton CI IP4 ...139 E6
Urban Rd IP16 ...129 D6
US 100th Bomb Group Meml Mus* IP21 ...21 D4
Uvedale Gdns IP6 ...125 E4
Uxbridge Cres IP3 ...140 C1

V

Vale La
  Bury St Edmunds IP33 ...123 C3
  Kersey IP7 ...94 A6
  Stutton IP9 ...105 A6
Valentine Way IP30 ...64 F7
Valiant Rd IP31 ...33 D4
Valiant St 6 IP28 ...13 B1
Valley CI
  1 Brantham CO11 ...104 E5
  Halesworth IP19 ...118 E4
  Ipswich IP1 ...135 C1
Valley Farm* CO7 ...151 D1
Valley Farm Camargue Horses* IP13 ...127 A8
Valley Farm La IP7 ...94 E5
Valley Farm Rd IP12 ...147 B8
  Buxhall IP14 ...65 F3
  Wherstead IP9 ...143 A3
Valley Rd Battisford IP14 ...66 E1
  Chilton CO10 ...92 C6
  Great Bricett IP7 ...80 D6
  Ipswich IP1 ...135 B1
  Leiston IP16 ...129 E6
  Little Blakenham IP8 ...81 E4
Valley View CO10 ...77 C4
Valley Wash CO10 ...75 D4
Valley Way CB8 ...120 E3
Valley Wlk IP3 ...152 F5
Valleyview Dr IP4 ...140 F4
Vallibus CI 8 NR32 ...112 E4
Van Dyck CI 9 NR32 ...113 B6
Vandyck Rd IP3 ...144 A8
Vanners Rd CB9 ...132 E5
Vaughan St IP2 ...155 B1
Vaunces La IP21 ...21 E4
Vaunce's La IP21 ...21 E4
Vaux Ave CB9 ...132 C4
Velda CI NR33 ...114 F4
Ventris CI IP2 ...138 D5
Verdons La IP21 ...39 E4
Verdure CI 2 NR32 ...112 F5
Vere Gdns IP1 ...135 C2
Vermeer CI 5 NR32 ...113 B6
Vermont Cres IP4 ...155 C4
Vermont Rd IP4 ...155 C4
Verneuil Ave IP14 ...124 D3
Vernon St IP2 ...155 B1
Veyses End 3 CO7 ...103 E5
Vicarage CI CB8 ...59 E5
Vicarage Ct CO10 ...148 F3
Vicarage Gdns 10 IP14 ...53 F2
Vicarage Hill 7 IP12 ...147 A5
Vicarage La Acton CO10 ...92 A6
  Bramford IP8 ...134 B1
  Bungay NR35 ...110 E3
  Wherstead IP9 ...143 B5
  Woodditton CB8 ...60 B6
Vicarage Rd
  Belchamp St Paul CO10 ...90 D5
  Felixstowe IP11 ...152 D4
  Laxfield IP13 ...40 B3
  Newmarket CB8 ...121 B3
  Thetford IP24 ...16 C6
  Wingfield IP21 ...39 A8
  Winston IP14 ...54 A1
Victor Rd IP31 ...33 D4
Victoria CI 3 IP31 ...49 E4
Victoria Cres 2 CO11 ...104 E2
Victoria Hill IP13 ...117 C4
Victoria Mill Rd IP13 ...126 B2
Victoria Rd
  Aldeburgh IP15 ...130 E4
  Diss IP22 ...20 D2
  Felixstowe IP11 ...152 F3
  Haverhill CB9 ...132 B5
  Lowestoft NR33 ...114 E7
  Stowmarket IP14 ...124 C7
  Woodbridge IP12 ...147 A5
Victoria St
  Bury St Edmunds IP33 ...154 A2

Victoria St continued
  Felixstowe IP11 ...153 A4
  7 Harwich CO12 ...107 B2
  Ipswich IP1 ...139 A6
  16 Southwold IP18 ...119 D5
Victoria Terr
  3 Fressingfield IP21 ...39 E8
  Lowestoft NR33 ...115 D7
Victoria Way CB8 ...120 E7
Victory CI IP33 ...123 C2
Victory Rd Ipswich IP4 ...140 A7
  Leiston IP16 ...129 C5
View Point Rd IP11 ...153 H10
Viking CI IP12 ...84 B1
Viking Hts IP12 ...84 B1
Viking Rd IP14 ...124 C5
Villa Hill IP17 ...99 B7
Village Way
  Lowestoft NR33 ...113 B5
  Waldringfield IP12 ...98 D7
Vincent CI 7 Feltwell IP26 ...4 E5
  Ipswich IP1 ...138 E8
Vince's Rd IP32 ...20 D2
Vine CI IP31 ...17 E1
Vine Rd IP6 ...69 C2
Vinefields The IP33 ...154 C2
Vinery CI IP13 ...127 C6
Vinery Rd IP33 ...122 F3
Vines The IP17 ...128 D7
Vinesse Rd CO6 ...102 B2
Vineway The
  6 Harwich CO12 ...107 A2
  7 Harwich CO12 ...107 A2
Violet CI
  Bury St Edmunds IP32 ...123 F5
  Ipswich IP2 ...138 F4
Violet Hill Rd IP14 ...124 C7
Virginia Rd 11 IP28 ...30 A8
Vyces Rd IP13 ...126 B3

W

W Suffolk Hospl The IP33 ...123 A2
Wacker Field Rd 8 IP12 ...85 E8
Wadd La IP17 ...72 C6
Waddesdon Rd 8 CO12 ...107 B2
Waddlegoose La IP14 ...54 A5
Waddling La IP14 ...112 A7
Wadehall La NR34 ...10 B5
Wades Gr IP5 ...141 E7
Wades La Raydon IP7 ...94 E5
  Shotley IP9 ...106 E7
Wades Wood 1 IP30 ...50 D1
Wadgate Rd IP11 ...152 E4
Wadhurst Rd IP1 ...140 D3
Wainford CI 8 NR34 ...9 F4
Wainford Rd NR35 ...110 E5
Wainwright Way IP5 ...141 D8
Wainwright CI 4 NR32 ...113 A6
Wainwright Gdns IP6 ...81 F5
Wake Ave IP28 ...116 C5
Wakeshall La CO10 ...90 B4
Walberswick Nature Reserve* IP17 ...43 B4
Walberswick Way 8 NR32 ...113 A3
Walcot Rd IP22 ...20 D3
Walcot Rise IP22 ...20 D3
Walcott Wlk NR33 ...115 B5
Waldegrave CI 3 CO11 ...104 D2
Waldegrave Rd IP11 ...152 A8
Waldingfield Rd 10 Acton CO10 ...92 B7
  Chilton CO10 ...148 F8
Waldingfield Prim Sch IP12 ...98 D7
Waldringfield Rd IP12 ...84 C1
Walker CI IP4 ...140 C5
Walker Gdns NR34 ...26 C5
Walks The NR34 ...10 A8
Wall La CO11 ...105 C2
Wallace Rd IP1 ...138 E8
Waller's Gr IP2 ...138 F4
Wallow La IP7 ...80 D6
Walls The CO11 ...104 E2
Walmer CI NR33 ...115 A5
Walmer Rd IP1 ...115 A5
Walnut CI Acton CO10 ...92 B8
  Felixstowe IP11 ...153 D7
  Hopton IP22 ...18 C1
  16 Lakenheath IP27 ...13 F2
Walnut Gr IP28 ...30 A4
Walnut Tree CI 1 IP8 ...134 A2
Walnut Tree La
  3 Harkstead IP9 ...106 A5
  Sudbury CO10 ...148 B5
Walnut Tree Mdw IP14 ...68 B6
Walnuts La IP13 ...127 B5
Walnuts The
  Beccles NR34 ...111 E4
  3 Ufford IP13 ...84 F7
Walnuttree Hospl CO10 ...148 B5
Walpole La IP19 ...41 D5
Walpole Rd
  Bramfield IP19 ...41 E4
  Halesworth IP19 ...118 A1
Walsham Le Willows Sch IP31 ...35 C2
Walsham Rd
  Finningham IP14 ...36 A1
  Finningham IP14 ...36 B1
  6 Ixworth IP31 ...34 B1
  Wattisfield IP22 ...35 C3
Walsingham CI 6 CO10 ...92 B3

Walsingham Rd IP33 ...122 D3
Walters CI 9 NR31 ...3 B7
Waltham CI IP7 ...139 A2
Walton Ave IP11 ...152 C3
Walton E 5 Fordham CB7 ...29 A1
  1 Stowmarket IP14 ...124 B8
Walton Rd NR32 ...113 D1
Walton Way IP28 ...30 B5
Wamil Way IP28 ...116 B4
Wangford Rd
  Lakenheath IP27 ...13 F7
  Reydon IP18 ...26 D1
  Southwold IP18 ...119 B8
  Uggeshall NR34 ...26 A3
  Westhall IP19 ...25 B4
Wannock CI NR33 ...114 D4
Wantisden Cnr IP12 ...86 A6
Ward Rd IP8 ...138 B2
Wardlaw CI 10 IP14 ...53 F2
Wardley CI IP22 ...138 D1
Wardley Hill Rd NR35 ...8 D8
Ware Rd IP7 ...149 D3
Wareham Ave IP3 ...140 D3
Warene CI 3 IP13 ...126 C3
Warham Rd CO12 ...106 F1
Warren Ave IP28 ...30 A4
Warren Chase IP5 ...141 E7
Warren CI Elmswell IP30 ...50 E2
  Lakenheath IP27 ...109 D5
Warren Heath Ave IP3 ...140 D2
Warren Heath Rd IP3 ...140 D2
Warren Hill Rd IP12 ...146 E4
Warren La
  Ashen IP9 ...106 D4
  Elmswell IP30 ...50 E2
  27 Martlesham Heath IP5 ...98 A8
  Woolpit IP30 ...50 F1
Warren Loke NR31 ...2 B7
Warren Rd
  Great Yarmouth NR31 ...3 B8
  Herringswell CB8 ...46 A8
  Hopton on Sea NR31 ...3 C7
  Lowestoft NR32 ...113 D4
  Red Lodge IP28 ...30 C8
Warren's La NR34 ...10 A2
Warrington Rd IP1 ...155 A4
Warrington St CB8 ...121 A2
Warwick Ave
  Halesworth IP19 ...118 C5
  Woodbridge IP12 ...146 F6
Warwick Rd IP4 ...139 E6
Wash La Beccles NR34 ...111 B2
  Boxford CO6 ...102 F3
  Burgh St Peter NR34 ...10 C8
  Dennington IP13 ...55 E6
  Frostenden NR34 ...26 C3
  Great Finborough IP14 ...124 A5
  Hinderclay IP22 ...35 E8
  Kessingland NR34 ...11 C1
  Mendlesham IP14 ...52 E3
  Reydon IP18 ...26 D2
  St Peter, South Elmham NR35 ...23 F7
  Shelfanger IP22 ...20 B6
  Stanton IP31 ...34 F3
  Topcroft NR35 ...7 A8
  Wenhaston With Mells Hamlet IP19 ...118 E1
  Wilby IP21 ...58 B8
  Witnesham IP6 ...83 A6
Washington St
  7 Mildenhall IP28 ...13 B1
  12 Mildenhall IP28 ...30 A8
Wassicks La IP14 ...51 E3
Watch House Hill NR35 ...110 E4
Water La
  Athelington IP21 ...38 F1
  Barnardiston CB9 ...75 B4
  Barnham IP24 ...16 C2
  Botesdale IP22 ...35 F5
  3 Bures CO8 ...101 C5
  Cavendish CO10 ...75 E5
  Debenham IP14 ...53 F2
  Denston CB8 ...75 F7
  Garboldisham IP22 ...18 D4
  Great Bradley CB8 ...74 C8
  Great Horkesley CO6 ...102 D7
  Great Wenham IP7 ...94 E4
  Helions Bumpstead CB9 ...88 B4
  Kersey IP7 ...94 A6
  Layham IP7 ...149 F1
  Lowestoft NR32 ...113 C2
  Polstead CO6 ...102 F8
  Steeple Bumpstead CB9 ...88 D3
  Sturmer CB9 ...133 D3
  Thelnetham IP22 ...18 E1
  Thornham Magna IP23 ...37 A1
  Weybread IP21 ...22 D4
  Worlingworth IP13 ...54 D8
Water Mill La IP21 ...36 F6
Water Run The IP7 ...79 F7
Water St CO10 ...78 D4
Watercourse The CB8 ...121 A4
Waterford Rd IP1 ...134 D2
Watering CI 11 IP6 ...81 C3
Watering La IP17 ...72 C7
Watering Rd IP14 ...38 D5
Waterloo Ave
  Leiston IP16 ...129 B6
  4 Roydon IP22 ...20 A3
Waterloo CI CB8 ...120 D8
Waterloo Rd
  4 Ipswich IP1 ...139 A7

Waterloo Rd continued
  Lowestoft NR33 ...115 D7
Sotterley NR34 ...26 D7
Watermill CI IP7 ...149 E2
Watermill Rd IP12 ...98 C5
Waters Ave NR33 ...114 C3
Waterside IP13 ...29 C5
Waterworks Rd 12 IP28 ...30 A8
Waterworks St IP4 ...155 C2
Watery La IP13 ...146 A8
Watson Way IP12 ...99 E4
Watsons CI 3 NR31 ...3 C7
Watson's Hill IP27 ...79 F1
Watt CI IP12 ...99 E4
Wattisfield Rd IP33 ...35 C2
Wattisham Airfield IP7 ...80 C6
Wattisham Airfield Mus* IP7 ...80 C6
Wattisham Rd IP7 ...79 F4
Waveney CI 3 IP17 ...128 C4
Waveney Cres NR33 ...115 B7
Waveney Hill
  Carlton Colville NR32 ...114 B8
  Lowestoft NR32 ...112 B1
Waveney Hts IP21 ...21 F2
Waveney Rd
  Beccles NR34 ...111 B4
  Bungay NR35 ...110 D3
  16 Bury St Edmunds IP32 ...48 C5
  Ditchingham NR35 ...110 D8
  Felixstowe IP11 ...152 C3
  Ipswich IP1 ...138 E8
  10 Lowestoft NR32 ...115 D8
Waveney Sports & Leisure Ctr NR32 ...113 C3
Waveney Terr 4 CB9 ...132 E5
Waveney Valley Swimming Pool NR35 ...110 D2
Way Bank La CO9 ...89 C7
Wayne CI NR32 ...113 B5
Wayside CI IP14 ...124 D3
Weald The NR32 ...112 E2
Weatheralls CI 9 CB7 ...28 D4
Weaver CI IP1 ...138 D8
Weavers CI
  2 Hadleigh IP7 ...149 D6
  4 Lavenham CO10 ...78 D4
Weavers Croft 2 IP30 ...22 C6
Weavers Dr 6 CO10 ...77 A2
Weavers La CO10 ...148 C5
Weavers Marsh La IP17 ...41 E2
Weavers Way IP5 ...82 A5
Webb Rd IP14 ...124 D3
Webb St 3 IP12 ...139 C3
Webb's CI IP14 ...124 C3
Webbs CI IP5 ...141 C7
Webster St NR35 ...110 A4
Weddell Rd CB9 ...133 A4
Weeting Heath Nature Reserve* IP27 ...5 C3
Weeting Prim Sch IP27 ...5 E3
Weir PI IP10 ...98 D2
Weirs Dro CB5 ...44 A6
Welbeck CI IP7 ...152 C7
Welbourne Way NR34 ...10 C4
Welburn CI 6 IP12 ...85 D8
Welch Rd NR33 ...115 A5
Welham La IP28 ...47 D5
Well Bottom CB8 ...45 A4
Well La 8 CO10 ...90 A8
Well St IP33 ...154 B2
Wellesley Rd
  Ipswich IP1 ...139 F5
  Troston IP31 ...33 D4
Wellington CI IP28 ...30 A6
Wellington Esplanade NR33 ...115 C6
Wellington Rd
  Eye IP23 ...117 D3
  4 Feltwell IP26 ...4 E5
  12 Harwich CO12 ...107 C3
  12 Lowestoft NR33 ...115 C6
  8 Mildenhall IP28 ...30 A8
  10 Troston IP31 ...33 D5
Wellington St
  7 Ipswich IP1 ...139 A7
  16 Newmarket CB8 ...121 A3
Wells CI IP4 ...139 E6
Wells Cnr IP17 ...39 F2
Wells Rd IP28 ...116 B5
Wells Hall Com Prim Sch CO10 ...148 F2
Wells Hall Rd CO10 ...148 F3
Wells' La IP20 ...22 D5
Wells Rd IP20 ...22 D5
Wembley Ave NR34 ...111 B4
Wendy CI 7 IP26 ...106 C8
Wenham
  East Bergholt CO7 ...151 D8
  Hintlesham CO7 ...150 A2
Wenham Rd IP6 ...150 E8
Wenhaston La IP19 ...42 D5
Wenhaston Prim Sch IP19 ...42 C6
Wenhaston Rd IP19 ...118 D8
Wenhaston Way 2 NR32 ...112 F3
Wensleydale 5 NR33 ...114 E3
Wentford View 1 CO10 ...76 A1
Wentworth CI
  14 Fornham All Saints IP28 ...48 C5
  Hadleigh IP7 ...149 F5

Wentworth Dr
  Felixstowe IP11 ...153 C6
  7 Ipswich IP8 ...138 C2
  10 Mildenhall IP28 ...116 A5
Wentworth Rd IP15 ...130 F4
Wentworth Way 2 NR33 ...114 F4
Wesel Ave IP11 ...153 A4
Wesley CI NR34 ...111 B2
Wesley End Rd CO9 ...89 B2
Wesley Way IP1 ...138 F8
West Dock Rd CO12 ...106 F3
West Dr
  Mildenhall IP28 ...116 B4
  Soham CB7 ...28 C4
West Dr Cres CB7 ...28 C4
West Gr Gdns CB7 ...28 C4
West End CB8 ...60 B5
West End La
  Great Thurlow CB9 ...74 B4
  18 Haverhill CB9 ...132 E6
West End Rd IP11 ...155 A2
West Gr NR33 ...115 A3
West Hall Rd
  1 Mundford IP26 ...6 B8
  Walsham-le-willows IP22 ...35 F3
West Harling Rd NR16 ...18 B8
West Herne La IP22 ...19 A1
West Lane IP4 ...140 C8
West Mdws IP14 ...134 C4
West Mill Gn IP9 ...104 F7
West Rd
  Bury St Edmunds IP33 ...122 E4
  Ipswich IP3 ...140 E1
West Row Prim Sch IP28 ...29 F7
West Row Rd IP28 ...116 A5
West Side CI NR32 ...113 C5
West St Harwich CO12 ...107 B3
  Icklingham IP28 ...31 C4
  Isleham CB7 ...29 B5
  Rickinghall Inferior IP22 ...35 E3
West Stow Anglo-Saxon Village* IP28 ...31 F2
West Stow Ctry Pk* IP28 ...31 F2
West Stow Rd IP28 ...32 B1
West Suffolk Coll IP33 ...122 E6
West Tofts Rd IP26 ...6 D7
West View IP14 ...124 B6
West View Gdns 4 IP23 ...36 D2
West Wood 9 IP31 ...49 A5
Westbourne High Sch IP1 ...134 F1
Westbourne Rd IP1 ...134 F1
Westbury Ave IP33 ...122 D5
Westbury Rd IP4 ...140 B8
Westend La CB9 ...133 F8
Westerfield Hall* IP6 ...135 E6
Westerfield La IP6 ...136 A5
Westerfield Rd
  Ipswich IP1 ...155 C4
  Westerfield IP6 ...135 E3
Westerfield Sta IP6 ...135 E3
Westerings The 1 CO6 ...102 C5
Western Ave
  Felixstowe IP11 ...153 C6
  Haverhill CB9 ...132 C7
Western CI 4 Feltwell IP26 ...4 D5
  Ipswich IP4 ...140 F4
Western Way IP33 ...122 D6
Western's End 6 CO10 ...104 E4
Westfield CO10 ...90 B8
Westfield Com Prim Sch IP6 ...135 C5
Westgate Gdns IP33 ...122 E3
Westgate IP16 ...73 F6
Westgate Cty Prim Sch IP33 ...154 A1
Westgate St
  Bury St Edmunds IP33 ...154 C1
  Ipswich IP1 ...155 B3
  Long Melford CO10 ...77 E1
  Methall IP21 ...39 B5
Westhall Rd NR32 ...113 B5
Westholme CI IP12 ...146 F4
Westholme Rd IP1 ...135 A1
Westhorpe 3 CB5 ...44 A6
Westhorpe Rd IP14 ...52 A8
Westland 2 IP5 ...98 A8
Westleton Rd NR33 ...114 D6
Westleton Rd IP17 ...57 E8
Westleton Way 17 IP11 ...152 D5
Westley Bottom Rd CB8 ...59 A4
Westley La IP29 ...122 B3
Westley Mid Sch IP29 ...122 C5
Westley Rd IP28 ...122 B8
Westley Way IP31 ...50 E7
Westminster CI IP4 ...140 B5
Westminster Dr IP33 ...122 D3
Westmorland CI CO11 ...105 A2
Westmorland Rd IP11 ...153 D7
Weston Colville Rd CB8 ...59 E1
Weston Rds NR33 ...113 B5
Weston Way CB8 ...120 C6
Westropps 6 CO10 ...91 E7
Westward Deals CB9 ...133 F8
Westward House IP16 ...129 C6
Westwood Ave
  Ipswich IP1 ...139 A8
  Lowestoft NR33 ...114 C6
Wet La CO4 ...102 F3

Wetherby Cl IP1 ....135 B3
Wetherden Rd
  Elmswell IP14 ....50 F2
  Great Ashfield IP31 .....51 B6
Wetheringsett CE Prim Sch
  IP14 ....53 A5
Wexford Rd IP1 ....134 D2
Weyland Rd IP6 ....83 A6
Weylands Cl IP14 ....62 D7
Whalebone Cnr CO4 ....103 C4
Whaplod Rd NR32 ......113 E1
Wharf La 3 CO8 ....101 C4
Wharfedale NR33 ....114 F3
Wharfedale Rd IP3 ......42 F6
Wharton St 3 NR35 ....110 B4
Whatfield CE Prim Sch
  IP7 ....80 C1
Whatfield Rd
  Aldham IP7 ....94 C7
  Elmsett IP7 ....80 E7
Whatfield Way IP14 ...124 E3
Wheatacre Dr 3 NR32 ...3 C4
Wheatcroft Rd NR33 ..114 D4
Wheatfields
  3 Botesdale IP22 ......36 A6
  4 Thurston IP31 ......49 E4
Wheatheaf Cl CO11 ....105 E2
Wheatsheaf La CO11 ..105 E2
Wheelbarrow La IP20 ..23 F5
Wheeler's La IP31 ......51 A5
Wheelwrights The
  IP11 ....152 C8
Whepstead Rd
  Hawstead IP29 ....63 B7
  Horringer IP29 ....57 B2
Wherry Rd 3 NR35 ....110 D3
Wherstead Rd IP2 .....155 B1
Whin Marsh 6 IP15 ...130 E5
Whinfield Cl IP17 .....128 D3
Whinfield 15 IP5 ....98 A8
Whinfield Ave 25 CO12 ...106 F1
Whinfield Cl IP5 ....98 A8
Whinneys The IP5 .....141 D8
Whinyard Way 3 IP11 ..153 D7
Whiskin Cl 7 NR32 ....112 D2
Whitby Rd
  Bury St Edmunds IP33 ...122 D3
  Ipswich IP4 ....139 F8
White Elm Rd IP30 .....50 C1
White Elm St IP3 ......139 E4
White Foot La IP13 .....83 E6
White Hall Cl CO10 .....92 C5
White Hart La IP30 .....28 D4
White Horse Cr 4 IP11 ..153 C6
White Horse Hill IP9 ..142 D1
White Horse Rd IP13 ...64 D7
White Horse Rd
  Capel St. Mary IP9 ...150 F3
  East Bergholt CO7 ....151 D3
  Kedington IP29 ....93 F7
White Horse St 4 NR32 ..113 E2
White House Farm La
  IP21 ....22 B6
White House Gdns
  NR34 ....111 A4
White House Rd IP1 ...134 D2
White Lion Rd NR34 ...10 B8
White Mdw 5 IP14 .....51 A1
White Womans La IP12 ..85 B7
Whitedike Dro IP26 .....4 B4
Whitegates CO8 ....121 B3
Whitehall Rd IP14 ......51 F1
Whitehouse Ind Est
  IP1 ....134 C3
Whitehouse Jun Sch
  IP1 ....134 E1
Whitehouse La
  Belchamp Otten CO10 ...90 D5
  Earsham NR35 ....7 C5
  Stowupland IP14 ......67 D8
Whitepost Cnr IP14 ....54 C1
Whites Cl IP21 ....39 B4
Whites Field CO7 .....151 B5
Whitethorn Rd IP3 ....140 F1
Whitewood Wlk 8 IP7 ...13 F2
Whiting Rd NR32 ......112 C2
Whiting St IP33 ....154 B1
Whitland Cl IP2 ....143 A8
Whitlands 6 CO10 ......77 A3
Whitlock Dr CO9 ....89 F1
Whittle Rd IP2 ....138 F6
Whitton Church La
  IP1 ....134 F4
Whitton Cl NR33 ......114 C6
Whitton Com Prim Sch
  IP1 ....134 E3
Whitton Gn Prim Sch
  NR33 ....114 F5
Whitton Leyer IP8 ....135 A4
Whitwell Holw Day Hospl
  IP17 ....128 B3
Whitworth Cl IP2 .....138 D2
Whyteway IP19 ....24 B4
Wick La CO12 ....107 A1
Wick Rd Langham CO4 ..103 C2
  Stoke-by-nayland CO6 ..103 A6
Wicken Rd CO7 ....28 D1
Wickham Com Prim Sch
  IP13 ....127 B6
Wickham La 4 IP14 ....52 A6
Wickham Mkt FC
  IP13 ....127 C6
Wickham Mkt Sta 3 IP12 ..71 C2
Wickham Rd IP22 ......52 F7
Wickhambrook Ct 8
  IP11 ....152 C4

Wickhambrook Prim Sch
  CB8 ....61 E2
Wickhambrook Rd
  IP29 ....62 A5
Wicklow La IP14 ......134 D2
Wicks La IP14 ....67 D7
Widgeon Cl IP22 .....138 F3
Wiggin Cl IP28 ....116 D2
Wiggs Acre NR34 ......10 C4
Wigg's Wlk 3 NR32 ....3 D4
Wigmore Cl IP2 ......138 F1
Wignall St CO11 .....104 C2
Wigston Rd IP33 .....122 C3
Wigwam Mill IP22 .....19 F1
Wilberforce St IP1 ...139 A6
Wilby CE Prim Sch
  IP21 ....39 B2
Wilby La IP13 ....39 B2
Wilby Rd IP21 ....39 A4
Wilbye Cl IP22 ....123 E4
Wild Acres 18 CB5 .....44 A5
Wild Tracks Offroad Activity
  Pk* CB7 ....45 E7
Wilde St NR32 ....113 E2
Wilde St Est IP28 .....13 D1
Wilderness Cl 3 IP20 ...22 D5
Wilderness Hill IP8 ....95 F6
Wilderness La
  Harleston IP20 ....22 D6
  Woodbridge IP12 ....147 A6
Wildflower Way NR35 ..110 B3
Wilding Dr IP5 ....141 D7
Wilding Rd IP8 ....138 C1
Wildmere La IP21 ......13 D1
Wilford Bridge Rd
  IP12 ....147 D7
Wilford Bridge Spur
  IP12 ....147 D7
Wilkinson Dr IP5 .....141 C6
Wilkinson Way IP12 ..147 A6
Wilks Rd IP14 ....123 B2
Willby Ave IP22 ......20 D3
Willcox Ave IP33 .....122 C1
Willoughby Cl IP11 ...71 A7
Willoughby Rd IP2 ...138 F5
Willow Cl
  Badwell Ash IP31 .....50 F8
  6 Claydon IP6 ....134 C8
  Haverhill CB9 ....132 B7
  Stradbroke IP21 ......39 B5
  8 Sudbury CO10 ....148 C4
  Worlington NR34 .....111 F3
  Wortwell IP20 ....23 A8
Willow Cres CB8 .....121 B2
Willow Gn IP13 ....94 E7
Willow St 3 CO6 .....102 C5
Willow La
  Bedingham NR35 ......7 B7
  Broome NR35 ....8 E7
  Cotton IP14 ....52 B6
Willow Marsh La
  Darsham IP17 ....42 A1
  Yoxford IP17 ....41 F2
Willow Rd NR33 ......115 A2
Willow Tree Cl IP3 ...127 B6
Willow Way
  3 Great Brickett IP7 ...80 D6
  2 Harwich CO12 .....106 F1
Willow Wlk 18 IP20 ...22 D5
Willowcroft Rd IP1 ...135 A2
Willrede Cl NR34 .....111 B3
Wilmslow Ave IP14 ..146 E5
Wilmslow Dr IP8 .....138 C1
Wilson Rd Hadleigh IP7 ...149 F5
  Ipswich IP8 ....138 B1
  Lowestoft NR33 .....115 C5
Wilton Rd IP26 ....4 E5
Wimbledon Ave IP27 ...14 E8
Wimborne Ave IP33 ..140 D4
Wimpole Cl IP5 ......140 F6
Wincanton Cl IP4 ....136 A1
Winchester Cl IP14 ..124 B6
Winchester Gdns 6 IP6 ..82 B5
Winchester Rd IP33 ..122 D4
Winchester Way IP2 ..142 F8
Windermere Cl IP3 ...141 A6
Windermere Pk NR32 ..113 A4
Windermere Rd
  6 Felixstowe IP11 ....153 D7
  Stowmarket IP14 ....124 C6
Windga La IP14 ....51 D1
Windham Rd CO10 ...148 E6
Winding Piece 4 IP30 ..49 D4
Windings Rd 4 IP27 ...80 F1
Windmill Cl
  Boxted CO4 ....102 F2
  Ramsey & Parkeston
  CO12 ....106 C1
  Soham CB7 ....36 F2
  3 Somersham IP8 .....81 C3
Windmill Gn 10 IP31 ...34 E4
Windmill Hill
  Capel St Mary IP9 ...150 C3
  Exning CB8 ....120 C8
  Long Melford CO10 ...77 D1
Windmill La IP21 ......38 F8

Windmill Rd IP20 .....23 A7
Windmill Rise
  Bury St Edmunds IP33 ...154 A1
  Hundon CO10 ....75 D4
  1 Wetherden IP14 ....51 A1
Windrush Rd IP14 ....141 C8
Windsor Circ
  1 Lakenheath IP27 ....14 A3
  Lakenheath IP27 .....109 F1
Windsor Cl
  7 Barnham IP24 ......16 C2
  Lawshall IP29 ....63 D2
Windsor Rd
  Felixstowe IP11 .....152 E3
  Ipswich IP1 ....138 F7
  Lowestoft NR33 .....115 C7
  Newmarket CB8 .....120 E4
  Southwold IP18 .....119 B8
Windward Way NR33 ..114 E5
Windyridge Rd IP30 ...65 D5
Winfarthing Rd IP22 ...20 B6
Winfrith Rd IP3 ......140 D4
Wingfield Mews IP14 ...68 B6
Wingfield Rd
  Lakenheath IP27 ....109 D7
  Syleham IP21 ....21 F1
  Weybread IP21 ....22 C2
Wingfield St
  Bungay NR35 ....110 B3
  Ipswich IP4 ....155 C2
Wings Rd IP27 ....109 C6
Winnipeg Rd NR32 ...113 D2
Winsford Rd IP32 ....123 E6
Winston Ave
  Ipswich IP4 ....140 C8
  Lowestoft NR33 .....114 E7
Winston Cl
  5 Felixstowe IP11 ...152 D5
  13 Kessingland NR33 ..11 C1
Winston Rd
  Southwold IP18 .....119 C7
  Winston IP14 ....53 F1
Winthrop Rd IP3 .....140 D4
Winthrops The CO10 ...93 B4
Wissett Cl IP19 ......118 A4
Wissett Rd
  Chediston IP19 ....41 B8
  Halesworth IP19 .....118 A5
  Wissett IP19 ....24 D1
Wissett Way NR32 ...113 B4
Wissey View 2 IP6 .....6 B8
Wissington Uplands
  IP6 ....82 F5
Wiston Hall* CO6 ....102 A5
Wiston Rd CO6 ....102 B4
Withers Pl 2 CB7 .....29 A1
Withersdale Rd
  Mendham IP20 ....23 A5
  Weybread IP21 ....22 D4
Withersfield Rd
  Haverhill CB9 ....132 C7
  Withersfield CB9 .....74 C4
Withipoll St IP4 .....155 C3
Witnesham Church La
  IP6 ....82 F5
Witney Gn NR4 ....136 C7
Witney Rd 3 NR33 ...115 A3
Wittons La IP21 ......38 C7
Wix Rd CO12 ....106 C1
Wik The Bacton IP14 ...51 D5
  Beccles NR34 ....111 B6
  Ipswich IP5 ....141 B8
Wollaston Cl 3 IP22 ..122 D8
Wollaston Rd NR32 ..113 D1
Wolsey Art Gall* IP1 ...155 B3
Wolsey Gdns IP11 ...153 A3
Wolsey Rd 4 IP11 ....124 C7
Wolsey St IP1 ....155 B2
Wolves Farm La IP7 ...94 E6
Wood Cl
  1 Bentwaters Airfield
  IP12 ....85 D8
  Kenninghall NR16 .....19 A8
  Tostock IP30 ....50 B3
Wood Farm La IP18 ...26 C2
Wood Farm Rd IP13 ..83 C5
Wood La Bedingham NR35 ...7 C6
  Bressingham IP22 ....19 E6
  Dallinghoo IP13 .....70 B1
  Dickleburgh & Rushall
  IP21 ....21 C2
  Fressingfield IP21 ....40 A6
  Henstead with Hulver Street
  NR34 ....26 E7
  Hepworth IP22 ....35 A6
  Oulton NR32 ....112 C3
  Reydon IP18 ....26 C1
  Scole IP21 ....21 C4
  Thelnetham IP22 .....35 C6
Wood Rd
  Badingham IP13 ......56 B6
  Woolpit IP30 ....65 F8
Wood Side IP14 ......124 B5
Wood View 4 IP17 ....56 F8
Woodbridge Mus The*
  IP12 ....147 A5
Woodbridge Prim Sch
  IP12 ....147 A5
Woodbridge Rd
  Alderton IP12 ....99 D3
  Bredfield IP13 ....84 C7
  Butley IP12 ....86 A5

Woodbridge Rd continued
  Framlingham IP13 ...126 C3
  Grundisburgh IP13 ...83 E6
  Ipswich IP1 ....155 C3
  Sutton IP12 ....85 A1
  Tunstall IP12 ....71 E1
  Waldringfield IP12 ...98 D6
  Wantisden IP12 ......85 E5
Woodbridge Rd E
  Ipswich IP4 ....140 C2
  Rushmere St Andrew
  IP4 ....140 C2
Woodbridge Rd S IP12 ..146 F5
Woodbridge Sta 147 B4
Woodchurch Ave 6
  NR33 ....114 C4
Woodcock Cl CB9 ....133 A5
Woodcock Rd IP22 ...138 E2
Woodcrofts Cl IP29 ...63 A1
Woodcutters Way
  IP27 ....109 D7
Wooditton Rd
  Kirtling CB8 ....60 D3
  Newmarket CB8 .....121 A1
  Wooditton CB8 ....60 B6
Woodfield Cl NR34 ...25 E7
Woodfield Dr IP14 ...124 E5
Woodfield La
  Stowmarket IP14 ....124 D4
  Stutton IP9 ....105 C5
Woodfields IP21 ......39 A4
Woodgates Rd CO7 ..151 D7
Woodhall Bsns Pk
  IP29 ....148 D8
Woodhall Cl CO10 ...148 C7
Woodhall CP Sch
  CO10 ....148 D8
Woodhall Rd CO10 ..148 C8
Woodhouse La IP14 ..141 C2
Woodland Ave NR34 ..111 F4
Woodland Cl
  Onehouse IP14 ....66 C6
  Risby IP28 ....47 D5
  Thurston IP31 ....49 E3
Woodland Dr
  Bungay NR35 ....110 B1
  Ellingham NR35 ....8 E7
Woodland Pl IP31 .....49 A6
Woodlands
  1 Chelmondiston IP9 ...106 C8
  Hadleigh IP7 ....149 B7
  Mildenhall IP28 .....117 A5
Woodlands Ave 4
  NR33 ....114 C3
Woodlands Bsns Pk
  IP28 ....49 B3
Woodlands Rd
  Holbrook IP9 ....105 E8
  Raydon IP7 ....94 F2
  Rushbrooke with Rougham
  IP30 ....49 B3
Woodlands Rise IP27 ..14 D8
Woodlands The NR32 ..113 B8
Woodlands Way
  Bramford IP8 ....134 C4
  Mildenhall IP28 ....116 F5
Woodlark Cl IP7 .....138 E1
Woodley Com Sch
  IP14 ....124 B7
Woodpecker Ave 2
  NR33 ....114 D5
Woodpecker Rd IP2 ..138 D3
Woodruff Rd IP3 .....140 E2
Woods Cl
  Ditchingham NR35 ...110 B7
  Sturmer CB9 ....133 C3
Woods Loke E NR32 ..112 B7
Woods Loke Prim Sch
  NR32 ....112 F0
Woods Loke W NR32 ..112 F3
Woodside
  Beccles NR34 ....111 D3
  Brampton with Stoven
  NR34 ....25 C5
Woodside Bsns Pk IP31 ..32 F2
Woodside Cl
  Bury St Edmunds IP33 ...123 B1
  Lowestoft NR33 .....114 C3
Woodspring Cl 12 IP14 ..139 A2
Woodsprone Ave IP1 ..135 C1
Woodthorpe Cl IP7 ..149 F5
Woodthorpe Rd IP7 ..149 E5
Woodville Rd IP4 ....139 F5
Woodward Ave IP14 ...51 F6
Woodhall St 2 IP33 ..154 B2
Woodlands Cl IP1 ....139 A6
Woollards Gdns 3 CO10 ..91 E8
Woolmers Cl IP14 ...124 D4
Woolmers La IP14 ...124 D5
Woolmongers IP7 .....82 A5
Woolnough Cl 4 CB9 ..88 D3
Woolnough Rd IP12 ..146 F6
Woolnoughs The 2
  IP5 ....141 D7
Woolpit Prim Sch NR30 ..50 D1
Woolpit Rd IP31 ......49 A7
Woolverstone Cl IP2 ..138 D1
Worcester Cl 5 IP32 ..123 E6
Worcester Rd IP3 ....144 A8
Wordsworth Cres IP1 ...134 E1
Wordsworth Rd
  4 Bury St Edmunds IP32 ...48 C5
  2 Stowmarket IP14 ..124 B8
Worell Dr NR34 ......111 E4

Wet - Yor 183
Workhouse Hill
  Boxted CO4 ....102 F3
  Hartest IP29 ....77 B8
Workhouse La IP17 ...57 E2
Workhouse Rd
  Little Horkesley CO6 ..102 B2
  Thornham Magna IP23 ...37 A1
Workshop La IP10 ...145 C5
World's End La IP14 ..65 F2
World's End Rd IP14 ..55 B4
Worlingham Hall*
  NR34 ....111 F5
Worlingham Mid Sch
  NR34 ....111 F4
Worlingham Rd
  NR34 ....9 F4
Worlingham Way
  NR32 ....113 A4
Worlington
  Barton Mills IP28 .....30 E3
  Worlington IP28 .....116 A3
Worlingworth CE Prim Sch
  IP13 ....54 E7
Worlingworth Rd IP21 ..38 F3
Wortham Ling Nature
  Reserve* IP22 ....19 F2
Wortham Pl 1 CB9 ...132 E6
Wortham Prim Sch
  IP22 ....36 E7
Worthing Rd NR32 ...113 D3
Wrabness Local Nature
  Reserve* IP9 ....105 E2
Wrabness Rd CO12 ..106 C1
Wrabness Sta CO11 ..106 A2
Wragg Dr IP28 ....121 A6
Wratting Rd
  Great Thurlow CB9 ...74 D5
  Haverhill CB9 ....132 E7
Wren Ave IP2 ....138 D3
Wren Cl
  Mildenhall IP28 .....116 D4
  1 Stowmarket IP14 ...67 A5
  18 Thurstow IP31 ....49 E4
Wrens Pk 2 IP11 ....153 D7
Wriggle St IP13 ....70 A7
Wright Cl IP14 ....124 D3
Wright La IP6 ....141 D8
Wright Rd IP13 ......140 C2
Wrights Way
  Leavenheath CO6 ....102 A7
  Woolpit IP30 ....50 C1
Wroxham Rd IP3 ....139 F3
Wyatt Cl IP30 ....50 F3
Wyatt Way IP24 ......16 B7
Wyatts La CO10 .....101 B8
Wye Rd IP1 ....140 A2
Wyken Rd IP31 ....34 D3
Wykes Bishop St 3 IP3 ..139 E4
Wymering Rd 10 IP18 ..119 D5
Wyncoll's La IP7 .....94 B2
Wyndham Way CB8 ..121 A6
Wynterton Cl IP3 ....140 B1
Wynton Rise IP14 ...124 E6
Wytchwoods The IP14 ...68 E6
Wyvern Rd IP3 ......140 C1
Wyverstone Rd IP31 ...51 B7

Y
Yale Bsns Pk IP3 ....144 F8
Yarmouth Pl 3 CB9 ..132 E6
Yarmouth Rd
  Corton NR32 ....113 A8
  Ditchingham NR35 ..110 D7
  Geldeston NR34 ......9 A7
  Ipswich IP1 ....139 A6
  Kirby Cane NR35 .....8 E7
  Lound NR32 ....2 F7
  Lowestoft NR32 .....113 B5
  Melton IP12 ....84 E6
  Ufford IP13 ....127 B1
  Woodbridge IP12 ...147 B8
Yarrow Dr NR33 .....114 C4
Yaxley Hall La IP23 ...37 C4
Yaxley Rd IP23 ......37 C3
Yeldham Pl CB9 .....132 E6
Yeoman Cres IP7 ...149 E5
Yeoman Rd IP11 ....152 D3
Yeoman Way IP7 ...149 E5
Yeoman's Cl NR35 ...110 C3
Yeovil Rd NR33 ......113 C2
Yerril Gdns CB8 ....132 C5
Yew Cl 1 IP27 ....13 F2
Yew Ct IP2 ....139 A3
Yew Tree Rise IP13 ..127 C7
Yewlands Gr IP30 .....65 A4
Yewtree Gr IP5 .....140 F7
Yewtree Rise IP8 ...138 C1
York Cl
  Bury St Edmunds IP33 ...122 E5
  8 Mildenhall IP28 ....30 A8
  Sudbury CO10 ......148 C6
York Cres 12 Claydon IP6 ..82 B5
  Claydon IP6 ....134 C8
York Rd
  Bury St Edmunds IP33 ...154 A2
  Felixstowe IP11 .....153 A4
  Foxhall IP5 ....98 A7
  Haverhill CB9 ....132 C5
  Ipswich IP3 ....140 A4
  Lowestoft NR32 .....113 C1
  Southwold IP18 .....119 B5
  Sudbury CO10 ......148 C6
York Terr IP33 ......154 A2